SECOND EDITION

Programming
Visual Basic .NET

Jesse Liberty

O'REILLY®

Beijing · Cambridge · Farnham · Köln · Paris · Sebastopol · Taipei · Tokyo

Programming Visual Basic .NET, Second Edition
by Jesse Liberty

Copyright © 2003, 2002 O'Reilly & Associates, Inc. All rights reserved.
Printed in the United States of America.

Published by O'Reilly & Associates, Inc., 1005 Gravenstein Highway North, Sebastopol, CA 95472.

O'Reilly & Associates books may be purchased for educational, business, or sales promotional use. Online editions are also available for most titles (*safari.oreilly.com*). For more information, contact our corporate/institutional sales department: (800) 998-9938 or *corporate@oreilly.com*.

Editor:	Valerie Quercia
Production Editor:	Jane Ellin
Cover Designer:	Pam Spremulli
Interior Designer:	Bret Kerr

Printing History:

January 2002:	First Edition by Dave Grundgeiger.
April 2003:	Second Edition by Jesse Liberty.

Nutshell Handbook, the Nutshell Handbook logo, and the O'Reilly logo are registered trademarks of O'Reilly & Associates, Inc. Many of the designations used by manufacturers and sellers to distinguish their products are claimed as trademarks. Where those designations appear in this book, and O'Reilly & Associates, Inc. was aware of a trademark claim, the designations have been printed in caps or initial caps. IntelliSense, Microsoft, MS-DOS, Visual Basic, Visual Studio, Windows, and Windows NT are registered trademarks, and Visual C# is a trademark of Microsoft Corporation. The association between the image of a catfish and the topic of Visual Basic .NET is a trademark of O'Reilly & Associates, Inc.

While every precaution has been taken in the preparation of this book, the publisher and author assume no responsibility for errors or omissions, or for damages resulting from the use of the information contained herein.

ISBN: 0-596-00438-9

[M]

Table of Contents

Part III.   VB.NET and the .NET CLR

Preface

In July 2000, Microsoft announced the release of its new .NET platform, which represented a major change in the way people think about programming. .NET facilitates object-oriented Internet development. Visual Basic .NET (VB.NET) is a programming language that was adapted from its predecessor, Visual Basic 6, specifically for the purpose of writing applications for the .NET platform. This new version of the Visual Basic language is well suited for developing distributed web applications.

About This Book

Programming Visual Basic .NET, Second Edition, is a tutorial, both on the VB.NET language and on writing .NET applications with VB.NET. If you are already proficient in a programming language, you may be able to skim a number of the early chapters, but be sure to read through Chapter 1, which provides an overview of the language and the .NET platform. If you are new to programming, you'll want to read the book as the King of Hearts instructed the White Rabbit in *Alice's Adventures in Wonderland*: "Begin at the beginning, and go on till you come to the end: then stop."

How This Book Is Organized

Part I focuses on the details of the VB.NET language. Part II explains how to write .NET programs, and Part III describes how to use Visual Basic .NET with the .NET Common Language Runtime library.

Part I, The Visual Basic .NET Language

Chapter 1, *Visual Basic .NET and the .NET Framework*, introduces you to the VB.NET language and the .NET platform.

Chapter 2, *Getting Started: "Hello World"*, presents a simple application that prints the words "Hello World" to a console window, and gives a line-by-line analysis of the code.

Chapter 3, *Language Fundamentals*, introduces the basic syntax and structure of the VB.NET language, including the intrinsic types, variables, statements, and expressions.

Chapter 4, *Object-Oriented Programming*, explains the principles behind and goals of this programming methodology, including the three pillars of object-oriented programming: encapsulation, specialization, and polymorphism.

Chapter 5, *Classes and Objects*, introduces the key concepts of programmer-defined types (classes) and instances of those types (objects). Classes and objects are the building blocks of object-oriented programming.

Chapter 6, *Inheritance and Polymorphism*, explores two of the key concepts behind object-oriented programming and demonstrates how you might implement them in your code.

Chapters 7 and 8 introduce *Structures* and *Interfaces,* respectively, both close cousins to classes. Structures are lightweight objects that are more restricted than classes, and that make fewer demands on the operating system and on memory. Interfaces are contracts; they describe how a class will work so that other programs can interact with your objects in well-defined ways.

Object-oriented programs often create a great many objects. It is often convenient to group these objects and manipulate them together. Chapter 9, *Arrays, Indexers, and Collections*, explores the collection classes provided by the Framework Class Library and how to create your own collection types as well.

Chapter 10, *Strings*, discusses the manipulation of strings of characters, the VB.NET String class, and regular expression syntax.

Chapter 11, *Exceptions*, explains how to handle errors and abnormal conditions that may arise in relation to your programs.

Both Windows and web applications are event-driven. In VB.NET, events are first-class members of the language. Chapter 12, *Delegates and Events*, focuses on how events are managed, and how *delegates* (object-oriented type-safe callback mechanisms) are used to support event handling.

Part II, Programming with VB.NET

Parts II and III will be of interest to all readers, regardless of programming experience. These sections explore the details of the .NET platform.

Part II details how to write .NET programs, both desktop applications with Windows Forms and web applications with Web Forms. In addition, Part II describes database interactivity and how to create web services.

On top of this infrastructure sits a high-level abstraction of the operating system, designed to facilitate object-oriented software development. This top tier includes ASP.NET and Windows Forms. ASP.NET includes both Web Forms, for rapid development of web applications, and Web Services, for creating web objects with no user interface.

VB.NET provides a Rapid Application Development (RAD) model similar to that previously available only in Visual Basic. Chapter 13, *Building Windows Applications*, describes how to use this RAD model to create professional-quality Windows programs using the Windows Forms development environment.

Whether intended for the Web or for the desktop, most applications depend on the manipulation and management of large amounts of data. Chapter 14, *Accessing Data with ADO.NET*, explains the ADO.NET layer of the .NET Framework and explains how to interact with Microsoft SQL Server and other data providers.

Chapter 15, *Building Web Applications with Web Forms*, combines the RAD techniques demonstrated in Chapter 13 with the data techniques from Chapter 14 to demonstrate how to build web applications with Web Forms.

Not all applications have a user interface. Chapter 16, *Programming Web Services*, focuses on the second half of ASP.NET technology. A web service is a distributed application that provides functionality via standard web protocols, most commonly XML and HTTP.

Part III, VB.NET and the .NET CLR

A runtime is an environment in which programs are executed. The *Common Language Runtime* (CLR) is the heart of .NET. It includes a data typing system that is enforced throughout the platform and that is common to all languages developed for .NET. The CLR is responsible for processes such as memory management and reference counting of objects.

Another key feature of the .NET CLR is *garbage collection*. In VB.NET, the developer is not responsible for destroying objects. Endless hours spent searching for memory leaks are a thing of the past; the CLR cleans up after you when your objects are no longer in use. The CLR's garbage collector checks the heap for unreferenced objects and frees the memory used by these objects.

The .NET platform and class library extend upward into the middle-level platform, where you find an infrastructure of supporting classes, including types for interprocess communication, XML, threading, I/O, security, diagnostics, and so on. The middle tier also includes the data-access components collectively referred to as ADO.NET that are discussed in Chapter 14.

Part III of this book discusses the relationship of VB.NET to the Common Language Runtime and the Framework Class Library.

Chapter 17, *Assemblies and Versioning*, distinguishes between private and public assemblies and describes how assemblies are created and managed. In .NET, an *assembly* is a collection of files that appears to the user to be a single DLL or executable. An assembly is the basic unit of reuse, versioning, security, and deployment.

.NET assemblies include extensive metadata about classes, methods, properties, events, and so forth. This metadata is compiled into the program and retrieved programmatically through reflection. Chapter 18, *Attributes and Reflection*, explores how to add metadata to your code, how to create custom attributes, and how to access this metadata through reflection. It goes on to discuss dynamic invocation, in which methods are invoked with late (runtime) binding, and ends with a demonstration of *reflection emit*, an advanced technique for building self-modifying code.

The .NET Framework was designed to support web-based and distributed applications. Components created in VB.NET may reside within other processes on the same machine or on other machines across the network or across the Internet. *Marshaling* is the technique of interacting with objects that aren't really there, while *remoting* comprises techniques for communicating with such objects. Chapter 19, *Marshaling and Remoting*, elaborates.

The Framework Class Library provides extensive support for asynchronous I/O and other classes that make explicit manipulation of threads unnecessary. However, VB.NET does provide extensive support for *Threads and Synchronization*, discussed in Chapter 20.

Conventions Used in This Book

The following font conventions are used in this book:

- *Italic* is used for pathnames, filenames, Internet addresses, and new terms where they are defined.
- `Constant Width` is used for code examples, command lines and options that should be typed verbatim, and VB.NET keywords.
- `Constant Width Italic` is used for replaceable items, such as variables or optional elements, within syntax lines or code.
- **`Constant Width Bold`** is used for emphasis within program code.

Pay special attention to notes set apart from the text with the following icons:

 This is a tip. It contains useful supplementary information about the topic at hand.

 This is a warning. It helps you solve or avoid annoying problems.

Support

As part of my responsibilities as author, I provide ongoing support for my books through my web site. You can also obtain the source code for all of the examples in this book at my site:

http://www.LibertyAssociates.com

On this web site, you'll also find access to a book-support discussion group with a section set aside for questions about VB.NET. Before you post a question, however, please check the FAQ (Frequently Asked Questions) list and the errata file on my web site. If you check these files and still have a question, then please go ahead and post to the discussion center.

The most effective way to get help is to ask a very precise question or even to create a very small program that illustrates your area of concern or confusion. You may also want to check the various newsgroups and discussion centers on the Internet. Microsoft offers a wide array of newsgroups, and Developmentor (*http://www. develop.com*) has a wonderful .NET email discussion list.

We'd Like to Hear from You

We have tested and verified the information in this book to the best of our ability, but you may find that features have changed (or even that we have made mistakes!). Please let us know about any errors you find, as well as your suggestions for future editions, by writing to:

O'Reilly & Associates, Inc.
1005 Gravenstein Highway North
Sebastopol, CA 95472
(800) 998-9938 (in the U.S. or Canada)
(707) 829-0515 (international/local)
(707) 829-0104 (fax)

We have a web page for the book, where we list examples, and any plans for future editions. You can access this information at:

http://www.oreilly.com/catalog/progvbdotnet2

You can also send messages electronically. To be put on the mailing list or request a catalog, send email to:

info@oreilly.com

To comment on the book, send email to:

bookquestions@oreilly.com

For more information about this book and others, as well as additional technical articles and discussion on the VB.NET and the .NET Framework, see the O'Reilly & Associates web site:

http://www.oreilly.com

and the O'Reilly .NET DevCenter:

http://www.oreillynet.com/dotnet

Acknowledgments

To ensure that *Programming Visual Basic .NET* is accurate, complete, and targeted at the needs and interests of professional programmers, I enlisted the help of some of the brightest programmers I know, including Dan Hurwitz, Seth Weiss, Sue Lynch, and Daniel Creeron.

John Osborn signed me to O'Reilly, for which I will forever be in his debt. Valerie Quercia, Jane Ellin, and Tatiana Diaz helped make this book better than what I'd written. Daniel Creeron tested all the code and redid a number of the illustrations for 1.1 compliance. Tim O'Reilly provided support and resources, and I'm grateful.

PART I

The Visual Basic .NET Language

CHAPTER 1

Visual Basic .NET and the .NET Framework

Programming Visual Basic .NET is a comprehensive guide to the .NET version of the Visual Basic language and its use as a tool for programming on Microsoft's .NET platform. One learns VB.NET specifically to create .NET applications; pretending otherwise would miss the point of the language. Thus, this book does not consider VB.NET in a vacuum but places the language firmly in the context of Microsoft's .NET platform and in the development of desktop and Internet applications.

This chapter introduces both the Visual Basic .NET language and the .NET platform, including the .NET Framework.

Visual Basic and .NET

Once upon a time there was a programming language called Basic, which stood for Beginner's All-purpose Symbolic Instruction Code. As the name suggests, Basic was intended to be as simple and accessible as possible for those unfamiliar with programming.

Then in 1991 Microsoft unveiled Visual Basic, a retooling of Basic that changed the way user interfaces were written. Visual Basic can still lay claim to being one of the most popular programming languages ever developed.

Visual Basic .NET is Microsoft's reengineering of Visual Basic for the .NET platform. VB.NET departs in some significant ways from earlier versions of Visual Basic. In fact, some early adopters of VB.NET started calling it VB.*NOT*. VB.NET has evolved into a full-fledged object-oriented commercial software development package. Yet VB.NET also retains some of the inherent simplicity of its predecessors.

VB.NET has a number of features that help it maintain backwards compatibility with Visual Basic 6 (VB6). Other features have been added specifically to adapt Visual Basic to object-oriented programming and the .NET platform.

VB.NET provides support in the language to find bugs early in the development process. This makes for code that is easier to maintain and programs that are more reliable. VB.NET does not support some features available in other languages (e.g., pointers) that make for unsafe code.

In the past, you might have learned a language like C or Java without much concern about the platform on which you would be programming. These cross-platform language were as comfortable on a Unix box as they were on a PC running Windows.

VB.NET, however, is a version of the Visual Basic language written specifically for .NET. While .NET may become cross-platform some day soon—a Unix port is already available—for now, the overwhelming majority of .NET programs will be written to run on a machine running Windows.

Stepchild No Longer

VB.NET represents a significant step forward for Visual Basic programmers. In the past, VB has been (unfairly) cast as a second-class "toy" language that was not up to the challenge of enterprise-level software development.

Whatever the merits of that accusation for VB6 and its predecessors, it is manifestly untrue for VB.NET. The code produced by Visual Basic .NET is (nearly) identical to that produced by C# or any other compiler designed for .NET. There is *no* performance or size penalty to writing with Visual Basic .NET.

In fact, the differences between Visual Basic .NET and C# are entirely syntactic. That is, one language uses semicolons, the other does not. One language uses brackets, the other parentheses. The differences are so simple, and so straightforward, that converting a C# program to Visual Basic .NET is an entirely mechanical operation, one that can be performed by a simple program; such programs are already available on the Web.

The truth is that there is no Visual Basic .NET language, nor is there a C# language. There is, in fact, a single .NET language called MSIL (Microsoft Intermediate Language). Both Visual Basic .NET and C# compilers produce MSIL code, and the code they produce is nearly identical!

The .NET Platform

In July, 2000, Microsoft announced the .NET platform. .NET is a development framework that provides a fresh application programming interface (API) to the services and APIs of classic Windows operating systems, especially the Windows 2000 family, while bringing together a number of disparate technologies that emerged from Microsoft during the late 1990s. Among the latter are COM+ component services, the ASP web development framework, a commitment to XML and object-oriented design, support for new web services protocols such as SOAP, WSDL, and UDDI, and a focus on the Internet, all integrated within the DNA architecture.

SOAP:- Simple Object Access Protocol
WSDL: Web Services Definition Language

UDDI: Universal Description Discovery and Integration protocol.

Microsoft says it is devoting 80% of its research and development budget to .NET and its associated technologies. The results of this commitment to date are impressive. For one thing, the scope of .NET is huge. The platform consists of four separate product groups:

- A set of languages, including Visual Basic .NET, C#, JScript .NET, and Managed C++; a set of development tools, including Visual Studio .NET; a comprehensive class library for building web services and web and Windows applications; and the *Common Language Runtime* (CLR) to execute objects built within this framework.

- A set of .NET Enterprise Servers, formerly known as SQL Server 2000, Exchange 2000, BizTalk 2000, and so on, that provide specialized functionality for relational data storage, email, B2B commerce, etc.

- An offering of commercial web services, .NET My Services; for a fee, developers can use these services in building applications that require knowledge of user identity, etc.

- New .NET-enabled non-PC devices, from cell phones to game boxes.

The .NET Framework

Microsoft .NET supports not only language independence, but also language integration. This means that you can inherit from classes, catch exceptions, and take advantage of polymorphism across different languages. The .NET Framework makes this possible with a specification called the *Common Type System* (CTS) that all .NET components must obey. For example, everything in .NET is an object of a specific class that derives from the root class called System.Object. The CTS supports the general concept of classes, interfaces, delegates (which support callbacks), reference types, and value types.

Additionally, .NET includes a *Common Language Specification* (CLS), which provides a series of basic rules that are required for language integration. The CLS determines the minimum requirements for being a .NET language. Compilers that conform to the CLS create objects that can interoperate with one another. The entire Framework Class Library (FCL) can be used by any language that conforms to the CLS. Complete coverage of the FCL classes is beyond the scope of this book. For more information on these classes, see *VB.NET Language in a Nutshell* (Roman, Petrusha, and Lomax, O'Reilly).

The .NET Framework sits on top of the operating system, which can be any flavor of Windows from Win 98 forward,* and consists of a number of components.

---

* Because of the architecture of the CLR, the operating system can potentially be any variety of Unix or another operating system altogether.

Currently, the .NET Framework consists of:

- Four official languages: VB.NET, C#, Managed C++, and JScript .NET
- The Common Language Runtime, an object-oriented platform for Windows and web development that all these languages share
- A number of related class libraries, collectively known as the Framework Class Library (FCL).

Figure 1-1 breaks down the .NET Framework into its system architectural components.

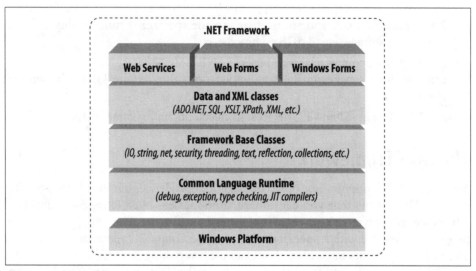

Figure 1-1. .NET Framework architecture

The most important component of the .NET Framework is the CLR, which provides the environment in which programs are executed. The CLR includes a virtual machine, analogous in many ways to the Java virtual machine. At a high level, the CLR activates objects, performs security checks on them, lays them out in memory, executes them, and garbage-collects them. (The Common Type System is also part of the CLR.)

In Figure 1-1, the layer on top of the CLR is a set of framework base classes, followed by an additional layer of data and XML classes, plus another layer of classes intended for web services, Web Forms, and Windows Forms. Collectively, these classes are known as the Framework Class Library, one of the largest class libraries in history and one that provides an object-oriented API to all the functionality that the .NET platform encapsulates. With more than 4,000 classes, the FCL facilitates rapid development of desktop, client/server, and other web services and applications.

The set of framework base classes, the lowest level of the FCL, is similar to the set of classes in Java. These classes support rudimentary input and output, string manipulation, security management, network communication, thread management, text manipulation, reflection and collections functionality, etc.

Above this level is a tier of classes that extend the base classes to support data management and XML manipulation. The data classes support persistent management of data that is maintained on backend databases. These classes include the Structured Query Language (SQL) classes to let you manipulate persistent data stores through a standard SQL interface. Additionally, a set of classes called ADO.NET allows you to manipulate persistent data. The .NET Framework also supports a number of classes to let you manipulate XML data and perform XML searching and translations.

Extending the framework base classes and the data and XML classes is a tier of classes geared toward building applications using three different technologies: Web Services, Web Forms, and Windows Forms. Web Services include a number of classes that support the development of lightweight distributed components, which will work even in the face of firewalls and NAT software. Because Web Services employ standard HTTP and SOAP as underlying communications protocols, these components support plug-and-play across cyberspace.

Web Forms and Windows Forms allow you to apply Rapid Application Development techniques to building web and Windows applications. Simply drag and drop controls onto your form, double-click a control, and write the code to respond to the associated event.

For a more detailed description of the .NET Framework, see .NET Framework Essentials, by Thuan Thai and Hoag Lam (O'Reilly).

Compilation and the MSIL

In .NET, programs are not compiled into executable files; they are compiled into *Microsoft Intermediate Language* (MSIL) files, which the CLR then executes. The MSIL (often shortened to IL) files that Visual Basic .NET produces are *identical* to the IL files that other .NET languages produce; the platform is language-agnostic. A key fact about the CLR is that it is *common*; the same runtime supports development in VB.NET as well as in C#.

VB.NET code is compiled into IL when you build your project. The IL is saved in a file on disk. When you run your program, the IL is compiled again, using the *Just In Time* (JIT) compiler (a process often called *JIT'ing*). The result is machine code, executed by the machine's processor.

The standard JIT compiler runs *on demand*. When a method is called, the JIT compiler analyzes the IL and produces highly efficient machine code, which runs very fast. The JIT compiler is smart enough to recognize when the code has already been compiled, so as the application runs, compilation happens only as needed. As .NET applications run, they tend to become faster and faster, as the already-compiled code is reused.

The CLS means that all .NET languages produce very similar IL code. As a result, objects created in one language can be accessed and derived from another. Thus it is possible to create a base class in C# and derive from it in VB.NET.

The VB.NET Language

The VB.NET language is disarmingly simple, with relatively few keywords and a dozen built-in datatypes, but VB.NET is highly expressive when it comes to implementing modern programming concepts. VB.NET includes all the support for structured, component-based, object-oriented programming that one expects of a modern language.

At the heart of any object-oriented language is its support for defining and working with classes. Classes define new types, allowing you to extend the language to better model the problem you are trying to solve. VB.NET contains keywords for declaring new classes and their methods and properties, and for implementing encapsulation, inheritance, and polymorphism, the three pillars of object-oriented programming.

VB.NET also supports *interfaces*, a means of making a contract with a class for services that the interface stipulates. In VB.NET, a class can inherit from only a single parent, but a class can implement multiple interfaces. When it implements an interface, a VB.NET class in effect promises to provide the functionality the interface specifies.

VB.NET also provides support for structures. A *structure* is a restricted, lightweight type that, when instantiated, makes fewer demands on the operating system and on memory than a conventional class does. A structure can't inherit from a class or be inherited from, but a structure can implement an interface.

VB.NET provides component-oriented features, such as properties, events, and declarative constructs (called *attributes*). Component-oriented programming is supported by the CLR's support for storing metadata with the code for the class. The metadata describes the class, including its methods and properties, as well as its security needs and other attributes, such as whether it can be serialized; the code contains the logic necessary to carry out its functions. A compiled class is thus a self-contained unit; therefore, a hosting environment that knows how to read a class' metadata and code needs no other information to make use of it. Using VB.NET and the CLR, it is possible to add custom metadata to a class by creating custom attributes. Likewise, it is possible to read class metadata using CLR types that support reflection.

An *assembly* is a collection of files that appear to the programmer to be a single dynamic link library (DLL) or executable (EXE). In .NET, an assembly is the basic unit of reuse, versioning, security, and deployment. The CLR provides a number of classes for manipulating assemblies.

CHAPTER 2

Getting Started: "Hello World"

It is a time-honored tradition to start a programming book with a "Hello World" program. In this chapter, we will create, compile, and run a simple "Hello World" program written in Visual Basic .NET. The analysis of this brief program will introduce key features of the Visual Basic .NET language.

Example 2-1 illustrates the fundamental elements of a very simple Visual Basic .NET program.

Example 2-1. A simple "Hello World" program in VB.NET

```
Module HelloWorld
' every console app starts with Main
    Sub Main( )
        System.Console.WriteLine("Hello World")
    End Sub
End Module
```

That is the entire program. Compiling and running it displays the words "Hello World" at the console.

Examining Your First Program

The single greatest challenge when learning to program is that you must learn everything before you can learn anything. Even this simple program uses many features of the language that will be discussed in coming chapters, including statements, methods, objects, strings, inheritance, blocks, libraries, and polymorphism.

This chapter provides a whirlwind tour of a number of these concepts. I'll then spend the rest of the book expanding on these areas and showing how they can be applied to create .NET applications.

Each program consists of a series of statements, which are instructions to the compiler. In VB.NET, as in previous versions of Visual Basic, every statement ends with a carriage return/linefeed; you create one by pressing the Enter key.

The first line in Example 2-1 defines a programming unit known as a *module*. In this case, the module is named HelloWorld:

```
Module HelloWorld
```

You begin each module definition using the Module keyword, as in the preceding code line. Likewise, you end each module definition with this line:

```
End Module
```

Within the HelloWorld module you define a *method*, or programming routine, called Main( ). The Main( ) method is the "entry point" for every VB.NET console application; it is where your program begins. Within the HelloWorld module, the Main( ) method is defined from lines 3 through 5. Notice the Sub keyword to signal the beginning of the subroutine and the End Sub line to conclude the method:

```
Sub Main( )
    System.Console.WriteLine("Hello World")
End Sub
```

Typically, one method calls another. The called method will do work, and it can return a value to the calling method. In VB.NET, as in previous versions of VB, methods come in two flavors: a method that returns a value is called a *function*; a method that does not return a value is called a *sub* (subroutine).

Main( ) is called by the operating system (when the program is invoked). Every method name is followed by opening and closing parentheses:

```
Sub Main( )
```

As the parentheses imply, it is possible to pass values into a method so that the method can manipulate or use those values. These values are called parameters or arguments to the method. In this case, Main( ) has no arguments. (Method arguments are covered in Chapter 5.) Within Main( ) is a single line of code:

```
System.Console.WriteLine("Hello World")
```

This line of code calls a method (WriteLine) on an object (Console) within the System namespace. Let's take that apart, piece by piece.

Classes and Objects

A *class* defines a type. An *object* is an individual instance of a class. In the preceding example, Console is an object that represents your screen. The Console class defines what it means to be a Console object; it defines what Console objects can do and what information Console objects can store (these characteristics are known as the object's *state*).

Similarly, the class Button defines what it means to be a button. The Button class defines that Button objects can be clicked, drawn, etc., and it defines what information they can store (e.g., the text label on the button). The individual buttons on a form are instances of the Button class; in other words, the individual buttons are

Button objects. Each object has its own state. For example, each Button object has its own text label. One button might read "OK", while another reads "Push Me". Classes and objects are described in detail in Chapter 5.

Namespaces

In the HelloWorld program, the Console class is defined within the System *namespace*. Each VB.NET class must have a unique name. Console is only one of a tremendous number of useful types that are part of the .NET Framework Class Library. Each class has a name, and thus the FCL contains thousands of names, such as ArrayList, FileDialog, DataException, EventArgs, and so on. Names and more names; hundreds, thousands, even tens of thousands of names.

This presents a problem. No developer can possibly memorize all the names that the .NET Framework uses, and sooner or later you are likely to create an object and give it a name that has already been used. What will happen if you develop your own Hashtable class, only to discover that it conflicts with the Hashtable class that .NET provides?

You certainly could rename your Hashtable class mySpecialHashtable, for example, but that is a losing battle. New Hashtable types are likely to be developed, and distinguishing between their type names and yours would be a nightmare.

The solution to this problem is provided by the namespace. A namespace restricts a name's scope, making it meaningful only within the defined namespace. Namespaces can help you organize and compartmentalize your types. System is one of the default namespaces VB.NET provides.

However, when you write a complex Visual Basic .NET program, you might want to create your own namespace hierarchy. There is no limit to how deep this hierarchy can be. The goal of namespaces is to help you divide and conquer the complexity of your object hierarchy.

For instance, assume that I tell you that Jim is an engineer. The word "engineer" is used for many things in English and can cause confusion. Does Jim design buildings? Write software? Run a train?

In English I might clarify by saying "he's a scientist" or "he's a train engineer." A Visual Basic .NET programmer could tell you that Jim is a Science.Engineer rather than a Train.Engineer. The namespace (in this case, Science or Train) restricts the scope of the word that follows. It creates a "space" in which that name is meaningful.

Further, it might happen that Jim is not just any kind of Science.Engineer. Perhaps Jim graduated from MIT with a degree in software engineering, not civil engineering (are civil engineers especially polite?). Thus, the object that is Jim might be defined more specifically as a Science.Software.Engineer. This classification implies that the namespace Software is meaningful within the namespace Science, and that Engineer in this context is meaningful within the namespace Software. If later you learn that Charlotte is a Transportation.Train.Engineer, you will not be confused as to what kind of engineer she is. The two uses of Engineer can coexist, each within its own namespace.

Similarly, if it turns out that .NET has a Hashtable class within its System.Collections namespace, and that I have also created a Hashtable class within a ProgVB-NET.DataStructures namespace, there is no conflict because each exists in its own namespace.

The WriteLine( ) Method

The Console class has a method, WriteLine(), that displays a line of text to the screen. The complete identification for the WriteLine() method includes the class and namespace to which it belongs, separated by the *dot operator*, as follows:

```
System.Console.WriteLine("Hello World")
```

The WriteLine() method declares a single parameter, the text string you want to display. When you pass in a string to the method, the string is an argument. In our sample program, the string "Hello World" corresponds to the parameter the method expects; thus, the string is displayed to the screen.

If you will be using many objects from the same namespace, you can save typing by telling the compiler about that namespace. You do so by adding an Imports declaration to the top of your program:

```
Imports System
```

Once you add this line, you can use the Console class name without explicitly identifying its namespace (System). Thus, if you add the preceding Imports declaration, you can rewrite the contents of Main() as follows:

```
Console.WriteLine("Hello World")
```

The Dot Operator (.)

In Example 2-1, the dot operator (.) is used both to access a method (and data) in a class (in this case, the method WriteLine()), and to restrict the class name to a specific namespace (in this case, to locate Console within the System namespace). This works well because in both cases we are "drilling down" to find the exact thing we want. The top level is the System namespace (which contains all the System objects that the Framework provides); the Console type exists within that namespace, and the WriteLine() method is a member function of the Console type.

The compiler will check the namespace you identified (System) and it will find the Console class defined there.

The compiler will check the namespace you identified (System) and it will find the Console class defined there.

 Visual Studio .NET automatically (and invisibly) adds the Imports System statement for you (as well as several other commonly used namespaces). Thus, if you write this Hello World program in Visual Studio .NET, you do not need to explicitly add the Imports System statement. However, keep in mind that you may need to explicitly import other namespaces for more complicated programs.

Since the method (or sub) is defined within the module, you do not close the module until you have closed the method. Thus, the program ends with the sequence:

```
        End Sub
End Module
```

Comments

This discussion has omitted a single line in our program. Just before the start of the Main( ) method appears a comment (here in bold):

```
' every console app starts with Main
Sub Main( )
        System.Console.WriteLine("Hello World")
```

A comment is just a note to yourself. You insert comments to make the code more readable. You can place comments anywhere in your program that you think the explanation will be helpful; they have no effect on the running program.

In VB.NET, comments begin with a single quotation mark. The quote indicates that everything to the right on the same line is a comment and will be ignored by the VB.NET compiler.

Writing and Building Your Programs

There are two obvious ways to enter, compile, and run the programs in this book. You can enter the text into a text editor like Notepad and then use the command-line compiler, or you can use the Visual Studio .NET Integrated Development Environment (IDE) to write the code and then request that the IDE call the compiler for you.

The job of the compiler is to turn your source code into a working program. It turns out to be just slightly more complicated than that because .NET uses an intermediate language called Microsoft Intermediate Language (MSIL, sometimes abbreviated to IL). The compiler reads your source code and produces IL. The .NET Just In Time (JIT) compiler then reads your IL code and produces an executable application in memory.

Using a Text Editor

You can enter source code like the "Hello World" program from Example 2-1 in any text editor, such as Notepad. You then save the code in a text file. For instance, you might name the file containing the "Hello World" program *HelloWorld.vb*.

You can then compile the source code by opening the Visual Studio .NET Command Prompt. In order to ensure that your compiler environment variables are set properly (so that your compiler will work properly) you will want to open a special DOS box provided in the .NET SDK. After installing the SDK, you will typically find this program at:

```
"C:\Program Files\Microsoft Visual Studio .NET 2003\Common7\Tools\vsvars32.bat"
```

I recommend that you save a shortcut to this on your desktop, but you can also open the Visual Studio .NET Command Prompt by using the menu sequence

```
Start -> Programs -> Microsoft Visual Studio .NET 2003 -> Visual Studio .NET Tools ->
Visual Studio .NET Command Prompt
```

On the command line, enter the name of the VB.NET compiler program, *vbc*, passing in the source, as in the following:

```
vbc HelloWorld.vb
```

The Microsoft VB.NET compiler will compile your code; when you display the directory you'll find that the compiler has produced an executable file called *HelloWorld.exe*. Type *HelloWorld* at the command prompt, and your program will execute, as shown in Figure 2-1.

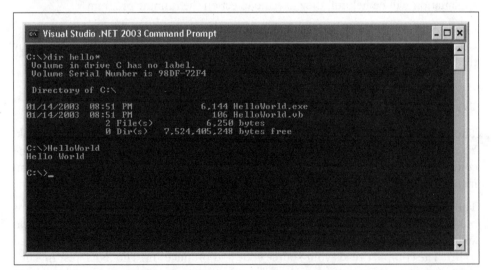

Figure 2-1. Executing HelloWorld.exe

If you prefer, you can compile the program in debug mode:

```
vbc /debug HelloWorld.vb
```

The /debug command-line switch inserts symbols in the code, which helps when you run your program in a debugger, introduced later in this chapter.

Just In Time Compilation

Compiling *HelloWorld.vb* using *vbc* creates an executable (*.exe*) file. Keep in mind, however, that the *.exe* file contains op-codes written in Microsoft Intermediate Language (MSIL), which is introduced in Chapter 1.

Interestingly, if you wrote this application in C# or any other language compliant with the .NET Common Language Specification (CLS), compiling it would produce the same MSIL. By design Intermediate Language code created from different languages is virtually indistinguishable, which is the point of having a common language specification in the first place.

In addition to producing the IL code (which is similar in spirit to Java's byte-code), the compiler creates a read-only segment of the *.exe* file in which it inserts a standard Win32 executable header. The compiler designates an entry point within the read-only segment; the operating system loader jumps to that entry point when you run the program, just as it would for any Windows program.

The operating system cannot execute the IL code, however, and that entry point does nothing but jump to the .NET Just In Time compiler (also introduced in Chapter 1). The JIT produces native CPU instructions, as you might find in a normal *.exe*. The key feature of a JIT compiler, however, is that functions are compiled only as they are used, just in time for execution.

Using Visual Studio .NET

Rather than writing your program in Notepad and compiling it at the command line, you can write and compile your program using the Visual Studio .NET Integrated Development Environment. The IDE provides enormous advantages. These include automatic indentation, IntelliSense word completion, color coding, and integration with the help files. Most important, the IDE includes a powerful debugger and a wealth of other tools.

I strongly recommend that you spend some time exploring the Visual Studio .NET Integrated Development Environment. This is your principal tool as a .NET developer, and you want to learn to use it well. Time invested up front in getting comfortable with Visual Studio .NET will pay for itself many times over. The following pages provide only a short overview of some of the IDE's most basic capabilities. To get the most out of Visual Studio .NET, spend the time to explore and read the documentation. It is a very powerful tool that will serve you well.

Creating the "Hello World" program

To create the "Hello World" program in the IDE, first open Visual Studio .NET. You can use the Visual Studio .NET desktop icon or select Visual Studio .NET from your Start menu, using the following sequence:

```
Start -> Programs -> Microsoft Visual Studio .NET 2003
```

Then choose File->New Project from the menu toolbar. This will invoke the New Project window. Figure 2-2 shows the New Project window.

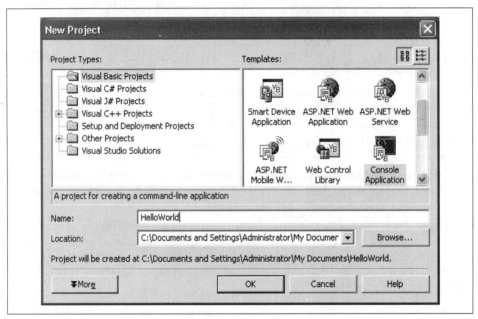

Figure 2-2. New Project dialog lets you choose a project template

To open a project to contain your application, select Visual Basic .NET Projects in the Project Type window and select Console Application in the Templates window. You can now enter a name for the project (e.g., HelloWorld) and select a directory in which to store your files. Then click OK, and a new window will appear in which you can enter the code, as shown in Figure 2-3.

Visual Studio .NET creates a module named Module1, which you are free to rename. When you rename the module, be sure to also change the name of the default file (*Module1.vb*). To reproduce Example 2-1, for instance, you change the name of Module1 to HelloWorld, and rename the *Module1.vb* file (listed in the Solution Explorer window) to *HelloWorld.vb*.

Finally, Visual Studio .NET creates a program skeleton. Replace the code provided by Visual Studio .NET with the code shown in Example 2-1.

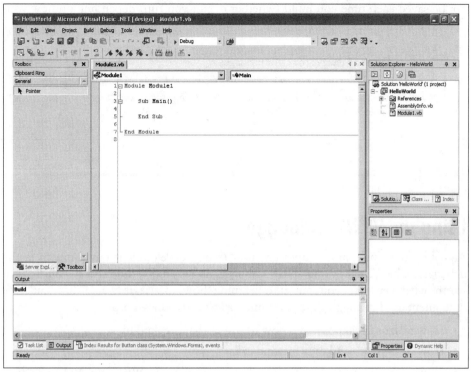

Figure 2-3. The IDE

Compiling and running "Hello World"

Once you've entered the code you want, you are ready to compile and run the program. There are many ways to compile and run the "Hello World" program from within Visual Studio .NET. Typically you can accomplish every task by choosing commands from the Visual Studio .NET menu toolbar, by using buttons, or, in many cases, by using key-combination shortcuts.

For example, you can test your program within the debugger by pressing F5 (or by choosing Debug->Start), or you can run outside the debugger by pressing Ctrl-F5 (or by choosing Debug->Start Without Debugging) or by clicking the Start button, as shown in Figure 2-4. In either case, this will build your program and run it.

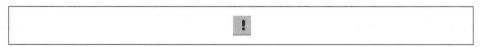

Figure 2-4. Start without debugging button

You can build your program without running it (e.g., just to check for compile errors) by pressing Ctrl-Shift-B, or by choosing Build->Build Solution or by clicking the Build button as shown in Figure 2-5. Updates to your source code may or may not be saved each time you build (whether or not you run) depending on how your options are set (Tools->Options).

 You may receive the error message:

    'Sub Main' was not found in 'HelloWorld.Module1'

To fix this, double-click on the error message, and then choose HelloWorld as the startup object.

Figure 2-5. Build button icon

Using the VS.NET Debugger

Arguably, the single most important tool in any development environment is the debugger. The Visual Studio .NET debugger is very powerful, and it will be well worth whatever time you put into learning how to use it well. That said, the fundamentals of debugging are very simple. The three key skills are:

- How to set a breakpoint and how to run to that breakpoint
- How to step into and over method calls
- How to examine and modify the value of variables, member data, and so forth

This chapter does not reiterate the entire debugger documentation, but these skills are so fundamental that it does provide a crash (pardon the expression) course.

The debugger can accomplish the same thing in many ways—typically via menu choices, buttons, and so forth. The simplest way to set a breakpoint is to click in the lefthand margin. The IDE will mark your breakpoint with a red dot, as shown in Figure 2-6.

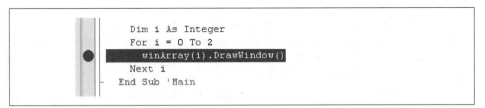

Figure 2-6. A breakpoint

 Discussing the debugger requires code examples. The code shown here is from Chapter 6, and you are not expected to understand how it works yet (though if you program in VB6, you'll probably get the gist of it).

To run the debugger you can choose Debug->Start or just press F5. The program will compile and run to the breakpoint, at which time it will stop and a yellow arrow will indicate the next statement for execution, as in Figure 2-7.

```
        Dim i As Integer
        For i = 0 To 2
            winArray(i).DrawWindow()
        Next i
    End Sub 'Main
```

Figure 2-7. The breakpoint hit

After you've hit your breakpoint it is easy to examine the values of various objects. For example, you can find the value of the variable i just by putting the cursor over it and waiting a moment, as shown in Figure 2-8.

```
    For i = 0 To 2
        winArray(i).DrawWindow()
    Next i              i = 0
```

Figure 2-8. Showing a value

The debugger IDE also provides a number of very useful windows, such as a Locals window that displays the values of all the local variables (see Figure 2-9).

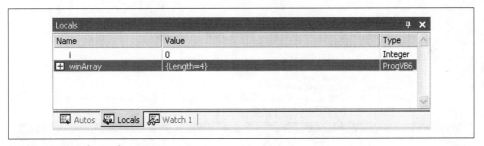

Figure 2-9. Locals window

Intrinsic types such as integers simply show their value (see i above), but objects show their type and have a plus (+) sign. You can expand these objects to see their internal data, as shown in Figure 2-10. You'll learn more about objects and their internal data in upcoming chapters.

You can step into the next method by pressing F11. Doing so steps into the DrawWindow() method of the WindowClass, as shown in Figure 2-11.

You can see that the next execution statement is now WriteLine() in DrawWindow(). The Locals window has updated to show the current state of the objects.

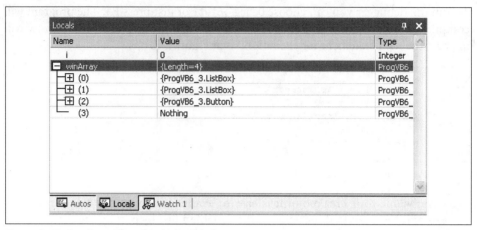

Figure 2-10. Locals window object expanded

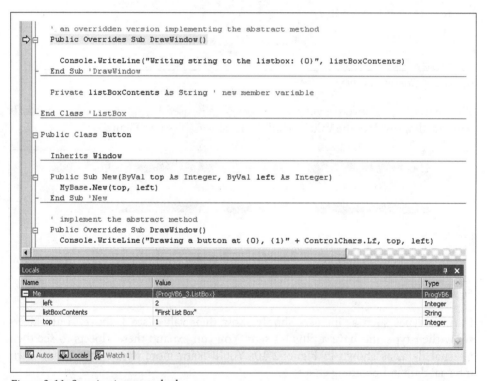

Figure 2-11. Stepping into a method

There is much more to learn about the debugger, but this brief introduction should get you started. You can answer many programming questions by writing short demonstration programs and examining them in the debugger. A good debugger is, in some ways, the single most powerful teaching tool for a programming language.

CHAPTER 3

Language Fundamentals

Chapter 2 demonstrates a very simple Visual Basic .NET program. Nonetheless, there is sufficient complexity in creating even that little program that some of the pertinent details had to be skipped over. This chapter illuminates these details by delving more deeply into the syntax and structure of the Visual Basic .NET language itself.

This chapter discusses the type system in Visual Basic .NET, drawing a distinction between built-in types (Integer, Boolean, etc.) and user-defined types (types you create, such as classes and interfaces). The chapter also covers programming fundamentals such as how to create and use variables and constants. It then goes on to introduce enumerations, strings, identifiers, expressions, and statements.

The second part of the chapter explains and demonstrates the use of branching, using statements such as If, Do, Do...While, and For. Also discussed are operators, including the assignment, logical, relational, and mathematical operators. Although Visual Basic .NET is principally concerned with the creation and manipulation of objects, it is best to start with the fundamental building blocks: the elements from which objects are created. These include the built-in types that are an intrinsic part of the Visual Basic .NET language as well as the syntactic elements of Visual Basic .NET.

VB.NET Versus VB6

If you're an experienced VB6 programmer, you might be tempted to skim through this chapter. However, you should take note of the following significant differences between VB6 and VB.NET:

- The Visual Basic .NET equivalent to the VB6 Currency type is the Decimal type. While these two types are for most purposes interchangeable, they differ in terms of precision. The Decimal type is a fixed-precision number with up to 28 digits, plus the position of the decimal point. Decimal values require the suffix "m" or "M".

- In VB.NET, the VB6 Variant type is eliminated.

- While in VB6, Char is a single-character String, in Visual Basic .NET Char is a type in its own right.

- Microsoft no longer recommends Hungarian* notation in public identifiers. Meaningful identifiers should be used (studentAge rather than x01) but no type-identifier prefix is needed or recommended.

- In VB.NET, enumerations are formal types, and so an explicit conversion is required to convert between an Enum type and an intrinsic type (such as Integer, Boolean, etc.).

- In VB6 enumerations are just aliases for integer values. In VB.NET, enumerations are actual types, and you must access enumerated constants using the fully qualified name of the enumeration (e.g., Temperature.FreezingPoint).

- In VB.NET, there is no Set statement; however properties have Set and Get accessors, as described in Chapter 5.

VB.NET Types

Visual Basic .NET can (and should) be treated as a strongly typed language. In a strongly typed language you must declare the type of each object you create (e.g., Integer, Decimal, String, Window, Button, etc.) and the compiler will help you prevent bugs by enforcing that only data of the right type is assigned to those objects. You tell the compiler you want Visual Basic .NET to be strongly typed by adding the line:

```
Option Strict On
```

to the top of every source code file. While this is optional it is good programming practice, and this book will assume that Option Strict is set On from now on. You can make this the default in Visual Studio .NET (starting in Version 1.1.) by choosing the menu items `Tools->Options->Projects->VB Defaults` and setting the default to Option Strict On.

The type of an object signals to the compiler the size of that object (e.g., Integer indicates an object of 4 bytes) and its capabilities (e.g., Buttons can be drawn, pressed, and so forth).

Like C++ and Java, Visual Basic .NET divides types into two sets: *intrinsic* (built-in) types that the language offers and *user-defined* types that the programmer defines.

---

* Hungarian notation was named to honor its inventor, Charles Simonyi of Microsoft, who was Hungarian. The idea was to prefix identifiers with letters indicating their type. Thus, an integer variable might be named iAge, a long variable might be named lTotal. Some of the prefixes were rather obscure, such as lpszName (with lpsz signifying "long pointer to a string ending in zero"). In any case, Hungarian notation does not lend itself to object-oriented programming (in which there may be thousands of types defined) and so is now deprecated in public identifiers. What you do with private identifiers is entirely up to you.

Visual Basic .NET also divides the set of types into two other categories: *value* types and *reference* types.[*] The principal difference between value and reference types is the manner in which their values are stored in memory. A value type holds its actual value in memory allocated on the stack (or it is allocated as part of a larger reference type object). The address of a reference type variable sits on the stack, but the actual object is stored on the heap.

If you have a very large object, putting it on the heap has many advantages. Chapter 5 discusses the various advantages and disadvantages of working with reference types; the current chapter focuses on the intrinsic value types available in Visual Basic .NET.

Working with Built-in Types

The Visual Basic .NET language offers the usual cornucopia of intrinsic (built-in) types one expects in a modern language, each of which maps to an underlying type supported by the .NET Common Language Specification (CLS). Mapping the Visual Basic .NET primitive types to the underlying .NET type ensures that objects created in Visual Basic .NET can be used interchangeably with objects created in any other language compliant with the .NET CLS, such as C#.

Each type has a specific and unchanging size. An Integer, for example, is always 4 bytes because it maps to an Int32 in the .NET CLS. Table 3-1 lists the built-in value types offered by Visual Basic .NET.

Table 3-1. VB.NET built-in value types

Type	Size (in bytes)	.NET Type	Description
Boolean	1	Boolean	True or false.
Byte	1	Byte	Unsigned (values 0–255).
Char	2	Char	Unicode characters.
Date	8	DateTime	1/1/0001 at 0:00:0000 through 12/31/9999 at 23:59:59.
Decimal	16	Decimal	Fixed-precision up to 28 digits and the position of the decimal point. This is typically used in financial calculations. Requires the suffix "m" or "M".
Double	8	Double	Double-precision floating point; holds the values from approximately +/-5.0 * 10^{-324} to approximate +/-1.8 * 10^{308} with 15–16 significant figures.
Integer	4	Int32	Signed Integer values between –2,147,483,648 and 2,147,483,647.
Long	8	Int64	Signed integers ranging from -9,223,372,036,854,775,808 to 9,223,372,036,854,775,807.
Short	2	Int16	Signed (short) (values –32,768 to 32,767).
Single	4	Single	Floating point number. Holds the values from approximately +/-1.5 * 10^{-45} to approximate +/-3.4 * 10^{38} with 7 significant figures.
String		String	A sequence of Unicode characters.

[*] All the intrinsic types are value types except for Object (discussed in Chapter 5) and String (discussed in Chapter 10). All user-defined types are reference types except for structures (discussed in Chapter 7).

The Stack and the Heap

A stack is a data structure used to store items on a last-in first-out basis (like a stack of dishes at the buffet line in a restaurant). *The* stack refers to an area of memory supported by the processor, on which the local variables are stored.

In Visual Basic .NET, value types (e.g., integers) are allocated on the stack—an area of memory is set aside for their value, and this area is referred to by the name of the variable.

Reference types (e.g., objects) are allocated on the heap. When an object is allocated on the heap its address is returned, and that address is assigned to a reference.

The garbage collector destroys objects on the stack sometime after the stack frame they are declared within ends. Typically a stack frame is defined by a function. Thus, if you declare a local variable within a function (as explained later in this chapter) the object will be marked for garbage collection after the function ends.

Objects on the heap are garbage collected sometime after the final reference to them is destroyed.

In addition to these primitive types, Visual Basic .NET has two other value types: Enum (considered later in this chapter) and Structure (see Chapter 7). Chapter 6 discusses other subtleties of value types, such as forcing value types to act as reference types through a process known as *boxing*, and the fact that value types do not "inherit."

Choosing a Built-in Type

Typically you decide which size Integer to use (Integer, Short, or Long) based on the magnitude of the value you want to store. For example, an Integer can only hold the values of approximately negative 2 billion through positive 2 billion, but a Long can hold values from negative 9 quintillion through positive 9 quintillion. So if you have to count, for example, all the people in the world, you would need to use a Long.

Single, Double, and Decimal offer varying degrees of size and precision for rational numbers. For most small fractional numbers, Single is fine.

The Char type represents a Unicode character. If you want to assign a single character literal to a Char variable, and Option Strict is On (as it should be), you must use the literal type character C to force the String to the Char data type. For example, you might write:

```
Dim myChar As Char
myChar = "X"C
```

The character literal C following the String "X" forces the conversion to the Char type.

Converting Built-in Types

Objects of one type can be converted into objects of another type. This is called *casting*.

Casting can be either narrowing or widening. A widening cast is one in which the conversion is to a type that can accommodate every possible value in the existing variable type. For example, an Integer can accommodate every possible value held by a Short. Thus, casting from Short to Integer is a widening conversion.

A narrowing cast is one in which the conversion is to a type that may not be able to accommodate every possible value in the existing variable type. For example, a Short can accommodate only some of the values that an Integer variable might hold. Thus, casting from an Integer to a Short is a narrowing conversion.

In VB.NET, conversions are invoked either implicitly or explicitly. Widening casts are implicit. In an implicit conversion, the compiler makes the conversion with no special action by the developer:

```
Dim myInteger As Integer = 5
Dim myDouble As Double = myInteger ' implicit cast
```

Narrowing casts, on the other hand, must be explicit if Option Strict is On:

```
Dim mySecondInteger As Integer = myDouble ' error! won't compile
```

With an explicit conversion, the developer must use a special function to signal the cast:

```
Dim mySecondInteger As Integer = CType(myDouble, Integer) 'ok
```

The semantics of an explicit conversion are: "Hey! Compiler! I know what I'm doing." This is sometimes called "hitting it with the big hammer" and can be very useful or very painful, depending on whether your thumb is in the way of the nail.

Visual Basic .NET provides a number of explicit casting methods:

CBool()
> Converts any valid string or numeric expression to Boolean. Numeric non-zero values are converted to True, zero is converted to False. The Strings "True" and "False" are converted to True and False, respectively.

CByte()
> Converts numeric expression in range 0 to 255 to Byte; rounds fractional part.

CChar()
> Returns the first character of a String as a Char.

CDate()
> Converts any valid representation of a date or time to the Date type (e.g., "April 15, 2003" is converted to the corresponding Date type).

CDbl()

Converts any expression that can be evaluated as a number to a Double if it is in the range of a Double.

CDec()

Converts any expression that can be evaluated as a number to a Decimal if it is in the range of a Decimal.

CInt()

Converts any expression that can be evaluated as a number to an Integer if it is in the range of an Integer; rounds fractional part.

CLng()

Converts any expression that can be evaluated as a number to a Long if it is in the range of a Long; rounds fractional part.

CObj()

Converts any expression that can be interpreted as an Object to an Object.

CShort()

Converts any expression that can be evaluated as a number to a Short if it is in the range of a Short.

CStr()

If Boolean, converts to the String "True" or "False." If the expression can be interpreted as a date, returns a String expression of the date. For numeric expressions, the returned String represents the number.

CType()

This is a general purpose conversion function that uses the syntax:

```
CType(expression, typename)
```

where *expression* is an expression or a variable, and *typename* is the data type to convert to. You can rewrite the following code:

```
System.Console.WriteLine( _
    "Freezing point of water: {0}", _
    CInt(Temperatures.FreezingPoint))
```

to the more generic:

```
System.Console.WriteLine( _
    "Freezing point of water: {0}", _
    CType(Temperatures.FreezingPoint, Integer))
```

Identifiers

Identifiers are names that programmers choose for their types, methods, variables, constants, objects, and so forth. An identifier must begin with a letter or an underscore.

The Microsoft naming conventions suggest using *Camel notation* (initial lowercase such as someName) for variable names (see the next section) and *Pascal notation* (initial uppercase such as SomeOtherName) for method names and most other identifiers. (Examples are provided later in this chapter and in subsequent chapters.)

Identifiers cannot clash with keywords. Thus, you cannot create a variable named Integer or Module. In addition, Visual Basic .NET identifiers are *not* case-sensitive, so myVariable and MyVariable are treated as the same variable names.

Variables and Constants

A variable is a storage location with a type. The type will be one of the intrinsic types (variables of user-defined types are called objects, and are explained in Chapter 5). In the examples in the earlier section "Converting Built-in Types," both myInteger and myDouble are variables. Variables can have values assigned to them, and those values can be changed programmatically.

WriteLine( )

The .NET Framework provides a useful method for writing output to the screen. The details of this method, System.Console.WriteLine( ), will become clearer as we progress through the book, but the fundamentals are straightforward. You call WriteLine( ) in Example 3-1, passing in a String that you want printed to the console (the screen) and, optionally, parameters that will be substituted. In the following example:

```
System.Console.WriteLine("After assignment, myInteger: {0}", myInteger)
```

the String "After assignment, myInteger:" is printed as-is, followed by the value in the variable myInteger. The location of the substitution parameter {0} specifies where the value of the first output variable, myInteger, will be displayed, in this case at the end of the String. We'll see a great deal more about WriteLine( ) in later chapters.

You create a variable by declaring its type and then giving it a name. You can initialize the variable when you declare it, and you can assign a new value to that variable at any time, changing the value held in the variable. Example 3-1 initializes the variable myInteger with the value 7, displays that value, reassigns the variable with the value 5, and displays it again.

Example 3-1. Initializing and assigning a value to a variable

```
Option Strict On
Imports System

Module Module1
    Sub Main( )
        Dim myInteger As Integer = 7
        Console.WriteLine("Initialized, myInteger: {0}", _
```

Example 3-1. Initializing and assigning a value to a variable (continued)

```
            myInteger)
        myInteger = 5
        Console.WriteLine("After assignment, myInteger: {0}", _
            myInteger)
    End Sub
End Module
```

```
Output:
Initialized, myInteger: 7
After assignment, myInteger: 5
```

Default Values

If you create a variable but do not initialize it with a value, Visual Basic .NET will provide a default value for you. The default values for the intrinsic types are as follows:

- Numeric types (Decimal, Double, Integer, Long, Short, and Single) will be assigned the value 0.
- The Char type will be assigned the value " " .
- The Boolean type will be assigned the value False.
- The Date type will be assigned 12:00:00 am, 1/1/0001.

Constants

Variables are a powerful tool, but there are times when you want to manipulate a defined value, one whose value you want to ensure remains constant. For example, you might need to work with the Fahrenheit freezing and boiling points of water in a program simulating a chemistry experiment. Your program will be clearer if you name the variables that store these values FreezingPoint and BoilingPoint, but you do not want to permit their values to be reassigned. How do you prevent reassignment? The answer is to use a constant. A *constant* is a variable whose value cannot be changed.

Constants come in three flavors: *literals*, *symbolic constants*, and *enumerations*. In this assignment:

```
    x = 32
```

the value 32 is a literal constant. The value of 32 is always 32. You can't assign a new value to 32; you can't make 32 represent the value 99 no matter how you might try.

Symbolic constants assign a name to a constant value. You declare a symbolic constant using the Const keyword and the following syntax:

```
    Const value As type = identifier
```

A constant must be initialized when it is declared, and once initialized it cannot be altered. For example:

```
Const FreezingPoint As Integer = 32
```

In this declaration, 32 is a literal constant and FreezingPoint is a symbolic constant of type Integer. Example 3-2 illustrates the use of symbolic constants.

Example 3-2. Using symbolic constants

```
Option Strict On
Imports System
Module Module1
    Sub Main( )
        Const FreezingPoint As Integer = 32 ' Farenheit
        Const BoilingPoint As Integer = 212
        Console.WriteLine("Freezing point of water: {0}", _
            FreezingPoint)
        Console.WriteLine("Boiling point of water: {0}", _
            BoilingPoint)
        ' BoilingPoint = 100
    End Sub
End Module
```

Example 3-2 creates two symbolic Integer constants: FreezingPoint and BoilingPoint. As a matter of style, constant names are written in Pascal notation (initial uppercase), but this is certainly not required by the language.

These constants serve the same purpose as always using the *literal* values 32 and 212 for the freezing and boiling points of water in expressions that require them, but because these constants have names they convey far more meaning. Also, if you decide to switch this program to Celsius, you can reinitialize these constants at compile time to 0 and 100, respectively, and all the rest of the code ought to continue to work.

To prove to yourself that the constant cannot be reassigned, try uncommenting the assignment to BoilingPoint:

```
BoilingPoint = 100
```

When you recompile you should receive this error:

```
Constant cannot be the target of an assignment
```

Enumerations

Enumerations provide a powerful alternative to constants. An enumeration is a distinct value type, consisting of a set of named constants (called the *enumerator list*).

In Example 3-2, you created two related constants:

```
Const FreezingPoint As Integer = 32
Const BoilingPoint As Integer = 212
```

You might wish to add a number of other useful constants as well to this list, such as:

```
Const LightJacketWeather As Integer = 60
Const SwimmingWeather As Integer = 72
Const WickedCold As Integer = 0
```

This process is somewhat cumbersome, and there is no logical connection among these various constants. Visual Basic .NET provides the *enumeration* to solve these problems:

```
Public Enum Temperatures
    CelsiusMeetsFahrenheit = -40
    WickedCold = 0
    FreezingPoint = 32
    LightJacketWeather = 60
    SwimmingWeather = 72
    BoilingPoint = 212
End Enum 'Temperatures
```

Every enumeration has an underlying type, which can be any integral type (Integer, Short, Long, etc.) except for Char. The syntax of an enumeration is:

```
[attributes] [access modifiers] Enum identifier [As base-type]

    enumerator-list [ = constant-expression ]
End Enum
```

The optional attributes and modifiers are considered later in this book. For now, let's focus on the rest of this declaration. An enumeration begins with the keyword Enum, which is generally followed by an identifier, such as:

```
Enum Temperatures
```

The *base-type* is the underlying type for the enumeration. If you leave out this optional value (and often you will) it defaults to Integer, but you are free to use any of the integral types (e.g., Short, Long). For example, the following fragment declares an enumeration of Longs:

```
Enum ServingSizes As Long
    Small = 1
    Regular = 2
    Large = 3
End Enum
```

Example 3-3 rewrites Example 3-2 to use an enumeration.

Example 3-3. Using enumerations to simplify your code

```
Option Strict On
Imports System
Module Module1

    Enum Temperatures
        CelsiusMeetsFahrenheit = -40
        WickedCold = 0
```

Example 3-3. Using enumerations to simplify your code (continued)

```
        FreezingPoint = 32
        LightJacketWeather = 60
        SwimmingWeather = 72
        BoilingPoint = 212
    End Enum 'Temperatures

    Sub Main( )
        Console.WriteLine("Freezing point of water: {0}", _
            CType(Temperatures.FreezingPoint, Integer))
        Console.WriteLine("Boiling point of water: {0}", _
            CType(Temperatures.BoilingPoint, Integer))
    End Sub
End Module
```

In this example, the EnumType of each of the enumerated values is Temperatures. As you can see, an Enum (e.g., WickedCold) must be qualified by its Enumtype (e.g., Temperatures.WickedCold). This was optional in VB6, but it is mandated in VB.NET.

When you want to display the value of an enumerated constant, rather than its name, you must cast the constant to its underlying type (Integer). The Integer value is passed to WriteLine( ), and that value is displayed.

Each constant in an enumeration corresponds to a numerical value; in this case, an Integer. If you don't specifically set it otherwise, the enumeration begins at 0 and each subsequent value counts up from the previous.

If you create the following enumeration:

```
Enum SomeValues
    First
    Second
    Third = 20
    Fourth
End Enum
```

the value of First will be 0, Second will be 1, Third will be 20, and Fourth will be 21.

> Enums are formal types; therefore an explicit conversion is required to convert between an Enum type and an integral type.

Strings

It is nearly impossible to write a Visual Basic .NET program without creating strings. A String object holds a string of characters.

You declare a String variable using the `String` keyword much as you would create an instance of any object:

```
Dim myString As String
```

A string literal is created by placing double quotes around a string of letters:

```
"Hello World"
```

It is common to initialize a string variable with a string literal:

```
Dim myString As String = "Hello World"
```

Strings will be covered in much greater detail in Chapter 10.

Whitespace

In the Visual Basic .NET language, spaces and tabs are considered to be "whitespace" (so named because you see only the white of the underlying "page"). Extra whitespace is generally ignored in Visual Basic .NET statements. Thus, you can write:

```
myVariable = 5
```

or:

```
myVariable    =                    5
```

and the compiler will treat the two statements as identical. In fact, Visual Studio .NET will automatically discard the extra white space and close up the second version so that it resembles the first!

The exception to this rule is that whitespace within strings is not ignored. If you write:

```
Console.WriteLine("Hello World")
```

each space between "Hello" and "World" is treated as another character in the string.

Most of the time the use of whitespace is intuitive. The key is to use whitespace to make the program more readable to the programmer; the compiler is indifferent.

However, there are instances in which the use of whitespace is quite significant. Although the expression:

```
Dim x As Integer = 5
```

is the same as:

```
Dim x As Integer=5
```

it is not the same as:

```
Dimx As Integer = 5
```

The compiler knows that the whitespace on either side of the assignment operator is extra, but the whitespace between the keyword Dim and the identifier x is *not* extra, and is required. This is not surprising; the whitespace allows the compiler to parse the keyword Dim rather than some unknown term Dimx. You are free to add as much or as little whitespace between Dim and x as you care to, but there must be at least one whitespace character (typically a space or tab).

Statements

In Visual Basic .NET a complete program instruction is called a *statement*. Programs consist of sequences of Visual Basic .NET statements. Each statement must end with a new line:

```
Dim x As Integer      ' a statement
x = 23                ' another statement
Dim y As Integer = x  ' yet another statement
```

It is possible to combine two (or more) statements on a single line by separating the statements with the colon operator:

```
Dim x As Integer = 23 : Dim y As Integer = 25
```

While this is legal, it is uncommon because it makes the code more difficult to read.

A statement that evaluates to a value (e.g., to a Boolean value) is called an *expression*.

Branching

Visual Basic .NET statements are evaluated in order. The compiler starts at the beginning of a statement list and makes its way to the bottom. This would be entirely straightforward, and terribly limiting, were it not for branching. There are two types of branches in a Visual Basic .NET program: *unconditional branching* and *conditional branching*.

Program flow is also affected by looping and iteration statements, which are signaled by the keywords If, Select Case, For, Do, While, and For Each. Iteration is discussed later in this chapter, and For Each is considered in Chapter 9. For now, let's consider some of the more basic methods of conditional and unconditional branching.

Unconditional Branching Statements

An unconditional branch is created by invoking a method. When the compiler encounters the name of a method it stops execution in the current method and branches to the newly "called" method. When that method returns a value, execution picks up in the original method on the line just below the method call. Example 3-4 illustrates.

Example 3-4. Calling a method

```
Option Strict On
Imports System
Module Module1
```

Example 3-4. Calling a method (continued)

```
Sub Main( )
    Console.WriteLine("In Main! Calling SomeMethod( )...")
    SomeMethod( )
    Console.WriteLine("Back in Main( ).")
End Sub 'Main

Sub SomeMethod( )
    Console.WriteLine("Greetings from SomeMethod!")
End Sub 'SomeMethod

End Module

Output:
In Main! Calling SomeMethod( )...
Greetings from SomeMethod!
Back in Main( ).
```

Program flow begins in Main( ) and proceeds until SomeMethod( ) is invoked (invoking a method is sometimes referred to as "calling" the method). At that point program flow branches to the method. When the method completes, program flow resumes at the next line after the call to that method.

 You can create an unconditional branch by using one of the unconditional branch keywords: Goto, Exit, Return, or Throw. The first three of these are discussed later in this chapter, while the final statement, Throw, is discussed in Chapter 11.

Conditional Branching Statements

While methods branch unconditionally, often you will want to branch within a method depending on a condition that you evaluate while the program is running. This is known as *conditional branching*. Conditional branching statements allow you to write logic such as "If you are over 25 years old, then you may rent a car."

VB.NET provides a number of constructs that allow you to write conditional branches into your programs. A conditional branching statement is signaled by keywords such as If and Select Case; these constructs are described in the following sections.

If Statements

The simplest branching statement is If. An If statement says, "If a particular condition is true, then execute the statement; otherwise skip it." (The condition is a *Boolean expression*. An expression is a statement that evaluates to a value. A Boolean expression evaluates to either true or false.)

The formal description of an If statement is:

```
If expression Then
    statements
End If
```

This formal definition states that the If statement takes an expression and Then executes the *statements* until the End If, but only if the *expression* evaluates to true.

An alternative one-line version is:

```
If expression Then statement
```

 Many VB.NET developers avoid the single-line If statement because it can be confusing and thus difficult to maintain.

Example 3-5 illustrates the use of an If statement.

Example 3-5. Using the If statement

```
Option Strict On
Imports System
Module Module1

    Sub Main( )

        Dim valueOne As Integer = 10
        Dim valueTwo As Integer = 20
        Dim valueThree As Integer = 30

        Console.WriteLine("Testing valueOne against valueTwo...")
        If valueOne > valueTwo Then
            Console.WriteLine( _
                "ValueOne: {0} larger than ValueTwo: {1}", _
                valueOne, valueTwo)
        End If

        Console.WriteLine("Testing valueThree against valueTwo...")
        If valueThree > valueTwo Then
            Console.WriteLine( _
                "ValueThree: {0} larger than ValueTwo: {1}", _
                valueThree, valueTwo)
        End If
        Console.WriteLine("Testing is valueTwo > 15 (one line)...")
        If valueTwo > 15 Then Console.WriteLine("Yes it is")

    End Sub 'Main

End Module
Output:
Testing valueOne against valueTwo...
Testing valueThree against valueTwo...
```

Example 3-5. Using the If statement (continued)

```
ValueThree: 30 larger than ValueTwo: 20
Testing is valueTwo > 15 (one line)...
Yes it is
```

In this simple program, you declare three variables, valueOne, valueTwo, and valueThree, with the values 10, 20, and 30, respectively. In the first If statement, you test whether valueOne is greater than valueTwo:

```
If valueOne > valueTwo Then
    Console.WriteLine( _
        "ValueOne: {0} larger than ValueTwo: {1}", valueOne, valueTwo)
End If
```

Because valueOne (10) is less than valueTwo (20), this If statement fails (the condition returns false), and thus the body of the If statement (the statements between the If and the End If) doesn't execute.

> The test for greater-than uses the greater-than operator (>), which is discussed in detail later in this chapter.

You then test whether valueThree is greater than valueTwo:

```
If valueThree > valueTwo Then
    Console.WriteLine( _
        "ValueThree: {0} larger than ValueTwo: {1}", valueThree, valueTwo)
End If
```

Since valueThree (30) *is* greater than valueTwo (20), the test returns true, and thus the statement executes. The statement in this case is the call to the WriteLine() method, shown in bold in the preceding sample code.

Finally, you use a one-line If statement to test whether valueTwo is greater than 15. Since this evaluates true, the statement that follows executes, and the words "Yes it is" are displayed.

```
If valueTwo > 15 Then Console.WriteLine("Yes it is")
```

The output reflects that the first If statement fails, but the second and third succeed:

```
Testing valueOne against valueTwo...
Testing valueThree against valueTwo...
ValueThree: 30 larger than ValueTwo: 20
Testing is valueTwo > 15 (one line)...
Yes it is
```

VB6 programmers take note: In Visual Basic .NET, variables created within nested scope (e.g., within an If statement) are scoped to that statement and are not visible outside the nested scope. Thus the following code:

```
If someValue > someOtherValue Then
    Dim tempValue As Integer = 5
    ' other code here
End If
myValue = tempValue  'error!
```

will generate a compile error at the last line:

```
Name 'tempValue' is not declared
```

because the variable tempValue was declared within the If statement and thus is not visible outside the If statement.

If . . . Else Statements

Often, you will find that you want to take one set of actions when the condition tests true and a different set of actions when the condition tests false. This allows you to write logic such as, "If you are over 25 years old, then you may rent a car; *otherwise*, you must take the train."

The *otherwise* portion of the logic is executed in the Else statement. For example, you can modify Example 3-5 to print an appropriate message whether or not valueOne is greater than valueTwo, as shown in Example 3-6.

Example 3-6. The Else statement

```
Option Strict On
Imports System
Module Module1

    Sub Main( )

        Dim valueOne As Integer = 10
        Dim valueTwo As Integer = 20
        Dim valueThree As Integer = 30

        Console.WriteLine("Testing valueOne against valueTwo...")
        If valueOne > valueTwo Then
            Console.WriteLine( _
                "ValueOne: {0} larger than ValueTwo: {1}", valueOne, valueTwo)
        Else
            Console.WriteLine( _
                "Nope, ValueOne: {0} is NOT larger than valueTwo: {1}", _
                valueOne, valueTwo)
        End If
    End Sub 'Main

End Module
```

Example 3-6. The Else statement (continued)

```
Output:
Testing valueOne against valueTwo...
Nope, ValueOne: 10 is NOT larger than valueTwo: 20
```

Because the test in the If statement fails (valueOne is *not* larger than valueTwo), the body of the If statement is skipped and the body of the Else statement is executed. Had the test succeeded, the If statement body would execute and the Else statement would be skipped.

Nested If Statements

It is possible, and not uncommon, to nest If statements to handle complex conditions. For example, suppose you need to write a program to evaluate the temperature and return the following types of information:

- If the temperature is 32 degrees or lower, the program should warn you about ice on the road.

- If the temperature is exactly 32 degrees, the program should tell you that there may be ice patches.

- If the temperature is higher than 32 degrees, the program should assure you that there is no ice.*

There are many good ways to write this program. Example 3-7 illustrates one approach, using nested If statements.

Example 3-7. Nested If statements

```
Option Strict On
Imports System
Module Module1


  Sub Main( )
     Dim temp As Integer = 32

     If temp <= 32 Then
        Console.WriteLine("Warning! Ice on road!")
        If temp = 32 Then
           Console.WriteLine("Temp exactly freezing, beware of water.")
        Else
           Console.WriteLine("Watch for black ice! Temp: {0}", temp)
        End If 'temp = 32
     End If 'temp <= 32
  End Sub 'Main
```

---

* This book does not warranty the absence of ice. Drive carefully and observe all speed limits. Offer void where prohibited. Your mileage may vary.

Example 3-7. Nested If statements (continued)

```
End Module
Output:
Warning! Ice on road!
Temp exactly freezing, beware of water.
```

The logic of Example 3-7 is that it tests whether the temperature is less than or equal to 32. If so, it prints a warning:

```
If temp <= 32 Then
        Console.WriteLine("Warning! Ice on road!")
```

The program then uses a second If statement, nested within the first, to check whether the temp is equal to 32 degrees. If so, it prints one message ("Temp exactly freezing, beware of water."); if not, the temp must be less than 32 and an Else is executed, causing the program to print the next message ("Watch for black ice . . ."). Because the second If statement is nested within the first If, the logic of the Else statement is: "Since it has been established that the temp is less than or equal to 32, and it isn't equal to 32, it must be less than 32."

 The less-than-or-equal-to operator <= is described under "Relational Operators," later in this chapter.

ElseIf

The ElseIf statement allows you to perform a related sequence of Ifs. The logic of ElseIf is that if the first If evaluates false, then evaluate the first ElseIf. The first If/ElseIf statement to evaluate true will have its statements executed (and no others will even be evaluated). If none of the statements evaluates true, the final Else clause is executed. Example 3-8 uses ElseIf to perform the same actions as Example 3-7.

Example 3-8. The ElseIf statement

```
Option Strict On
Imports System
Module Module1

    Sub Main( )
        Dim temp As Integer = -32

        If temp > 32 Then
            Console.WriteLine("Safe driving...")
        ElseIf temp = 32 Then
            Console.WriteLine("Warning, 32 degrees, watch for ice and water")
        ElseIf temp > 0 Then
            Console.WriteLine("Watch for ice...")
        ElseIf temp = 0 Then
            Console.WriteLine("Temperature = 0")
        Else
```

Example 3-8. The ElseIf statement (continued)

```
        Console.WriteLine("Temperatures below zero, Wicked Cold!")
      End If
   End Sub 'Main

End Module
Output:
Temperatures below zero, Wicked Cold!
```

IIF: If and Only IF

A very common idiom is to test an expression and to assign a value to a variable based on the result of that test. For example, you might want to find the larger of two values. You can certainly do so with an If...Else statement, as shown in Example 3-9.

Example 3-9. Set max value with If...Else

```
Option Strict On
Imports System
Module Module1

    Sub Main( )

        Dim valueOne As Integer = 10
        Dim valueTwo As Integer = 20
        Dim maxValue As Integer

        If valueOne > valueTwo Then
            maxValue = valueOne
        Else
            maxValue = valueTwo
        End If

        Console.WriteLine("ValueOne: {0}, valueTwo: {1},  maxValue: {2}", _
            valueOne, valueTwo, maxValue)
    End Sub 'Main

End Module
Output:
ValueOne: 10, valueTwo: 20,  maxValue: 20
```

Because If...Else is such a common task, however, Visual Basic .NET provides a special keyword, IIF, to test an expression and return one of two values. (The letters that make up the keyword are meant to suggest "If and only IF" and that is also the way you should read the keyword.) The IIF statement takes three arguments:

- The Boolean expression to be evaluated
- The value to return if the expression is true
- The value to return if the expression is false

The logic of an IIF statement is this: If valueOne is greater than valueTwo, return the value in valueOne and assign it to maxValue, otherwise return the value in valueTwo and assign that to maxValue.

Thus, you can rewrite Example 3-9, eliminating the If...Else block with a single IIF statement, as shown in Example 3-10.

Example 3-10. The IIF statement

```
Option Strict On
Imports System
Module Module1

    Sub Main( )

        Dim valueOne As Integer = 10
        Dim valueTwo As Integer = 20
        Dim maxValue As Integer

        maxValue = CInt(IIf((valueOne > valueTwo), valueOne, valueTwo))

        Console.WriteLine("ValueOne: {0}, valueTwo: {1},  maxValue: {2}", _
            valueOne, valueTwo, maxValue)
    End Sub 'Main

End Module
```

The IIF statement is defined to take a Boolean expression and two objects and return an object. Thus, the return value must be cast to an Integer.

Select Case Statements

Nested If statements and long sequences of ElseIf statements are hard to read, hard to get right, and hard to debug. When you have a complex set of choices to make, the Select Case statement is a more powerful alternative. The logic of a Select Case statement is this: "Pick a matching value and act accordingly." The syntax is as follows:

```
Select [ Case ] testExpression
[ Case expressionList
    [ statements ] ]
[ Case Else
    [ else-statements] ]
End Select
```

It is easiest to understand this construct in the context of a sample program. In Example 3-11, a value of 15 is assigned to the variable targetInteger. The Select Case statement tests for the values 5, 10, and 15. If one matches, the associated statement is executed.

Example 3-11. Using Select Case

```
Option Strict On
Imports System
Module Module1

    Sub Main( )
        Dim targetInteger As Integer = 15

        Select targetInteger
           Case 5
              Console.WriteLine("5")
           Case 10
              Console.WriteLine("10")
           Case 15
              Console.WriteLine("15!")
           Case Else
              Console.WriteLine("Value not found")
        End Select
    End Sub 'Main

End Module

Output:
15!
```

The output shows that 15 matched, and the associated statement was executed, displaying the value "15!". If none of the values matched, any statements following Case Else would be executed.

Note that Case also allows you to check a variable against a range of values. You can combine Case with the keywords Is and To to specify the ranges, as illustrated in Example 3-12. Note that the target value (targetInteger) has been changed to 7.

Example 3-12. Testing for a range of values

```
Option Strict On
Imports System

Module Module1

    Sub Main( )
        Dim targetInteger As Integer = 7

        Select Case targetInteger
           Case Is < 10
              Console.WriteLine("Less than 10")
           Case 10 To 14
              Console.WriteLine("10-14")
           Case 15
              Console.WriteLine("15!")
           Case Else
              Console.WriteLine("Value not found")
        End Select
```

Example 3-12. Testing for a range of values (continued)

```
    End Sub 'Main

End Module
```

Output:
Less than 10

In Example 3-12, the first test examines whether targetInteger is less than 10. You specify this by combining Case with the Is keyword followed by the less-than operator and the number 10 to specify the range:

```
    Case Is < 10
```

You then use Case with the To keyword to specify a range of 10 through 14:

```
    Case 10 To 14
```

The preceding Case will match any value of 10 through 14, inclusive.

You are not restricted to just testing for a numeric value. You can also test for String values. In fact, you can test ranges of String values, examining whether a target value fits alphabetically within the range, as shown in Example 3-13.

Example 3-13. Testing alphabetic ranges

```
Option Strict On
Imports System
Module Module1

    Sub Main( )

        Dim target As String = "Milo"

        Select Case target

            Case "Alpha" To "Lambda "
                Console.WriteLine("Alpha To Lambda executed")
            Case "Lamda" To "Zeta"
                Console.WriteLine("Lambda To Zeta executed")
            Case Else
                Console.WriteLine("Else executed")
        End Select
    End Sub 'Main

End Module
```

Output:
Lambda To Zeta executed

Example 3-13 tests whether the string "Milo" fits within the alphabetic range between the strings "Alpha" and "Lambda"; then it tests whether "Milo" fits within the range between the strings "Lambda" and "Zeta." Both ranges are inclusive. Clearly the second range encompasses the string "Milo" and the output bears that out.

You can also simply test whether one string matches another. The following case tests whether the string "Milo" is the same as the string "Fred":

```
Dim target As String = "Milo"

Select Case target
    Case "Fred"
        Console.WriteLine("Fred")
```

But clearly "Milo" does not equal "Fred."

You can also combine a series of tests in a single Case statement, separating them by commas. Thus you could test whether "Milo" matches either of the strings "Fred" or "Joe" and also whether it falls within the (admittedly small) alphabetic range that comes before "Alpha" using the following code:

```
Dim target As String = "Milo"

Select Case target
    Case "Fred", "Joe", Is < "Alpha"
        Console.WriteLine("Joe or Fred or < Alpha")
```

Clearly "Milo" would not match any of these cases; but changing the target string to "Aardvark" would get you somewhere.

Iteration (Looping) Statements

There are many situations in which you will want to do the same thing again and again, perhaps slightly changing a value each time you repeat the action. This is called *iteration* or *looping*. Typically, you'll iterate (or loop) over a set of items, taking the same action on each. This is the programming equivalent to an assembly line. On an assembly line, you might take a hundred car bodies and put a windshield on each one as it comes by. In an iterative program, you might work your way through a collection of text boxes on a form, retrieving the value from each in turn and using those values to update a database.

VB.NET provides an extensive suite of iteration statements, including Do, For, and For Each. You can also create a loop by using a statement called Goto. This chapter considers the use of Goto, Do, and For. However, you'll have to wait until Chapter 9 to learn more about For Each.

Creating Loops with Goto

Goto is the most primitive kind of unconditional branching statement, and it is not much used in modern programming. Its most common usage was to create looping statements, and in fact, the Goto statement is the seed from which all other looping statements have been germinated. Unfortunately, it is a semolina seed, producer of spaghetti code and endless confusion.

Programs that use Goto statements jump around a great deal. Goto can cause your method to loop back and forth in ways that are difficult to follow.

If you were to try to draw the flow of control in a program that makes extensive use of Goto statements, the resulting morass of intersecting and overlapping lines might look like a plate of spaghetti; hence the term "spaghetti code." Spaghetti code is a contemptuous epithet; no one wants to write spaghetti code.

Most experienced programmers properly shun the Goto statement, but in the interest of completeness, here's how you use it:

1. Create a label.
2. Goto that label.

The label is an identifier followed by a colon. You place the label in your code, and then you use the Goto keyword to jump to that label. The Goto command is typically tied to an If statement, as illustrated in Example 3-14.

Example 3-14. Using Goto

```
Option Strict On
Imports System

Module Module1

    Sub Main( )
        Dim counterVariable As Integer = 0

repeat:  ' the label
        Console.WriteLine("counterVariable: {0}", counterVariable)

        ' increment the counter
        counterVariable += 1

        If counterVariable < 10 Then
            GoTo repeat ' the dastardly deed
        End If
    End Sub 'Main

End Module

Output:
counterVariable: 0
counterVariable: 1
counterVariable: 2
counterVariable: 3
counterVariable: 4
counterVariable: 5
counterVariable: 6
counterVariable: 7
counterVariable: 8
counterVariable: 9
```

This code is not terribly complex; you've used only a single Goto statement. However, with multiple such statements and labels scattered through your code, tracing the flow of execution becomes very difficult.

It was the phenomenon of spaghetti code that led to the creation of alternatives, such as the Do loop.

The Do Loop

The semantics of a Do loop are, "Do this work while a condition is true" or "Do this work until a condition becomes true." You can test the condition either at the top or at the bottom of the loop. If you test at the bottom of the loop, the loop will execute at least once.

The Do loop can even be written with no conditions, in which case it will execute indefinitely, until it encounters an Exit Do statement.

Do loops come in a number of varieties, some of which require additional keywords such as While and Until. The syntax for these various Do loops follows. Note that in each case, the BooleanExpression can be any expression that evaluates to a Boolean value of true or false.

```
Do While boolean-expression
    statements
Loop

Do Until boolean-expression
    statements
Loop

Do
    statements
Loop While boolean-expression

Do
    statements
Loop Until boolean-expression

Do
    statements
Loop
```

In the first type of Do loop, Do While, the *statements* in the loop execute only while the *boolean-expression* returns true. Example 3-15 shows a Do While loop, which in this case does no more than increment a counterVariable from 0 to 9, printing a statement to that effect to the console for each iteration of the loop.

Example 3-15. Using Do While

```
Option Strict On
Imports System
```

Example 3-15. Using Do While (continued)

```
Module Module1

    Sub Main( )
        Dim counterVariable As Integer = 0

        Do While counterVariable < 10
            Console.WriteLine("counterVariable: {0}", counterVariable)
            counterVariable = counterVariable + 1
        Loop ' While counterVariable < 10

    End Sub 'Main

End Module

Output:
counterVariable: 0
counterVariable: 1
counterVariable: 2
counterVariable: 3
counterVariable: 4
counterVariable: 5
counterVariable: 6
counterVariable: 7
counterVariable: 8
counterVariable: 9
```

The second version of Do, Do Until, executes until the *boolean-expression* returns true, using the following syntax:

```
Do Until boolean-expression
    statements
Loop
```

Example 3-16 modifies Example 3-15 to use Do Until.

Example 3-16. Using Do Until

```
Option Strict On
Imports System

Module Module1

    Sub Main( )
        Dim counterVariable As Integer = 0

        Do Until counterVariable = 10
            Console.WriteLine("counterVariable: {0}", counterVariable)
            counterVariable = counterVariable + 1
        Loop ' Until counterVariable = 10

    End Sub 'Main

End Module
```

The output from Example 3-16 is identical to that of Example 3-15.

 Be very careful when looping to a specific value. If the value is never reached, or skipped over, your loop can continue without end.

Do While and Do Until are closely related; which you use will depend on the semantics of the problem you are trying to solve. That is, use the construct that represents how you think about the problem. If you are solving this problem: "Keep winding the box until the Jack pops up," then use a Do Until loop. If you are solving this problem: "As long as the music plays, keep dancing," then use a Do While loop.

In order to make sure a Do While or Do Until loop runs at least once, you can test the condition at the end of the loop:

```
Do
    statements
Loop While boolean-expression

Do
    statements
Loop Until boolean-expression
```

If your counterVariable were initialized to 100, but you wanted to make sure the loop ran once anyway, you might use the Do Loop...While construct, as shown in Example 3-17.

Example 3-17. Do Loop While

```
Option Strict On
Imports System

Module Module1

    Sub Main( )
        Dim counterVariable As Integer = 100

        Do
            Console.WriteLine("counterVariable: {0}", counterVariable)
            counterVariable = counterVariable + 1
        Loop While counterVariable < 10

    End Sub 'Main

End Module

Output:
counterVariable: 100
```

While Loops

VB.NET offers a While loop construct that is closely related to the Do While loop, albeit less popular. The syntax is:

```
While Boolean-expression
    statements
End While
```

The logic of this is *identical* to the basic Do While loop, as demonstrated by the following code:

```
Option Strict On
Imports System
Module Module1

    Sub Main( )
      Dim counterVariable As Integer = 0

      While counterVariable < 10
          Console.WriteLine("counterVariable: {0}",
          counterVariable) counterVariable =
          counterVariable + 1
      End While

    End Sub 'Main

End Module

Output:
counterVariable: 0
counterVariable: 1
counterVariable: 2
counterVariable: 3
counterVariable: 4
counterVariable: 5
counterVariable: 6
counterVariable: 7
counterVariable: 8
counterVariable: 9
```

Because the While loop was deprecated in VB6, and because its logic is identical to the more common Do While loop, many VB.NET programmers eschew the While loop construct. It is included here for completeness.

The final Do loop construct is a loop that never ends because there is no condition to satisfy:

```
Do
    statements
Loop
```

The only way to end this construct is to deliberately break out of the loop using the Exit Do statement, described in the next section.

Breaking Out of a Do Loop

You can break out of any Do loop with the Exit Do statement. You *must* break out of the final Do construct:

```
Do
    statements
Loop
```

because otherwise it will never terminate. You typically use this construct when you do not know in advance what condition will cause the loop to terminate (e.g., the termination can be in response to user action).

By using Exit Do within an If statement, as shown in Example 3-18, you can basically mimic the Do Loop...While construct demonstrated in Example 3-17.

Example 3-18. Using Exit Do

```
Option Strict On
Imports System

Module Module1

    Sub Main( )
        Dim counterVariable As Integer = 0

        Do
            Console.WriteLine("counterVariable: {0}", counterVariable)
            counterVariable = counterVariable + 1

            ' test whether we've counted to 9, if so, exit the loop
            If counterVariable > 9 Then
                Exit Do
            End If
        Loop

    End Sub 'Main

End Module

Output:
counterVariable: 0
counterVariable: 1
counterVariable: 2
counterVariable: 3
counterVariable: 4
counterVariable: 5
counterVariable: 6
counterVariable: 7
counterVariable: 8
counterVariable: 9
```

In Example 3-17, you would loop indefinitely if the If statement did not set up a condition and provide an exit via Exit Do. However, as written, Example 3-19 exits the loop when counterVariable becomes greater than 9. You typically would use either the Do While or Do Loop...While construct to accomplish this, but there are many ways to accomplish the same thing in VB.NET. In fact, VB.NET offers yet another alternative, the While loop, as described in the sidebar.

The For Loop

When you need to iterate over a loop a specified number of times, you can use a For loop with a counter variable. The syntax of the For loop is:

```
For variable = expression To expression [ Step expression ]
    statements
Next [ variable-list ]
```

The simplest and most common use of the For statement is to create a variable to count through the iterations of the loop. For example, you might create an integer variable loopCounter that you'll use to step through a loop ten times, as shown in Example 3-19. Note that the Next keyword is used to mark the end of the For loop.

Example 3-19. Using a For loop

```
Option Strict On
Imports System

Module Module1

  Sub Main( )

     Dim loopCounter As Integer
     For loopCounter = 0 To 9
        Console.WriteLine("loopCounter: {0}", loopCounter)
     Next

  End Sub 'Main

End Module

Output:
loopCounter: 0
loopCounter: 1
loopCounter: 2
loopCounter: 3
loopCounter: 4
loopCounter: 5
loopCounter: 6
loopCounter: 7
loopCounter: 8
loopCounter: 9
```

The variable (loopCounter) can be of any numeric type. For example, you might initialize a Single rather than an Integer, and step up through the loop from 0.5 to 9, as shown in Example 3-20.

Example 3-20. Loop with a Single counter

```
Option Strict On
Imports System

Module Module1

    Sub Main( )

        Dim loopCounter As Single
        For loopCounter = 0.5 To 9
            Console.WriteLine("loopCounter: {0}", loopCounter)
        Next

    End Sub 'Main

End Module
```

```
Output:
loopCounter: 0.5
loopCounter: 1.5
loopCounter: 2.5
loopCounter: 3.5
loopCounter: 4.5
loopCounter: 5.5
loopCounter: 6.5
loopCounter: 7.5
loopCounter: 8.5
```

The loop steps up by 1 on each iteration because that is the default step value. The next step would be 9.5, which would be above the upper limit (9) you've set. Thus, the loop ends at loopCounter 8.5.

You can override the default step value of 1 by using the keyword Step. For example, you can modify the step counter in the previous example to .5, as shown in Example 3-21.

Example 3-21. Adjusting the step counter

```
Option Strict On
Imports System

Module Module1

    Sub Main( )

        Dim loopCounter As Single
        For loopCounter = 0.5 To 9 Step 0.5
            Console.WriteLine("loopCounter: {0}", loopCounter)
```

Example 3-21. Adjusting the step counter (continued)

```
    Next

    End Sub 'Main

End Module

Output:
loopCounter: 0.5
loopCounter: 1
loopCounter: 1.5
loopCounter: 2
loopCounter: 2.5
loopCounter: 3
loopCounter: 3.5
loopCounter: 4
loopCounter: 4.5
loopCounter: 5
loopCounter: 5.5
loopCounter: 6
loopCounter: 6.5
loopCounter: 7
loopCounter: 7.5
loopCounter: 8
loopCounter: 8.5
loopCounter: 9
```

Controlling a For Loop Using Next

You can specify which counter variable the Next statement updates. Thus, rather than writing Next in the previous example, you could have written:

```
    Next loopCounter
```

One place where you might want to name the variable being incremented is with a nested loop. For example, in Example 3-22 you create an outer loop to count through the values 3 to 6, and an inner loop to count the values 10 to 12.

Example 3-22. Using Next

```
Option Strict On
Imports System

Module Module1
    Sub Main( )
        Dim inner As Integer
        Dim outer As Integer
        For outer = 3 To 6
            For inner = 10 To 12
                Console.WriteLine("{0} * {1} = {2}", _
                    outer, inner, outer * inner)
            Next inner
        Next outer
```

Example 3-22. Using Next (continued)

```
    End Sub
End Module
```

```
Output:
3 * 10 = 30
3 * 11 = 33
3 * 12 = 36
4 * 10 = 40
4 * 11 = 44
4 * 12 = 48
5 * 10 = 50
5 * 11 = 55
5 * 12 = 60
6 * 10 = 60
6 * 11 = 66
6 * 12 = 72
```

Notice that the inner loop runs through each value for each value in the outer loop (that is, 10–12 is repeated for each of 3, 4, 5, and 6).

Once again, you are free to leave off the name of the variable you are incrementing because Visual Basic .NET can keep track of the inner and outer loop statements for you. Thus, you can rewrite the loop as:

```
For outer = 3 To 6
    For inner = 10 To 12
        Console.WriteLine("{0} * {1} = {2}", _
            outer, inner, outer * inner)
    Next
Next
```

On the other hand, you can combine the two Next statements into one, in which case you *do* need the variable name:

```
For outer = 3 To 6
    For inner = 10 To 12
        Console.WriteLine("{0} * {1} = {2}", _
            outer, inner, outer * inner)
Next inner, outer
```

 VB.NET programmers generally prefer using individual Next statements rather than combining Next statements on one line because it makes for code that is easier to understand and to maintain.

Operators

An *operator* is a symbol (e.g., =, +, >, &) that causes VB.NET to take an action. That action might be an assignment of a value to a variable, the addition of two values, a comparison of two values, concatenation of strings, etc.

In the previous sections, you've seen a number of operators at work. For example, the assignment operator (=) has been used to assign a value to a variable:

```
Dim myVariable As Integer
myVariable = 15
```

In the code shown above, the value 15 is assigned to the Integer variable myVariable. In the section on branching you saw more sophisticated operators, such as the greater-than comparison operator (>) used to compare two values:

```
If valueOne > valueTwo Then
```

The preceding If statement compares valueOne with valueTwo; if the former is larger than the latter, the test evaluates true, and the If statement executes.

The following sections will consider many of the operators used in VB.NET in some detail.

Mathematical Operators

VB.NET uses seven mathematical operators: five for standard calculations (+, -, *, /, and \), a sixth to return the remainder when dividing integers (Mod), and a seventh for exponential operations (^). The following sections consider the use of these operators.

Simple arithmetic operators (+, -, *, /, \)

VB.NET offers five operators for simple arithmetic: the addition (+), subtraction (-), and multiplication (*) operators work as you might expect. Adding two numbers returns their sum, subtracting returns their difference, and multiplying returns their product.

VB.NET offers *two* division operators: / and \. The forward slash or right-facing division operator (/) returns a floating-point answer. In other words, this operator allows for a fractional answer; there is no remainder. Thus, if you use this operator to divide 12 by 5 (12/5), the answer is 2.4. This answer is returned as a Double.

If you assign the returned value to an Integer variable, the decimal part is lopped off, and the result will be 2. If Option Strict is turned On (as it should be), you must explicitly cast the assigned value to an Integer, because this is a narrowing cast.

The backslash or left-facing division operator (\) performs integer division; that is, it returns an integer value and discards any remainder. Thus, if you use the integer division operator to divide 12 by 5 (12\5), the return value is truncated to the integer 2, with VB.NET discarding the remainder of 4. However, no cast is needed (even with Option Strict On) because you've explicitly asked for the integer value. Example 3-23 illustrates integer and fractional division.

Example 3-23. Arithmetic operators

```
Option Strict On
Imports System

Module Module1

    Sub Main( )

        Dim twelve As Integer = 12
        Dim five As Integer = 5
        Dim intAnswer As Integer
        Dim doubleAnswer As Double

        Console.WriteLine("{0} + {1} = {2}", _
            twelve, five, twelve + five)

        Console.WriteLine("{0} - {1} = {2}", _
            twelve, five, twelve - five)

        Console.WriteLine("{0} * {1} = {2}", _
            twelve, five, twelve * five)

        ' integer division
        intAnswer = twelve \ five
        doubleAnswer = twelve \ five
        Console.WriteLine("{0} \ {1} = [integer] {2}  [double] {3}", _
            twelve, five, intAnswer, doubleAnswer)

        ' explicit cast required to assign to integer
        intAnswer = CInt(twelve / five)
        doubleAnswer = twelve / five
        Console.WriteLine("{0} / {1} = [integer] {2}  [double] {3}", _
            twelve, five, intAnswer, doubleAnswer)

    End Sub 'Main( )
End Module
Output:
12 + 5 = 17
12 - 5 = 7
12 * 5 = 60
12 \ 5 = [integer] 2  [double] 2
12 / 5 = [integer] 2  [double] 2.4
```

In Example 3-23, you first declare two variables named twelve and five, which are initialized to contain the values 12 and 5, respectively:

```
Dim twelve As Integer = 12
Dim five As Integer = 5
```

You then pass the sum, difference, and product of twelve and five to the Console.WriteLine( ) method:

```
Console.WriteLine("{0} + {1} = {2}", _
    twelve, five, twelve + five)
```

```
Console.WriteLine("{0} - {1} = {2}", _
    twelve, five, twelve - five)

Console.WriteLine("{0} * {1} = {2}", _
    twelve, five, twelve * five)
```

The results are just as you would expect:

```
12 + 5 = 17
12 - 5 = 7
12 * 5 = 60
```

The type of the variable to which you assign the answer affects the value that is ultimately saved. You cannot assign a floating-point answer to a variable of type Integer. So, even if you perform standard division and receive a fractional answer, if you assign that answer to an Integer variable, the result will be truncated—just as if you had used integer division (\) to begin with!

For example, you might create two local variables, intAnswer and doubleAnswer, to hold two quotients:

```
Dim intAnswer As Integer
Dim doubleAnswer As Double
```

You then divide twelve by five twice. The first time you use integer division:

```
intAnswer = twelve \ five
doubleAnswer = twelve \ five
```

The result returned by integer division, using the (\) operator, is always an integer. Thus, it does not matter whether you assign the result of integer division to a variable of type Integer or to a variable of type Double. This is reflected in the output:

```
12 \ 5 = [integer] 2  [double] 2
```

You then divide again, using the standard division operator (/), which allows for fractional answers:

```
intAnswer = CInt(twelve / five)
doubleAnswer = twelve / five
```

The standard division operator returns a floating-point answer, which can be accommodated by a variable of type Double (as in your variable doubleAnswer). But assigning the result to an Integer variable (like intAnswer) casts the result to an Integer (and, because Option Strict is On, requires an explicit cast operator). The fractional portion is discarded, as shown in the output:

```
12 / 5 = [integer] 2  [double] 2.4
```

Self-assignment operators

It is not uncommon to want to add a value to a variable and store the result back in the variable itself.

```
x = x + 5
```

While in mathematics the preceding line would make no sense, in Visual Basic .NET this is read "add 5 to x and store the results in x." Similarly, you might subtract 5 from x, and store the result in x:

```
x = x - 5
```

These statements are so common that, like many other languages, Visual Basic .NET implements a form of shorthand known as self-assignment. There are self-assignment variants of all the mathematical operators:

```
x += 5  ' x = x + 5
x -= 5  ' x = x - 5
x *= 5  ' x = x * 5
x /= 5  ' x = x / 5
x \= 5  ' x = x \ 5
```

You can also use self-assignment with strings:

```
Dim myString As String = "Hello "
myString += "World"
```

After these two statements, myString contains the string "Hello World".

The modulus operator (Mod) to return remainders

To find the remainder in integer division, use the modulus operator (Mod). For example, the statement 17 Mod 4 returns 1 (the remainder after integer division).

The modulus operator turns out to be more useful than you might at first imagine. When you perform modulus *n* on a number that is a multiple of *n*, the result is zero. Thus 80 Mod 10 = 0 because 80 is an even multiple of 10. This fact allows you to set up loops in which you take an action every *n*th time through the loop, by testing a counter to see if Mod*n* is equal to zero, as illustrated in Example 3-24.

Example 3-24. Using the modulus operator (Mod)

```
Option Strict On
Imports System

Module Module1

    Sub Main()

        Dim counter As Integer

        ' count from 1 to 100
        For counter = 1 To 100
            ' display the value
            Console.Write("{0} ", counter)

            ' every tenth value, display a tab and the value
            If counter Mod 10 = 0 Then
                Console.WriteLine(vbTab & counter)
            End If
```

Example 3-24. Using the modulus operator (Mod) (continued)

```
    Next counter

  End Sub ' Main

End Module
```

```
Output:
1 2 3 4 5 6 7 8 9 10      10
11 12 13 14 15 16 17 18 19 20     20
21 22 23 24 25 26 27 28 29 30     30
31 32 33 34 35 36 37 38 39 40     40
41 42 43 44 45 46 47 48 49 50     50
51 52 53 54 55 56 57 58 59 60     60
61 62 63 64 65 66 67 68 69 70     70
71 72 73 74 75 76 77 78 79 80     80
81 82 83 84 85 86 87 88 89 90     90
91 92 93 94 95 96 97 98 99 100    100
```

In Example 3-24, the value of the counter variable is incremented by 1 each time through the For loop. Within the loop, the value of counter modulus 10 (counter Mod 10) is compared with zero. When they are equal (counter modulus 10 is zero), the value of counter is evenly divisible by 10, and the value is printed in the righthand column.

The code in Example 3-24 uses the vbTab constant to represent a tab character.

The exponentiation operator (^)

The final arithmetic operator is the exponentiation operator (^), which raises a number to the power of the exponent. Example 3-25 raises the number 5 to a power of 4.

Example 3-25. The exponentiation operator

```
Option Strict On
Imports System
Module Module1

  Sub Main( )

    Dim value As Integer = 5
    Dim power As Integer = 4

    Console.WriteLine("{0} to the {1}th power is {2}", _
      value, power, value ^ power)

  End Sub ' End of the Main( ) method definition
```

Example 3-25. The exponentiation operator (continued)

```
End Module
```

```
Output:
5 to the 4th power is 625
```

String Concatenation Operators (&, +)

Visual Basic .NET offers two operators for *concatenating* strings: the concatenation operator (&) and the addition operator (+). Since the addition operator doubles as a concatenation operator, most VB.NET programmers prefer to use the concatenation operator (&) operator for concatenating, in order to avoid confusion with addition.

If you start with two strings, as in the following:

```
Dim s1 As String = "Hello "
Dim s2 As String = "World"
```

you can concatenate the two strings together (append the second to the first) to create a new string (s3 in this case):

```
Dim s3 As String
s3 = s1 & s2
Console.WriteLine(s3)
```

The output is:

```
Hello World
```

Note that it is possible to use the + operator to produce the same result:

```
Dim s3 As String
s3 = s1 + s2
Console.WriteLine(s3)
```

Again, the output is:

```
Hello World
```

Relational Operators

Relational operators are used to compare two values and then return a Boolean (i.e., true or false). The greater-than operator (>), for example, returns true if the value on the left of the operator is greater than the value on the right. Thus, 5>2 returns the value true, while 2>5 returns the value false.

The relational operators for VB.NET are shown in Table 3-2. This table assumes two variables: bigValue and smallValue, in which bigValue has been assigned the value 100 and smallValue the value 50.

Table 3-2. Relational operators (assumes bigValue = 100 and smallValue = 50)

Name	Operator	Given this statement:	The expression evaluates to:
Equals	=	bigValue = 100	True
		bigValue = 80	False
Not Equal	<>	bigValue <> 100	False
		bigValue <> 80	True
Greater than	>	bigValue > smallValue	True
Greater than or equal to	>= or =>	bigValue >= smallValue	True
		smallValue => bigValue	False
Less than	<	bigValue < smallValue	False
Less than or equal to	<= or =<	smallValue <= bigValue	True
		bigValue =< smallValue	False

Each of these relational operators acts as you might expect. Notice that some of the operators are composed of two characters. For example, the greater than or equal to operator is created using the greater than symbol (>) and the equals sign (=). Notice that you can place these symbols in either order (>= or =>) to form the greater than or equal to operator.

In VB.NET, the equality operator and the assignment operator are represented by the same symbol, the equals sign (=). In the following code line, the symbol is used in each of these ways:

```
If myX = 5 Then myX = 7
```

The first use of the = symbol is as the equality operator ("if myX is equal to 5"); the second use is as the assignment operator ("set myX to the value 7"). The compiler figures out how the symbol is to be interpreted according to the context.

Logical Operators Within Conditionals

If statements test whether a condition is true. Often you will want to test whether two conditions are both true, or only one is True, or neither is True. VB.NET provides a set of logical operators for this, as shown in Table 3-3. This table assumes two variables, x and y, in which x has the value 5, and y the value 7.

Table 3-3. Logical operators (assumes x = 5 and y = 7)

Operator	Given this statement:	The expression evaluates to:	Logic
And	x = 3 And y = 7	False	Both must be true to evaluate true.
Or	x = 3 Or y = 7	True	Either or both must be true to evaluate true.
XOr	X = 5 XOr y = 7	False	True only if one (and only one) statement is true.
Not	Not x = 3	True	Expression must be false to evaluate true.

The And operator tests whether two statements are both true. The first line in Table 3-3 includes an example that illustrates the use of the And operator:

```
x = 3 And y = 7
```

The entire expression evaluates false because one side (x = 3) is false. (Remember that x = 5 and y = 7.)

With the Or operator, either or both sides must be true; the expression is false only if both sides are false. So, in the case of the example in Table 3-3:

```
x = 3 Or y = 7
```

the entire expression evaluates true because one side (y = 7) is true.

The XOr logical operator (which stands for eXclusive Or) is used to test if one (and only one) of the two statements is correct. Thus, the example from Table 3-3:

```
x = 5 XOr y = 7
```

evaluates false because both statements are true. (The XOr statement is false if both statements are true, or if both statements are false; it is true only if one, and only one, statement is true.)

With the Not operator, the statement is true if the expression is false, and vice versa. So, in the accompanying example:

```
Not x = 3
```

the entire expression is true because the tested expression (x = 3) is false. (The logic is: "It is true that it is not true that x is equal to 3.")

All of these examples appear in context in Example 3-26.

Example 3-26. The logical operators

```
Option Strict On
Imports System
Module Module1

    Sub Main( )

        Dim x As Integer = 5
        Dim y As Integer = 7

        Dim andValue As Boolean
        Dim orValue As Boolean
        Dim xorValue As Boolean
        Dim notValue As Boolean

        andValue = x = 3 And y = 7
        orValue = x = 3 Or y = 7
        xorValue = x = 3 Xor y = 7
        notValue = Not x = 3

        Console.WriteLine("x = 3 And y = 7. {0}", andValue)
```

Example 3-26. The logical operators (continued)

```
      Console.WriteLine("x = 3 Or y = 7. {0}", orValue)
      Console.WriteLine("x = 3 Xor y = 7. {0}", xorValue)
      Console.WriteLine("Not x = 3. {0}", notValue)

   End Sub 'Main

End Module

Output:
x = 3 And y = 7. False
x = 3 Or y = 7. True
x = 3 Xor y = 7. True
Not x = 3. True
```

Short-Circuit Evaluation

Consider the following code snippet:

```
      Dim x As Integer = 7
      If (x < 8) Or (x > 12) Then
```

The If statement here is a bit complicated. Everything in the If statement must evaluate true for the If statement to be true. Within the If statement are two expressions (x < 8) and (x > 12) separated by the keyword Or. It turns out that x is less than 8, so it does not matter whether or not x is greater than 12, and there is no logical reason for the compiler to evaluate the second term (i.e., after the Or).

As it stands, however, the second term will be evaluated. You can instruct the compiler not to evaluate the second term if the first term is true, by changing the Or keyword to OrElse:

```
      If (x < 8) OrElse (x > 12) Then
```

You can prove to yourself that the evaluation was short-circuited by moving the comparisons (less than and greater than) to methods, as shown in Example 3-27.

Example 3-27. Short-circuit evaluation using OrElse

```
Option Strict On
Imports System
Module Module1

      Function IsBigger( _
      ByVal firstVal As Integer, _
      ByVal secondVal As Integer) _
         As Boolean

         If firstVal > secondVal Then
            Return True
         Else
            Return False
         End If
```

Example 3-27. Short-circuit evaluation using OrElse (continued)

```
    End Function

    Function IsSmaller( _
    ByVal firstVal As Integer, _
    ByVal secondVal As Integer) _
        As Boolean

        If firstVal < secondVal Then
            Return True
        Else
            Return False
        End If

    End Function

    Sub Main( )

        Dim x As Integer = 7
        If IsSmaller(x, 8) OrElse IsBigger(x, 12) Then
            Console.WriteLine("x < 8 OrElse x > 12")
        Else
            Console.WriteLine("Not True that x < 8 OrElse x > 12")
        End If

    End Sub 'Main

End Module
```

In Example 3-27 you create two methods, IsBigger and IsSmaller. Each takes two parameters. IsBigger returns true if the first parameter is larger than the second, IsSmaller returns true if the first parameter is smaller than the second.

If you write Example 3-27 in Visual Studio .NET and then put a break point on the If statement in Main( ), you can see the evaluation of the two sides of the OrElse statement. The compiler will step into IsBigger, but will never step into IsSmaller. Since IsBigger returned true, IsSmaller need not be called.

Change the value of x to 15 and you will find that both IsBigger and IsSmaller are invoked. Since IsBigger returns false, the compiler must test IsSmaller to see if it might return true.

You can accomplish short-circuit evaluation for the And keyword by using the keyword AndAlso. If you leave x set to 15, but change the If statement in Main( ) to the following:

```
    If IsSmaller(x, 8) AndAlso IsBigger(x, 12) Then
```

you will see the compiler step into IsSmaller but never step into IsBigger. Since the IsSmaller method returns false, there is no need to test IsBigger. AndAlso requires that both parts of the statement evaluate true. Once you have the first side evaluate false, there is no need to test the second side.

Operator Precedence

The compiler must know the order in which to evaluate a series of operators. For example, if you write:

```
myVariable = 5 + 7 * 3
```

there are three operators for the compiler to evaluate (=, +, and *).

The compiler could evaluate this equation from left to right, which would:

1. Assign the value 5 to myVariable.
2. Add 7 to the 5, resulting in 12.
3. Multiply the result (12) by 3, giving a final answer of 36.

However, because the assignment is done in step 1, the final value of 36 would then be thrown away. This is clearly not what is intended.

The rules of precedence tell the compiler which operators to evaluate first. As is the case in algebra, multiplication has higher precedence than addition, so 5 + 7 * 3 is equal to 26 rather than 36. Both addition and multiplication have higher precedence than assignment, so the compiler will do the math, and then assign the result (26) to myVariable only after the math is completed. In VB.NET, parentheses are used to change the order of precedence much as they are in algebra. Thus, you can change the result by writing:

```
myVariable = (5+7) * 3
```

Grouping the elements of the assignment in this way causes the compiler to add 5+7, multiply the result by 3, and then assign that value (36) to myVariable.

Within a single line of code, operators are evaluated in the following order:

- Mathematical
- Concatenation
- Relational/Comparison
- Logical

Relational operators are evaluated left to right. Mathematical operators are evaluated in this order:

- Exponentiation (^)
- Division and multiplication (/, *)
- Integer division (\)
- Modulus operator (Mod)
- Addition and subtraction (+,-)

The logical operators are evaluated in this order:

- Not
- And
- Or
- XOr

In some complex equations, you might need to nest parentheses to ensure the proper order of operations. For example, assume I want to know how many seconds my family wastes each morning. It turns out that the adults spend 20 minutes over coffee each morning and 10 minutes reading the newspaper. The children waste 30 minutes dawdling and 10 minutes arguing.

Here's my algorithm:

```
(((minDrinkingCoffee + minReadingNewspaper) * numAdults) +
 ((minDawdling + minArguing) * numChildren)) * secondsPerMinute
```

Although this works, it is hard to read and hard to get right. It's much easier to use interim variables:

```
wastedByEachAdult = minDrinkingCoffee +  minReadingNewspaper
wastedByAllAdults = wastedByEachAdult * numAdults
wastedByEachKid = minDawdling  + minArguing
wastedByAllKids = wastedByEachKid * numChildren
wastedByFamily = wastedByAllAdults + wastedByAllKids
totalSeconds = wastedByFamily * 60
```

The latter example uses many more interim variables, but it is far easier to read, understand, and (most important) debug. As you step through this program in your debugger, you can see the interim values and make sure they are correct.

A more complete listing is shown in Example 3-28.

Example 3-28. Using parentheses and interim variables

```
Option Strict On
Imports System
Module Module1

    Sub Main( )
        Dim minDrinkingCoffee As Integer = 5
        Dim minReadingNewspaper As Integer = 10
        Dim minArguing As Integer = 15
        Dim minDawdling As Integer = 20

        Dim numAdults As Integer = 2
        Dim numChildren As Integer = 2

        Dim wastedByEachAdult As Integer
        Dim wastedByAllAdults As Integer
        Dim wastedByEachKid As Integer
        Dim wastedByAllKids As Integer
```

Example 3-28. Using parentheses and interim variables (continued)

```
    Dim wastedByFamily As Integer
    Dim totalSeconds As Integer

    wastedByEachAdult = minDrinkingCoffee + minReadingNewspaper
    wastedByAllAdults = wastedByEachAdult * numAdults
    wastedByEachKid = minDawdling + minArguing
    wastedByAllKids = wastedByEachKid * numChildren
    wastedByFamily = wastedByAllAdults + wastedByAllKids
    totalSeconds = wastedByFamily * 60

    Console.WriteLine("Each adult wastes {0} minutes", wastedByEachAdult)
    Console.WriteLine("Each child wastes {0} mintues", wastedByEachKid)
    Console.WriteLine("Total minutes wasted by entire family: {0}", _
            wastedByFamily)
    Console.WriteLine("Total wasted seconds: {0}", totalSeconds)


  End Sub ' End of Main( ) module definition

End Module
Output:
Each adult wastes 15 minutes
Each child wasts 35 mintues
Total minutes wasted by entire family: 100
Total wasted seconds: 6000
```

CHAPTER 4

Object-Oriented Programming

Windows and web programs are enormously complex. Programs present information to users in graphically rich ways, offering complicated user interfaces, complete with drop-down and pop-up menus, buttons, listboxes, and so forth. Behind these interfaces, programs model complex business relationships, such as those among customers, products, orders, and inventory. You can interact with such a program in hundreds, if not thousands, of different ways, and the program must respond appropriately every time.

To manage this enormous complexity, programmers have developed a technique called object-oriented programming. It is based on a very simple premise: you manage complexity by modeling its essential aspects. The closer your program models the problem you are trying to solve, the easier it is to understand (and thus to write and to maintain) that program.

Programmers refer to the problem you are trying to solve and all the information you know about that problem as the *problem domain*. For example, if you are writing a program to manage the inventory and sales of a company, the problem domain would include everything you know about how the company acquires and manages inventory, makes sales, handles the income from sales, tracks sales figures, and so forth. The sales manager and the stock room manager would be problem domain experts who can help you understand the problem domain.

A well-designed object-oriented program will be filled with objects from the problem domain. At the first level of design, you'll think about how these objects interact, and what their *state, capabilities,* and *responsibilities* are.

State
> A programmer refers to the current conditions and values of an object as that object's state. For example, you might have an object representing a customer. The customer's state includes the customer's address, phone number, and email, as well as the customer's credit rating, recent purchase history, and so forth.

Capabilities

The customer has many capabilities, but a developer only cares about modeling those that are relevant to the problem domain. Thus a customer object might be able to buy an item, return an item, increase his credit rating, and so forth.

Responsibilities

Along with capabilities come responsibilities. The customer object is responsible for managing its own address. In a well-designed program, no other object needs to know the details of the customer's address. The address might be stored as data within the customer object, or it might be stored in a database, but it is up to the customer object to know how to retrieve and update his own address.

Of course, all of the objects in your program are just *metaphors* for the objects in your problem domain.

Metaphors

Many of the concepts used throughout this book, and any book on programming, are actually metaphors. We get so used to the metaphors we forget that they are metaphors. You are used to talking about a window on your program, but of course there is no such thing; there is just a rectangle with text and images in it. It looks like a window into your document so we call it a window. Of course, you don't actually have a document either, just bits in memory. No folders, no buttons, these are all just metaphors.

There are many levels to these metaphors. The window metaphor is enhanced by an image drawn on your monitor. That image is created by lighting tiny dots on the screen, called pixels. These pixels are lit in response to instructions written in your VB.NET program. Each VB.NET instruction is really a metaphor; the actual instructions read by your computer are in *assembly language*, low-level instructions that are fed to the underlying computer chip. These assembly instructions map to a series of 1s and 0s that the chip understands. Of course, the 1s and 0s are just metaphors for electricity in wires. When two wires meet, we measure the amount of electricity and if there is a threshold amount we call it 1, otherwise 0. You get the idea.

Good metaphors can be very powerful. The art of object-oriented programming is really the art of conceiving of good metaphors.

Creating Models

Humans are model-builders. We create models of the world to manage complexity and to help us understand problems we're trying to solve. You see models all the time. Maps are models of roadways. Globes are models of the Earth. Chemical symbols are models of chemical interactions. Atomic models are representations of the interaction of sub-atomic particles.

Models are simplifications. There is little point to a model that is as complex as the object in the problem domain. If you had a map of the United States that had every rock, blade of grass, and bit of dirt in the entire country, the map would have to be as big as the country itself.* Your road atlas of the U.S. eschews all sorts of irrelevant detail, focusing only on those aspects of the problem domain (e.g., the country's roads) that are important to solving the problem (e.g., getting from one place to another). If you want to drive from Boston to New York City, you don't care where the trees are; you care where the exits and interchanges are located. Therefore, the network of roads is what appears on the atlas.

Albert Einstein once said, "Things should be made as simple as possible, but not any simpler." A model must be faithful to those aspects of the problem domain that are relevant. For example, a road map must provide accurate relative distances. The distance from Boston to New York must be proportional to the actual driving distance. If one inch represents 25 miles at the start of the trip, it must represent 25 miles throughout the trip, or the map will be unusable.

A good object-oriented design is an accurate model of the problem you are trying to solve. Your design choices will influence not only how you solve the problem, but in fact they will influence how you think about the problem. A good design, like a good model, allows you to examine the relevant details of the problem without confusion.

Classes and Objects

The most important metaphors in object-oriented programming are the class and the object.

A *class* defines a new type of thing. The class defines the common characteristics of every object of that new type. For example, you might define a class Car. Ever car will share certain characteristics (wheels, brakes, accelerator, and so forth). You drive a particular car, but your car and my car both belong to the class of Cars; they are of type Car.

An *object* is an individual instance of a type. Each individual car (your particular car, my particular car) is an instance of the class Car, and thus is an object. An object is just a thing.

We perceive the world to be composed of things. Look at your computer. You do not see various bits of plastic and glass amorphously merging with the surrounding environment. You naturally and inevitably see distinct things: a computer, a keyboard, a monitor, speakers, pens, paper. Things.

---

* To borrow a joke from comedian Steven Wright: "I have a map of the world. One inch equals one inch. I live at E5."

More importantly, even before you decide to do it, you've categorized these things. You immediately classify the computer on your desk as a specific instance of a type of thing: this computer is one of the type Computer. This pen is an instance of a more general type of thing, Pens. It is so natural you can't avoid it, and yet the process is so subtle, it's difficult to articulate. When I see my dog Milo, I can't help but see him *as a dog*, not just as an individual entity. Milo is an instance, Dog is a class.

The theory behind object-oriented programming is that for computer programs to accurately model the world, the programs should reflect this human tendency to think about things and types of things. In VB.NET you do that by creating a class to define a type and creating an object to model a thing.

Class Relationships

The heart of object-oriented design is establishing relationships among the classes. Classes interact and relate to one another in various ways.

The simplest interaction is when a method in one class is used to call a method in a second class. For example, the Manager class might have a method that calls the UpdateSalary() method on an object of type Employee. We then say that the Manager class and the Employee class are *associated*. Association among classes simply means they interact.

Some complicated types are *composed* of other types. For example, an automobile might be composed of wheels, engine, transmission, and so forth. You might model this by creating a Wheel class, an Engine class, and a Transmission class. You could then create an Automobile class, and each automobile would have four instances of the Wheel class, and one instance each of the Engine and Transmission class. Another way to view this relationship is to say that the Automobile class *aggregates* the Wheel, Engine, and Transmission classes.

This process of aggregation (or composition) allows you to build very complex classes from relatively simple classes. The .NET Framework provides a String class to handle text strings. You might create your own Address class out of five text strings (address line 1, address line 2, city, state, and zip). You might then create a second class, Employee, that has an instance of Address as one of its members.

The Three Pillars of Object-Oriented Programming

Object-oriented programming is built on three sturdy pillars: *encapsulation*, *specialization*, and *polymorphism*.

Each class should be fully encapsulated; that is, it should define the state and responsibilities of that type. For example, if you create an Employee object, that Employee object should fully define all there is to know, from the perspective of your program, about each Employee. You do not, typically, want to have one class that defines the Employee's work information, and a second, unrelated class that defines the Employee's contact information. Instead, you want to encapsulate all this information inside the Employee class, perhaps by aggregating the contact information as a member of the Employee class.

Specialization allows you to establish hierarchical relationships among your classes. For example, you can define a Manager to be a specialized type of an Employee and an Employee to be a specialized type of Person. This allows you to leverage the state and abilities of an Employee object in the more specialized form of the Manager.

Polymorphism allows you to treat a group of objects in a similar way and have the objects sort out how to implement the programming instructions. For instance, suppose you have a collection of Employee objects and you want to tell each Employee to give herself a raise. It turns out that Employees get a straight 5% raise, while raises for Managers are determined by how well they've fulfilled their annual objectives. With polymorphism, you can tell each object in the collection to give itself a raise, and the right thing happens regardless of the real type of the object. That is, each employee gets 5%, while each manager gets the appropriate raise based on objectives.

Encapsulation

The first pillar of object-oriented programming is *encapsulation*. The idea behind encapsulation is that you want to keep each type or class discreet and self-contained. This allows you to change the implementation of one class without affecting any other class.

A class that provides a method that other classes can use is called a *server*. A class that uses that method is called a *client*. The goal of encapsulation is that you can change the details of how a server does its work without breaking anything in the implementation of the client.

This is accomplished by drawing a bright and shining line between the *public interface* of a class and its *private implementation*. The public interface is a contract issued by your class that says, I promise to be able to do this work. Specifically, you'll see that a public interface says call this method, with these parameters, and I'll do this work and return this value. A client can rely on a public interface not to change. If the public interface does change, then the client must be recompiled and perhaps redesigned.

The private implementation, on the other hand, is private to the server. The designer of the server class is free to change *how* it does the work promised in the public interface, so long as it continues to fulfill the terms of its implicit contract: it must take the given parameters, do the promised work, and return the promised value.

For example, you might have a public method that promises as follows: Give me a dollar amount and a number of years, and I'll return the net present value. How you compute that amount is your business; if a client supplies a dollar amount and a number of years, you must return the net present value. You might implement that initially by keeping a table of values. You might change that at a later time to compute the value using the appropriate algebra. That is your business, and does not affect the client. As long as you don't change the public interface (e.g., as long as you don't change the number or type of parameters expected or change the type of the return value), your clients will not break while you change the implementation.

Specialization and Generalization

The second pillar, specialization, is implemented in VB.NET by declaring that a new class derives from an existing class. When you do so, the specialized class inherits the characteristics of the more general class. The specialized class is called a *derived* class, while the more general class is known as a *base* class.

The specialization relationship is referred to as the *is-a* relationship. A dog *is a* mammal, a car *is a* vehicle. (Dog would be derived from the base class Mammal, Car from the base class Vehicle.)

Specialization allows you to create a family of objects. In Windows a button *is a* control. A listbox *is a* control. Controls have certain characteristics (color, size, location) and certain abilities (can be drawn, can be selected). These characteristics and abilities are inherited by all of their derived types. This allows for a very powerful form of reuse. Rather than cutting and pasting code from one type to another, the shared fields and methods are inherited by the derived type. If you change how a shared ability is implemented, you do not have to update code in every derived type; they inherit the changes.

For example, a Manager is a special type of Employee. The Manager adds new capabilities (hiring, firing, rewarding, praising) and a new state (annual objectives, management level, etc.). The Manager, however, also inherits the characteristics and capabilities common to all Employees. Thus a Manager has an address, a name, an employee ID, and Managers can be given raises, can be laid off, and so forth. You'll see specialization at work in Chapter 6.

Polymorphism

Polymorphism, the third pillar of object-oriented programming, is closely related to inheritance. The prefix *poly* means many; *morph* means form. Thus, polymorphism refers to the ability of a single type or class to take many forms.

The essence of polymorphism is this: at times you will know you have a collection of a general type, for example a collection of Controls. You do not know (or care) what the specific subtype each of your controls is (one may be a button, another a listbox, etc.). The important thing is that you know they all inherit shared abilities (e.g., the Draw() method) and that you can treat them all as controls. If you write a programming instruction that tells each control to draw itself, this is implemented properly on a per-control basis (i.e., buttons draw as buttons, listboxes draw as listboxes, etc.). You do not need to know how each subtype accomplishes this; you only need to know that each type is defined to be able to draw.

Polymorphism allows you to treat a collection of disparate derived types (buttons, listboxes, etc.) as a group. You treat the general group of controls the same way, and each individual control does the right thing according to its specific type. Chapter 6 provides more concrete examples.

Object-Oriented Analysis and Design

The steps to take before programming anything are analysis and design. Analysis is the process of understanding and detailing the problem you are trying to solve. Design is the actual planning of your solution.

With trivial problems (e.g., computing the Fibonacci series*), you may not need an extensive analysis period, but with complex business problems, the analysis process can take weeks or even months. One powerful analysis technique is to create what are called use-case scenarios, in which you describe in some detail how the system will be used. Among the other considerations in the analysis period are determining your success factors (how do you know if your program works) and writing a specification of your program's requirements.

Once you've analyzed the problem, you design the solution. Key to the design process is imagining the classes you will use and their inter-relationships. You might design a simple program on the fly, without this careful planning; but in any serious business application, you will want to take some time to think through the issues.

There are many powerful design techniques you might use, most of which are beyond the scope of this book. One interesting controversy that has arisen recently is between traditional object-oriented design on the one hand† and eXtreme programming on the other.‡

---

* The Fibonacci series is the sum of the values 0,1,1,2,3,5,8,13... The series is named for Fibonacci, who in 1202 investigated how fast rabbits could breed in ideal circumstances. The series works by adding the previous two numbers to get the next (thus 8 is the sum of 5+3).

† See *The Unified Modeling Language User Guide*, *The Unified Software Development Process*, and *The Unified Modeling Language Reference Manual*, all by Grady Booch, Ivar Jacobson, and James Rumbaugh (Addison-Wesley).

‡ See *Planning Extreme Programming* by Kent Beck and Martin Fowler (Addison-Wesley).

There are other competing approaches as well. How much time you put into these topics will depend, in large measure, on the complexity of the problems you are trying to solve, and the size of your development team.

 My personal approach to managing complexity is to keep team size very small. I have worked on large development teams, and over the years I've come to believe that the ideal size is three. Three highly skilled programmers can be incredibly productive, and with three you don't need a manager. Three people can have only one conversation at a time. Three people can never be evenly split on a decision. One day I'll write a book on programming in teams of three, but this isn't it, and so we'll stay focused on VB.NET programming, rather than on design debates.

About the Examples in This Book

Object-oriented programming is designed to help you manage complex programs. Unfortunately, it is very difficult to show complex problems and their solutions in a tutorial on VB.NET. The complexity of these problems gets in the way of what you're trying to learn about.

The examples in this book will be extremely simple. The simplicity may hide some of the motivation for the technique, but the simplicity makes the technique clearer. You'll have to take it on faith, for now, that these techniques scale up well to very complex problems.

The beginning chapters of this book focus on the syntax of VB.NET. You need the syntax of the language to be able to write a program at all, but it's important to keep in mind that the syntax of any language is less important than its semantics. The meaning of what you are writing and why you're writing it are the real focus of object-oriented programming and thus of this book.

Don't let concern with syntax get in the way of understanding the semantics. The compiler can help you get the syntax right (if only by complaining when you get it wrong), and the documentation can remind you of the syntax, but understanding the semantics, the meaning of the construct, is the hard part. Throughout this book, I work hard to explain not only *how* you do something, but *why* and *when* you do it.

CHAPTER 5

Classes and Objects

Chapter 3 discusses the primitive types built into the VB.NET language, such as Integer, Long, and Single. The true power of VB.NET, however, lies in its capacity to let the programmer define new types to suit particular problems. It is this ability to create new types that characterizes an object-oriented language. You specify new types in VB.NET by declaring and defining *classes*.

Particular instances of a class are called *objects*. The difference between a class and an object is the same as the difference between the concept of a Dog and the particular dog who is shedding on your carpet as you read this. You can't play fetch with the definition of a Dog, only with an instance.

A Dog class describes what dogs are like: they have weight, height, eye color, hair color, disposition, and so forth. They also have actions they can perform, such as eat, walk, bark, and sleep. A particular dog (such as my dog Milo) will have a specific weight (62 pounds), height (22 inches), eye color (black), hair color (yellow), disposition (angelic), and so forth. He is capable of all the actions—methods, in programming parlance—of any dog (though if you knew him you might imagine that eating is the only method he implements).

The huge advantage of classes in object-oriented programming is that classes *encapsulate* the characteristics and capabilities of a type in a single, self-contained unit. Suppose, for instance, you want to sort the contents of a Windows listbox control. The listbox control is defined as a class. One of the properties of that class is that it knows how to sort itself. Sorting is encapsulated within the class, and the details of how the listbox sorts itself are not made visible to other classes. If you want a listbox sorted, you just tell the listbox to sort itself, and it takes care of the details.

So, you simply write a method that tells the listbox to sort itself—and that's what happens. How it sorts is of no concern; *that* it does so is all you need to know. As noted in Chapter 4, this is called encapsulation, which, along with polymorphism and inheritance, is one of three cardinal principles of object-oriented programming. Polymorphism and inheritance are discussed in Chapter 6.

An old programming joke asks, How many object-oriented programmers does it take to change a light bulb? Answer: none, you just tell the light bulb to change itself.* This chapter explains the VB.NET language features that are used to specify new classes. The elements of a class—its behaviors and its state—are known collectively as its *class members*.

Class behavior is created by writing methods (sometimes called member functions). A method is a small routine that every object of the class can execute. For example, a Dog class might have a bark method, a listbox class might have a sort method.

Class state is maintained by fields (sometimes called member variables). Fields can be primitive types (e.g., an Integer to hold the age of the dog, a set of strings to hold the contents of the listbox), or fields can be objects of other classes (e.g., an Employee class might have a field of type Address).

Finally, classes can also have properties, which act like methods to the creator of the class, but look like fields to clients of the class. A client is any object that interacts with instances of the class.

Defining Classes

When you define a new class, you define the attributes of all objects of that class, as well as their behaviors. For example, if you are creating your own windowing operating system, you might want to create screen widgets (known as controls in Windows). One control of interest might be a listbox, which is very useful for presenting a list of choices to the user and enabling the user to select from the list.

Listboxes have a variety of characteristics: height, width, location, and text color, for example. Programmers have also come to expect certain behaviors of listboxes: they can be opened, closed, sorted, and so on.

Object-oriented programming allows you to create a new type, ListBox, which encapsulates these characteristics and capabilities.

To define a new type or class, you first declare it and then define its methods and fields. You declare a class using the Class keyword. The complete syntax is as follows:

```
[attributes] [access-modifiers] Class identifier
[Inherits classname]
    {class-body}
End Class
```

Attributes are used to provide special metadata about a class (that is, information about the structure or use of the class) and are covered in Chapter 18.

---

* Alternate answer: "None, Microsoft has changed the standard to darkness."

Access modifiers are discussed later in this chapter. (Typically, your classes will use the keyword Public as an access modifier.)

The *identifier* is the name of the class that you provide. Typically, VB.NET classes are named with nouns (e.g., Dog, Employee, ListBox). The naming convention (not required, but strongly encouraged) is to use Pascal notation. In Pascal notation you use no underbars or hyphens, but if the name has two words (Golden Retriever) you push the two words together, each word beginning with an uppercase letter (Golden-Retriever).

The optional Inherits statement is discussed in Chapter 6.

The member definitions make up the *class-body* and are enclosed between the Class and End Class keywords.

```
Public Class Dog
    Dim age As Integer   'the dog's age
    Dim weight As Integer  'the dog's weight
    Public Sub Bark()
      '....
    End Sub
End Class
```

All the things a Dog can do are described by methods within the class definition of Dog. The dog's attributes, or state, are described by the fields (member variables), such as age and weight.

Instantiating Objects

To make an actual instance, or object, of the Dog class, you must declare the object, and you must allocate memory for the object. These two steps combined are necessary to create, or *instantiate,* the object.

First, you declare the object by writing the access modifier (in this case, Dim), followed by an identifier (milo) for the object or instance of the class, the As keyword, and the type or class name (Dog):

```
Dim milo As Dog   'declare milo to be an instance of Dog
```

This is not unlike the way you create a local variable. Notice also that like with variables, the identifier for the object uses Camel Notation. Camel Notation is just like Pascal Notation except that the very first letter is lowercase. Thus, a variable or object name might be myDog, designatedDriver, or plantManager.

The declaration alone doesn't actually create an instance, however. To create an instance of a class you must also allocate memory for the object using the keyword New:

```
milo = New Dog()   'allocate memory for milo
```

You can combine the declaration of the Dog type with the memory allocation into a single line:

```
Dim milo As New Dog( )
```

This declares milo to be an object of type Dog and also creates a new instance of Dog. You'll see what the parentheses are for later in this chapter in the discussion of the constructor.

In VB.NET, *everything* happens within a class. "But wait," I hear you cry, "we have been creating modules!" Yes, you've been writing code using modules, but when you compile your application a class is created for you from that module. This is VB.NET's strategy to continue to use modules (as VB6 did) but still comply with the .NET approach that everything is a class. (See the next section, "Modules Are Classes," for further explanation.)

Given that everything happens within a class, no methods can run outside of a class, not even Main(). The Main() method is the entry point for your program; it is called by the operating system, and it is where execution of your program begins. Typically, you'll create a small module to house Main():

```
Module modMain
    Public Sub Main( )
        ...
    End Sub
End Module
```

The compiler will turn this module into a class for you, as explained in the next section. However, it is somewhat more efficient for you to declare the class yourself:

```
Public Class Tester
    Public Sub Main( )
        Dim testObject As New Tester( )
    End Sub
    ' other members
End Class
```

In the preceding code, you create the Tester class explicitly. Even though Tester was created to house the Main() method, you've not yet instantiated any objects of type Tester. To do so you would write:

```
Dim testObject As New Tester( ) 'make an instance of Tester
```

As you'll see later in this chapter, creating an instance of the Tester class allows you to call other methods on the object you've created (testObject).

One way to understand the difference between a class and an instance (object) of that class is to consider the distinction between the type Integer and a variable of type Integer.

You can't assign a value to a type:

```
Integer = 5  ' error
```

Instead, you assign a value to an object of that type, in this case, a variable of type Integer:

```
Dim myInteger As Integer
myInteger = 5 'ok
```

Similarly, you can't assign values to fields in a class; you must assign values to fields in an object. Thus, you can't write:

```
Dog.weight = 5
```

This is not meaningful. It isn't true that every Dog's weight is 5 pounds. You must instead write:

```
milo.weight = 5
```

This says that a particular Dog's weight (milo's weight) is 5 pounds.

Modules Are Classes

You can see the relationship between modules and classes very easily. Begin by creating a new VB.NET console application called ModuleTest, as shown in Example 5-1.

Example 5-1. ModuleTest

```
Module Module1

    Sub Main()
      Console.WriteLine("Hello from Module")
    End Sub

End Module
```

Using Visual Studio .NET, build this program and run it. Building the program saves an executable version on disk. Open ILDasm, which is the Intermediate Language Disassembler. ILDasm is a tool provided with the SDK that allows you to look at the Intermediate Language code produced by your program.

You might need to search for ILDasm on your disk. It is typically found in:

```
Program Files\Microsoft Visual Studio .NET 2003\FrameworkSDK\Bin
```

Open ILDasm and make the following menu choices: File->Open.

Navigate to your *ModuleTest* directory, and then navigate into the *bin* directory. Double-click on the *.exe* file. Expand the project, and you'll find a declaration of a class. Double-click on the class, and you'll see that Module1 has been declared to be a class, as shown in Figure 5-1.

Memory Allocation: The Stack Versus the Heap

Objects created within methods are called local variables. They are local to the method, as opposed to belonging to the object, as member variables do. The object

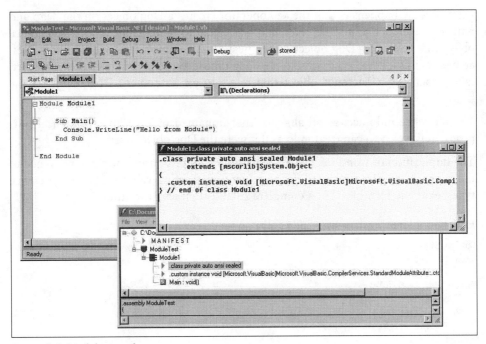

Figure 5-1. Modules are classes

is created within the method, used within the method, and then destroyed when the method ends. Local objects are not part of the object's state; they are temporary value holders, useful only within the particular method.

Local variables of intrinsic types such as Integer are created on a portion of memory known as *the stack*. The stack is allocated and de-allocated as methods are invoked. When you start a method, all the local variables are created on the stack. When the method ends, local variables are destroyed.

These variables are referred to as *local* because they exist (and are visible) only during the lifetime of the method. They are said to have *local scope*. When the method ends, the variable goes out of scope and is destroyed.

VB.NET divides the world of types into value types and reference types. Value types are created on the stack. All the intrinsic types (Integer, Long, etc.) are value types, and thus are created on the stack.

Classes, on the other hand, are reference types. Reference types are created on an undifferentiated block of memory known as *the heap*. When you declare an instance of a reference type, what you actually are declaring is a reference. A reference is a variable that refers to another object. The reference acts like an alias for the object. That is, when you write:

```
Dim milo As New Dog()
```

what actually happens is that the New operator creates a Dog object on the heap and returns a reference to it. That reference is assigned to milo. Thus, milo is a reference object that refers to a Dog object on the heap. It is common to say that milo is a reference to a Dog, or even that milo is a Dog object, but technically that is incorrect. milo is actually a reference object that refers to an (unnamed) Dog object on the heap.

The reference milo acts as an alias for that unnamed object. For all practical purposes, however, you can treat milo as if it were the Dog object itself.

The implication of using references is that you can have more than one reference to the same object. To see this difference between creating value types and reference types, examine Example 5-2. A complete analysis follows the output.

Example 5-2. Creating value types and reference types

```
Option Strict On
Imports System

Public Module Module1

    Public Class Dog
        Public weight As Integer
    End Class


    Public Class Tester

        Public Shared Sub Main( )
            Dim testObject As New Tester( )
            testObject.Run( )
        End Sub

        Public Sub Run( )
            ' create an integer
            Dim firstInt As Integer = 5

            ' create a second integer
            Dim secondInt As Integer = firstInt

            ' display the two integers
            Console.WriteLine( _
                "firstInt: {0} secondInt: {1}", firstInt, secondInt)

            ' modify the second integer
            secondInt = 7

            ' display the two integers
            Console.WriteLine( _
                "firstInt: {0} secondInt: {1}", firstInt, secondInt)

            ' create a dog
```

Example 5-2. Creating value types and reference types (continued)

```
        Dim milo As New Dog( )

        ' assign a value to weight
        milo.weight = 5

        ' create a second reference to the dog
        Dim fido As Dog = milo

        ' display their values
        Console.WriteLine( _
            "Milo: {0}, fido: {1}", milo.weight, fido.weight)

        ' assign a new weight to the second reference
        fido.weight = 7

        ' display the two values
        Console.WriteLine( _
            "Milo: {0}, fido: {1}", milo.weight, fido.weight)
    End Sub

End Class

End Module
Output:
firstInt: 5 secondInt: 5
firstInt: 5 secondInt: 7
Milo: 5, fido: 5
Milo: 7, fido: 7
```

In Example 5-2, you create a class named Tester within your module. (Remember that the module itself will be converted to a class at compile time; that class will contain the Tester class.) You must mark Main( ) with the keyword Shared. (The Shared keyword is covered later in this chapter.)

Within Main( ), you create an instance of the Tester class and you call the Run( ) method on that instance:

```
    Public Shared Sub Main( )
        Dim testObject As New Tester( )
        testObject.Run( )
    End Sub
```

Run( ) begins by creating an integer, firstInt, and initializing it with the value 5. The second integer, secondInt, is then created and initialized with the value in firstInt. Their values are displayed as output:

```
    firstInt: 5 secondInt: 5
```

Because Integer is a value type, a copy of the value is made, and secondInt is an independent second variable, as illustrated in Figure 5-2.

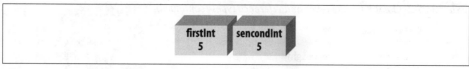

Figure 5-2. secondInt is a copy of firstInt

Then the program assigns a new value to secondInt:

```
secondInt = 7
```

Because these variables are value types, independent of one another, the first variable is unaffected. Only the copy is changed, as illustrated in Figure 5-3.

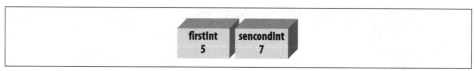

Figure 5-3. Only the copy is changed

When the values are displayed, they are now different:

```
firstInt: 5 secondInt: 7
```

Your next step is to create a simple Dog class with only one member: a public variable `weight`.

 Generally you will not make member variables public. The `weight` field was made public to simplify this example. The use of the `Public` keyword and other access modifiers is explained later in this chapter.

You instantiate a Dog object and save a reference to that Dog object in the reference milo:

```
Dim milo As New Dog( )
```

You assign the value 5 to milo's weight field:

```
milo.weight = 5
```

You commonly say that you've set milo's weight to 5, but actually you've set the weight of the unnamed object on the heap to which milo refers, as shown in Figure 5-4.

Next you create a second reference to Dog and initialize it by setting it equal to milo. This creates a new reference to the same object on the heap.

```
Dim fido As Dog = milo
```

Notice that this is syntactically similar to creating a second Integer variable and initializing it with an existing Integer, as you did before:

```
Dim secondInt As Integer = firstInt
Dim fido As Dog = milo
```

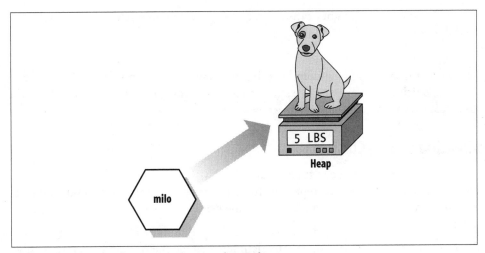

Figure 5-4. milo is a reference to an unnamed Dog object

The difference is that Dog is a reference type, so fido is not a copy of milo; it is a second reference to the same object to which milo refers. That is, you now have an object on the heap with two references to it, as illustrated in Figure 5-5.

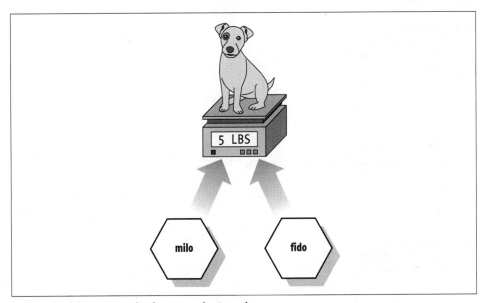

Figure 5-5. fido is a second reference to the Dog object

When you change the weight of that object through the fido reference:

```
fido.weight = 7
```

you are changing the weight of the same object to which milo refers. This is reflected in the output:

```
Milo: 7, fido: 7
```

It isn't that fido is changing milo, it is that by changing the (unnamed) object on the heap to which fido refers, you are simultaneously changing the value of milo because they refer to the same unnamed object.

Creating a Time Class

Now consider a class to keep track of and display the time of day. The internal state of the class must be able to represent the current year, month, date, hour, minute, and second. You probably would also like the class to display the time in a variety of formats.

You might implement such a class by defining a single method and six variables, as shown in Example 5-3.

Example 5-3. The Time class

```
Option Strict On
Imports System

Public Class Time
    ' Private variables
    Private year As Integer
    Private month As Integer
    Private date As Integer
    Private hour As Integer
    Private minute As Integer
    Private second As Integer
    ' Public methods
    Public Sub DisplayCurrentTime()
        Console.WriteLine("Stub for DisplayCurrentTime")
    End Sub 'DisplayCurrentTime
End Class 'Time

Module Module1

    Sub Main()
        Dim timeObject As New Time()
        timeObject.DisplayCurrentTime()
    End Sub

End Module
```

This code creates a new user-defined type: Time. The Time class definition begins with the declaration of a number of member variables: Year, Month, Date, Hour, Minute, and Second. The keyword Private indicates that these values can only be called by methods of this class. The Private keyword is an access modifier, the use of which is explained later in this chapter.

Many VB.NET programmers prefer to put all of the member fields together, either at the very top or the very bottom of the class declaration, though that is not required by the language.

The only method declared within the Time class is the method DisplayCurrentTime(). The DisplayCurrentTime() method is defined as a sub procedure or subroutine; as explained in Chapter 2, that means it will not return a value to the method that invokes it. For now, the body of this method has been "stubbed out."

Stubbing out a method is a temporary measure you might use when you first write a program to allow you to think about the overall structure without filling in every detail when you create a class. When you stub out a method body, you leave out the internal logic and just mark the method, as done here, perhaps with a message to the console:

```
Public Sub DisplayCurrentTime( )
    Console.WriteLine("Stub for DisplayCurrentTime")
End Sub 'DisplayCurrentTime
```

When you create the project, VS.NET creates the module, named Module1. Within the module, you define your Main() method, and within Main() you can instantiate a Time object:

```
Module Module1
    Sub Main( )
        Dim timeObject As New Time( )
```

Because timeObject is an instance of Time, Main() can make use of the DisplayCurrentTime() method available with objects of that type and call it to display the time:

```
timeObject.DisplayCurrentTime( )
```

You invoke a method on an object by writing the name of the object (timeObject) followed by the dot operator (.), followed by the method name and parameter list in parentheses (in this case, empty). You'll see how to pass in values to initialize the member variables in the discussion of constructors, later in this chapter.

Access Modifiers

An access modifier determines which class methods—including methods of other classes—can see and use a member variable or method within a class. Table 5-1 summarizes the VB.NET access modifiers.

Table 5-1. Access modifiers

Access modifier	Restrictions
Public	No restrictions. Members that are marked Public are visible to any method of any class.
Private	The members in class A that are marked Private are accessible only to methods of class A.

Table 5-1. Access modifiers (continued)

Access modifier	Restrictions
Protected	The members in class A that are marked `Protected` are accessible to methods of class A and also to methods of classes derived from class A. The `Protected` access modifier is used with derived classes, as explained in Chapter 6.
Friend	The members in class A that are marked `Friend` are accessible to methods of any class in A's assembly.[a]
Protected Friend	The members in class A that are marked `Protected Friend` are accessible to methods of class A, to methods of classes derived from class A, and also to any class in A's assembly. This is effectively `Protected` *or* `Friend` (There is no concept of `Protected` *and* `Friend`.)

[a] An assembly is a collection of files that appear to the programmer as a single executable (exe) or DLL.

The Time class and its DisplayCurrentTime( ) method are both declared public so that any other class can make use of them. If DisplayCurrentTime( ) had been private, it would not be possible to invoke DisplayCurrentTime from any method of any class other than methods of Time. In Example 5-3, DisplayCurrentTime( ) was invoked from a method of Tester (not Time), and this was legal because both the class (Time) and the method (DisplayCurrentTime) were marked public.

> It is good programming practice to explicitly set the accessibility of all methods and members of your class.

Method Arguments

The behavior of a class is defined by the methods of that class. To make your methods as flexible as possible, you can define parameters: information passed into the method when the method is invoked. Thus, rather than having to write one method when you want to sort your ListBox from A–Z and a second method when you want to sort it from Z–A, you define a more general Sort( ) method and pass in a parameter specifiying the order of the sort.

Methods can take any number of parameters.* The parameter list follows the method name and is enclosed in parentheses. Each parameter's type is identified along with the name of the parameter using the As keyword.

For example, the following declaration defines a sub procedure (thus, it returns no value) named MyMethod( ) which takes two parameters, an integer and a button:

```
Sub MyMethod (firstParam As Integer, secondParam As Button)
    ' ...
End Sub
```

---

* The terms "argument" and "parameter" are often used interchangeably, though some programmers insist on differentiating between the parameter declaration and the arguments passed in when the method is invoked.

Within the body of the method, the parameters act as local variables, as if you had declared them in the body of the method and initialized them with the values passed in. Example 5-4 illustrates how you pass values into a method, in this case values of type Integer and Single.

 The Visual Studio .NET editor will mark your parameters as ByVal, indicating that the parameter is passed "by value."

ByVal firstParam As Integer

When a parameter is passed by value, a copy is made. This is as opposed to passing "by reference." The ByVal keyword and its implications are discussed later in this chapter.

Example 5-4. Passing parameters

```
Option Strict On
Imports System

Public Class TestClass
    Sub SomeMethod( _
        ByVal firstParam As Integer, _
        ByVal secondParam As Single)

        Console.WriteLine( _
            "Here are the parameters received: {0}, {1}", _
            firstParam, secondParam)

    End Sub
End Class

Module Module1

    Sub Main( )
        Dim howManyPeople As Integer = 5
        Dim pi As Single = 3.14F

        Dim tc As New TestClass( )
        tc.SomeMethod(howManyPeople, pi)

    End Sub

End Module

Output:
Here are the parameters received: 5, 3.14
```

If Option Strict is On, when you pass in a Single with a decimal part (3.14) you must append the letter F (3.14F) to signal to the compiler that the value is a Single, and not a Double.

The method SomeMethod( ) takes an Integer and a Single and displays them using Console.WriteLine( ). The parameters, which are named firstParam and second-Param, are treated as local variables within SomeMethod( ).

In the calling method (Main), two local variables (howManyPeople and pi) are created and initialized. These variables are passed as the arguments to SomeMethod( ). The compiler maps howManyPeople to firstParam and pi to secondParam, based on their relative positions in the parameter list.

Constructors

In Example 5-3, notice that the statement that creates the Time object looks as though it is invoking a method:

```
Dim timeObject As New Time( )
```

In fact, a method *is* invoked whenever you instantiate an object. This method is called a *constructor*. Each time you define a class you are free to define your own constructor, but if you don't, the compiler will provide one for you invisibly and automatically. The job of a constructor is to create the object specified by a class and to put it into a valid state. Before the constructor runs, the object is just a blob of memory; after the constructor completes, the memory holds a valid instance of the class.

The Time class of Example 5-3 does not define a constructor. As noted earlier, if you do not declare a constructor the compiler provides one for you. The constructor provided by the compiler creates the object but takes no other action.

Any constructor that takes no arguments is called a *default constructor*. It turns out that the constructor provided by the compiler takes no arguments, and hence is a default constructor. This terminology has caused a great deal of confusion. You can create your own default constructor, and if you do not create a constructor at all, the compiler will create a default constructor for you, by default.

If you do not explicitly initialize your member variables, they are initialized to default values (integers to 0, strings to the empty string, etc.). Table 5-2 lists the default values assigned to primitive types.

Table 5-2. Types and their default values

Type	Default value
Numeric (Integer, Long, etc.)	0
Boolean	False
Char	'\0' (null)
Enum	0
Reference	null

Typically, you'll want to define your own constructor and provide it with arguments, so that the constructor can set the initial state for your object. In Example 5-3, you want to pass in the current year, month, date, and so forth, so that the object is created with meaningful data.

You declare a constructor like any other member method except:

- The constructor is always named New.
- Constructors are declared using the Sub keyword (which means there is no return value).

If there are arguments to be passed, you define an argument list just as you would for any other method. Example 5-5 declares a constructor for the Time class that accepts six integer arguments.

Example 5-5. Creating a constructor

```
Option Strict On
Imports System

Public Class Time
    ' Private variables
    Private year As Integer
    Private month As Integer
    Private date As Integer
    Private hour As Integer
    Private minute As Integer
    Private second As Integer
    ' Public methods
    Public Sub DisplayCurrentTime()
        Console.WriteLine("{0}/{1}/{2} {3}:{4}:{5}", _
            month, date, year, hour, minute, second)
    End Sub 'DisplayCurrentTime

    ' Constructor
    Public Sub New( _
ByVal theYear As Integer, _
ByVal theMonth As Integer, _
ByVal theDate As Integer, _
ByVal theHour As Integer, _
ByVal theMinute As Integer, _
ByVal theSecond As Integer)

        year = theYear
        month = theMonth
        date = theDate
        hour = theHour
        minute = theMinute
        second = theSecond
    End Sub

End Class 'Time
```

Example 5-5. Creating a constructor (continued)

```
Module Module1

    Sub Main( )
        Dim timeObject As New Time(2005, 3, 25, 9, 35, 20)
        timeObject.DisplayCurrentTime( )
    End Sub

End Module
```

Output:
3/25/2005 9:35:20

In this example, the constructor (Sub New) takes a series of integer values and initializes all the member variables based on these parameters. When the constructor finishes, the values have been initialized. When DisplayCurrentTime( ) is called in Main( ), the values are displayed.

Try commenting out one of the assignments and running the program again. You'll find that each member variable is initialized by the compiler to 0. Integer member variables are set to 0 if you don't otherwise assign them. Remember that value types (e.g., integers) must be initialized; if you don't tell the constructor what to do, it will set default values.

Initializers

It is possible to initialize the values of member variables with an *initializer*, instead of having to do so in the constructor. You create an initializer by assigning an initial value to a class member:

```
Private second As Integer = 30
```

Assume that the semantics of the Time object are such that no matter what time is set, the seconds are always initialized to 30. You might rewrite your Time class to use an initializer so that the value of Second is always initialized, as shown in Example 5-6.

Example 5-6. Using an initializer

```
Option Strict On
Imports System

Public Class Time
    ' Private variables
    Private year As Integer
    Private month As Integer
    Private date As Integer
    Private hour As Integer
    Private minute As Integer
    Private second As Integer = 30
```

Example 5-6. Using an initializer (continued)

```
' Public methods
Public Sub DisplayCurrentTime( )
    Console.WriteLine("{0}/{1}/{2} {3}:{4}:{5}", _
        month, date, year, hour, minute, second)
End Sub 'DisplayCurrentTime

Public Sub New( _
ByVal theYear As Integer, _
ByVal theMonth As Integer, _
ByVal theDate As Integer, _
ByVal theHour As Integer, _
ByVal theMinute As Integer)
    year = theYear
    month = theMonth
    date = theDate
    hour = theHour
    minute = theMinute
End Sub


End Class 'Time

Module Module1

    Sub Main( )
        Dim timeObject As New Time(2005, 3, 25, 9, 35)
        timeObject.DisplayCurrentTime( )
    End Sub

End Module


Output:
3/25/2005 9:35:30
```

If you do not provide a specific initializer, the constructor will initialize each integer member variable to zero (0). In the case shown, however, the Second member is initialized to 30:

```
Private second As Integer = 30
```

Copy Constructors

A *copy constructor* creates a new object by copying variables from an existing object of the same type. For example, you might want to pass a Time object to a Time constructor so that the new Time object has the same values as the old one.

VB.NET does not provide a copy constructor, so if you want one you must provide it yourself. Such a constructor copies the elements from the original object into the new one:

```
Public Sub New(ByVal existingObject As Time)
    year = existingObject.Year
    month = existingObject.Month
    date = existingObject.Date
    hour = existingObject.Hour
    minute = existingObject.Minute
    second = existingObject.Second
End Sub
```

A copy constructor is invoked by instantiating an object of type Time and passing it the name of the Time object to be copied:

```
Dim t2 As New Time(existingObject)
```

Here an existing Time object (existingObject) is passed as a parameter to the copy constructor that will create a new Time object (), as shown in Example 5-7.

Example 5-7. Copy constructor

```
Option Strict On
Imports System

Public Class Time
    ' Private variables
    Private year As Integer
    Private month As Integer
    Private date As Integer
    Private hour As Integer
    Private minute As Integer
    Private second As Integer = 30

    ' Public methods
    Public Sub DisplayCurrentTime()
        Console.WriteLine("{0}/{1}/{2} {3}:{4}:{5}", _
            month, date, year, hour, minute, second)
    End Sub 'DisplayCurrentTime

    Public Sub New( _
    ByVal theYear As Integer, _
    ByVal theMonth As Integer, _
    ByVal theDate As Integer, _
    ByVal theHour As Integer, _
    ByVal theMinute As Integer)
        year = theYear
        month = theMonth
        date = theDate
        hour = theHour
        minute = theMinute
        second = theSecond
    End Sub

    Public Sub New(existingObject As Time)
        year = existingObject.Year
        month = existingObject.Month
```

Example 5-7. Copy constructor (continued)

```
      date = existingObject.Date
      hour = existingObject.Hour
      minute = existingObject.Minute
      second = existingObject.Second
   End Sub


End Class 'Time

Module Module1

   Sub Main( )
      Dim timeObject As New Time(2005, 3, 25, 9, 35)
      Dim t2 As New Time(timeObject)
      timeObject.DisplayCurrentTime( )
      t2.DisplayCurrentTime( )
   End Sub

End Module

Output:
3/25/2005 9:35:30
3/25/2005 9:35:30
```

The Me Keyword

The keyword Me refers to the current instance of an object. The Me reference is a hidden reference to every non-shared method of a class; shared methods are discussed later in this chapter. Each method can refer to the other methods and variables of that object by way of the Me reference.

The Me reference is typically used in any of three ways. The first way is to qualify instance members that have the same name as parameters, as in the following:

```
Public Sub SomeMethod(ByVal Hour As Integer)
   Me.Hour = Hour
End Sub
```

In this example, SomeMethod( ) takes a parameter (Hour) with the same name as a member variable of the class. The Me reference is used to resolve the ambiguity. While Me.Hour refers to the member variable, Hour refers to the parameter.

> The argument in favor of this style, which is often used in constructors, is that you pick the right variable name and then use it both for the parameter and for the member variable. The counter-argument is that using the same name for both the parameter and the member variable can be confusing.

The second use of the Me reference is to pass the current object as a parameter to another method, as in the following code:

```
Public Sub myMethod( )
    Dim someObject As New SomeType( )
    someObject.SomeMethod(Me)
End Sub
```

In this code snippet, you call a method on an object, passing in the Me reference. This allows the method you're calling access to the methods and properties of the current object.

The third use of the Me reference is with indexers, which are covered in Chapter 9.

You can also use the Me reference to make the copy constructor more explicit:

```
Public Sub New(ByVal that As Time)
    Me.year = that.year
    Me.month = that.month
    Me.date = that.date
    Me.hour = that.hour
    Me.minute = that.minute
    Me.second = that.second
End Sub
```

In this snippet, Me refers to the current object (the object whose constructor is running), and that refers to the object passed in.

> The keyword Me always refers to the current object; the argument name that was chosen for convenience.

Using Shared Members

The properties and methods of a class can be either *instance members* or *shared members*. Instance members are associated with instances of a type, while shared members are associated with the class, and not with any particular instance. Methods are instance methods unless you explicitly mark them with the keyword Shared.

The vast majority of methods will be instance methods. The semantics of an instance method are that you are taking an action on a specific object. From time to time, however, it is convenient to be able to invoke a method without having an instance of the class, and for that you will use a shared method.

You can access a shared member through the name of the class in which it is declared. For example, suppose you have a class named Button and have instantiated objects of that class named btnUpdate and btnDelete.

Suppose that the Button class has an instance method Draw( ) and a shared method GetButtonCount( ). The job of Draw( ) is to draw the current button; the job of GetButtonCount( ) is to return the number of buttons currently visible on the form.

You access an instance method through an instance of the class; that is, through an object:

```
btnUpdate.SomeMethod( )
```

You can access a shared method in the same way:

```
btnUpdate.GetButtonCount( )
```

You can also access a shared method through the class name (rather than through an instance):

```
Button.GetButtonCount( )
```

This allows you to access the shared method without having an instance of the class.

A common use of shared member variables, or fields, is to keep track of the number of instances/objects that currently exist for your class. In Example 5-8, you create a Cat class. The Cat class might be used in a pet-store simulation. For this example, the Cat class has been stripped to its absolute essentials. Analysis follows.

Example 5-8. Shared fields

```
Option Strict On
Imports System

Class Cat
    Private Shared instances As Integer = 0
    Private weight As Integer
    Private name As String

    Public Sub New(ByVal name As String, ByVal weight As Integer)
        instances += 1
        Me.name = name
        Me.weight = weight
    End Sub

    Public Shared Sub HowManyCats( )
        Console.WriteLine("{0} cats adopted", instances)
    End Sub

    Public Sub TellWeight( )
        Console.WriteLine("{0} is {1} pounds", _
        name, weight)
    End Sub

End Class 'Cat

Module Module1

    Sub Main( )
        Cat.HowManyCats( )
        Dim frisky As New Cat("Frisky", 5)
        frisky.TellWeight( )
```

Example 5-8. Shared fields (continued)

```
    Cat.HowManyCats()
    Dim whiskers As New Cat("Whiskers", 7)
    whiskers.TellWeight()  ' instance method
    whiskers.HowManyCats() ' shared method through instance
    Cat.HowManyCats()       ' shared method through class name
  End Sub

End Module
```

```
Output:
0 cats adopted
Frisky is 5 pounds
1 cats adopted
Whiskers is 7 pounds
2 cats adopted
2 cats adopted
```

The Cat class begins by defining a shared member variable, instances, that is initialized to zero. This shared member field will keep track of the number of Cat objects created. Each time the constructor (Sub New) runs (creating a new object), the instances field is incremented.

The Cat class also defines two instance fields: name and weight. These track the name and weight of each individual Cat object.

The Cat class defines two methods: HowManyCats() and TellWeight(). HowManyCats() is shared. The number of cats is not an attribute of any given Cat, it is an attribute of the entire class. TellWeight() is an instance method. The name and weight of each cat is per instance (i.e., each Cat has his own name and weight).

The Main() method accesses the shared HowManyCats() method directly, through the class:

```
    Cat.HowManyCats()
```

Main() then creates an instance of Cat and accesses the instance method TellWeight() through an instance (frisky) of Cat:

```
    Dim frisky As New Cat("Frisky", 5)
    frisky.TellWeight()
```

Each time a new Cat is created, HowManyCats() reports the increase.

You access the instance method through the object, but you can access the shared method either through an object or through the class name:

```
    whiskers.TellWeight()
    whiskers.HowManyCats()
    Cat.HowManyCats()
```

Destroying Objects

Unlike many other programming languages (C, C++, Pascal, etc.), VB.NET provides garbage collection. Your objects are destroyed when you are done with them. You do not need to worry about cleaning up after your objects unless you use unmanaged resources. An unmanaged resource is an operating system feature outside of the .NET Framework, such as a file handle or a database connection. If you do control an unmanaged resource, you will need to explicitly free that resource when you are done with it. Implicit control over this resource is provided with a Finalize() method, which will be called by the garbage collector when your object is destroyed:

```
Protected Overrides Sub Finalize()
  ' release non-managed resources
  MyBase.Finalize()
End Sub
```

The Protected keyword is described in the "Access Modifiers" section earlier in this chapter. For a discussion of the Overrides and MyBase keywords, see Chapter 6.

It is not legal to call Finalize() explicitly. Finalize() will be called by the garbage collector. If you do handle precious unmanaged resources (such as file handles) that you want to close and dispose of as quickly as possible, you ought to implement the IDisposable interface. (You will learn more about interfaces in Chapter 8.) The IDisposable interface requires that you create a method named Dispose() that will be called by your clients.

If you provide a Dispose() method, you should stop the garbage collector from calling your object's destructor. To stop the garbage collector, you call the shared method GC.SuppressFinalize(), passing in the Me reference for your object. Your Finalize() method can then call your Dispose() method. Thus, you might write:

```
Public Class Testing
    Implements IDisposable
    Dim is_disposed As Boolean = False

    Protected Sub Dispose(ByVal disposing As Boolean)
        If Not is_disposed Then
            If disposing Then
                Console.WriteLine("Not in destructor, OK to reference other objects")
            End If
            ' perform cleanup for this object
            Console.WriteLine("Disposing...")
        End If
        Me.is_disposed = True
    End Sub

    Public Sub Dispose() Implements IDisposable.Dispose
        Dispose(True)
        'tell the GC not to finalize
        GC.SuppressFinalize(Me)
    End Sub
```

```
Protected Overrides Sub Finalize()
    Dispose(False)
    Console.WriteLine("In destructor.")
End Sub

End Class
```

Overloading Methods and Constructors

Often you'll want to have more than one method with the same name. The most common example of this is to have more than one constructor. Having more than one constructor allows you to create the object with different parameters. For example, if you were creating a Time object, you might have circumstances where you want to create the Time object by passing in the date, hours, minutes, and seconds. Other times, you might want to create a Time object by passing in an existing Time object. Still other times, you might want to pass in just a date, without hours and minutes. Overloading the constructor allows you to provide these various options.

Let's return to the Time class you created in Example 5-3. It might be convenient to create a Time class object by passing in a DateTime object (provided by the Framework). On the other hand, it might also be convenient to pass in the hour, minute, second, and date. Some clients might prefer one or the other constructor; you can provide both and the client can decide which better fits the situation.

In order to overload your constructor, you must make sure that each constructor has a unique *signature*. The signature of a method is composed of its name and its parameter list. Two methods differ in their signatures if they have different names or different parameter lists.

Of course, constructors must all have the same name, as every constructor is named with the name of the class. Therefore, to overload the constructor, you must vary the parameter list. Parameter lists can differ by having different numbers or types of parameters.

The following four lines of code show how you might distinguish methods by varying the signature:

```
Public Sub MyMethod(p1 As Integer)
Public Sub MyMethod(p1 As Integer, p2 As Integer) 'different number
Public Sub MyMethod(p1 As Integer, s1 As String)  'different types
Public Sub SomeMethod(p1 As Integer) 'different name
```

The first three methods are all overloads of the myMethod() method. The first differs from the second and third in the number of parameters. The second closely resembles the third version, but the second parameter in each is a different type. In the second method, the second parameter (p2) is an integer; in the third method, the second parameter (s1) is a string. These changes to the number or type of parameters are sufficient changes in the signature to allow the compiler to distinguish the methods.

The fourth method differs from the other three methods by having a different name. This is not method overloading, just different methods, but it illustrates that two methods can have the same number and type of parameters if they have different names. Thus, the fourth and first have the same parameter list, but their names are different.

A class can have any number of methods, as long as each one's signature differs from that of all the others. Example 5-9 illustrates a Time class with two constructors, one that takes a DateTime object, and the other that takes six integers.

Example 5-9. Overloading a method

```
Option Strict On
Imports System

Public Class Time
    ' private member variables
    Private year As Integer
    Private month As Integer
    Private dayOfMonth As Integer
    Private hour As Integer
    Private minute As Integer
    Private second As Integer


    ' public accessor methods
    Public Sub DisplayCurrentTime( )
        Console.WriteLine( _
        "{0}/{1}/{2} {3}:{4}:{5}", _
        month, dayOfMonth, year, hour, minute, second)
    End Sub 'DisplayCurrentTime


    ' constructors
    Public Sub New(ByVal dt As DateTime)
        year = dt.Year
        month = dt.Month
        dayOfMonth = dt.Day
        hour = dt.Hour
        minute = dt.Minute
        second = dt.Second
    End Sub 'New


    Public Sub New( _
    ByVal year As Integer, _
    ByVal month As Integer, _
    ByVal dayOfMonth As Integer, _
    ByVal hour As Integer, _
    ByVal minute As Integer, _
    ByVal second As Integer)
        Me.year = year
```

Example 5-9. Overloading a method (continued)

```
        Me.month = month
        Me.dayOfMonth = dayOfMonth
        Me.hour = hour
        Me.minute = minute
        Me.second = second
    End Sub 'New

End Class 'Time


Module Module1

    Sub Main( )
        Dim currentTime As DateTime = DateTime.Now
        Dim time1 As New Time(currentTime)
        time1.DisplayCurrentTime( )
        Dim time2 As New Time(2005, 11, 18, 11, 3, 30)
        time2.DisplayCurrentTime( )
    End Sub

End Module

Output:
5/1/2002 8:53:05
11/18/2005 11:3:30
```

The Time class in Example 5-9 has two constructors. If a function's signature consisted only of the function name, the compiler would not know which constructors to call when constructing the new Time objects time1 and time2. However, because the signature includes the parameters and their types, the compiler is able to match the constructor call for time1 with the constructor whose signature requires a DateTime object.

```
    Dim currentTime As New DateTime( )
    Dim time1 As New Time(currentTime)
    time1.DisplayCurrentTime( )
```

Likewise, the compiler is able to associate the time2 constructor call with the constructor method whose signature specifies six integer arguments:

```
    Dim time2 As New Time(2005, 11, 18, 11, 3, 30)
    time2.DisplayCurrentTime ( )
```

 When you overload a method, you must change the signature (i.e., the name, number, or type of the parameters). You are free, as well, to change the return type, but this is optional. Changing only the return type does not overload the method, and creating two methods with the same signature but differing return types will generate a compile error.

Encapsulating Data with Properties

It is generally desirable to designate the member variables of a class as Private (using the Private keyword). This means that only member methods of that class can access their value. You make member variables private to support *data hiding*, which is part of the encapsulation of a class.

Typically, most methods will be public (designated by the Public keyword). The public members of your class constitute a contract between your class and the *clients* of your class. Any object that interacts with your class is a client. Your public methods promise that if the client calls them with the right parameters, they will perform the promised action. *How* your methods perform that object is not part of the public contract. That is up to your class.

You can also have some private methods, known as helper methods, whose job it is to do work for methods of your class, but which are not available to clients. The private member variables and private methods are not part of your public contract; they are hidden details of the implementation of your class.

Object-oriented programmers are told that member variables should be private. That is fine, but how do you provide access to this data to your clients? The answer for VB.NET programmers is properties.

Properties allow clients to access class state as if they were accessing member fields directly, while actually implementing that access through a class method.

This is ideal. The client wants direct access to the state of the object. The class designer, however, wants to hide the internal state of his class (perhaps in class fields), and provide indirect access through a method. The property provides both: the illusion of direct access for the client, the reality of indirect access for the class developer.

By decoupling the class state from the method that accesses that state, the designer is free to change the internal state of the object as needed. When the Time class is first created, the Hour value might be stored as a member variable. When the class is redesigned, the Hour value might be computed, or retrieved from a database. If the client had direct access to the original Hour member variable, the change to computing the value would break the client. By decoupling and forcing the client to go through a property, the Time class can change how it manages its internal state without breaking client code.

In short, properties provide the data hiding required by good object-oriented design. Example 5-10 creates a property called Hour, which is then discussed in the paragraphs that follow.

It is a convention in VB.NET to give your private member variables names with a prefix to distinguish them from the property name. For example, you might prefix every member variable with the letter m (for member), thus mMinute and mHour. You are then free to use the unprefixed version (Hour and Minute) for the property. By convention, properties are named with Pascal notation (first letters are uppercase).

Example 5-10. Properties

```
Option Strict On
Imports System

Public Class Time
    ' private member variables
    Private mYear As Integer
    Private mMonth As Integer
    Private mDayOfMonth As Integer
    Private mHour As Integer
    Private mMinute As Integer
    Private mSecond As Integer

    Property Hour( ) As Integer
        Get
            Return mHour
        End Get
        Set(ByVal Value As Integer)
            mHour = Value
        End Set
    End Property


    ' public accessor methods
    Public Sub DisplayCurrentTime( )
        Console.WriteLine( _
        "{0}/{1}/{2} {3}:{4}:{5}", _
        mMonth, mDayOfMonth, mYear, Hour, mMinute, mSecond)
    End Sub 'DisplayCurrentTime


    ' constructors
    Public Sub New(ByVal dt As DateTime)
        mYear = dt.Year
        mMonth = dt.Month
        mDayOfMonth = dt.Day
        mHour = dt.Hour
        mMinute = dt.Minute
        mSecond = dt.Second
    End Sub 'New


    Public Sub New( _
    ByVal mYear As Integer, _
    ByVal mMonth As Integer, _
```

Example 5-10. Properties (continued)

```
      ByVal mDayOfMonth As Integer, _
      ByVal mHour As Integer, _
      ByVal mMinute As Integer, _
      ByVal mSecond As Integer)
         Me.mYear = mYear
         Me.mMonth = mMonth
         Me.mDayOfMonth = mDayOfMonth
         Me.Hour = mHour
         Me.mMinute = mMinute
         Me.mSecond = mSecond
      End Sub 'New

End Class 'Time


Module Module1

   Sub Main( )
      Dim currentTime As DateTime = DateTime.Now
      Dim time1 As New Time(currentTime)
      time1.DisplayCurrentTime( )

      'extract the hour to a local variable
      Dim theHour As Integer = time1.Hour

      'display the local variable
      Console.WriteLine("Retrieved the hour: {0}", _
        theHour)

      'add one to the local variable
      theHour += 1

      'write the time back to the object
      time1.Hour = theHour

      'display the result
      Console.WriteLine("Updated the hour: {0}", _
        time1.Hour)

   End Sub

End Module

Output:
5/1/2002 8:56:59
Retrieved the hour: 8
Updated the hour: 9
```

You create a property with this syntax:

```
Property Identifier( ) As Type
   Get
      statements
```

```
        End Get

    Set(ByVal Value As Type)
        statements
    End Set
End Property
```

If you create the property in Visual Studio .NET however, the editor will provide extensive help with the syntax. For example, once you type:

```
Property Minute As Integer
```

the IDE will reformat your property as follows:

```
Property Minute( ) As Integer
    Get

    End Get
    Set(ByVal Value As Integer)

    End Set
End Property
```

In Example 5-10, Hour is a property. Its declaration creates two *accessors*: Get and Set.

```
Property Hour( ) As Integer
    Get
        Return mHour
    End Get
    Set(ByVal Value As Integer)
        mHour = Value
    End Set
End Property
```

Each accessor has an *accessor-body* that does the work of retrieving and setting the property value. The property value might be stored in a database (in which case the accessor would do whatever work is needed to interact with the database), or it might just be stored in a private member variable (in this case, mHour):

```
Private mHour As Integer
```

The Get Accessor

The body of the Get accessor is similar to a class method that returns an object of the type of the property. In Example 5-10, the accessor for the Hour property is similar to a method that returns an integer. It returns the value of the private member variable mHour in which the value of the property has been stored:

```
Get
    Return mHour
End Get
```

In this example, the value of mHour is returned, but you could just as easily retrieve an Integer value from a database or compute it on the fly.

Whenever you reference the property (other than to assign to it), the Get accessor is invoked to read the value of the property. For example, in the following code the value of the Time object's Hour property is assigned to a local variable. What actually happens is that the Get accessor is called, which returns the value of the Hour member variable, and that value is assigned to the local variable named theHour:

```
Dim time1 As New Time(currentTime)
Dim theHour As Integer = time1.Hour
```

The Set Accessor

The Set accessor sets the value of a property. Set has an implicit parameter, Value, that represents the assigned value. That is, when you write:

```
Minute = 5
```

the compiler passes the value you are assigning (5) to the Set statement as the Value parameter. You can then set the member variable to that value using the keyword:

```
mMinute = Value
```

The advantage of this approach is that the client can interact with the properties directly, without sacrificing the data hiding and encapsulation sacrosanct in good object-oriented design.

ReadOnly and WriteOnly Properties

At times you may want to create a property that allows the client to retrieve a value but not to set it. You can mark your property ReadOnly, as in the following:

```
ReadOnly Property Hour( ) As Integer
```

Doing so allows you (and forces you) to leave out the Set accessor in your property. If you do add a Set accessor, the compiler will complain with the message:

```
Properties declared 'ReadOnly' cannot have a 'Set'
```

If you leave out the Set accessor and then try to assign to the property, the compiler will complain with the message:

```
Property 'Hour' is 'ReadOnly'
```

In short, marking the property ReadOnly enlists the compiler in enforcing that you can not use that property to set a value.

Similarly, you can mark a property WriteOnly:

```
WriteOnly Property Hour( ) As Integer
```

Doing so will cause the compiler to enforce that your property must have a Set and must not have a Get accessor. If you leave out the Get or Set without marking the property WriteOnly or ReadOnly, respectively, you will receive a compile error.

You are not permitted to combine ReadOnly with WriteOnly, but this is not much of a burden.

Passing Parameters by Value and by Reference

Visual Basic .NET differentiates between *value types* and *reference types*. All the intrinsic types (Integer, Long, etc.), as well as structures (described in Chapter 7) are value types. Classes are reference types, as are interfaces (described in Chapter 8).

By default, value types are passed into methods by value. This means that when a value object is passed to a method, a temporary copy of the object is created within that method. Once the method completes, the copy is discarded.

When you pass a reference type to a method a copy is made of the reference as well. The key difference is that the original reference and its copy both refer to the same actual object (on the heap). Changes you make through the copy of the reference are reflected back in the calling method. Thus, even though you are passing a copy of the reference you are "passing by reference"—that is, you are giving the method you are calling a reference to the actual object which it can modify.

Although passing by value is the normal case, there are times when you will want to pass value objects by reference. Visual Basic .NET allows you to make your intention explicit by using either the ByVal keyword or the ByRef keyword, as explained in the following sections.

Passing Parameters by Value

In many of the method calls shown in the previous sections, the parameters were marked with the keyword ByVal. This indicates that the arguments are passed to the method by value; that is, a copy of the argument is passed to the method. Examine the code in Example 5-11. Try to guess what the output will be before reading further.

Example 5-11. Using the ByVal parameter

```
Option Strict On
Imports System

Public Class Tester

    Public Sub Run( )
        ' declare a variable and initialize to 5
        Dim theVariable As Integer = 5
```

Example 5-11. Using the ByVal parameter (continued)

```
     ' display its value
     Console.WriteLine("In Run. theVariable: {0}", _
     theVariable)

     ' call a method and pass in the variable
     Doubler(theVariable)

     ' return and display the value again
     Console.WriteLine("Back in Run. theVariable: {0}", _
     theVariable)

 End Sub

 Public Sub Doubler(ByVal param As Integer)

     ' display the value that was passed in
     Console.WriteLine("In Method1. Received param: {0}", _
     param)

     'Double the value
     param *= 2

     ' Display the doubled value before returning
     Console.WriteLine( _
     "Updated param. Returning new value: {0}", _
     param)

 End Sub

End Class 'Tester


Module Module1

 Sub Main( )
    Dim t As New Tester( )
    t.Run( )
 End Sub

End Module
```

In Example 5-11, the Main( ) method does nothing but instantiate a Tester object and call Run( ). In Run( ), you create a local variable, theVariable, and initialize its value to 5, which you then display:

```
Dim theVariable As Integer = 5
Console.WriteLine("In Run. theVariable: {0}", _
theVariable)
```

You pass theVariable to the Doubler( ) method, which displays the value, doubles it, and then redisplays it before returning:

```
Public Sub Doubler(ByVal param As Integer)

    Console.WriteLine("In Method1. Received param: {0}", _
    param)

    param *= 2

    Console.WriteLine( _
    "Updated param. Returning new value: {0}", _
    param)

End Sub
```

When you return from the call to Doubler(), you display the value of theVariable again. What is the value that is now displayed?

```
Console.WriteLine("Back in Run. theVariable: {0}", _
theVariable)
```

As shown in the output, the value of the variable that was passed in to Doubler() is, in fact, doubled in the Doubler() method, but is *unchanged* in the calling method (Run):

```
Output:
In Run. theVariable: 5
In Method1. Received param: 5
Updated param. Returning new value: 10
Back in Run. theVariable: 5
```

The value of the parameter was passed by value, and thus a copy was made in the Doubler() method. This copy was doubled, but the original value was unaffected.

Passing Parameters by Reference

Visual Basic .NET also supports passing parameters by reference using the ByRef keyword. You can test this by making one tiny change to Example 5-11, changing the parameter of Doubler() from ByVal to ByRef:

```
Public Sub Doubler(ByRef param As Integer)
```

The rest of the program remains completely unchanged. Run the program again and compare the new output with the original:

```
Output:
In Run. theVariable: 5
In Method1. Received param: 5
Updated param. Returning new value: 10
Back in Run. theVariable: 10
```

The value of the argument to the method is now passed by reference. That is, rather than a copy being made, a reference to the object itself is passed, as illustrated in Figure 5-6. The object referred to by param is now the variable declared in Run(). Thus, when you change it in Doubler(), the change is reflected back in the Run() method.

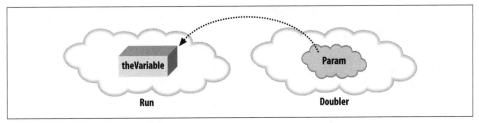

Figure 5-6. Passing arguments by reference

Passing Reference Types by Value

Earlier, you saw how you can create a copy of a reference to an object and then have the two references refer to the same object. Similarly, when you pass a reference as a parameter, a copy of the parameter is made, but that is a copy of a reference, and the two references refer to the same object. You can see the effect by modifying Example 5-11 to pass an object, rather than an Integer, by value. The complete listing is shown in Example 5-12. Analysis follows the output.

Example 5-12. Passing a reference as a parameter

```
Option Strict On
Imports System

Public Class Cat

    Private mWeight As Integer

    Public Sub New(ByVal weight As Integer)
        mWeight = weight
    End Sub

    Public Property Weight( ) As Integer
        Get
            Return mWeight
        End Get
        Set(ByVal Value As Integer)
            mWeight = Value
        End Set
    End Property

    Public Overrides Function ToString( ) As String
        Return mWeight.ToString( )
    End Function

End Class

Public Class Tester

    Public Sub Run( )
        'declare a Cat and initialize to 5
```

Example 5-12. Passing a reference as a parameter (continued)

```
    Dim theVariable As New Cat(5)

    'display its value
    Console.WriteLine("In Run. theVariable: {0}", _
    theVariable)

    'call a method and pass in the variable
    Doubler(theVariable)

    'return and display the value again
    Console.WriteLine("Back in Run. theVariable: {0}", _
    theVariable)

End Sub

Public Sub Doubler(ByVal param As Cat)
    'display the value that was passed in
    Console.WriteLine("In Method1. Received param: {0}", _
    param)

    'double the value
    param.Weight = param.Weight * 2

    'display the doubled value before returning
    Console.WriteLine( _
    "Updated param. Returning new value: {0}", _
    param)

End Sub

End Class 'Tester


Module Module1

Sub Main( )
    Dim t As New Tester( )
    t.Run( )
End Sub

End Module

Output:
In Run. theVariable: 5
In Method1. Received param: 5
Updated param. Returning new value: 10
Back in Run. theVariable: 10
```

Example 5-12 begins by defining a very simple Cat class:

```
    Public Class Cat
```

The class has a single private member variable, mWeight, and a property (Weight) to get and set the value of that variable:

```
Private mWeight As Integer

Public Property Weight() As Integer
   Get
      Return mWeight
   End Get
   Set(ByVal Value As Integer)
      mWeight = Value
   End Set
End Property
```

The constructor allows you to initialize a Cat object by passing in an integer value for its weight:

```
Public Sub New(ByVal weight As Integer)
   mWeight = weight
End Sub
```

Finally, you override the ToString() method so that when you display the Cat object, its weight is displayed:

```
Public Overrides Function ToString() As String
   Return mWeight.ToString()
End Function
```

Example 5-12 changes Example 5-11 as little as possible. The Run() method still creates a local object named theVariable, but this time it is a Cat rather than an integer:

```
Dim theVariable As New Cat(5)
```

The value of theVariable is displayed and then passed to the Doubler() method:

```
Console.WriteLine("In Run. theVariable: {0}", _
theVariable)
Doubler(theVariable)
```

In Example 5-12, the Doubler() method is changed to make the parameter be a Cat rather than an integer. Note that the parameter is marked ByVal. The Cat reference will be passed by value, and a copy of the reference will be made:

```
Public Sub Doubler(ByVal param As Cat)
```

Within Doubler(), the value of the parameter is displayed, doubled, and then displayed again:

```
Console.WriteLine("In Method1. Received param: {0}
param)

param.Weight = param.Weight * 2

Console.WriteLine( _
"Updated param. Returning new value: {0}", _
param)
```

Back in Run( ), the value of theVariable is displayed:

```
Console.WriteLine("Back in Run. theVariable: {0}", _
theVariable)
```

This is *identical* to Example 5-11 in which the integer value of theVariable was unchanged after returning from Doubler( ). This time, however, the value *is* changed, even though the object was passed by value. The difference is that integers are value types, and classes are reference types.

CHAPTER 6

Inheritance and Polymorphism

Chapter 5 demonstrates how to create new types by declaring classes. The current chapter explores the relationship among objects in the real world and how to model these relationships in your code. This chapter focuses on *specialization*, which is implemented in VB.NET through *inheritance*. This chapter also explains how instances of more specialized classes can be treated as if they were instances of more general classes, a process known as *polymorphism*. This chapter ends with a consideration of *not inheritable* classes, which cannot be specialized, and a discussion of the root of all classes, the Object class, as well as a brief overview of nested classes.

Specialization and Generalization

Classes and their instances (objects) do not exist in a vacuum but rather in a network of interdependencies and relationships, just as we, as social animals, live in a world of relationships and categories. One of the most important relationships among objects in the real world is *specialization*, which can be described as an *is-a* relationship. When we say that a Dog *is-a* mammal, we mean that the dog is a specialized kind of mammal. It has all the characteristics of any mammal (it bears live young, nurses with milk, has hair, etc.), but it specializes these characteristics to the familiar characteristics of *canine domesticus*. A Cat is also a mammal. As such we expect it to share certain characteristics with the dog that are generalized in Mammal, but to differ in those characteristics that are specialized in Cat.

The specialization and generalization relationships are both reciprocal and hierarchical. They are reciprocal because specialization is the obverse side of the coin from generalization. Thus, Dog and Cat specialize Mammal, and Mammal generalizes from Dog and Cat.

These relationships are hierarchical because they create a relationship tree, with specialized types branching off from more generalized types. As you move up the hierarchy you achieve greater *generalization*. You move up toward Mammal to generalize that Dogs and Cats and Horses all bear live young. As you move down the hierarchy you specialize. Thus, the Cat specializes Mammal in having claws (a characteristic) and purring (a behavior).

Similarly, when you say that ListBox and Button *are* Windows, you indicate that there are characteristics and behaviors of Windows that you expect to find in both of these types. In other words, Window generalizes the shared characteristics of both ListBox and Button, while each specializes its own particular characteristics and behaviors.

The Unified Modeling Language (UML) is a standardized "language" for describing an object-oriented system. In the UML, classes are represented as boxes. The name of the class appears at the top of the box, and (optionally) methods and members can be listed in the sections within the box.

In the UML, you model specialization relationships as shown in Figure 6-1. Note that the arrow points from the more specialized class up to the more general class. In the figure, the more specialized Button and ListBox classes point up to the more general Window class.

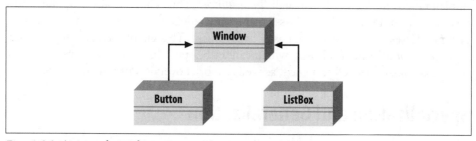

Figure 6-1. An is-a relationship

It is not uncommon for two classes to share functionality. When this occurs, you can *factor out* these commonalities into a shared base class, which is more general than the more specialized classes. This provides you with greater reuse of common code, and with code that is easier to maintain.

For example, suppose you started out creating a series of objects as illustrated in Figure 6-2.

After working with RadioButtons, CheckBoxes, and Command buttons for a while, you realize that they share certain characteristics and behaviors that are more specialized than Window but more general than any of the three. You might factor these common traits and behaviors into a common base class, Button, and rearrange your inheritance hierarchy as shown in Figure 6-3. This is an example of how generalization is used in object-oriented development.

The UML diagram in Figure 6-3 depicts the relationship among the factored classes and shows that both ListBox and Button derive from Window, and that Button is in turn specialized into CheckBox and Command. Finally, RadioButton derives from CheckBox. You can thus say that RadioButton is a CheckBox, which in turn is a Button, and that Buttons are Windows.

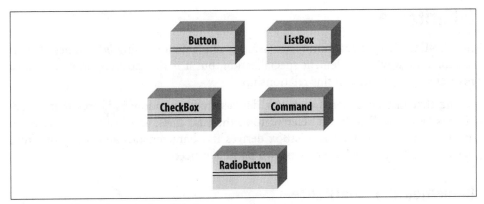

Figure 6-2. Objects deriving from Window

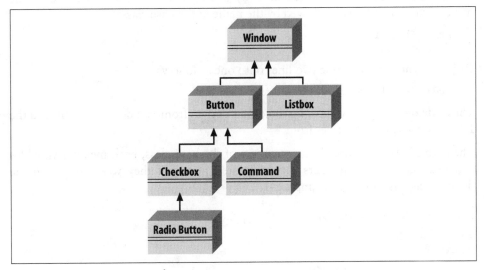

Figure 6-3. Factoring a Button class

This is not the only, or even necessarily the best, organization for these objects, but it is a reasonable starting point for understanding how these types (classes) relate to one another.

> Actually, although this might reflect how some widget hierarchies are organized, I am very skeptical of any system in which the model does not reflect how I perceive reality, and when I find myself saying that a RadioButton is a CheckBox, I have to think long and hard about whether that makes sense. I suppose a RadioButton *is* a kind of checkbox. It is a checkbox that supports the idiom of mutually exclusive choices. That said, it is a bit of a stretch and might be a sign of a shaky design.

Inheritance

In VB.NET, the specialization relationship is implemented using *inheritance*. This is not the only way to implement specialization, but it is the most common and most natural way to implement this relationship.

Saying that ListBox inherits from (or derives from) Window indicates that it specializes Window. Window is referred to as the *base* class, and ListBox is referred to as the *derived* class. That is, ListBox derives its characteristics and behaviors from Window and then specializes to its own particular needs.

Implementing Inheritance

In VB.NET, you create a derived class by adding the Inherits keyword after the name of the derived class, followed by the name of the base class:

```
Public Class ListBox
    Inherits Window
```

Or you might combine these two lines onto one as follows:

```
Public Class ListBox : Inherits Window
```

This code declares a new class, ListBox, that derives from Window. You can read the Inherits keyword as "derives from."

The derived class inherits all the members of the base class, both member variables and methods. These members can be treated just as if they were created in the derived class, as shown in Example 6-1.

Example 6-1. Deriving a new class

```
Option Strict On
Imports System

Public Class Window

    ' constructor takes two integers to
    ' fix location on the console
    Public Sub New(ByVal top As Integer, ByVal left As Integer)
        Me.top = top
        Me.left = left
    End Sub 'New

    ' simulates drawing the window
    Public Sub DrawWindow()
        Console.WriteLine("Drawing Window at {0}, {1}", top, left)
    End Sub 'DrawWindow

    ' these members are private and thus invisible
    ' to derived class methods; we'll examine this
    ' later in the chapter
```

Example 6-1. Deriving a new class (continued)

```
    Private top As Integer
    Private left As Integer

End Class 'Window

' ListBox derives from Window
Public Class ListBox

    Inherits Window

    ' constructor adds a parameter
    Public Sub New(ByVal top As Integer, ByVal left As Integer, ByVal theContents As
String)
        MyBase.New(top, left) ' call base constructor
        mListBoxContents = theContents
    End Sub 'New

    ' a shadow version (note keyword) because in the
    ' derived method we change the behavior
    Public Shadows Sub DrawWindow( )
        MyBase.DrawWindow( ) ' invoke the base method
        Console.WriteLine("Writing string to the listbox: {0}", mListBoxContents)
    End Sub 'DrawWindow

    Private mListBoxContents As String ' new member variable

End Class 'ListBox

Module Module1

    Sub Main( )
        ' create a base instance
        Dim w As New Window(5, 10)
        w.DrawWindow( )

        ' create a derived instance
        Dim lb As New ListBox(20, 30, "Hello world")
        lb.DrawWindow( )
    End Sub

End Module

Output:
Drawing Window at 5, 10
Drawing Window at 20, 30
Writing string to the listbox: Hello world
```

Example 6-1 starts with the declaration of the base class Window. This class implements a constructor and a simple DrawWindow() method. There are two private member variables, top and left. The program is analyzed in detail in the following sections.

Calling Base Class Constructors

In Example 6-1, the new class ListBox derives from Window and has its own constructor, which takes three parameters (top, left, and theContents). The ListBox constructor invokes the constructor of its parent by calling MyBase.New and passing in the parameters (using the ByVal keyword, as described in Chapter 5):

```
Public Sub New( _
    ByVal top As Integer, _
    ByVal left As Integer, _
    ByVal theContents As String)
    MyBase.New(top, left) ' call base constructor
    mListBoxContents = theContents
End Sub 'New
```

Because classes cannot inherit constructors, a derived class must implement its own constructor and can only make use of the constructor of its base class by calling it explicitly.

If the base class has an accessible default constructor, the derived constructor is not required to invoke the base constructor explicitly; instead, the default constructor is called implicitly. However, if the base class does not have a default constructor, every derived constructor *must* explicitly invoke one of the base class constructors using the MyBase keyword, which refers to the base class for the current object.

 As discussed in Chapter 5, if you do not declare a constructor of any kind, the compiler will create a default constructor for you. Whether you write it yourself or you use the one provided "by default" by the compiler, a default constructor is one that takes no parameters. Note, however, that once you do create a constructor of any kind (with or without parameters) the compiler does *not* create a default constructor for you.

Shadowing Base Methods

Also notice in Example 6-1 that ListBox implements a new version of DrawWindow():

```
Public Shadows Sub DrawWindow()
```

The keyword Shadows here indicates that the programmer is intentionally creating a new version of this method in the derived class.

In Example 6-1, the DrawWindow() method of ListBox hides and replaces the base class method. When you call DrawWindow() on an object of type ListBox, it is ListBox.DrawWindow() that will be invoked, not Window.DrawWindow(). Note, however, that ListBox.DrawWindow() can invoke the DrawWindow() method of its base class with the code:

```
MyBase.DrawWindow() 'invoke the base method
```

Controlling Access

The visibility of a class and its members can be restricted through the use of access modifiers, such as Public, Private, and Protected. As explained in Chapter 5, Public allows a member to be accessed by the member methods of other classes, while Private indicates that the member is visible only to member methods of its own class. The Protected keyword extends visibility to methods of derived classes.

Classes as well as their members can be designated with any of these accessibility levels. If a class member has a different access designation than the class, the more restricted access applies. Thus, if you define a class, SomeClass, as follows:

```
Public Class SomeClass
    '...
    Protected myValue As Integer
End Class 'SomeClass
```

the accessibility for myValue is protected even though the class itself is public. A *public class* is one that is visible to any other class that wishes to interact with it.

Polymorphism

There are two powerful aspects to inheritance. One is code reuse. When you create a ListBox class, you're able to reuse some of the logic in the base (Window) class.

What is arguably more powerful, however, is the second aspect of inheritance: *polymorphism*. *Poly* means many and *morph* means form. Thus, polymorphism refers to being able to use many forms of a type without regard to the details.

When the phone company sends your phone a ring signal, it does not know what type of phone is on the other end of the line. You might have an old-fashioned Western Electric phone that energizes a motor to ring a bell, or you might have an electronic phone that plays digital music.

As far as the phone company is concerned, it knows only about the "base type" phone and expects that any "instance" of this type knows how to ring. When the phone company tells your phone to *ring*, it simply expects the phone to "do the right thing." Thus, the phone company treats your phone polymorphically.

Creating Polymorphic Types

Because a ListBox *is-a* Window and a Button *is-a* Window, you expect to be able to use either of these types in situations that call for a Window. For example, a form might want to keep a collection of all the instances of Window it manages so that when the form is opened, it can tell each of its Windows to draw itself. For this operation, the form does not want to know which elements are list boxes and which are buttons; it just wants to tick through its collection and tell each to "draw." In short, the form wants to treat all its Window objects polymorphically.

Creating Polymorphic Methods

To create a method that supports polymorphism, you need only mark it as overridable in its base class. For example, to indicate that the method DrawWindow() of class Window in Example 6-1 is polymorphic, simply add the keyword Overridable to its declaration, as follows:

```
Public Overridable Sub DrawWindow( )
```

Now each derived class is free to implement its own version of DrawWindow() and the method will be invoked polymorphically. To do so, you simply override the base class overridable method by using the keyword Overrides in the derived class method definition, and then add the new code for that overridden method.

 Be careful to distinguish the keyword Overridable, which states that a method *can* be overridden in a derived class, from Overrides, which states that the method is being overridden in the current class. The former says "this method can be overridden if you'd like," the latter says, "Yes, please, I'm overriding the method right now."

In the following excerpt from Example 6-2 (which appears later in this section), List-Box derives from Window and implements its own version of DrawWindow():

```
Public Overrides Sub DrawWindow( )
    MyBase.DrawWindow( ) ' invoke the base method
    Console.WriteLine( _
      "Writing string to the listbox: {0}", listBoxContents)
End Sub 'DrawWindow
```

The keyword Overrides tells the compiler that this class has intentionally overridden how DrawWindow() works. Similarly, you'll override this method in another class, Button, also derived from Window.

In the body of Example 6-2, you'll create three objects: a Window, a ListBox, and a Button. You'll then call DrawWindow() on each:

```
Dim win As New Window(1, 2)
Dim lb As New ListBox(3, 4, "Stand alone list box")
Dim b As New Button(5, 6)
win.DrawWindow( )
lb.DrawWindow( )
b.DrawWindow( )
```

This works much as you might expect. The correct DrawWindow() object is called for each. So far, nothing polymorphic has been done.

The real magic starts when you create an array of Window objects.

Example 6-2 uses an array, which is a collection of objects, all of the same type. You create an array by indicating the type of objects to hold and then allocating space for a given number of those objects. For example, the following code declares winArray to be an array of three Window objects:

```
Dim winArray(3) As Window
```

You access the members of the array with parentheses. The first element is accessed with winArray(0), the second with winArray(1), and so forth. Arrays are explained in detail in Chapter 9.

Because a ListBox *is-a* Window, you are free to place a ListBox into an array of Windows. You can also place a Button into an array of Window objects because a Button is also a Window:

```
Dim winArray(3) As Window
winArray(0) = New Window(1, 2)
winArray(1) = New ListBox(3, 4, "List box in array")
winArray(2) = New Button(5, 6)
```

The first line of code declares an array named winArray that will hold three Window objects. The next three lines add new Window objects to the array. The first adds a Window. The second adds a ListBox (which is a Window because ListBox derives from Window), and the third adds a Button (Button also derives from Window).

What happens when you call DrawWindow() on each of these objects?

```
Dim offSet As Integer
For offSet = 0 To 2
    winArray(offSet).DrawWindow()
Next offSet
```

This code calls DrawWindow() on each element in the array in turn. The value offSet is initialized to zero and is incremented each time through the loop. The value of offSet is used as an index into the array.

All the compiler knows is that it has three Window objects and that you've called DrawWindow() on each. If you had not marked DrawWindow() as overridable, Window's original DrawWindow() method would be called three times.

However, because you did mark DrawWindow() as overridable, and because the derived classes override that method, when you call DrawWindow() on the array, the right thing happens for each object in the array. Specifically, the compiler determines the runtime type of the actual objects (a Window, a ListBox, and a Button) and calls the right method on each. This is the essence of polymorphism.

The runtime type of an object is the actual (derived) type. At compile time you do not have to decide what kind of objects will be added to your collection, so long as they all derive from the declared type (in this case Window). At runtime the actual type is discovered and the right method is called. This allows you to pick the actual type of objects to add to the collection while the program is running.

The complete code for this example is shown in Example 6-2.

Example 6-2. Virtual methods

```
Option Strict On
Imports System
Public Class Window

    ' constructor takes two integers to
    ' fix location on the console
    Public Sub New(ByVal top As Integer, ByVal left As Integer)
        Me.top = top
        Me.left = left
    End Sub 'New

    ' simulates drawing the window
    Public Overridable Sub DrawWindow()
        Console.WriteLine("Window: drawing Window at {0}, {1}", top, left)
    End Sub 'DrawWindow

    ' these members are protected and thus visible
    ' to derived class methods. We'll examine this
    ' later in the chapter
    Protected top As Integer
    Protected left As Integer

End Class 'Window

' ListBox derives from Window
Public Class ListBox

    Inherits Window

    ' constructor adds a parameter
    Public Sub New(ByVal top As Integer, ByVal left As Integer, ByVal contents As String)
        MyBase.New(top, left) ' call base constructor

        listBoxContents = contents
    End Sub 'New

    ' an overridden version (note keyword) because in the
    ' derived method we change the behavior
    Public Overrides Sub DrawWindow()
        MyBase.DrawWindow() ' invoke the base method
        Console.WriteLine( _
```

Example 6-2. Virtual methods (continued)

```vb
            "Writing string to the listbox: {0}", listBoxContents)
    End Sub 'DrawWindow

    Private listBoxContents As String ' new member variable

End Class 'ListBox

Public Class Button

    Inherits Window

    Public Sub New(ByVal top As Integer, ByVal left As Integer)
        MyBase.New(top, left)
    End Sub 'New

    ' an overridden version (note keyword) because in the
    ' derived method we change the behavior
    Public Overrides Sub DrawWindow()
        Console.WriteLine( _
            "Drawing a button at {0}, {1}" + ControlChars.Lf, top, Left)
    End Sub 'DrawWindow

End Class 'Button

Public Class Tester

    Shared Sub Main()
        Dim win As New Window(1, 2)
        Dim lb As New ListBox(3, 4, "Stand alone list box")
        Dim b As New Button(5, 6)

        win.DrawWindow()
        lb.DrawWindow()
        b.DrawWindow()

        Dim winArray(3) As Window
        winArray(0) = New Window(1, 2)
        winArray(1) = New ListBox(3, 4, "List box in array")
        winArray(2) = New Button(5, 6)

        Dim i As Integer
        For i = 0 To 2
            winArray(i).DrawWindow()
        Next i

    End Sub 'Main

End Class 'Tester

Output:
Window: drawing Window at 1, 2
Window: drawing Window at 3, 4
```

Example 6-2. Virtual methods (continued)

```
Writing string to the listbox: Stand alone list box
Drawing a button at 5, 6

Window: drawing Window at 1, 2
Window: drawing Window at 3, 4
Writing string to the listbox: List box in array
Drawing a button at 5, 6
```

Note that throughout this example, the new overridden methods are marked with the keyword Overrides:

```
Public Overrides Sub DrawWindow()
```

The compiler now knows to use the overridden method when treating these objects polymorphically. The compiler is responsible for tracking the real type of the object and for handling the "late binding" so that it is ListBox.DrawWindow() that is called when the Window reference really points to a ListBox object.

Versioning with Overridable and Overrides

In VB.NET, the programmer's decision to override an overridable method is made explicit with the Overrides keyword. This helps you release new versions of your code. Changes to the base class will not break existing code in the derived classes; the requirement to use the Overrides keyword helps prevent that problem.

Here's how: Assume for a moment that the Window base class of the previous example was written by Company A. Suppose also that the ListBox and RadioButton classes were written by programmers from Company B using a purchased copy of the Company A Window class as a base. The programmers in Company B have little or no control over the design of the Window class, including future changes that Company A might choose to make.

Now suppose that one of the programmers for Company B decides to add a Sort() method to ListBox:

```
Public Class ListBox
    Inherits Window
    Public Overridable Sub Sort()
       '...
    End Sub
```

This presents no problems until Company A, the author of Window, releases Version 2 of its Window class, and it turns out that the programmers in Company A have also added a Sort() method to their public class Window:

```
Public Class Window
    Public Overridable Sub Sort()
       '...
    End Sub
```

In other object-oriented languages (such as C++), the new overridable Sort() method in Window would now act as a base method for the overridable Sort() method in ListBox. The compiler would call the Sort() method in ListBox when you intend to call the Sort() in Window. In Java, if the Sort() in Window had a different return type, the class loader would consider the Sort() in ListBox to be an invalid override and would fail to load.

VB.NET prevents this confusion. In VB.NET, an overridable function is always considered to be the root of dispatch; that is, once VB.NET finds an overridable method, it looks no further up the inheritance hierarchy. If a new overridable Sort() function is introduced into Window, the runtime behavior of ListBox is unchanged.

When ListBox is compiled again, however, the compiler generates a warning:

```
Module1.vb(31) : warning BC40005: sub 'Sort' shadows an
overridable method in a base class. To override the
base method, this method must be declared 'Overrides'.
```

To remove the warning, the programmer must indicate what he intends. He can mark the ListBox Sort() method Shadows, to indicate that it is *not* an override of the Overridable method in Window:

```
Public Class ListBox
    Inherits Window

    Public Shadows Sub Sort()
        '...
    End Sub 'Sort
```

This action removes the warning. If, on the other hand, the programmer does want to override the method in Window, he need only use the Overrides keyword to make that intention explicit:

```
Public Class ListBox
    Inherits Window

    Public Overrides Sub Sort()
        '...
    End Sub 'Sort
```

Abstract Methods and Classes

Each type of Window has a different shape and appearance. Drop-down list boxes look very different from Buttons. Clearly, every subclass of Window *should* implement its own DrawWindow() method—but so far, nothing in the Window class enforces that they must do so. To require subclasses to implement a method of their base, you need to designate that method as *abstract*.

You designate a method as abstract by placing the MustOverride keyword at the beginning of the method definition, as follows:

```
MustOverride Public Sub DrawWindow ()
```

An MustOverride method has no implementation. It creates a method name and signature that must be implemented in all derived classes. Furthermore, making one or more methods of any class MustOverride has the side effect of making the class abstract; an abstract class must be marked with the keyword MustInherit.

Classes marked with MustInherit establish a base for derived classes, but it is not legal to instantiate an object of a class marked MustInherit. Once you declare a method with MustOverride, you prohibit the creation of any instances of that class.

If one or more methods of the class are MustOverride, the class definition must be marked MustInherit, as in the following:

```
MustInherit Public Class Window
```

Thus, if you were to designate DrawWindow() MustOverride in the Window class, the Window class would thus become MustInherit. Then you could derive from Window, but you could not create any Window objects/instances. If the Window class is an abstraction, there is no such thing as a Window object; only objects derived from Window.

Making Window.DrawWindow() MustOverride means that each class derived from Window would have to implement its own DrawWindow() method. If the derived class failed to implement the MustOverride method, that derived class would also be MustInherit, and again no instances would be possible. Example 6-3 illustrates the use of MustInherit and MustOverride.

Example 6-3. An abstract class and method

```
Option Strict On
Imports System

MustInherit Public Class Window

    ' constructor takes two integers to
    ' fix location on the console
    Public Sub New(top As Integer, left As Integer)
        Me.top = top
        Me.left = left
    End Sub 'New

    ' simulates drawing the window
    ' notice: no implementation
    Public MustOverride Sub DrawWindow()

    Protected top As Integer
    Protected left As Integer

End Class 'Window

' ListBox derives from Window
Public Class ListBox
```

Example 6-3. An abstract class and method (continued)

```
    Inherits Window

    ' constructor adds a parameter
    Public Sub New(top As Integer, left As Integer, contents As String)
        MyBase.New(top, left) ' call base constructor

        listBoxContents = contents
    End Sub 'New


    ' an overridden version implementing the abstract method
    Public Overrides Sub DrawWindow( )

        Console.WriteLine("Writing string to the listbox: {0}", listBoxContents)
    End Sub 'DrawWindow

    Private listBoxContents As String ' new member variable

End Class 'ListBox

Public Class Button

    Inherits Window

    Public Sub New(top As Integer, left As Integer)
        MyBase.New(top, left)
    End Sub 'New

    ' implement the abstract method
    Public Overrides Sub DrawWindow( )
        Console.WriteLine("Drawing a button at {0}, {1}" + ControlChars.Lf, top, left)
    End Sub 'DrawWindow

End Class 'Button

Public Class Tester

    Shared Sub Main( )
        Dim winArray(3) As Window
        winArray(0) = New ListBox(1, 2, "First List Box")
        winArray(1) = New ListBox(3, 4, "Second List Box")
        winArray(2) = New Button(5, 6)

        Dim i As Integer
        For i = 0 To 2
            winArray(i).DrawWindow( )
        Next i
    End Sub 'Main

End Class 'Tester

Output:
```

Example 6-3. An abstract class and method (continued)

```
Writing string to the listbox: First List Box
Writing string to the listbox: Second List Box
Drawing a button at 5, 6
```

The Idea Behind Abstraction

MustInherit classes should not just be an implementation trick; they should represent the idea of an abstraction that establishes a "contract" for all derived classes. In other words, MustInherit classes mandate the public methods of the classes that will implement the abstraction.

The idea of a MustInherit Window class ought to lay out the common characteristics and behaviors of all windows, even though you never intend to instantiate the abstraction Window itself.

A MustInherit class serves to implement the abstraction "Window" that will be manifest in the various concrete instances of Window, such as browser window, frame, button, list box, drop-down, and so forth. The MustInherit class establishes what a Window is, even though we never intend to create a "Window" per se. An alternative to using MustInherit is to define an interface, as described in Chapter 8.

In Example 6-3, the Window class has been declared MustInherit and therefore cannot be instantiated. If you replace the first array member:

```
winArray(0) = New ListBox(1, 2, "First List Box")
```

with this code:

```
winArray(0) = New Window(1, 2)
```

the program will generate the following error:

```
C:\...Module1.vb(63): 'New' cannot be used on class 'DebuggingVB.Window' because it
contains a 'MustOverride' member that has not been overridden.
```

You can instantiate the ListBox and Button objects because these classes override the MustOverride method, thus making the classes *concrete* (i.e., not abstract).

NotInheritable Classes

The opposite side of the design coin from MustInherit is NotInheritable. Just as classes marked with MustInherit are considered *abstract*, classes marked with NotInheritable are considered *sealed*. Although an abstract class is intended to be derived-from and to provide a template for its subclasses to follow, a sealed class does not allow classes to derive from it at all. The NotInheritable keyword placed before the class declaration precludes derivation. Classes are most often marked NotInheritable to prevent accidental inheritance.

If the declaration of Window in Example 6-3 is changed from MustInherit to NotInheritable, the program will fail to compile. If you try to build this project, the compiler will return the following error message:

```
C:\...Module1.vb(13): 'NotInheritable' classes cannot have members
declared 'MustOverride'.
```

Microsoft recommends using NotInheritable "when it will not be necessary to create derived classes"* and also when your class consists of nothing but shared methods and properties.

The Root of All Classes: Object

All VB.NET classes, of any type, are treated as if they ultimately derive from a single class, Object. Object is the (root) base class for all other classes.

A base class is the "parent" of a derived class. A derived class can be the base to further derived classes, creating an inheritance "tree" or hierarchy. A *root* class is the topmost class in an inheritance hierarchy. In VB.NET (and all CLS-compliant languages), the root class is Object. The nomenclature is a bit confusing until you imagine an upside-down tree, with the root on top and the derived classes below. Thus, the base class is considered to be "above" the derived class.

Object provides a number of methods that subclasses can and do override. These include Equals(), which determines if two objects are the same, GetType(), which returns the type of the object, and ToString(), which returns a string to represent the current object. Specifically, ToString() returns a string with the name of the class to which the object belongs. Table 6-1 summarizes the methods of Object.

Table 6-1. The Object class

Method	What it does
Equals( )	Evaluates whether two objects are equivalent.
Finalize( )	Cleans up non-memory resources; implemented by a destructor.
GetHashCode( )	Allows objects to provide their own hash function for use in collections (see Chapter 9).
GetType( )	Provides access to the type object.
MemberwiseClone( )	Creates copies of the object; should never be implemented by your type.
ReferenceEquals( )	Evaluates whether two objects refer to the same instance.
ToString( )	Provides a string representation of the object.

In Example 6-4, the Dog class overrides the ToString() method inherited from Object, to return the weight of the Dog. This example also takes advantage of the

---

* Visual Studio .NET Combined Collection: Base Class Usage Guidelines.

startling fact that intrinsic types (Integer, Long, etc.) can also be treated as if they derive from Object, and thus you can call ToString() on an integer variable! Calling ToString() on an intrinsic type returns a string representation of the variable's value.

Example 6-4. Overriding ToString

```
Option Strict On
Imports System

Public Class Dog

    Private weight As Integer
    ' constructor
    Public Sub New(ByVal weight As Integer)
        Me.weight = weight
    End Sub 'New

    ' override Object.ToString
    Public Overrides Function ToString() As String
        Return weight.ToString()
    End Function 'ToString

End Class 'Dog

Public Class Tester

    Shared Sub Main()
        Dim i As Integer = 5
        Console.WriteLine("The value of i is: {0}", i.ToString())

        Dim milo As New Dog(62)
        Console.WriteLine("My dog Milo weighs {0} pounds", milo.ToString())
    End Sub 'Main

End Class 'Tester

Output:
The value of i is: 5
My dog Milo weighs 62 pounds
```

The documentation for Object.ToString() reveals its signature:

```
Overridable Public Function ToString() As String
```

It is an overridable public method that returns a string and that takes no parameters. All the built-in types, such as Integer, derive from Object and so can invoke Object's methods.

 The Console class's Write() and WriteLine() methods call ToString() for you on objects that you pass in for display.

Example 6-4 overrides the Overridable ToString() function for Dog, so that calling ToString() on a Dog object will return a reasonable value. If you comment out the overridden function, the base method will be invoked. The base class default behavior is to return a string with the name of the class itself. Thus, the output would be changed to the meaningless:

```
My dog Milo weighs Dog pounds
```

 Classes do not need to declare explicitly that they derive from Object; the inheritance is implicit.

Boxing and Unboxing Types

Boxing and *unboxing* are the processes that enable value types (e.g., integers) to be treated as reference types (objects). The value is "boxed" inside an Object and subsequently "unboxed" back to a value type. It is this process that allowed you to call the ToString() method on the integer in Example 6-4.

Boxing Is Implicit

Boxing is an implicit conversion of a value type to the type Object. Boxing a value allocates an instance of Object and copies the value into the new object instance, as shown in Figure 6-4.

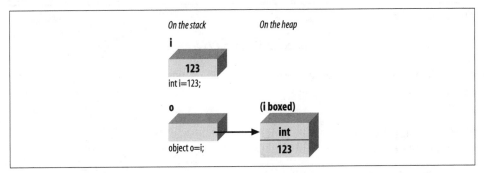

Figure 6-4. Boxing value types

Boxing is implicit when you provide a value type where a reference is expected. The compiler notices that you've provided a value type and silently boxes it within an object. You can, of course, explicitly cast the value type to a reference type, as in the following:

```
Dim myIntegerValue As Integer = 5
Dim myObject As Object = myIntegerValue ' explicitly cast to object
myObject.ToString()
```

This is not necessary, however, as the compiler will box the value for you, silently and with no action on your part:

```
Dim myIntegerValue As Integer = 5
myIntegerValue.ToString( ) ' boxed for you
```

Unboxing Must Be Explicit

To return the boxed object back to a value type, you must explicitly unbox it if Option Strict is On (as it should be). You will typically unbox by using the DirectCast( ) function or the CType( ) function. Figure 6-5 illustrates unboxing.

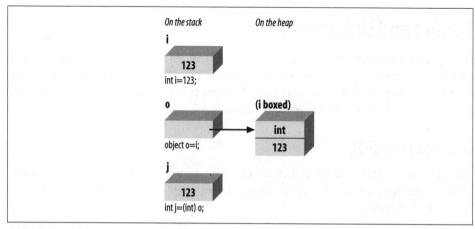

Figure 6-5. Unboxing

Boxing and unboxing are illustrated in Example 6-5.

Example 6-5. Boxing and unboxing

```
Option Strict On
Imports System

Public Class UnboxingTest
    Public Shared Sub Main( )

        Dim myIntegerVariable As Integer = 123

        ' boxing
        Dim myObjectVariable As Object = myIntegerVariable
        Console.WriteLine("myObjectVariable: {0}", _
            myObjectVariable.ToString( ))

        ' unboxing (must be explicit)
        Dim anotherIntegerVariable As Integer = _
            DirectCast(myObjectVariable, Integer)
        Console.WriteLine("anotherIntegerVariable: {0}", _
            anotherIntegerVariable)
```

Example 6-5. Boxing and unboxing (continued)

```
    End Sub
End Class
```

```
Output:
myObjectVariable: 123
anotherIntegerVariable: 123
```

Example 6-5 creates an integer myIntegerVariable and implicitly boxes it when it is assigned to the object myObjectVariable; then, to exercise the newly boxed object, its value is displayed by calling ToString().

The object is then explicitly unboxed and assigned to a new integer variable, anotherIntegerVariable, whose value is displayed to show that the value has been preserved.

Typically, you will wrap an unbox operation in a try block, as explained in Chapter 11. If the object being unboxed is null or is a reference to an object of a different type, an InvalidCastException error occurs.

As an alternative, you can use the TypeOf() function, as follows:

```
' unboxing (must be explicit)
If TypeOf (myObjectVariable) Is Integer Then
   Dim anotherIntegerVariable As Integer = _
       DirectCast(myObjectVariable, Integer)
   Console.WriteLine("anotherIntegerVariable: {0}", _
       anotherIntegerVariable)
 End If
```

Nested Classes

Classes have members, and it is entirely possible for the members of a class to be another user-defined type. Thus, a Button class might have a member of type Location, and a Location class might contain members of type Point. Finally, Point might contain members of type Integer.

At times, the contained class might exist only to serve the outer class, and there might be no reason for it to be otherwise visible. (In short, the contained class acts as a helper class.) You can define the helper class within the definition of the outer class. The contained, inner class is called a *nested* class, and the class that contains it is called, simply, the *outer* class.

Nested classes have the advantage of access to all the members of the outer class. That is, a method of a nested class can access private members of the outer class.

In addition, the nested class can be hidden from all other classes—that is, it can be private to the outer class.

Finally, a nested class that is public is accessed within the scope of the outer class. If Button is the outer class, and Location is the (public) inner class, you refer to Location as Button.Location, with the outer class (Button) acting (more or less) as a namespace or scope.

Example 6-6 features a nested class of Fraction named FractionArtist. The job of FractionArtist is to render the fraction on the console. In this example, the rendering is handled by a pair of simple WriteLine() statements.

Example 6-6. Using a nested class

```
Option Strict On
Imports System
Public Class Fraction

    Private numerator As Integer
    Private denominator As Integer

    Public Sub New( _
      ByVal numerator As Integer, ByVal denominator As Integer)
        Me.numerator = numerator
        Me.denominator = denominator
    End Sub 'New

    Public Overrides Function ToString() As String
        Return [String].Format("{0}/{1}", numerator, denominator)
    End Function 'ToString

    ' Nested Class
    Class FractionArtist
        Public Sub Draw(ByVal f As Fraction)
            Console.WriteLine("Drawing the numerator: {0}", f.numerator)
            Console.WriteLine( _
                "Drawing the denominator: {0}", f.denominator)
        End Sub 'Draw
    End Class 'FractionArtist

End Class 'Fraction

Public Class Tester
    Shared Sub Main()
        Dim f1 As New Fraction(3, 4)
        Console.WriteLine("f1: {0}", f1.ToString())

        Dim fa As New Fraction.FractionArtist()
        fa.Draw(f1)
    End Sub 'Main
End Class 'Tester
```

The nested class is shown in bold. The FractionArtist class provides only a single member, the Draw() method. What is particularly interesting is that Draw() has access to the private data members f.numerator and f.denominator, to which it would not have had access if it were not a nested class.

Notice in Main( ) that to declare an instance of this nested class, you must specify the type name of the outer class:

```
Dim fa As New Fraction.FractionArtist( )
```

FractionArtist is scoped to within the Fraction class.

CHAPTER 7

Structures

So far, the only user-defined type you've seen is the class. A second type of user-defined type is a *structure*. Structures are designed to be lightweight alternatives to classes. In this case, the term lightweight means that structures use fewer resources (i.e., less memory) than classes, but they offer less functionality.

Structures are similar to classes in that they can contain constructors, properties, methods, fields, operators, nested types, and indexers. There are, however, significant differences between classes and structures.

For example, structures don't support inheritance or destructors. More important, while a class is a reference type, a structure is a value type.

The current consensus is that you ought to use structures only for types that are small, simple, and similar in their behavior and characteristics to built-in types. For example, if you were creating a class to represent a point on the screen (x,y coordinates), you might consider using a structure rather than a class.

Structures are somewhat more efficient in their use of memory in arrays; however, they can be less efficient when used in collections (arrays and collections are discussed in Chapter 9). Collections expect references, and because structures are value types, they must be boxed. There is overhead in boxing and unboxing, and classes might be more efficient in large collections. Boxing and unboxing are discussed in Chapter 6. In this chapter, you will learn how to define and work with structures and how to use constructors to initialize their values.

Defining a Structure

The syntax for declaring a structure is almost identical to that for a class:

```
[attributes] [access-modifiers] Structure identifier
[Implements interface-list]

    structure-members
End Structure
```

Attributes are discussed in Chapter 18. *Access modifiers* (Public, Private, etc.) work just as they do with classes. (See Chapter 5 for a discussion of access modifiers.) The keyword Structure is followed by an *identifier* (the name of the structure). The optional *interface-list* is explained in Chapter 8. Within the body of the structure, you define fields and methods, also called the structure members, just as you do in a class.

Example 7-1 defines a structure named Location to hold x,y coordinates of an object displayed on the screen.

Example 7-1. Creating a structure

```
Option Strict On
Imports System
Namespace StructureDemonstration

    ' declare a Structure named Location
    Public Structure Location
        ' the structure has private data
        Private myXVal As Integer
        Private myYVal As Integer


        ' constructor
        Public Sub New( _
           ByVal xCoordinate As Integer, ByVal yCoordinate As Integer)
            myXVal = xCoordinate
            myYVal = yCoordinate
        End Sub 'New

        ' property

        Public Property XVal( ) As Integer
            Get
                Return myXVal
            End Get
            Set(ByVal Value As Integer)
                myXVal = Value
            End Set
        End Property

        Public Property YVal( ) As Integer
            Get
                Return myYVal
            End Get
            Set(ByVal Value As Integer)
                myYVal = Value
            End Set
        End Property

        ' Display the structure as a String
        Public Overrides Function ToString( ) As String
            Return String.Format("{0}, {1}", xVal, yVal)
```

Example 7-1. Creating a structure (continued)

```
        End Function 'ToString
    End Structure 'Location

    Class Tester
        Public Sub Run()
            ' create an instance of the structure
            Dim loc1 As New Location(200, 300)

            ' display the values in the structure
            Console.WriteLine("Loc1 location: {0}", loc1)

            ' invoke the default constructor
            Dim loc2 As New Location()
            Console.WriteLine("Loc2 location: {0}", loc2)

            ' pass the structure to a method
            myFunc(loc1)

            ' redisplay the values in the structure
            Console.WriteLine("Loc1 location: {0}", loc1)
        End Sub 'Run


        ' method takes a structure as a parameter
        Public Sub myFunc(ByVal loc As Location)
            ' modify the values through the properties
            loc.XVal = 50
            loc.YVal = 100
            Console.WriteLine("Loc1 location: {0}", loc)
        End Sub 'myFunc


        Shared Sub Main()
            Dim t As New Tester()
            t.Run()
        End Sub 'Main

    End Class 'Tester
End Namespace 'StructureDemonstration

Output:
Loc1 location: 200, 300
Loc2 location: 0, 0
Loc1 location: 50, 100
Loc1 location: 200, 300
```

The Location structure is defined as public, much as you might define a class.

```
    Public Structure Location
        ' the structure has private data
        Private myXVal As Integer
        Private myYVal As Integer
```

As with a class, you can define a constructor and properties for the structure. For example, you might create integer member variables myXVal and myYVal, and then provide public properties for them named XVal and YVal (see Chapter 5):

```
' constructor
Public Sub New( _
   ByVal xCoordinate As Integer, ByVal yCoordinate As Integer)
      myXVal = xCoordinate
      myYVal = yCoordinate
End Sub 'New

Public Property XVal( ) As Integer
    Get
         Return myXVal
    End Get
    Set(ByVal Value As Integer)
         myXVal = Value
    End Set
End Property

Public Property YVal( ) As Integer
    Get
         Return myYVal
    End Get
    Set(ByVal Value As Integer)
         myYVal = Value
    End Set
End Property
```

There is no difference in the way you create constructors and properties in structures and the way you do so in classes. However, you are not permitted to create a custom default constructor for a structure. That is, you cannot write a constructor with no parameters. Thus the following code would not compile:

```
' won't compile - no custom default
' constructors for structures
Public Sub New( )
    xVal = 5
    yVal = 10
End Sub 'New
```

Instead, the compiler creates a default constructor for you (whether or not you create other constructors), and that default constructor initializes all the member values to their default values (e.g., integers are initialized to zero).

The Run( ) method of the Tester class creates an instance of the Location structure named loc1, passing in the initial x,y coordinates of 200,300:

```
Dim loc1 As New Location(200, 300)
```

Loc1 is then passed to WriteLine( ) to display the x,y values:

```
Console.WriteLine("Loc1 location: {0}", loc1)
```

When you pass the loc1 object to Console.WriteLine( ), WriteLine( ) automatically invokes the overridable ToString( ) method on the object. Thus, Location.ToString( ) is invoked, which displays the x and y coordinates of the loc1 object:

```
Loc1 location: 200, 300
```

Before modifying the values in loc1, the example creates a second instance of the Location structure, named loc2, and displays its values:

```
Dim loc2 As New Location( )
Console.WriteLine("Loc2 location: {0}", loc2)
```

The creation of loc2 invokes the default constructor (note that no parameters are passed in). The output shows that the compiler-provided default constructor initialized the member variables to default values.

```
Loc2 location: 0, 0
```

You next pass your first structure, loc1, whose values are 200,300, to a method, myFunc( ). In that method, the parameter is a Location object named loc. Within the myFunc( ) method, the XVal property is used to set the x coordinate to 50, and the YVal property is used to set the y coordinate to 100; then the new value is displayed using WriteLine( ):

```
Public Sub myFunc(ByVal loc As Location)
    ' modify the values through the properties
    loc.XVal = 50
    loc.YVal = 100
    Console.WriteLine("Loc1 location: {0}", loc)
End Sub 'myFunc
```

As expected, the results show the modification:

```
Loc1 location: 50, 100
```

When you return to the calling method (Run( )), the values of loc1 are displayed, showing they are unchanged from before the call to myFunc( ):

```
Loc1 location: 200, 300
```

When you passed loc1 to myFunc( ), the structure was passed by value (structures, like the intrinsic types, are value types). A copy was made, and it was on that copy that you changed the values to 50 and 100. The original Location structure (loc1) was unaffected by the changes made within myFunc( ).

No Inheritance

Unlike classes, structures do not support inheritance. Structures implicitly derive from Object (as do all types in VB.NET, including the built-in types) but cannot inherit from any other class or structure. Structures are also implicitly *not-inheritable* (that is, no class or structure can derive from a structure). See Chapter 6 for a discussion of inheritance and not-inheritable classes.

No Initialization

You cannot initialize an instance field in a structure. Thus, it is illegal to write:

```
Private xVal As Integer = 50
Private yVal As Integer = 100
```

though this kind of initialization is perfectly legal in a class. You must instead set the value of your member fields in the body of the constructor. As noted earlier, the default constructor (provided by the compiler) will set all the member variables to their default value.

Public Member Data?

Structures are designed to be simple and lightweight. While private member data promotes data hiding and encapsulation, some programmers feel it is overkill for structures. They make the member data public, thus simplifying the implementation of the structure. Other programmers feel that properties provide a clean and simple interface, and that good programming practice demands data hiding even with simple lightweight objects. Which you choose is a matter of design philosophy; the language will support either approach.

Calling the Default Constructor

As mentioned earlier, if you do not create a constructor, an implicit default constructor will be called by the compiler. You can see this at work by commenting out the constructor in Example 7-1:

```
'Public Sub New( _
'    ByVal xCoordinate As Integer, ByVal yCoordinate As Integer)
'        myXVal = xCoordinate
'        myYVal = yCoordinate
'End Sub 'New
```

and replacing the first line in Main() with one that creates an instance of Location without passing values:

```
'Dim loc1 As New Location(200, 300)
Dim loc1 As New Location( )
```

Because there is now no constructor at all, the implicit default constructor is called. The output looks like this:

```
Loc1 location: 0, 0
Loc2 location: 0, 0
```

The default constructor has initialized the member variables to zero.

Creating Structures Without New

Because loc1 is a structure (not a class), it is created on the stack. Thus, in Example 7-1, when the New keyword is called:

```
Dim loc1 As New Location(200, 300)
```

the resulting Location object is created on the stack.

The New keyword calls the Location constructor. However, unlike with a class, it is possible to create a structure without using New at all. This is consistent with how built-in type variables (such as Integer) are defined and is illustrated in Example 7-2.

 Creating structures without the keyword New brings little advantage and can create programs that are harder to understand, more error prone, and more difficult to maintain! Proceed at your own risk.

Example 7-2. Creating a structure without New

```
Option Strict On
Imports System
Namespace StructureDemonstration

    ' declare a structure named Location
    Public Structure Location
        ' the Structure has private data
        Private myXVal As Integer
        Private myYVal As Integer

        Public Sub New( _
            ByVal xCoordinate As Integer, ByVal yCoordinate As Integer)
            myXVal = xCoordinate
            myYVal = yCoordinate
        End Sub 'New

        ' property

        Public Property XVal( ) As Integer
            Get
                Return myXVal
            End Get
            Set(ByVal Value As Integer)
                myXVal = Value
            End Set
        End Property

        Public Property YVal( ) As Integer
            Get
                Return myYVal
            End Get
            Set(ByVal Value As Integer)
                myYVal = Value
```

Example 7-2. Creating a structure without New (continued)

```
        End Set
    End Property

    ' display the structure as a String
    Public Overrides Function ToString( ) As String
        Return String.Format("{0}, {1}", XVal, YVal)
    End Function 'ToString
End Structure 'Location

Class Tester
    Public Sub Run( )
        ' create an instance of the structure
        Dim loc1 As Location  ' no call to the constructor
        loc1.XVal = 75
        loc1.YVal = 225

        ' display the values in the structure
        Console.WriteLine("Loc1 location: {0}", loc1)
    End Sub 'Run

    Shared Sub Main( )
        Dim t As New Tester( )
        t.Run( )
    End Sub 'Main

End Class 'Tester
End Namespace 'StructureDemonstration
```

In Example 7-2, you initialize the local variables directly, before passing the object to WriteLine( ):

```
loc1.XVal = 75
loc1.YVal = 225
```

If you were to comment out one of the assignments and recompile:

```
Public Sub Run( )
    Dim loc1 As Location  ' no call to the constructor
    loc1.XVal = 75
    ' loc1.YVal = 225

    ' display the values in the Structure
    Console.WriteLine("Loc1 location: {0}", loc1)
End Sub 'Run
```

the unassigned value (YVal) would be initialized to its default value (in this case, 0):

```
loc1.XVal = 75
loc1.YVal = 0
```

CHAPTER 8

Interfaces

An *interface* is a contract that guarantees to a client how a class or structure will behave. When a class implements an interface, it tells any potential client "I guarantee I'll support the methods, properties, events, and indexers of the named interface." (See Chapter 5 for information about methods and properties, see Chapter 12 for information about events, and see Chapter 9 for coverage of indexers.)

An interface offers an alternative to a `MustInherit` class (see Chapter 6) for creating contracts among classes and their clients. These contracts are made manifest using the `Interface` keyword, which declares a reference type that encapsulates the contract.

Syntactically, an interface is like a class that has only `MustInherit` methods. A `MustInherit` class serves as the base class for a family of derived classes, while interfaces are meant to be mixed in with other inheritance trees.

When a class implements an interface, it must implement all the methods of that interface; in effect the class says "I agree to fulfill the contract defined by this interface."

Inheriting from a `MustInherit` class implements the *is-a* relationship, introduced in Chapter 4. Implementing an interface defines a different relationship that we've not seen until now: the *implements* relationship. These two relationships are subtly different. A car *is a* vehicle, but it might *implement* the CanBeBoughtWithABigLoan capability (as can a house, for example).

When specifying interfaces, it is easy to get confused about who is responsible for what. There are three concepts to keep clear:

The interface
> This is the contract. By convention, interface names begin with a capital I; thus, your interface might have a name like IPrintable. The IPrintable interface might describe a Print( ) method.

The implementing class

    This is the class that agrees to the contract described by the interface. For example, Document might be a class that implements the IPrintable interface, and thus provides a Print( ) method.

The client class

    This is a class that calls methods from the implementing class. For example, you might have an Editor class that calls the Document class's Print( ) method.

Interfaces are a critical addition to any framework, and they are used extensively throughout .NET. For example, the collection classes (array lists, stacks, and queues) are defined, in large measure, by the interfaces they implement. (The collection classes are explained in detail in Chapter 9.)

In this chapter, you will learn how to create, implement, and use interfaces. You'll learn how one class can implement multiple interfaces. You will also learn how to make new interfaces by combining existing interfaces or by extending (deriving from) an existing interface. Finally, you will learn how to test whether a class has implemented an interface.

Defining an Interface

The syntax for defining an interface is very similar to the syntax for defining a class or a structure:

```
[attributes] [access-modifier] Interface identifier
[interface-bases]
interface-body
End Interface
```

The optional *attributes* are discussed in Chapter 18. *Access modifiers* (Public, Private, etc.) work just as they do with classes. (See Chapter 5 for more about access modifiers.) The Interface keyword is followed by an *identifier* (the interface name). It is common (but not required) to begin the name of your interface with a capital I.

Thus, IStorable, ICloneable, IClaudius, etc. The optional list of *interface-bases* is discussed in the section titled "Extending Interfaces," later in this chapter.

The body of the interface is terminated with the keywords `End Interface`.

Interfaces Versus Abstract Base Classes

Programmers learning VB.NET often ask about the difference between an interface and an abstract (`MustInherit`) base class. The key difference is subtle: a `MustInherit` base class serves as the base class for a family of derived classes, while an interface is meant to be mixed in with other inheritance trees.

Inheriting from a `MustInherit` class implements the *is-a* relationship, introduced in Chapter 4. Implementing an interface defines a different relationship, one we've not seen until now: the *implements* relationship. These two relationships are subtly different. A car *is a* vehicle, but it might *implement* the CanBeBoughtWithABigLoan capability (as can a house, for example).

Suppose you want to create an interface to define the contract for data being stored to a database or file. Your interface will define the methods and properties a class will need to implement in order to be stored. You decide to call this interface IStorable.

In this interface, you might specify two methods, Read() and Write(), and a property, Status, which appear in the interface body:

```
Interface IStorable
    Sub Read( )
    Sub Write(object)
    Property Status( ) As Integer
End Interface
```

Note that when declaring the methods of the interface, you provide a prototype:

```
Sub Read( )
```

but no implementation and no `End Function`, `End Sub`, or `End Property` statement. Notice also that the IStorable method declarations do not include access modifiers (e.g., `Public`, `Private`, `Protected`, `Friend`). In fact, providing an access modifier generates a compile error. Interface methods are implicitly public because an interface is a contract meant to be used by other classes.

Implementing an Interface

Suppose you are the author of a Document class that specifies that Document objects can be stored in a database. You decide to have Document implement the IStorable interface. It isn't required that you do so, but by implementing the IStorable interface you signal to potential clients that the Document class can be used just

---

like any other IStorable object. This will, for example, allow your clients to add your Document objects to a collection of IStorable objects, and to otherwise interact with your Document in this very general and well-understood way.

To implement the IStorable interface, you must do two things:

1. Declare a particular class that implements the interface, using the Implements keyword. The following code declares that the Document class implements IStorable:

```
Public Class Document
        Implements IStorable
```

 The colon operator allows you to put two statements on a single line. It is not uncommon to write:

```
        Public Class Document : Implements IStorable
```

2. Implement each of the interface methods, events, properties, and so forth, and explicitly mark each member as implementing the corresponding interface member. The following code would implement the IStorable interface's Read() method:

```
Public Sub Read() Implements IStorable.Read
    Console.WriteLine("Implementing the Read Method for IStorable")
End Sub 'Read
```

 Note that with Sub and Function, the Implements keyword goes on the same line as the method definition, and so no colon is needed.

Visual Studio .NET will assist you in this effort through IntelliSense. When you enter the keyword Implements, IntelliSense prompts you with the various interfaces, as shown in Figure 8-1.

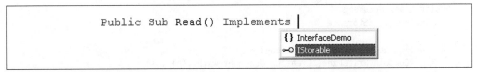

Figure 8-1. IntelliSense helps with Implements

Once you enter the name of the interface, IntelliSense can help you identify which member you are implementing, as shown in Figure 8-2.

Your definition of this class might look like this:

```
Public Class Document : Implements IStorable

    Public Sub Read() Implements IStorable.Read
    '...
```

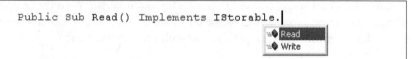

```
Public Sub Read() Implements IStorable.
                                        Read
                                        Write
```

Figure 8-2. Choosing a method from an interface

```
    End Sub 'Read

    Public Sub Write(ByVal o As Object) Implements IStorable.Write
    '...
    End Sub 'Write

    Public Property Status() As Integer Implements IStorable.Status
    '...
    End Property
End Class 'Document
```

It is now your responsibility, as the author of the Document class, to provide a meaningful implementation of the IStorable methods and property. Having designated Document as implementing IStorable, you must implement all the IStorable members, or you will generate an error when you compile. Defining and implementing the IStorable interface is illustrated in Example 8-1.

Example 8-1. Document class implementing IStorable

```
Option Strict On
Imports System
Namespace InterfaceDemo
    ' define the interface
    Interface IStorable
        Sub Read()
        Sub Write(ByVal obj As Object)
        Property Status() As Integer
    End Interface 'IStorable

    ' create a class which implements the IStorable interface
    Public Class Document
        Implements IStorable

        Public Sub New(ByVal s As String)
            Console.WriteLine("Creating document with: {0}", s)
        End Sub 'New

        ' implement the Read method
        Public Sub Read() Implements IStorable.Read
            Console.WriteLine("Implementing the Read Method for IStorable")
        End Sub 'Read

        ' implement the Write method
        Public Sub Write(ByVal o As Object) Implements IStorable.Write
            Console.WriteLine( _
                "Implementing the Write Method for IStorable")
```

Example 8-1. Document class implementing IStorable (continued)

```
        End Sub 'Write

        ' implement the property
        Public Property Status() As Integer Implements IStorable.Status
            Get
                Return myStatus
            End Get
            Set(ByVal Value As Integer)
                myStatus = Value
            End Set
        End Property

        ' store the value for the property
        Private myStatus As Integer = 0

    End Class 'Document

    Class Tester

        Public Sub Run()
            Dim doc As New Document("Test Document")
            doc.Status = -1
            doc.Read()
            Console.WriteLine("Document Status: {0}", doc.Status)
        End Sub 'Run

        Public Shared Sub Main()
            Dim t As New Tester()
            t.Run()
        End Sub 'Main

    End Class 'Tester

End Namespace 'InterfaceDemo

Output:
Creating document with: Test Document
Implementing the Read Method for IStorable
Document Status: -1
```

Example 8-1 defines a simple interface, IStorable, with two methods, Read() and Write(), and a property, Status, of type Integer:

```
        ' define the interface
        Interface IStorable
            Sub Read()
            Sub Write(ByVal obj As Object)
            Property Status() As Integer
        End Interface 'IStorable
```

Notice that the IStorable method declarations for Read() and Write() do not include access modifiers, as was explained earlier, because interface methods are implicitly public so that they can be used by other classes. Once you've defined the IStorable interface, you can define classes that implement the interface. Keep in mind that you cannot create an instance of an interface; instead you instantiate a class that implements the interface.*

The class implementing the interface must fulfill the contract exactly and completely. Thus, your Document class must provide a Read() and a Write() method and the Status property.

```
' create a class which implements the IStorable interface
Public Class Document
    Implements IStorable

    Public Sub New(ByVal s As String)
        Console.WriteLine("Creating document with: {0}", s)
    End Sub 'New

    ' implement the Read method
    Public Sub Read() Implements IStorable.Read
        Console.WriteLine("Implementing the Read Method for IStorable")
    End Sub 'Read

    ' implement the Write method
    Public Sub Write(ByVal o As Object) Implements IStorable.Write
        Console.WriteLine( _
            "Implementing the Write Method for IStorable")
    End Sub 'Write

    ' implement the property
    Public Property Status() As Integer Implements IStorable.Status
        Get
            Return myStatus
        End Get
        Set(ByVal Value As Integer)
            myStatus = Value
        End Set
    End Property

    ' store the value for the property
    Private myStatus As Integer = 0

End Class 'Document
```

How the Document class fulfills the requirements of the interface, however, is entirely up to you as the class designer. Although IStorable dictates that Document must have a Status property, it does not know or care whether Document stores the actual status as a member variable or looks it up in a database. Example 8-1 implements the Status property by returning and setting the value of a private member variable, myStatus.

---

* As will be demonstrated later in this chapter, you can make variables of an interface type, but you must assign to those variables objects of the implementing type.

Implementing More Than One Interface

Multiple inheritance refers to the ability to derive from more than one class. Visual Basic .NET does not support multiple inheritance. Classes can derive from only one class. If they don't explicitly derive from a class, then they implicitly derive from the Object class.

Classes can, however, implement any number of interfaces. The ability to implement multiple interfaces accomplishes much the same thing as the ability to derive from more than one class. In fact, many object-oriented programmers would argue that implementing multiple interfaces is superior to multiple inheritance because it provides the equivalent capabilities with less confusion.

When you design your class you can choose not to implement any interfaces, you can implement a single interface, or you can implement two or more interfaces. For example, in addition to IStorable, you might have a second interface, ICompressible, for files that can be compressed to save disk space. If your Document class can be stored and it can also be compressed, you might choose to have Document implement both the IStorable and ICompressible interfaces.

 Both IStorable and ICompressible are interfaces created for this book and are not part of the standard .NET Framework.

Example 8-2 shows the complete listing of the new ICompressible interface and demonstrates how you modify the Document class to implement the two interfaces.

Example 8-2. IStorable and ICompressible, implemented by Document

```
Option Strict On
Imports System
Namespace InterfaceDemo

    Interface IStorable
        Sub Read( )
        Sub Write(ByVal obj As Object)
        Property Status( ) As Integer
    End Interface 'IStorable

    ' here's the new interface
    Interface ICompressible
        Sub Compress( )
        Sub Decompress( )
    End Interface 'ICompressible

    ' Document implements both interfaces
    Public Class Document

        Implements ICompressible, IStorable
```

```vb
        ' the document constructor
        Public Sub New(ByVal s As String)
            Console.WriteLine("Creating document with: {0}", s)
        End Sub 'New

        ' implement IStorable
        Public Sub Read() Implements IStorable.Read
            Console.WriteLine("Implementing the Read Method for IStorable")
        End Sub 'Read

        Public Sub Write(ByVal o As Object) Implements IStorable.Write
            Console.WriteLine( _
              "Implementing the Write Method for IStorable")
        End Sub 'Write

        Public Property Status() As Integer Implements IStorable.Status
            Get
                Return myStatus
            End Get
            Set(ByVal Value As Integer)
                myStatus = Value
            End Set
        End Property

        ' implement ICompressible
        Public Sub Compress() Implements ICompressible.Compress
            Console.WriteLine("Implementing Compress")
        End Sub 'Compress

        Public Sub Decompress() Implements ICompressible.Decompress
            Console.WriteLine("Implementing Decompress")
        End Sub 'Decompress

        ' hold the data for IStorable's Status property
        Private myStatus As Integer = 0

End Class 'Document

    Class Tester

        Public Sub Run()
            Dim doc As New Document("Test Document")
            doc.Status = -1
            doc.Read()
            doc.Compress()
            Console.WriteLine("Document Status: {0}", doc.Status)
        End Sub 'Run

        Shared Sub Main()
            Dim t As New Tester()
            t.Run()
        End Sub 'Main
```

```
    End Class 'Tester

End Namespace 'InterfaceDemo

Output:
Creating document with: Test Document
Implementing the Read Method for IStorable
Implementing Compress
Document Status: -1
```

As Example 8-2 shows, you declare the fact that your Document class will implement two interfaces by changing the declaration (in the list of interface bases) to indicate that both interfaces are implemented, separating the two interfaces with commas:

```
    Public Class Document
        Implements ICompressible, IStorable
```

After you've done this, the Document class must also implement the methods specified by the ICompressible interface. ICompressible has only two methods, Compress() and Uncompress(), which are specified as:

```
    Interface ICompressible
        Sub Compress()
        Sub Decompress()
    End Interface 'ICompressible
```

These methods do no more than display notification messages to the console; in effect the methods are stubbed out.

```
    Public Sub Compress() Implements ICompressible.Compress
        Console.WriteLine("Implementing Compress")
    End Sub 'Compress

    Public Sub Decompress() Implements ICompressible.Decompress
        Console.WriteLine("Implementing Decompress")
    End Sub 'Decompress
```

Casting to an Interface

You can access the members (i.e., methods and properties) of an interface through the object of any class that implements the interface. Thus, you can access the methods and properties of IStorable through the Document object, as if they were members of the Document class:

```
    Dim doc As New Document("Test Document")
    doc.Status = -1
    doc.Read()
```

Alternatively, you can create an instance of the interface, and then use that interface to access the methods of that interface:

```
Dim isDoc As IStorable = doc
isDoc.status = 0
isDoc.Read( )
```

In Chapter 9, you'll see that at times you may create collections of objects that implement a given interface (e.g., a collection of storable objects). You can manipulate them without knowing their real type—so long as they implement IStorable. For instance, you won't know that you have a Document object; rather, you'll know only that the object in question implements IStorable. You can create a variable of type IStorable and cast your Document to that type. You can then access the IStorable methods through the IStorable variable.

When you cast you say to the compiler, "Trust me, I know this object is really of this type." In this case you are saying, "Trust me, I know this document really implements IStorable, so you can treat it as an IStorable."

As stated earlier, you cannot instantiate an interface directly—that is, you cannot write:

```
IStorable isDoc As New IStorable( )
```

You can, however, create an instance of the implementing class, and then create an instance of the interface:

```
Dim isDoc As IStorable = doc
```

(isDoc is a reference to an IStorable object.) This is considered a widening conversion (from Document to the IStorable interface), and so there is no need for an explicit cast.

In general, it is a better design decision to access the interface methods through an interface reference. Thus, it was better to use isDoc.Read( ), than doc.Read( ), in the previous example. Access through an interface allows you to treat the interface polymorphically. In other words, you can have two or more classes implement the interface, and then by accessing these classes only through the interface, you can ignore their real runtime type and treat them simply as instances of the interface. You'll see the power of this technique in Chapter 9.

Testing for Interface Implementation

There may be instances in which you do not know in advance (at compile time) that an object supports a particular interface. For instance, given a collection of objects, you might not know whether each object in the collection implements IStorable, ICompressible, or both.

You can find out what interfaces are implemented by a particular object by casting blindly and then catching the exceptions that arise when you've tried to cast the object to an interface it hasn't implemented. The code to cast Document to ICompressible might be:

```
Dim icDoc As ICompressible = doc
icDoc.Compress()
```

If it turns out that if Document implements only the IStorable interface but not the ICompressible interface:

```
Public Class Document
    Implements IStorable
```

the cast to ICompressible will fail to compile (assuming Option Strict is On as it should be). If you turn Option Strict off, the code will compile, but at runtime, because of the illegal cast, the program will throw an exception:

```
System.InvalidCastException: Specified cast is not valid.
```

 Exceptions are used to report errors and are covered in detail in Chapter 11.

You could then catch the exception and take corrective action, but this approach is ugly and evil and you should not do things this way. This is like testing whether a gun is loaded by firing it; it's dangerous and it annoys the neighbors.

Rather than firing blindly, you would like to be able to ask the object if it implements an interface, in order to then invoke the appropriate methods; to do so you will use the Is operator.

TypeOf...Is

The TypeOf...Is expression lets you query whether an object implements an interface. The syntax of the expression is:

TypeOf *expression* **Is** *type*

This expression evaluates true if the tested *expression* (which must be a reference type, such as an instance of a class) can be safely cast to *type* (e.g., an interface) without throwing an exception.

Example 8-3 illustrates the use of the TypeOf and Is keywords to test whether a Document object implements the IStorable and ICompressible interfaces.

Example 8-3. Using the TypeOf and Is keywords

```
Option Strict On
Imports System
Namespace InterfaceDemo

    Interface IStorable
        Sub Read()
```

Example 8-3. Using the TypeOf and Is keywords (continued)

```vb
        Sub Write(ByVal obj As Object)
        Property Status() As Integer
    End Interface 'IStorable

    ' here's the new interface
    Interface ICompressible
        Sub Compress()
        Sub Decompress()
    End Interface 'ICompressible

    ' document implements only IStorable
Public Class Document

    Implements IStorable

    ' the document constructor
    Public Sub New(ByVal s As String)
        Console.WriteLine("Creating document with: {0}", s)
    End Sub 'New

    ' implement IStorable
    Public Sub Read() Implements IStorable.Read
        Console.WriteLine("Implementing the Read Method for IStorable")
    End Sub 'Read

    Public Sub Write(ByVal o As Object) Implements IStorable.Write
        Console.WriteLine( _
          "Implementing the Write Method for IStorable")
    End Sub 'Write

    Public Property Status() As Integer Implements IStorable.Status
        Get
            Return Status
        End Get
        Set(ByVal Value As Integer)
            Status = Value
        End Set
    End Property

    ' hold the data for IStorable's Status property
    Private myStatus As Integer = 0

End Class 'Document

Class Tester

    Public Sub Run()
        Dim doc As New Document("Test Document")

        ' only cast if it is safe
        If TypeOf doc Is IStorable Then
            Dim isDoc As IStorable = doc
```

Example 8-3. Using the TypeOf and Is keywords (continued)

```
            isDoc.Read( )
        Else
            Console.WriteLine("Could not cast to IStorable")
        End If

        ' this test will fail
        If TypeOf doc Is ICompressible Then
            Dim icDoc As ICompressible = doc
            icDoc.Compress( )
        Else
            Console.WriteLine("Could not cast to ICompressible")
        End If
    End Sub 'Run

    Shared Sub Main( )
        Dim t As New Tester( )
        t.Run( )
    End Sub 'Main

End Class 'Tester

End Namespace 'InterfaceDemo

Output:
Creating document with: Test Document
Implementing the Read Method for IStorable
Could not cast to ICompressible
```

In Example 8-3, the Document class implements only IStorable:

```
Public Class Document
    Implements IStorable
```

In the Run( ) method of the Tester class, you create an instance of Document:

```
Dim doc As New Document("Test Document")
```

and you test whether that instance is an IStorable (that is, does it implement the IStorable interface?):

```
If TypeOf doc Is IStorable Then
```

If so, you create an instance of the IStorable interface and call an interface method (isDoc.Read):

```
Dim isDoc As IStorable = doc
isDoc.Read( )
```

You then repeat the test with ICompressible, and if the test fails, you print an error message:

```
If TypeOf doc Is ICompressible Then
    Dim icDoc As ICompressible = CType(doc, ICompressible)
    icDoc.Compress( )
Else
```

```
        Console.WriteLine("Could not cast to ICompressible")
    End If
```

The output shows that the first test (IStorable) succeeds (as expected) and the second test (of ICompressible) fails, also as expected:

```
Implementing the Read Method for IStorable
Could not cast to ICompressible
```

Extending Interfaces

It is possible to extend an existing interface to add new methods or members, or to modify how existing members work. For example, you might extend ICompressible with a new interface, ICompressible2, which extends the original interface with a method to keep track of the bytes saved.

The following code creates a new interface named ICompressible2 that is identical to ICompressible except that it adds the method LogSavedBytes():

```
Interface ICompressible2
    Inherits ICompressible
    Sub LogSavedBytes( )
End Interface 'ICompressible2
```

 Notice that your new interface (ICompressible2) inherits from the base interface (ICompressible). Classes can inherit only from a single class, but interfaces can inherit from more than one interface, as shown later in this chapter.

Classes are now free to implement either ICompressible or ICompressible2, depending on whether they need the additional functionality. If a class does implement ICompressible2, it must implement all the methods of both ICompressible2 and also ICompressible. Objects of that type can be cast either to ICompressible2 or to ICompressible.

In Example 8-4, you'll extend ICompressible to create ICompressible2. You'll then cast the Document first to be of type IStorable, then to be of type ICompressible2. Finally, you'll cast the Document object to ICompressible. This last cast is safe because any object that implements ICompressible2 must also have implemented ICompressible (the former is a superset of the latter). This is the same logic that says you can cast any object of a derived type to an object of a base type (that is, if Student derives from Human, then all Students are Human, even though not all Humans are Students).

Example 8-4. Extending interfaces

```
Option Strict On
Imports System
Namespace InterfaceDemo
```

Example 8-4. Extending interfaces (continued)

```
Interface IStorable
    Sub Read( )
    Sub Write(ByVal obj As Object)

    Property Status( ) As Integer
End Interface 'IStorable

' the Compressible interface is now the
' base for ICompressible2
Interface ICompressible
    Sub Compress( )
    Sub Decompress( )
End Interface 'ICompressible

' extend ICompressible to log the bytes saved
Interface ICompressible2
    Inherits ICompressible
    Sub LogSavedBytes( )
End Interface 'ICompressible2

' Document implements both interfaces
Public Class Document

    Implements ICompressible2, IStorable

    ' the document constructor
    Public Sub New(s As String)
        Console.WriteLine("Creating document with: {0}", s)
    End Sub 'New

    ' implement IStorable
    Public Sub Read( ) Implements IStorable.Read
        Console.WriteLine("Implementing the Read Method for IStorable")
    End Sub 'Read

    Public Sub Write(ByVal o As Object) Implements IStorable.Write
        Console.WriteLine( _
            "Implementing the Write Method for IStorable")
    End Sub 'Write

    Public Property Status( ) As Integer Implements IStorable.Status
        Get
            Return myStatus
        End Get
        Set(ByVal Value As Integer)
            myStatus = Value
        End Set
    End Property

    ' implement ICompressible
    Public Sub Compress( ) Implements ICompressible.Compress
        Console.WriteLine("Implementing Compress")
```

Example 8-4. Extending interfaces (continued)

```vb
        End Sub 'Compress

        Public Sub Decompress() Implements ICompressible.Decompress
            Console.WriteLine("Implementing Decompress")
        End Sub 'Decompress

        ' implement ICompressible2
        Public Sub LogSavedBytes() Implements ICompressible2.LogSavedBytes
            Console.WriteLine("Implementing LogSavedBytes")
        End Sub 'LogSavedBytes

        ' hold the data for IStorable's Status property
        Private myStatus As Integer = 0

End Class 'Document

Class Tester

    Public Sub Run()
        Dim doc As New Document("Test Document")

        If TypeOf doc Is IStorable Then
            Dim isDoc As IStorable = doc
            isDoc.Read()
        Else
            Console.WriteLine("Could not cast to IStorable")
        End If

        If TypeOf doc Is ICompressible2 Then
            Dim ilDoc As ICompressible2 = doc
            Console.Write("Calling both ICompressible and ")
            Console.WriteLine("ICompressible2 methods...")
            ilDoc.Compress()
            ilDoc.LogSavedBytes()
        Else
            Console.WriteLine("Could not cast to ICompressible2")
        End If

        If TypeOf doc Is ICompressible Then
            Dim icDoc As ICompressible = doc
            Console.WriteLine( _
                "Treating the object as Compressible... ")
            icDoc.Compress()
        Else
            Console.WriteLine("Could not cast to ICompressible")
        End If
    End Sub 'Run

    Shared Sub Main()
        Dim t As New Tester()
        t.Run()
    End Sub 'Main
```

Example 8-4. Extending interfaces (continued)

```
    End Class 'Tester

End Namespace 'InterfaceDemo

Output:
Creating document with: Test Document
Implementing the Read Method for IStorable
Calling both ICompressible and ICompressible2 methods...
Implementing Compress
Implementing LogSavedBytes
Treating the object as Compressible...
Implementing Compress
```

Example 8-4 starts by creating the ICompressible2 interface:

```
    Interface ICompressible2
        Inherits ICompressible
        Sub LogSavedBytes()
    End Interface 'ICompressible2
```

Notice that the syntax for extending an interface is the same as that for deriving from a class. This extended interface explicitly defines only one method, LogSavedBytes(); but of course any class implementing this interface must also implement the base interface (ICompressible) and all its members.

You define the Document class to implement both IStorable and ICompressible2:

```
    Public Class Document
        Implements ICompressible2, IStorable
```

You are now free to cast the Document object to IStorable, ICompressible, or to ICompressible2:

```
    If TypeOf doc Is IStorable Then
        Dim ilDoc As IStorable = doc

    If TypeOf doc Is ICompressible Then
        Dim icDoc As ICompressible = doc

    If TypeOf doc Is ICompressible2 Then
        Dim ic2Doc As ICompressible2 = doc
```

If you take a look back at the output, you'll see that all three of these casts succeed.

Combining Interfaces

You can also create new interfaces by combining existing interfaces and optionally adding new methods or properties. For example, you might decide to combine the definitions of IStorable and ICompressible2 into a new interface called IStorable-Compressible. This interface would combine the methods of each of the other two interfaces, but would also add a new method, LogOriginalSize(), to store the original size of the pre-compressed item:

```
Interface IStorableCompressible
Inherits IStorable, ICompressible2
    Sub LogOriginalSize( )
End Interface
```

Having created this interface, you can now modify Document to implement IStorableCompressible:

```
Public Class Document
    Implements IStorableCompressible
```

You are now free to cast the Document object to any of the four interfaces you've created so far:

```
If TypeOf doc Is IStorable Then
    Dim isDoc As IStorable = doc

If TypeOf doc Is ICompressible Then
    Dim icDoc As ICompressible = doc

If TypeOf doc Is ICompressible2 Then
    Dim ic2Doc As ICompressible2 = doc

If TypeOf doc Is IStorableCompressible Then
    Dim iscDoc As IStorableCompressible = doc
```

You can then use the four variables to invoke the appropriate methods from the various interfaces:

```
isDoc.Read( )
icDoc.Compress( )
ic2Doc.LogSavedBytes( )
iscDoc.LogOriginalSize( )
```

Remember that when you cast to the new, combined interface, you can invoke any of the methods of any of the interfaces it extends or combines. The preceding code invokes four methods of iscDoc (the IStorableCompressible object). Only one of the preceding methods is defined in IStorableCompressible, but all four are methods defined by interfaces that IStorableCompressible extends or combines.

Overriding Interface Implementations

An implementing class is free to mark any or all of the methods that implement the interface as overridable. Derived classes can then override or provide new implementations. For example, a Document class might implement the IStorable interface and mark the Read() and Write() methods as overridable. The Document might Read() and Write() its contents to a File type. The developer might later derive new types from Document, such as perhaps a Note or EmailMessage type. While the

Document class implements Read() and Write to save to a File, the Note class might implement Read() and Write() to read from and write to a database.

Example 8-5 strips down the complexity of the previous examples and illustrates overriding an interface implementation. In this example, you'll derive a new class named Note from the Document class.

Document implements the IStorable-required Read() method as an overridable method, and Note overrides that implementation.

 Notice that Document does not mark Write() as overridable. You'll see the implications of this decision in the analysis section that follows the output.

The complete listing is shown in Example 8-5 and analyzed in detail following.

Example 8-5. Overriding an interface implementation

```
Option Strict On

Imports Microsoft.VisualBasic
Imports System

Namespace OverridingInterfaces

    Interface IStorable
        Sub Read( )
        Sub Write( )
    End Interface

    ' simplify Document to implement only IStorable
    Public Class Document : Implements IStorable

        ' the document constructor
        Public Sub New(ByVal s As String)
            Console.WriteLine("Creating document with: {0}", s)
        End Sub

        ' make read virtual
        Public Overridable Sub Read( ) Implements IStorable.Read
            Console.WriteLine("Document Virtual Read Method for IStorable")
        End Sub

        ' NB: Not virtual!
        Public Sub Write( ) Implements IStorable.Write
            Console.WriteLine("Document Write Method for IStorable")
        End Sub

    End Class

    ' derive from Document
    Public Class Note : Inherits Document
```

Example 8-5. Overriding an interface implementation (continued)

```
        Public Sub New(ByVal s As String)
            MyBase.New(s)
            Console.WriteLine("Creating note with: {0}", s)
        End Sub

        ' override the Read method
        Public Overrides Sub Read()
            Console.WriteLine("Overriding the Read method for Note!")
        End Sub

        ' implement my own Write method
        Public Shadows Sub Write()
            Console.WriteLine("Implementing the Write method for Note!")
        End Sub

    End Class

    Class Tester

        Public Sub Run()
            ' create a Document object
            Dim theNote As Document = New Note("Test Note")

            ' cast the Document to IStorable
            If TypeOf theNote Is IStorable Then
                Dim isNote As IStorable = theNote
                isNote.Read()
                isNote.Write()
            End If

            Console.WriteLine(vbCrLf)

            ' direct call to the methods
            theNote.Read()
            theNote.Write()

            Console.WriteLine(vbCrLf)

            ' create a note object
            Dim note2 As New Note("Second Test")

            ' Cast the note to IStorable
            If TypeOf note2 Is IStorable Then
                Dim isNote2 As IStorable = note2
                isNote2.Read()
                isNote2.Write()
            End If
            Console.WriteLine(vbCrLf)

            ' directly call the methods
            note2.Read()
            note2.Write()
```

Example 8-5. Overriding an interface implementation (continued)

```
        End Sub

        Public Shared Sub Main( )
            Dim t As New Tester( )
            t.Run( )
        End Sub

    End Class

End Namespace
```

```
Output:
Creating document with: Test Note
Creating note with: Test Note
Overriding the Read method for Note!
Document Write Method for IStorable

Overriding the Read method for Note!
Document Write Method for IStorable

Creating document with: Second Test
Creating note with: Second Test
Overriding the Read method for Note!
Document Write Method for IStorable

Overriding the Read method for Note!
Implementing the Write method for Note!
```

In Example 8-5, the IStorable interface is simplified for clarity's sake:

```
Interface IStorable
    Sub Read( )
    Sub Write( )
End Interface
```

The Document class implements the IStorable interface:

```
Public Class Document : Implements IStorable
```

The designer of Document has opted to make the Read( ) method overridable but not to make the Write( ) method overridable:

```
Public Overridable Sub Read( ) Implements IStorable.Read
Public Sub Write( ) Implements IStorable.Write
```

 In a real-world application, you would almost certainly mark both as overridable, but I've differentiated them to demonstrate that the developer is free to pick and choose which methods can be overridden.

The new class, Note, derives from Document:

```
Public Class Note : Inherits Document
```

It is not necessary for Note to override Read() (it may shadow it instead), but it is free to do so and has done so here:

```
Public Overrides Sub Read()
```

To illustrate the implications of marking an implementing method as overridable, the Run() method calls the Read() and Write() methods in four ways:

- Through the base class reference to a derived object
- Through an interface created from the base class reference to the derived object
- Through a derived object
- Through an interface created from the derived object

As you'll see, the base class reference and the derived class reference act just as they always have: overridable methods are implemented polymorphically and non-overridable methods are not. The interfaces created from these references work just like the references themselves: overridable implementations of the interface methods are polymorphic, and non-overridable methods are not.

The one surprising aspect is this: when you call the non-polymorphic Write() method on the IStorable interface cast from the derived Note, you actually get the Document's Write() method. This is because Write() is implemented in the base class and is not overridable.

To accomplish the first two calls, a Document (base class) reference is created, and the address of a new Note (derived) object created on the heap is assigned to the Document reference:

```
Dim theNote As Document = New Note("Test Note")
```

An interface reference is created (isNote) and theNote is cast to the IStorable interface:

```
If TypeOf theNote Is IStorable Then
    Dim isNote As IStorable = theNote
```

You then invoke the Read() and Write() methods through that interface. The output reveals that the Read() method is responded to polymorphically and the Write() method is not, just as you would expect:

```
Overriding the Read method for Note!
Document Write Method for IStorable
```

The Read() and Write() methods are then called directly on the derived object itself:

```
theNote.Read()
theNote.Write()
```

and once again you see the polymorphic implementation has worked:

```
Overriding the Read method for Note!
Document Write Method for IStorable
```

In both cases, the Read( ) method of Note was called, but the Write( ) method of Document was called.

To prove to yourself that this is a result of the overriding method, you next create a second Note object, this time assigning its address to a reference to a Note. This will be used to illustrate the final cases (i.e., a call through a derived object and a call through an interface created from the derived object):

```
Dim note2 As New Note("Second Test")
```

Once again, when you cast to a reference, the overridden Read( ) method is called. When, however, methods are called directly on the Note object:

```
note2.Read( )
note2.Write( )
```

the output reflects that you've called a Note and not an overridden Document:

```
Overriding the Read method for Note!
Implementing the Write method for Note!
```

CHAPTER 9

Arrays, Indexers, and Collections

Most of the examples in previous chapters have dealt with one object at a time. In many applications, however, you will want to work with a group of objects all at the same time. A *collection* is a container that holds a group of objects. Collections are used to hold all the strings in a listbox, to hold all the employees in a company, to hold all the controls on a page, and so forth. This chapter will review the principal collection types offered by the .NET Framework.

The simplest collection in VB.NET is the *array*. This chapter examines the Array type in detail and also includes coverage of some of the more complicated collection types, including ArrayList, Collection, Queue, and Stack.

In addition, this chapter introduces the concept of indexers, a feature of VB.NET that makes it possible to create your own classes that can be treated like arrays.

Every collection type has certain shared characteristics. These are captured by the *collection interfaces*. The .NET Framework provides standard interfaces for enumerating, comparing, and creating collections. This chapter concludes with a discussion of the .NET collection interfaces and an example of how you can implement the collection interfaces in your own classes to give your objects collection semantics.

Arrays

An *array* is an indexed collection of objects, all of the same type. In this chapter, you will learn to work with three types of arrays: one-dimensional arrays, multidimensional rectangular arrays, and multidimensional jagged arrays.

To picture a one-dimensional array, imagine a series of mailboxes, all lined up one after the other. Each mailbox can hold exactly one object (one letter, one box, etc.). It turns out that all the mailboxes must hold the same kind of object; you declare the type of object the mailboxes will hold when you declare the array.

A multidimensional array allows you to create rows of mailboxes, one above the other. If all the rows are the same length, you have a rectangular array. If each row of mailboxes is a different length, you have a jagged array.

You can think of a multidimensional array as being like a grid of rows and columns in which each slot (mailbox) contains information. For example, each column might contain information pertinent to an employee. Each row would contain all the information for a single employee.

Most often you will deal with one-dimensional arrays, and if you do create multi-dimension arrays they will be two-dimensional—but larger multidimensional arrays (3D, 4D, etc.) are also possible.

A jagged array is a type of two-dimensional array in which each row can have a different number of columns. A jagged array is less of a grid, and more of an array of arrays—that is, an array in which the elements in one array are other arrays. This allows you to group a few arrays of varying sizes into a single array. For example, you might have an array of ten buttons, and a second array of five listboxes, and a third array of seven checkboxes. You can group all three into a jagged array of controls.

Declaring Arrays

In order to declare an array, you must use a constructor, but you are free to use it in a variety of ways. For example, you can use either an implicit or an explicit constructor, as in the following:

```
Dim myIntArray( ) As Integer  ' implicit constructor
Dim myIntArray As Integer = New Integer( ) {}' explicit constructor
```

Which type of constructor you use is a matter of personal preference.

Alternatively, you can specify the initial size of the array (that is, how many elements it will hold):

```
Dim myIntArray(6) As Integer   ' implicit constructor 6 members
Dim myIntArray As Integer = new Integer(6) ' explicit, 6 members
```

In all of these examples, the parentheses tell the VB.NET compiler that you are declaring an array, and the type specifies the type of the elements it will contain. In all of the arrays we have declared so far, myIntArray is an array of Integers. It is important to distinguish between the array itself (which is a collection of elements) and the component elements within the array. myIntArray is the array; its elements are the six integers it holds.

 While VB.NET arrays are reference types, created on the heap, the elements of an array are allocated based on their type. Thus, myIntArray is a reference type allocated on the heap, and the integer elements in myIntArray are value types, allocated on the stack. (While you can *box* a value type so that it can be treated like a reference type, as explained in Chapter 6, it is not necessary or desirable to box the integers in an array.) By contrast, an array that contains reference types, such as Employee or Button, will contain nothing but references to the elements, which are themselves created on the heap.

The Size of the Array

Arrays are zero-based,* which means that the index of the first element is always zero, as in myArray(0). The second element is element 1. Index 3 indicates the element that is offset from the beginning of the array by 3 elements—that is, the fourth element in the array. You access element 3 by writing:

```
myArray(3) ' return the 4th element (at offset 3)
```

You declare the initial size of the array (that is, how many elements it will hold) by specifying the upper bounds of the array. Both of the following declarations specify an array with seven elements; the first uses an implicit constructor for this purpose, the second an explicit constructor:

```
Dim myIntArray(6) As Integer  ' implicit constructor, 7 members
Dim myIntArray As Integer = New Integer(6) {}' explicit, 7 members
```

Note that these arrays have seven elements (not six) because with an upper bound of 6, the element indices are 0,1,2,3,4,5,6 for a total of 7 elements.

The ReDim Keyword

You can change the size of an array at any time using the ReDim keyword. Changing the size is commonly referred to as *redimensioning* the array.†

There are two ways to redimension an array. If you use the Preserve keyword, the data in the array is preserved; otherwise, all the data in the array is lost when it is resized using ReDim.

You can resize an array named myArray from its current size to 50 by writing:

```
ReDim myArray(50)
```

You can make the same change to myArray, but preserve the existing data in the array by writing:

```
ReDim preserve myArray(50)
```

At times, you will not want to resize an array to a particular size but rather to expand the array by a particular increment. For example, if you are adding items to an array, and you find you're about to run out of room, you might add 50 to the current size of the array. You can use the UBound property of the array which returns the current

---

* It is possible to create arrays that are not zero-based, but only with multidimensional arrays, and it is rarely a good idea. To do so you must use the CreateInstance() method of the Array class, and the resulting arrays are not compliant with the Common Language Specification.

† "Redimensioning" is a terribly misleading term. It suggests you are changing the dimensions of the array (which is described later in this chapter); in fact you are changing the array's size. Redimensioning should more properly be called resizing the array, but the terminology was established early in the history of Visual Basic, and it's too late now; we're stuck with the term redimensioning.

upper bound of the array. The following line resizes myArray to 50 elements larger than its current size:

```
ReDim Preserve myArray(UBound(myArray) + 50)
```

Understanding Default Values

When you create an array of value types, each element initially contains the default value for the type stored in the array. (See Table 5-2.) The following declaration creates an array (myIntArray) of six integers, each of whose value is initialized to 0, the default value for Integer types:

```
'six Integers with default values
Dim myIntArray As Integer = New Integer(6) {}
```

With an array of reference types, the elements are *not* initialized to their default values. Instead, they are initialized to Nothing. If you attempt to access any of the elements in an array of reference types before you have specifically initialized them, you will generate an exception (exceptions are covered in Chapter 11).

Assume you have created a Button class. You declare an array of Button objects (thus reference types) with the following statement:

```
Dim myButtonArray As Button( )
```

and you instantiate the actual array, to hold four Buttons, like this:

```
myButtonArray = New Button(3){}
```

Note that you can combine the two steps and write:

```
Dim myButtonArray As Button( ) = New Button(3) {}
```

In either case, unlike with the earlier integer example, this statement does *not* create an array with references to four Button objects. Since Button objects are reference types, this creates the array myButtonArray with four Nothing, or null, references. To use this array, you must first construct and assign a Button object for each reference in the array. This is called *populating* the array. You can construct the objects in a loop that adds them one by one to the array. Example 9-1 illustrates creating an array of value types (integers) and of reference types (Employee objects).

Example 9-1. Creating an array

```
Option Strict On
Imports System

'a simple class to store in the array
Public Class Employee
    Private empID As Integer
    'constructor
    Public Sub New(ByVal empID As Integer)
        Me.empID = empID
    End Sub
```

Example 9-1. Creating an array (continued)

```
End Class

Class Tester
    Public Sub Run( )
        Dim intArray As Integer( )
        Dim empArray As Employee( )
        intArray = New Integer(5) {}
        empArray = New Employee(3) {}

        'populate the array
        Dim i As Integer

        'for indices 0 through 3
        For i = 0 To empArray.Length - 1
            empArray(i) = New Employee(i + 5)
            i = i + 1
        Next
    End Sub

    Shared Sub Main( )
        Dim t As New Tester( )
        t.Run( )
    End Sub
End Class
```

Example 9-1 begins by creating a simple Employee class to add to the array. When Run( ) begins, two arrays are declared, one of type Integer, the other of type Employee:

```
Dim intArray As Integer( )
Dim empArray As Employee( )
```

The Integer array is populated with Integers set to zero. The Employee array is initialized with Nothing references.

 empArray does not have Employee objects whose member fields are set to Nothing; it does not have Employee objects at all. What is in the cubby holes of the array is just nulls. Nothing. Nada. When you create the Employee objects, you can then store them in the array.

You must populate the Employee array before you can refer to its elements:

```
For i = 0 To empArray.Length - 1
    empArray(i) = New Employee(i + 5)
    i = i + 1
Next
```

The exercise has no output. You've added the elements to the array, but how do you use them? How do you refer to them?

Accessing Array Elements

You access a particular element within an array using parentheses and a numeric value knows as an *index*, or *offset*. You access element 3 by writing:

```
myArray(3) ' return the 4th element (at offset 3)
```

Because arrays are objects, they have properties. One of the more useful properties of the Array class is Length, which tells you how many objects are in an array. Array objects can be indexed from 0 to Length–1. That is, if there are five elements in an array, their indices are 0,1,2,3,4.

In Example 9-2, you create an array of Employees and an array of integers, populate the Employee array, and then you print the values in each array.

Example 9-2. Accessing two simple arrays

```
Option Strict On
Imports System

Namespace ArrayDemo

    'a simple class to store in the array
    Public Class Employee

        Private empID As Integer

        'constructor
        Public Sub New(ByVal empID As Integer)
            Me.empID = empID
        End Sub 'New

        Public Overrides Function ToString() As String
            Return empID.ToString()
        End Function 'ToString
    End Class 'Employee

    Class Tester

        Public Sub Run()
            Dim intArray() As Integer
            Dim empArray() As Employee

            intArray = New Integer(5) {}
            empArray = New Employee(3) {}

            'populate the array
            Dim i As Integer
            For i = 0 To empArray.Length - 1
                empArray(i) = New Employee(i + 5)
            Next i

            Console.WriteLine("The Integer array...")
```

Example 9-2. Accessing two simple arrays (continued)

```
            For i = 0 To intArray.Length - 1
                Console.WriteLine(intArray(i).ToString())
            Next i

            Console.WriteLine(ControlChars.Lf + "The Employee array...")
            For i = 0 To empArray.Length - 1
                Console.WriteLine(empArray(i).ToString())
            Next i
        End Sub 'Run

        Shared Sub Main()
            Dim t As New Tester()
            t.Run()
        End Sub 'Main
    End Class 'Tester

End Namespace 'ArrayDemo

Output:
The Integer array...
0
0
0
0
0

The Employee array...
5
6
7
```

Example 9-2 starts with the definition of an Employee class that implements a constructor that takes a single integer parameter. The ToString() method inherited from Object is overridden to print the value of the Employee object's employee ID.

The Run() method declares and then instantiates a pair of arrays. The Integer array is automatically filled with Integers whose value is set to zero. The Employee array contents must be constructed by hand (or will contain values set to Nothing). To populate the array by hand, you construct each Employee object in turn, adding them to the Array as they are created:

```
Dim i As Integer
For i = 0 To empArray.Length - 1
    empArray(i) = New Employee(i + 5)
Next i
```

In this For loop, each Employee is created with a value equal to five more than its index in the array. These are arbitrary values used here to illustrate how to add Employee objects to the array.

Finally, the contents of the arrays are printed to ensure that they are filled as intended. The five Integers print their value first, followed by the three Employee objects.

 If you comment out the code in which the Employee objects are created, you'll generate an exception when you try to display the contents of the Employee array. This demonstrates that arrays of reference types are initialized with Nothing references.

```
Unhandled Exception: System.NullReferenceException: Object
reference not set to an instance of an object. at
InterfaceDemo.ArrayDemo.Tester.Run( ) in C:\...\InterfaceDemo\
Module1.vb:line 40   at InterfaceDemo.ArrayDemo.Tester.Main( )
in C:\...InterfaceDemo\Module1.vb:line 47
```

The For Each Statement

The For Each looping statement allows you to iterate through all the items in an array (or other collection), examining each item in turn. The syntax for the For Each statement is:

```
For Each identifier In collection
    statement
Next
```

The For Each statement creates a new object that will hold a reference to each of the objects in the collection, in turn, as you loop through the collection. For example, you might write:

```
Dim intValue As Integer
For Each intValue In intArray
```

Each time through the loop, the next member of intArray will be assigned to the integer variable intValue. You can then use that object to display the value, as in:

```
Console.WriteLine(intValue.ToString( ))
```

Similarly, you might iterate through the Employee array:

```
Dim e As Employee
For Each e In empArray
    Console.WriteLine(e)
Next
```

In the case shown here, e is an object of type Employee. For each turn through the loop, e will refer to the next Employee in the array.

Example 9-3 rewrites the Run( ) method of Example 9-2 to use a For Each loop, but is otherwise unchanged.

Example 9-3. For Each loop

```
Option Strict On
Imports System
```

Example 9-3. For Each loop (continued)

```
Public Sub Run( )
    Dim intArray( ) As Integer
    Dim empArray( ) As Employee

    intArray = New Integer(5) {}
    empArray = New Employee(3) {}

    'populate the array
    Dim i As Integer
    For i = 0 To empArray.Length - 1
        empArray(i) = New Employee(i + 5)
    Next i

    Console.WriteLine("The Integer array...")

    Dim intValue As Integer
    For Each intValue In intArray
        Console.WriteLine(intValue.ToString( ))
    Next
    Console.WriteLine("The Employee array...")
    Dim e As Employee
    For Each e In empArray
        Console.WriteLine(e)
    Next

End Sub 'Run

Output:
The Integer array...
0
0
0
0
0
The Employee array...
5
6
7
```

The output for Example 9-3 is identical to Example 9-2. However, rather than creating a For statement that measures the size of the array and uses a temporary counting variable as an index into the array:

```
For i = 0 To empArray.Length - 1
    Console.WriteLine(empArray(i).ToString( ))
Next i
```

you now iterate over the array with the For Each loop which automatically extracts the next item from within the array and assigns it to a temporary object you've

---

created in the head of the statement. In the following case, the temporary object is of type Employee (it is a reference to an Employee object) and is named e:

```
Dim e As Employee
For Each e In empArray
    Console.WriteLine(e)
Next
```

Since the object extracted from the array is of the appropriate type (i.e., e is a reference to an Employee), you can call any public method of Employee.

 It is generally a good idea for the length of the variable name to be proportional to its lifetime. Because i and e in the previous examples exist only momentarily, their names can be quite short. A variable that will last the life of a method deserves a larger name (e.g., temperature or weight), and a variable that will last the lifetime of an object might deserve an even longer name (estimatedGrossWeight).

Initializing Array Elements

Rather than assigning elements to the array as we have done so far, it is possible to initialize the contents of an array at the time it is instantiated. You do so by providing a list of values delimited by curly braces ({}). VB.NET provides two different syntaxes to accomplish the same task:

```
Dim myIntArray1( ) As Integer = { 2, 4, 5, 8, 10}
Dim myIntArray2( ) As Integer  = New Integer(4) { 2, 4, 6, 8, 10 }
```

There is no practical difference between these two statements, and most programmers will use the shorter syntax because we are, by nature, lazy. We are so lazy, we'll work all day to save a few minutes doing a task—which isn't so crazy if we're going to do that task hundreds of times! Example 9-4 again rewrites the Run( ) method of Example 9-4, this time demonstrating initialization of both arrays.

Example 9-4. Initializing array elements

```
Option Strict On
Imports System

Public Sub Run( )
    Dim intArray As Integer( ) = {2, 4, 6, 8, 10}
    Dim empArray As Employee( ) = _
      {New Employee(5), New Employee(7), New Employee(9)}

    Console.WriteLine("The Integer array...")
    Dim theInt As Integer
    For Each theInt In intArray
        Console.WriteLine(theInt.ToString( ))
    Next theInt

    Console.WriteLine("The Employee array...")
```

Example 9-4. Initializing array elements (continued)

```
    Dim e As Employee
    For Each e In empArray
        Console.WriteLine(e.ToString())
    Next e
End Sub 'Run
```

```
Output:
The Integer array...
2
4
6
8
10

The Employee array...
5
7
9
```

The ParamArray Keyword

What do you do if you need to pass parameters to a method but you don't know how many parameters you'll want to pass? It is possible that the decision on how many parameters you'll pass in won't be made until runtime.

VB.NET provides the `ParamArray` keyword to allow you to pass in a variable number of parameters. As far as the client (the calling method) is concerned, you pass in a variable number of parameters. As far as the implementing method is concerned, it has been passed an array, and so it can just iterate through the array to find each parameter!

For example, you can create a method called DisplayVals() that takes integers as parameters and displays them to the console:

```
    Public Sub DisplayVals(ByVal ParamArray intVals() As Integer)
        Dim i As Integer
        For Each i In intVals
            Console.WriteLine("DisplayVals {0}", i)
        Next i
    End Sub 'DisplayVals
```

The `ParamArray` keyword indicates that you can pass in any number of integers, and the method will treat them as if you had passed in an array of integers. Thus you can call this method from Run() with:

```
    DisplayVals(5, 6, 7, 8)
```

And the DisplayVals() method will treat this *exactly* as if you had written:

```
    Dim explicitArray() As Integer = {5, 6, 7, 8}
    DisplayVals(explicitArray)
```

And in fact, you are free to create such an array and send it in as the parameter, as demonstrated in Example 9-5.

Example 9-5. The ParamArray keyword

```
Option Strict On
Imports System

Namespace ArrayDemo

    Class Tester

        Public Sub Run()
            Dim a As Integer = 5
            Dim b As Integer = 6
            Dim c As Integer = 7
            Console.WriteLine("Calling with three Integers")
            DisplayVals(a, b, c)

            Console.WriteLine("Calling with four Integers")
            DisplayVals(5, 6, 7, 8)

            Console.WriteLine("Calling with an array of four Integers")
            Dim explicitArray() As Integer = {5, 6, 7, 8}
            DisplayVals(explicitArray)
End Sub 'Run

        'takes a variable number of Integers
        Public Sub DisplayVals(ByVal ParamArray intVals() As Integer)
            Dim i As Integer
            For Each i In intVals
                Console.WriteLine("DisplayVals {0}", i)
            Next i
        End Sub 'DisplayVals

        Shared Sub Main()
            Dim t As New Tester()
            t.Run()
        End Sub 'Main
    End Class 'Tester
End Namespace 'ArrayDemo

Output:
Calling with three Integers
DisplayVals 5
DisplayVals 6
DisplayVals 7

Calling with four Integers
DisplayVals 5
DisplayVals 6
DisplayVals 7
DisplayVals 8
```

Example 9-5. The ParamArray keyword (continued)

```
Calling with an array of four Integers
DisplayVals 5
DisplayVals 6
DisplayVals 7
DisplayVals 8
```

In Example 9-5, the first time you call DisplayVals( ) you pass in three integer variables:

```
Dim a As Integer = 5
Dim b As Integer = 6
Dim c As Integer = 7
DisplayVals(a, b, c)
```

The second time you call DisplayVals( ) you use four literal constants:

```
DisplayVals(5, 6, 7, 8)
```

In both cases, DisplayVals( ) treats the parameters as if they were declared in an array. In the final invocation, you explicitly create an array and pass that as the parameter to the method:

```
Dim explicitArray( ) As Integer = {5, 6, 7, 8}
DisplayVals(explicitArray)
```

Multidimensional Arrays

Arrays can be thought of as long rows of slots into which values can be placed. Once you have a picture of a row of slots, imagine ten rows, one on top of another. This is the classic two-dimensional array of rows and columns. The rows run across the array and the columns run up and down the array, as illustrated in Figure 9-1.

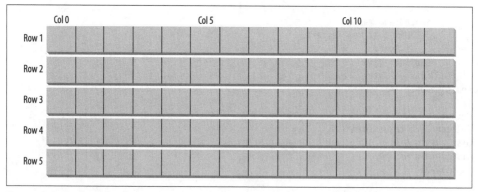

Figure 9-1. Rows and columns create a multidimensional array

A third dimension is possible but somewhat harder to picture. Imagine making your arrays three-dimensional, with new rows stacked atop the old two-dimensional array. OK, now imagine four dimensions. Now imagine ten.

Those of you who are not string-theory physicists have probably given up, as have I. Multidimensional arrays are useful, however, even if you can't quite picture what they would look like. You might, for example, use a four-dimensional array to track movement in three dimensions (x,y,z) over time.

VB.NET supports two types of multidimensional arrays: rectangular and jagged. In a rectangular array, every row is the same length. In a jagged array, however, each row can be a different length. In fact, you can think of each row in a jagged array as an array unto itself. Thus, a jagged array is actually an array of arrays.

Rectangular Arrays

A *rectangular array* is an array of two (or more) dimensions. In the classic two-dimensional array, the first dimension is the number of rows and the second dimension is the number of columns.

To declare and instantiate a two-dimensional rectangular array named rectangularArray that contains two rows and three columns of integers, you could use either of the following syntax lines:

```
Dim rectangularArray (,) As Integer
Dim rectangularArray As Integer(,)
```

Either line will create an empty two-dimensional array.

In Example 9-6, you create a two-dimensional array of integers, and you populate the array using two For loops. The outer For loop iterates once for each row, and the inner For loop iterates once for each column in each row:

```
Dim i As Integer
For i = 0 To rows - 1
    Dim j As Integer
    For j = 0 To columns - 1
        rectangularArray(i, j) = i + j
    Next j
Next i
```

You then use a second set of For loops to display the contents of the array:

```
For i = 0 To rows - 1
    Dim j As Integer
    For j = 0 To columns - 1
        Console.WriteLine( _
          "rectangularArray[{0},{1}] = {2}", _
          i, j, rectangularArray(i, j))
    Next j
Next i
```

Note that for the second loop you do not redeclare the variable i, because it was declared earlier. You *do*, however, redeclare j, because the first instance of j was declared within the scope of the earlier For loop, and so is not visible here.

The complete listing is shown in Example 9-6, followed by the output.

Example 9-6. Rectangular array

```
Option Strict On
Imports System

Namespace ArrayDemo

    Class Tester

        Public Sub Run( )
            Const rowsUB As Integer = 4
            Const columnsUB As Integer = 3

            'declare a 4x3 Integer array
            Dim rectangularArray(rowsUB, columnsUB) As Integer

            'populate the array
            Dim i As Integer
            For i = 0 To rowsUB - 1
                Dim j As Integer
                For j = 0 To columnsUB - 1
                    rectangularArray(i, j) = i + j
                Next j
            Next i

            'report the contents of the array
            For i = 0 To rowsUB - 1
                Dim j As Integer
                For j = 0 To columnsUB - 1
                    Console.WriteLine( _
                      "rectangularArray[{0},{1}] = {2}", _
                      i, j, rectangularArray(i, j))
                Next j
            Next i
        End Sub 'Run

        Shared Sub Main( )
            Dim t As New Tester( )
            t.Run( )
        End Sub 'Main
    End Class 'Tester

End Namespace 'ArrayDemo
```

Example 9-6. Rectangular array (continued)

```
Output:
rectangularArray[0,0] = 0
rectangularArray[0,1] = 1
rectangularArray[0,2] = 2
rectangularArray[1,0] = 1
rectangularArray[1,1] = 2
rectangularArray[1,2] = 3
rectangularArray[2,0] = 2
rectangularArray[2,1] = 3
rectangularArray[2,2] = 4
rectangularArray[3,0] = 3
rectangularArray[3,1] = 4
rectangularArray[3,2] = 5
```

In Example 9-6, you declare a pair of constant values to be used to specify the upper bound of the rows (rowsUB) and the upper bound of the columns (columnsUB) in the two-dimensional array:

```
Const rowsUB As Integer = 4
Const columnsUB As Integer = 3
```

Creating these constants allows you to refer to these values throughout the program; if you decide later to change the value of either, you only have to make the change in one location in your code.

You use these upper bounds to declare the array:

```
Dim rectangularArray(rowsUB, columnsUB) As Integer
```

Notice the syntax. The parentheses indicate that the type is an array, and the comma indicates the array has two dimensions; two commas would indicate three dimensions, and so on.

Just as you can initialize a one-dimensional array using bracketed lists of values, you can initialize a two-dimensional array using similar syntax:

```
Dim rectangularArray As Integer(,) = _
    {{0, 1, 2}, {3, 4, 5}, {6, 7, 8}, {9, 10, 11}}
```

The outer braces mark the entire array initialization; the inner braces mark each of the elements in the second dimension. Since this is a 4×3 array (four rows by three columns), you have four sets of three initialized values (12 in all). Example 9-7 rewrites the Run() method from Example 9-6 to use initialization.

Example 9-7. Initializing a two-dimensional array

```
Public Sub Run()
    Const rowsUB As Integer = 4
    Const columnsUB As Integer = 3

    'define and initialize the array
    Dim rectangularArray As Integer(,) = _
        {{0, 1, 2}, {3, 4, 5}, {6, 7, 8}, {9, 10, 11}}
```

Example 9-7. Initializing a two-dimensional array (continued)

```
    'report the contents of the array
    Dim i As Integer
    For i = 0 To rowsUB - 1
            Dim j As Integer
            For j = 0 To columnsUB - 1
                    Console.WriteLine( _
                      "rectangularArray[{0},{1}] = {2}", _
                      i, j, rectangularArray(i, j))
            Next j
    Next i
End Sub 'Run
```

```
Output:
rectangularArray[0,0] = 0
rectangularArray[0,1] = 1
rectangularArray[0,2] = 2
rectangularArray[1,0] = 3
rectangularArray[1,1] = 4
rectangularArray[1,2] = 5
rectangularArray[2,0] = 6
rectangularArray[2,1] = 7
rectangularArray[2,2] = 8
rectangularArray[3,0] = 9
rectangularArray[3,1] = 10
rectangularArray[3,2] = 11
```

As the output illustrates, the VB.NET compiler understands the syntax of your initialization; the objects are accessed with the appropriate offsets.

You might guess that this is a 12-element array, and that you can just as easily access an element at rectangularArray(0,3) as at rectangularArray(1,0), but if you try you will run right into an exception:

```
Unhandled Exception: System.IndexOutOfRangeException:
Index was outside the bounds of the array.
    at DebuggingVB.ArrayDemo.Tester.Run( ) in ...Module1.vb:line 13
    at DebuggingVB.ArrayDemo.Tester.Main( ) in ...Module1.vb:line 29
```

The specification rectangularArray(0,3) addresses the array element at row 1 in column 4 (offset 0,3). Since the array has been defined as having four rows and *three* columns, this position does not exist in the array. VB.NET arrays are smart and they keep track of their bounds. When you define a 4×3 array, you must treat it as such, and not as a 3×4 or a 12×1 array.

Had you written the initialization as:

```
Dim rectangularArray As Integer(,) = _
  { {0,1,2,3}, {4,5,6,7}, {8,9,10,11} }
```

you would instead have implied a 3×4 array, and rectangularArray(0,3) would be valid.

Jagged Arrays

A *jagged array* is an array of arrays. Specifically, a jagged array is a type of multidimensional array in which each row can be a different size from all the other rows. Thus, a graphical representation of the array has a "jagged" appearance, as in Figure 9-2.

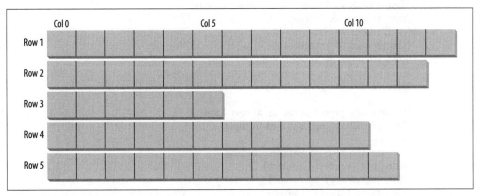

Figure 9-2. Jagged array

You can think of each row in a jagged array as an array unto itself—a one-dimensional array. Thus, technically speaking, a jagged array is an array of arrays. When you create a jagged array, you declare the number of rows in your array. Each row will hold a one-dimensional array, and each row can be of any length. To declare a jagged array you use the following syntax, where the number of pairs of parentheses indicates the number of dimensions of the array:

```
Dim identifier( )( ) As type
```

For example, you would declare a two-dimensional jagged array of integers named myJaggedArray as follows:

```
Dim myJaggedArray( )( ) As Integer
```

You address the elements in the array as follows: The array name followed by the offset into the array of arrays (the row), followed by the offset into the chosen array (the column within the chosen row). That is, to access the fifth element of the third array, you would write:

```
myJaggedArray(2)(4)
```

Remember that all arrays are zero-based. The third element is at offset 2, and the fifth element is at offset 4.

Example 9-8 creates a jagged array named myJaggedArray, initializes its elements, and then prints their content. To save space, the program takes advantage of the fact that integer array elements are automatically initialized to zero, and it initializes the values of only some of the elements.

Example 9-8. Jagged array

```
Option Strict On
Imports System

Namespace JaggedArray
    Public Class Tester
        Public Sub Run()
            Const rowsUB As Integer = 3   'upper bounds
            Const rowZero As Integer = 5
            Const rowOne As Integer = 2
            Const rowTwo As Integer = 3
            Const rowThree As Integer = 5

            Dim i As Integer

            'declare the jagged array as 4 rows high
            Dim jaggedArray(rowsUB)() As Integer

            'declare the rows of various lengths
            ReDim jaggedArray(0)(rowZero)
            ReDim jaggedArray(1)(rowOne)
            ReDim jaggedArray(2)(rowTwo)
            ReDim jaggedArray(3)(rowThree)

            'fill some (but not all) elements of the rows
            jaggedArray(0)(3) = 15
            jaggedArray(1)(1) = 12
            jaggedArray(2)(1) = 9
            jaggedArray(2)(2) = 99
            jaggedArray(3)(0) = 10
            jaggedArray(3)(1) = 11
            jaggedArray(3)(2) = 12
            jaggedArray(3)(3) = 13
            jaggedArray(3)(4) = 14

            For i = 0 To rowZero
                Console.WriteLine("jaggedArray(0)({0}) = {1}", _
                    i, jaggedArray(0)(i))
            Next

            For i = 0 To rowOne
                Console.WriteLine("jaggedArray(1)({0}) = {1}", _
                    i, jaggedArray(1)(i))
            Next

            For i = 0 To rowTwo
                Console.WriteLine("jaggedArray(2)({0}) = {1}", _
                    i, jaggedArray(2)(i))
            Next

            For i = 0 To rowThree
                Console.WriteLine("jaggedArray(3)({0}) = {1}", _
                    i, jaggedArray(3)(i))
```

Example 9-8. Jagged array (continued)

```
        Next
    End Sub

    Public Shared Sub Main( )
        Dim t As Tester = New Tester( )
        t.Run( )
    End Sub
End Class

End Namespace
```

```
Output:
jaggedArray(0)(0) = 0
jaggedArray(0)(1) = 0
jaggedArray(0)(2) = 0
jaggedArray(0)(3) = 15
jaggedArray(0)(4) = 0
jaggedArray(0)(5) = 0
jaggedArray(1)(0) = 0
jaggedArray(1)(1) = 12
jaggedArray(1)(2) = 0
jaggedArray(2)(0) = 0
jaggedArray(2)(1) = 9
jaggedArray(2)(2) = 99
jaggedArray(2)(3) = 0
jaggedArray(3)(0) = 10
jaggedArray(3)(1) = 11
jaggedArray(3)(2) = 12
jaggedArray(3)(3) = 13
jaggedArray(3)(4) = 14
jaggedArray(3)(5) = 0
```

Example 9-8 creates a jagged array with four rows:

```
Dim jaggedArray(rowsUB)( ) As Integer
```

Notice that the size of the second dimension is not specified. The columns in a jagged array vary by row; thus they are set by creating a new array for each row. Each of these arrays can have a different size:

```
ReDim jaggedArray(0)(rowZero)
ReDim jaggedArray(1)(rowOne)
ReDim jaggedArray(2)(rowTwo)
ReDim jaggedArray(3)(rowThree)
```

If you look back at the values of the constants (rowZero through rowThree), you'll be able to figure out that there are 15 slots in this array.

Notice that you use the keyword ReDim (discussed earlier) to dimension the internal arrays. Here it is being used to resize the internal arrays from their initial size of zero to the size you designate.

Once an array size is specified for each row, you need only populate the various members of each array (row) and then print out their contents to ensure that all went as expected.

Notice that when you accessed the members of the rectangular array, you put the indexes all within one set of parentheses:

```
rectangularArray(i,j)
```

while with a jagged array you need two sets of parentheses:

```
jaggedArray(3)(i)
```

You can keep this straight by thinking of the first as a single array of more than one dimension and the jagged array as an array of arrays.

System.Array

VB.NET implements arrays with the class System.Array. The Array class has a number of useful methods. Table 9-1 shows a few of the more important methods and properties of the System.Array class.

Table 9-1. Useful methods and properties of System.Array

Method or property	Description
Clear( )	Public shared method that sets a range of elements in the array to zero or to a null reference
Copy( )	Overloaded public shared method that copies a section of one array to another array
IndexOf( )	Overloaded public shared method that returns the index (offset) of the first instance of a value in a one-dimensional array
IsFixedSize	Public property that returns a value indicating whether the array has a fixed size
LastIndexOf( )	Overloaded public shared method that returns the index of the last instance of a value in a one-dimensional array
Length	Public property that returns the length of the array
Reverse( )	Overloaded public shared method that reverses the order of the elements in a one-dimensional array
Rank	Public property that returns the number of dimensions of the array
Sort( )	Overloaded public shared method that sorts the values in a one-dimensional array

The Array class's shared methods, Reverse( ) and Sort( ), make manipulation of the objects within the array very easy. Note, however, that to reverse or sort the elements of the array, they must be of a type that implements the IComparable interface, described in Chapter 8. The .NET Framework includes the String class, which does implement this interface, so we'll demonstrate both Reverse( ) and Sort( ) with Strings. The complete listing is shown in Example 9-9, followed by the output and analysis.

Example 9-9. Sort() and Reverse() methods of Array

```
Option Strict On
Imports System

Namespace ReverseAndSort
    Class Tester

        Public Shared Sub DisplayArray(ByVal theArray( ) As Object)
            Dim obj As Object
            For Each obj In theArray
                Console.WriteLine("Value: {0}", obj)
            Next obj
            Console.WriteLine(ControlChars.Lf)
        End Sub 'DisplayArray

        Public Sub Run( )
            Dim myArray As [String]( ) = {"Who", "is", "John", "Galt"}

            Console.WriteLine("Display myArray...")
            DisplayArray(myArray)

            Console.WriteLine("Reverse and display myArray...")
            Array.Reverse(myArray)
            DisplayArray(myArray)

            Dim myOtherArray As [String]( ) = _
              {"We", "Hold", "These", "Truths", "To", "Be", "Self", "Evident"}

            Console.WriteLine("Display myOtherArray...")
            DisplayArray(myOtherArray)

            Console.WriteLine("Sort and display myOtherArray...")
            Array.Sort(myOtherArray)
            DisplayArray(myOtherArray)
        End Sub 'Run

        Public Shared Sub Main( )
            Dim t As New Tester( )
            t.Run( )
        End Sub 'Main
    End Class 'Tester

End Namespace 'ReverseAndSort
```

Output:
```
Display myArray...
Value: Who
Value: is
Value: John
Value: Galt

Reverse and display myArray...
Value: Galt
```

Example 9-9. Sort( ) and Reverse( ) methods of Array (continued)

```
Value: John
Value: is
Value: Who

Display myOtherArray...
Value: We
Value: Hold
Value: These
Value: Truths
Value: To
Value: Be
Value: Self
Value: Evident

Sort and display myOtherArray...
Value: Be
Value: Evident
Value: Hold
Value: Self
Value: These
Value: To
Value: Truths
Value: We
```

Example 9-9 begins by creating myArray, an array of strings, containing the words:

```
"Who", "is", "John", "Galt"
```

This array is displayed, and then passed to the Array.Reverse( ) method, where it is displayed again to see that the array itself has been reversed:

```
Value: Galt
Value: John
Value: is
Value: Who
```

Similarly, the example creates a second array, myOtherArray, containing the words:

```
"We", "Hold", "These", "Truths",
"To", "Be", "Self", "Evident",
```

which is passed to the Array.Sort( ) method. Then Array.Sort( ) happily sorts them alphabetically:

```
Value: Be
Value: Evident
Value: Hold
Value: Self
Value: These
Value: To
Value: Truths
Value: We
```

The method to display the strings has been made somewhat generic by declaring the type passed in to be an array of objects:

```
Public Shared Sub DisplayArray(ByVal theArray( ) As Object)
```

The DisplayArray( ) method iterates through the array of objects, passing each to WriteLine( ). Since WriteLine( ) calls ToString( ) on objects, and since every object (including String) supports ToString( ), declaring the temporary variable obj to be of type Object works very well. Using objects has the advantage that you can reuse your DisplayArray( ) method with arrays of other types of objects, once you know how to implement the IComparable interface. Implementing interfaces is described in Chapter 8, and the IComparable interface, which is used with strings, is described in Chapter 10.

Indexers and the Default Property

Some classes contain their own internal collection. For example, you might write your own School class that would contain, as a private member variable, a collection of the Students enrolled in the school. You might then want to access the School class as if it were an array of Students. To do so, you would use the *default* property, which will allow you to write:

```
Dim joe As Student = mySchool(5)
```

accessing the sixth element in mySchool's internal collection!

As another example, suppose you create a listbox control named myListBox that contains a list of strings stored in a one-dimensional array, a private member variable named myStrings. A listbox control contains member properties and methods in addition to its array of strings. However, it would be convenient to be able to access the listbox array with an index, just as if the listbox were an array. For example, such a property would permit statements like the following:

```
Dim theFirstString As String = myListBox(0)
```

You implement this with the default property. Each class can have one default property, designated with the Default keyword. It is common to use the property name Item for the default property, but that is not required.

You can retrieve the default property with or without the property name. The following two code lines both retrieve the default property (which in this case, *is* called Item); the first uses the name, the second doesn't:

```
Dim theFirstString As String = myListBox.Item(0)
Dim theFirstString As String = myListBox(0)
```

In either case, the default property is acting as an *indexer*, a property used to index into the class as if it were a collection.

Example 9-10 declares a listbox control class that contains a simple array (strings) and a default property (Item) that acts as an indexer for accessing its contents. To keep the example simple, you'll strip the listbox control down to a few features.

The listing ignores everything having to do with being a user control and focuses only on the list of strings the listbox maintains and methods for manipulating them. In a real application, of course, these are a small fraction of the total methods of a listbox, whose principal job is to display the strings and enable user choice.

Example 9-10. Using an indexer

```
Option Strict On
Imports System

Namespace Indexers
    'a simplified ListBox control
    Public Class ListBoxTest
        Private strings(255) As String
        Private ctr As Integer = 0

        'initialize the listbox with strings
        Public Sub New(ByVal ParamArray initialStrings() As String)
            Dim s As String

            'copy the strings passed in to the constructor
            For Each s In initialStrings
                strings(ctr) = s
                ctr += 1
            Next
        End Sub

        'add a single string to the end of the listbox
        Public Sub Add(ByVal theString As String)
            If ctr >= Strings.Length Then
                ' handle bad index
            Else
                Strings(ctr) = theString
                ctr += 1
            End If
        End Sub

        'allow array-like access
        Default Public Property Item(ByVal index As Integer) As String
            Get
                If index < 0 Or index >= strings.Length Then
                    'handle bad index
                Else
                    Return strings(index)
                End If
            End Get
            Set(ByVal Value As String)
                If index >= ctr Then
                    'handle error
```

Example 9-10. Using an indexer (continued)

```
                Else
                    strings(index) = Value
                End If
            End Set
        End Property

        'publish how many strings you hold
        Public Function Count() As Integer
            Return ctr
        End Function
    End Class

Public Class Tester

    Public Sub Run()
        'create a new listbox and initialize
        Dim lbt As New ListBoxTest("Hello", "World")
        Dim i As Integer

        Console.WriteLine("After creation...")
        For i = 0 To lbt.Count - 1
            Console.WriteLine("lbt({0}): {1}", i, lbt(i))
        Next

        'add a few strings
        lbt.Add("Who")
        lbt.Add("Is")
        lbt.Add("John")
        lbt.Add("Galt")

        Console.WriteLine("After adding strings...")
        For i = 0 To lbt.Count - 1
            Console.WriteLine("lbt({0}): {1}", i, lbt(i))
        Next

        'test the access
        Dim subst As String = "Universe"
        lbt(1) = subst

        'access all the strings
        Console.WriteLine("After editing strings...")
        For i = 0 To lbt.Count - 1
            Console.WriteLine("lbt({0}): {1}", i, lbt(i))
        Next
    End Sub

    Public Shared Sub Main()
        Dim t As New Tester()
        t.Run()
    End Sub
End Class
```

Example 9-10. Using an indexer (continued)

```
End Namespace

Output:
After creation...
lbt(0): Hello
lbt(1): World

After adding strings...
lbt(0): Hello
lbt(1): World
lbt(2): Who
lbt(3): Is
lbt(4): John
lbt(5): Galt

After editing strings...
lbt(0): Hello
lbt(1): Universe
lbt(2): Who
lbt(3): Is
lbt(4): John
lbt(5): Galt
```

Example 9-10 begins by creating two private member variables, strings and ctr:

```
Private strings(255) As String
Private ctr As Integer = 0
```

In this program, the listbox maintains a simple array of strings, named (appropriately) strings. The member variable ctr keeps track of how many strings are added to the array.

The constructor initializes the array with the strings passed in as parameters. Because you cannot know how many strings will be added, you use the keyword ParamArray, as described earlier in this chapter:

```
Public Sub New(ByVal ParamArray initialStrings( ) As String)
    Dim s As String

    'copy the strings passed in to the constructor
    For Each s In initialStrings
        strings(ctr) = s
        ctr += 1
    Next
End Sub
```

Our focus is on the default property, Item, created using the following code:

```
Default Public Property Item(ByVal index As Integer) As String
```

In Example 9-10, the Get( ) method endeavors to implement rudimentary bounds checking, and, assuming the index requested is acceptable, it returns the value requested:

```
Get
    If index < 0 Or index >= strings.Length Then
        'handle bad index
    Else
        Return strings(index)
    End If
End Get
```

The Set( ) method checks to make sure that the index you are setting already has a value in the listbox. If not, it treats the set as an error; note that new elements can only be added using the Add( ) method with this approach. The Set( ) accessor takes advantage of the implicit parameter *value*, which represents whatever is assigned to the property.

```
Set(ByVal Value As String)
    If index >= ctr Then
        'handle error
    Else
        strings(index) = Value
    End If
End Set
```

Thus, if you write:

```
lbt(5) = "Hello World"
```

the compiler will call the default property Item's Set( ) method on your object and pass in the string "Hello World" as an implicit parameter-named value.

Default Properties and Assignment

In Example 9-10, you cannot assign to an index that does not have a value. Thus, if you write:

```
lbt(10) = "wow!"
```

you would trigger the error handler in the Set( ) method, which would note that the index you've passed in (10) is larger than the counter (6).

Of course, you can use the Set( ) method for assignment; you simply have to handle the indexes you receive. To do so, you might change the Set( ) method to check the Length property of the buffer rather than the current value of the counter (ctr). If a value was entered for an index that did not yet have a value, you would update ctr:

```
Set(ByVal Value As String)
    If index >= strings.Length Then
        'handle error
    Else
        strings(index) = Value
        if ctr < index + 1 then
          ctr = index + 1
        end if
    End If
End Set
```

This allows you to create a "sparse" array in which you can assign to offset 10 without ever having assigned to offset 9. Thus, if you were to write:

```
lbt(10) = "wow!"
```

the output would be:

```
lbt(0): Hello
lbt(1): Universe
lbt(2): Who
lbt(3): Is
lbt(4): John
lbt(5): Galt
lbt(6):
lbt(7):
lbt(8):
lbt(9):
lbt(10): wow!
```

In the Run() method of Example 9-10, you create an instance of the ListBoxTest class named lbt and pass in two strings as parameters:

```
Dim lbt As New ListBoxTest("Hello", "World")
```

You then call Add() to add four more strings:

```
lbt.Add("Who")
lbt.Add("Is")
lbt.Add("John")
lbt.Add("Galt")
```

Finally, you modify the second value (at index 1):

```
Dim subst As String = "Universe"
lbt(1) = subst
```

At each step, you display each value in a loop:

```
For i = 0 To lbt.Count - 1
    Console.WriteLine("lbt({0}): {1}", i, lbt(i))
Next
```

Indexing on Other Values

VB.NET does not require that you always use an integer value as the index to a collection. When you create a custom collection class and create your indexer, you are free to overload the default property so that a given collection can be indexed—for example, by an integer value or by a string value, depending on the needs of the client.

In the case of your listbox, you might want to be able to index into the listbox based on a string. Example 9-11 illustrates a string index. Example 9-11 is identical to Example 9-10 except for the addition of an overloaded default property, which can match a string, and findString(), a helper method created to support that index. The indexer calls findString() to return a record based on the value of the string provided.

Notice that the overloaded indexer of Example 9-11 and the indexer from Example 9-10 are able to coexist. The complete listing is shown, followed by the output, and then a detailed analysis.

Example 9-11. String indexer

```
Option Strict On
Imports System

Namespace Indexers
    'a simplified ListBox control
    Public Class ListBoxTest
        Private strings(255) As String
        Private ctr As Integer = 0

        'initialize the listbox with strings
        Public Sub New(ByVal ParamArray initialStrings() As String)
            Dim s As String

            'copy the strings passed in to the constructor
            For Each s In initialStrings
                strings(ctr) = s
                ctr += 1
            Next
        End Sub

        'add a single string to the end of the listbox
        Public Sub Add(ByVal theString As String)
            If ctr >= strings.Length Then
                ' handle bad index
            Else
                strings(ctr) = theString
                ctr += 1
            End If
        End Sub

        'allow array-like access
        Default Public Property Item( _
          ByVal index As Integer) As String
            Get
                If index < 0 Or index >= strings.Length Then
                    'handle bad index
                Else
                    Return strings(index)
                End If
            End Get
            Set(ByVal Value As String)
                If index >= ctr Then
                    'handle error
                Else
                    strings(index) = Value
                End If
            End Set
```

Example 9-11. String indexer (continued)

```
        End Property

        'index on string
        Default Public Property Item( _
           ByVal index As String) As String
           Get
               If index.Length = 0 Then
                   'handle bad index
               Else
                   Return strings(findString(index))
               End If
           End Get
           Set(ByVal Value As String)
               strings(findString(index)) = Value
           End Set
        End Property

        'helper method, given a string find
        'first matching record that starts with the target
        Private Function findString( _
           ByVal searchString As String) As Integer
           Dim i As Integer
           For i = 0 To strings.Length - 1
               If strings(i).StartsWith(searchString) Then
                   Return i
               End If
           Next
           Return -1
        End Function

        'publish how many strings you hold
        Public Function Count() As Integer
           Return ctr
        End Function
    End Class

Public Class Tester

    Public Sub Run()
        'create a new listbox and initialize
        Dim lbt As New ListBoxTest("Hello", "World")
        Dim i As Integer

        Console.WriteLine("After creation...")
        For i = 0 To lbt.Count - 1
            Console.WriteLine("lbt({0}): {1}", i, lbt(i))
        Next

        'add a few strings
        lbt.Add("Who")
        lbt.Add("Is")
        lbt.Add("John")
```

Example 9-11. String indexer (continued)

```
        lbt.Add("Galt")

        Console.WriteLine(vbCrLf & "After adding strings...")
        For i = 0 To lbt.Count - 1
            Console.WriteLine("lbt({0}): {1}", i, lbt(i))
        Next

        'test the access
        Dim subst As String = "Universe"
        lbt(1) = subst
        lbt("Hel") = "GoodBye"

        'access all the strings
        Console.WriteLine(vbCrLf & "After editing strings...")
        For i = 0 To lbt.Count - 1
            Console.WriteLine("lbt({0}): {1}", i, lbt(i))
        Next
    End Sub

    Public Shared Sub Main( )
        Dim t As New Tester( )
        t.Run( )
    End Sub
  End Class
End Namespace
```

```
Output:
lbt[0]: GoodBye
lbt[1]: Universe
lbt[2]: Who
lbt[3]: Is
lbt[4]: John
lbt[5]: Galt
```

In Example 9-11, the findString() method simply iterates through the strings held in strings until it finds a string that starts with the target string used in the index. If found, it returns the index of that string; otherwise it returns the value –1.

You can see in Main() that the user passes in a string segment to the index, just as was done with an integer:

```
lbt("Hel") = "GoodBye"
```

This calls the overloaded default property, which does some rudimentary error checking (in this case, making sure the string passed in has at least one letter) and then passes the value (Hel) to findString(). It gets back an index and uses that index to index into the strings array:

```
Return strings(findString(index))
```

The Set() accessor works in the same way:

```
Set(ByVal Value As String)
    strings(findString(index)) = Value
End Set
```

If the string does not match, a value of –1 is returned, which is then used as an index into strings. This action then generates an exception (System.NullReferenceException), as you can see by un-commenting the following line in Main():

```
lbt["xyz"] = "oops"
```

 The proper handling of not finding a string is, as they say, left as an exercise for the reader. You might consider displaying an error message or otherwise allowing the user to recover from the error. Exceptions are discussed in Chapter 11.

The Collection Interfaces: IEnumerable

While the Array is the simplest type of collection, there are times when you need additional functionality. The .NET Framework provides a number of already built and tested collection classes, including the ArrayList, Collection, Queue, and Stack. These standard classes are covered later in this chapter.

Chapter 8 introduced the concept of interfaces, which create a contract that a class can fulfill. Implementing an interface allows clients of the class to know exactly what to expect from the class. The .NET Framework provides a number of standard interfaces for enumerating, comparing, and creating collections.

These collection interfaces make it possible for you to write your own custom collection classes. By implementing the collection interfaces, your custom classes can provide the same semantics as the collection classes available through the .NET Framework. Table 9-2 lists the key collection interfaces and their uses.

Table 9-2. The collection interfaces

Interface	Purpose
IEnumerable	Designates a class that can be enumerated
IEnumerator	Designates a class that iterates over a collection; supports the For Each loop
ICollection	Implemented by all collections
IComparer	Compares two objects; used for sorting
IList	Used by collections that can be indexed
IDictionary	For key/value-based collections
IDictionaryEnumerator	Allows enumeration with For Each of a collection that supports IDictionary

This section will focus on the IEnumerable interface, using it to demonstrate how you can implement the collection interfaces in your own classes (allowing clients to treat your custom classes as if they were collections).

In Example 9-10, you developed a simple ListBoxTest class that provided an indexer for array-like semantics. That is, your ListBoxTest implemented its own indexer, so that you could treat the ListBoxTest object like it was an array:

```
myListBoxTest(5) = "Hello world"
Dim theText As String = myListBoxTest(1)
```

Of course, ListBoxTest is not an array; it is just a custom class that can be treated like an array because you gave it this indexer. You can make your ListBoxTest class even more like a real array by providing support for iterating over the contents of the array using the For Each statement. To provide support for the For Each statement, you'll need to implement the IEnumerable interface.

When you iterate over an array you visit each member in turn. Programmers talk about iterating over an array, iterating the array, iterating through the array, and enumerating the array. All of these terms are interchangeable.

The For Each statement will work with any class that implements the IEnumerable interface. Classes that implement the IEnumerable interface have a single method, GetEnumerator(), that returns an object that implements a second interface, IEnumerator.

Note the subtle difference in the names of these two interfaces: IEnumerable versus IEnumerator. The former designates a class that can be enumerated, the latter designates a class that does the actual enumeration.

The entire job of the IEnumerable interface is to define the GetEnumerator() method. The job of the GetEnumerator() method is to generate a specialized enumerator—that is, an instance of a class that implements a second interface, the IEnumerator interface. A class that implements IEnumerable can be enumerated. A class that implements IEnumerator knows how to enumerate an enumerable class (i.e., one that implements IEnumerable).

By implementing the IEnumerable interface, your ListBoxTest class is saying "you can enumerate my members, just ask me for my enumerator." The client asks the ListBoxTest for its enumerator by calling the GetEnumerator() method. What it gets back is an instance of a class that knows how to iterate over a listbox. That class, ListBoxEnumerator, will implement the IEnumerator interface.

This gets a bit confusing, so let's use an example. When you implement the IEnumerable interface for ListBoxTest, you are promising potential clients that ListBoxTest will support enumeration. That allows clients of your ListBoxTest class to write code like this:

```
Dim s As String
For Each s In ListBoxText
    '...
Next
```

You implement IEnumerable by providing the GetEnumerator() method, which returns an implementation of the IEnumerator interface. In this case, you'll return an instance of the ListBoxEnumerator class, and ListBoxEnumerator will implement the IEnumerator interface:

```
Public Function GetEnumerator() As IEnumerator _
      Implements IEnumerable.GetEnumerator
          Return New ListBoxEnumerator(Me)
End Function
```

The ListBoxEnumerator is a specialized instance of IEnumerator that knows how to enumerate the contents of your ListBoxTest class. Notice two things about this implementation. First, the constructor for ListBoxEnumerator takes a single argument, and you pass in the Me keyword. Doing so passes in a reference to the current ListBoxTest object, which is the object that will be enumerated. Second, notice that the ListBoxEnumerator is returned as an instance of IEnumerator. This implicit cast is safe because the ListBoxEnumerator class implements the IEnumerator interface.

 An alternative to creating a specialized class to implement IEnumerator is to have the enumerable class (ListBoxTest) implement IEnumerator itself. In that case, the IEnumerator returned by GetEnumerator() would be the ListBoxTest object, cast to IEnumerator.

Putting the enumeration responsibility into a dedicated class that implements IEnumerator (e.g., ListBoxEnumerator) is generally preferred to the alternative of letting the collection class (ListBoxTest) know how to enumerate itself. The specialized enumeration class encapsulates the responsibility of enumeration and the collection class (ListBoxTest) is not cluttered with a lot of enumeration code.

Because ListBoxEnumerator is specialized to know only how to enumerate ListBoxTest objects (and not any other enumerable objects), you will make ListBoxEnumerator a private class, contained within the definition of ListBoxTest. (The collection class is often referred to as the container class because it contains the members of the collection.) The complete listing is shown in Example 9-12, followed by a detailed analysis.

Example 9-12. Enumeration

```
Option Strict On

Imports System
```

Example 9-12. Enumeration (continued)

```
Imports System.Collections

Namespace Enumeration

    Public Class ListBoxTest : Implements IEnumerable
        Private strings() As String
        Private ctr As Integer = 0

        'private nested implementation of ListBoxEnumerator
        Private Class ListBoxEnumerator
            Implements IEnumerator
            'member fields of the nested ListBoxEnumerator class
            Private currentListBox As ListBoxTest
            Private index As Integer

            'public within the private implementation
            'thus, private within ListBoxTest
            Public Sub New(ByVal currentListBox As ListBoxTest)
                'a particular ListBoxTest instance is
                'passed in, hold a reference to it
                'in the member varaible currentListBox.
                Me.currentListBox = currentListBox
                index = -1
            End Sub

            'increment the index and make sure the
            'value is valid
            Public Function MoveNext() As Boolean _
              Implements IEnumerator.MoveNext
                index += 1
                If index >= currentListBox.strings.Length Then
                    Return False
                Else
                    Return True
                End If
            End Function

            Public Sub Reset() _
              Implements IEnumerator.Reset
                index = -1
            End Sub

            'current property defined as the
            'last string added to the listbox
            Public ReadOnly Property Current() As Object _
            Implements IEnumerator.Current
                Get
                    Return currentListBox(index)
                End Get
            End Property
        End Class  ' end nested class
```

Example 9-12. Enumeration (continued)

```
    'enumerable classes can return an enumerator
    Public Function GetEnumerator() As IEnumerator _
    Implements IEnumerable.GetEnumerator
        Return New ListBoxEnumerator(Me)
    End Function

    'initialize the listbox with strings
    Public Sub New( _
      ByVal ParamArray initialStrings() As String)
        'allocate space for the strings
        ReDim strings(7)

        'copy the strings passed in to the constructor
        Dim s As String
        For Each s In initialStrings
            strings(ctr) = s
            ctr += 1
        Next
    End Sub

    'add a single string to the end of the listbox
    Public Sub Add(ByVal theString As String)
        strings(ctr) = theString
        ctr += 1
    End Sub

    'allow array-like access
    Default Public Property Item( _
      ByVal index As Integer) As String
        Get
            If index < 0 Or index >= strings.Length Then
                ' handle bad index
                Exit Property
            End If
            Return strings(index)
        End Get
        Set(ByVal Value As String)
            strings(index) = Value
        End Set
    End Property

    'publish how many strings you hold
    Public Function GetNumEntries() As Integer
        Return ctr
    End Function

End Class

Public Class Tester
    Public Sub Run()
        'create a new listbox and initialize
        Dim currentListBox As New _
            ListBoxTest("Hello", "World")
```

Example 9-12. Enumeration (continued)

```
            'add a few strings
            currentListBox.Add("Who")
            currentListBox.Add("Is")
            currentListBox.Add("John")
            currentListBox.Add("Galt")

            'test the access
            Dim subst As String = "Universe"
            currentListBox(1) = subst

            'access all the strings
            Dim s As String
            For Each s In currentListBox
                Console.WriteLine("Value: {0}", s)
            Next
        End Sub

        Shared Sub Main()
            Dim t As New Tester()
            t.Run()
        End Sub
    End Class

End Namespace

Output:
Value: Hello
Value: Universe
Value: Who
Value: Is
Value: John
Value: Galt
Value:
Value:
```

The GetEnumerator() method of ListBoxTest passes a reference to the current object ListBoxEnumerator() to the enumerator, using the Me keyword:

```
    Return New ListBoxEnumerator(Me)
```

The enumerator will enumerate the members of the ListBoxTest object passed in as a parameter.

The class to implement the Enumerator is implemented as ListBoxEnumerator. The most interesting aspect of this code is the definition of the ListBoxEnumerator class. Notice that this class is defined within the definition of ListBoxTest. It is a nested class. It is also marked private; the only method that will ever instantiate a ListBoxEnumerator object is the GetEnumerator() method of ListBoxTest:

```
    'private nested implementation of ListBoxEnumerator
    Private Class ListBoxEnumerator
        Implements IEnumerator
```

ListBoxEnumerator is defined to implement the IEnumerator interface, which defines one property and two methods, as shown in Table 9-3.

Table 9-3. IEnumerator

Method or property	Description
Current	Property that returns the current element
MoveNext( )	Method that advances the enumerator to the next element
Reset( )	Method that sets the enumerator to its initial position, *before* the first element

The ListBoxTest object to be enumerated is passed in as an argument to the ListBox-Enumerator constructor, where it is assigned to the member variable currentList-Box. The constructor also sets the member variable index to –1, indicating that you have not yet begun to enumerate the object:

```
Public Sub New(ByVal currentListBox As ListBoxTest)
    Me.currentListBox = currentListBox
    index = -1
End Sub
```

 The number –1 is used as a signal to indicate that the enumerator is not yet pointing to any of the elements in the ListBoxTest object. You can't use the value 0, because 0 is a valid offset into the collection.

The MoveNext( ) method increments the index and then checks the length property of the strings array to ensure that you've not run past the end of the strings array. If you have run past the end, you return false; otherwise, you return true:

```
Public Function MoveNext( ) As Boolean _
    Implements IEnumerator.MoveNext
      index += 1
      If index >= currentListBox.strings.Length Then
          Return False
      Else
          Return True
      End If
End Function
```

The IEnumerator method Reset( ) does nothing but reset the index to –1. You can call Reset( ) any time you want to start over iterating the ListBoxTest object.

The Current property is implemented to return the current string. This is an arbitrary decision; in other classes, Current will have whatever meaning the designer decides is appropriate. However defined, every enumerator must be able to return the current member, as accessing the current member is what enumerators are for. The interface defines the Current property to return an object. Since strings are derived from Object, there is an implicit cast of the string to the more general Object type:

```
Public ReadOnly Property Current( ) As Object _
    Implements IEnumerator.Current
```

```
        Get
            Return currentListBox(index)
        End Get
    End Property
```

The call to For Each fetches the enumerator and uses it to enumerate over the array. Because For Each will display every string, whether or not you've added a meaningful value, in this example the strings array is initialized to hold only eight strings.

Now that you've seen how ListBoxTest implements IEnumerable, let's examine how the ListBoxTest object is used. The program begins by creating a new ListBoxTest object and passing two strings to the constructor:

```
Public Class Tester
    Public Sub Run()
        Dim currentListBox As New _
            ListBoxTest("Hello", "World")
```

When the ListBoxTest object (currentListBox) is created, an array of String objects is created with room for eight strings. The initial two strings passed in to the constructor are added to the array:

```
Public Sub New( _
    ByVal ParamArray initialStrings() As String)

    ReDim strings(7)

    Dim s As String
    For Each s In initialStrings
        strings(ctr) = s
        ctr += 1
    Next
End Sub
```

Back in Run(), four more strings are added using the Add() method, and the second string is updated with the word "Universe":

```
currentListBox.Add("Who")
currentListBox.Add("Is")
currentListBox.Add("John")
currentListBox.Add("Galt")

Dim subst As String = "Universe"
currentListBox(1) = subst
```

You iterate over the strings in currentListBox with a For Each loop, displaying each string in turn:

```
Dim s As String
For Each s In currentListBox
    Console.WriteLine("Value: {0}", s)
Next
```

The For Each loop checks that your class implements IEnumerable (and throws an exception if it does not) and invokes GetEnumerator():

```
Public Function GetEnumerator() As IEnumerator _
Implements IEnumerable.GetEnumerator
    Return New ListBoxEnumerator(Me)
End Function
```

GetEnumerator calls the ListBoxEnumerator constructor, thus initializing the index to −1.

```
Public Sub New(ByVal currentListBox As ListBoxTest)
    Me.currentListBox = currentListBox
    index = -1
End Sub
```

The first time through the loop, For Each automatically invokes MoveNext(), which immediately increments the index to 0 and returns true:

```
Public Function MoveNext() As Boolean _
    Implements IEnumerator.MoveNext
        index += 1
        If index >= currentListBox.strings.Length Then
            Return False
        Else
            Return True
        End If
End Function
```

The For Each loop then uses the Current property to get back the current string:

```
Public ReadOnly Property Current() As Object _
Implements IEnumerator.Current
    Get
        Return currentListBox(index)
    End Get
End Property
```

The Current property invokes the ListBoxTest's indexer, getting back the string stored at index 0. This string is assigned to the variable s defined in the For Each loop, and that string is displayed on the console. The For Each loop repeats these steps (call MoveNext(), access the Current property, display the string) until all the strings in the ListBoxTest object have been displayed.

.NET Collection Types: Beyond Array

The Array class is the simplest of the collection types provided with the .NET Framework. But the Framework provides a number of more powerful collection classes. The remaining pages of this chapter describe some of these very useful collection classes: ArrayList, Collection, Queue, and Stack.

Array Lists

Imagine that your program asks the user for input or gathers input from a web site. As it finds objects (strings, books, values, etc.), you would like to add them to an array, but you have no idea how many objects you'll collect in any given session.

It is difficult to use an array for such a purpose because you must declare the size of an Array object at compile time. If you try to add more objects than you've allocated memory for, the Array class will throw an exception. If you do not know in advance how many objects your array will be required to hold, you run the risk of declaring either too small an array (and running out of room) or too large an array (and wasting memory).

The .NET Framework provides a class designed for just this situation. The ArrayList class is an array whose size is dynamically increased as required. The ArrayList class provides many useful methods and properties. A few of the most important are shown in Table 9-4.

Table 9-4. ArrayList members

Method or property	Purpose
Add( )	Method to add an object to the ArrayList
Capacity	Property containing the number of elements the array can currently hold
Clear( )	Method that removes all elements from the ArrayList
Count	Property to return the number of elements currently in the array
GetEnumerator( )	Method that returns an enumerator to iterate an ArrayList
Insert( )	Method that inserts an element into ArrayList
Item( )	Method that gets or sets the element at the specified index; this is the indexer for the ArrayList class
RemoveAt( )	Method that removes the element at the specified index
Reverse( )	Method that reverses the order of elements in the ArrayList
Sort( )	Method that alphabetically sorts the ArrayList
ToArray( )	Method that copies the elements of the ArrayList to a new array

When you create an ArrayList, you do not define how many objects it will contain. You add to the ArrayList using the Add( ) method, and the list takes care of its own internal bookkeeping, as illustrated in Example 9-13.

Example 9-13. Using an ArrayList

```
Option Strict On
Imports System

Namespace ArrayListDemo
    'a class to hold in the array list
    Public Class Employee
        Private myEmpID As Integer
```

Example 9-13. Using an ArrayList (continued)

```vb
        Public Sub New(ByVal empID As Integer)
            Me.myEmpID = empID
        End Sub 'New

        Public Overrides Function ToString() As String
            Return myEmpID.ToString()
        End Function 'ToString

        Public Property EmpID() As Integer
            Get
                Return myEmpID
            End Get
            Set(ByVal Value As Integer)
                myEmpID = Value
            End Set
        End Property
    End Class 'Employee

Class Tester

    Public Sub Run()
        Dim empArray As New ArrayList()
        Dim intArray As New ArrayList()

        'populate the arraylists
        Dim i As Integer
        For i = 0 To 4
            empArray.Add(New Employee(i + 100))
            intArray.Add((i * 5))
        Next i

        'print each member of the array
        For Each i In intArray
            Console.Write("{0} ", i.ToString())
        Next i

        Console.WriteLine(ControlChars.Lf)

        'print each employee
        Dim e As Employee
        For Each e In empArray
            Console.Write("{0} ", e.ToString())
        Next e

        Console.WriteLine(ControlChars.Lf)
        Console.WriteLine("empArray.Capacity: {0}", empArray.Capacity)
    End Sub 'Run


    Shared Sub Main()
        Dim t As New Tester()
        t.Run()
```

Example 9-13. Using an ArrayList (continued)

```
      End Sub 'Main
   End Class 'Tester

End Namespace 'ArrayListDemo

Output:
0 5 10 15 20
100 101 102 103 104
empArray.Capacity: 16
```

Suppose you're defining two ArrayList objects, empArray to hold Employee objects, and intArray to hold integers:

```
Dim empArray As New ArrayList()
Dim intArray As New ArrayList()
```

Each ArrayList object has a property, Capacity, which is the number of elements the ArrayList is capable of storing.

 The default capacity for the ArrayList class is 16. You are free to set a different starting capacity for your ArrayList, but typically there is no need for you ever to do so.

You add elements to the ArrayList with the Add() method:

```
empArray.Add(New Employee(i + 100))
intArray.Add((i * 5))
```

When you add the 17th element, the capacity is automatically doubled to 32. If you change the For loop to:

```
For i = 0 To 17
```

the output looks like this:

```
0 5 10 15 20 25 30 35 40 45 50 55 60 65 70 75 80 85
100 101 102 103 104 105 106 107 108 109 110 111 112 113 114 115 116 117
empArray.Capacity: 32
```

Similarly, if you added a 33rd element, the capacity would be doubled to 64. The 65th element increases the capacity to 128, the 129th element increases it to 256, and so forth.

The Collection Class

Visual Basic .NET offers a generic collection class named, aptly, Collection. In many ways, the Collection object serves as an object-oriented alternative to Array, much as ArrayList does.

These two constructs (ArrayList and Collection) are very similar. Both offer Add() and Remove() methods as well as an Item property. The Collection class, however, overloads the Item property to take a string as a key into the collection. This allows the Collection class to act as a dictionary, associating keys with values. You can also use the Item property to access members of the collection by index value; however, the Collection uses a one-based index (i.e., the first element is index 1 rather than 0).

Example 9-14 illustrates the use of a Visual Basic .NET Collection object.

Example 9-14. Using a Collection object

```
Option Strict On
Imports System

Namespace CollectionDemo
    'a class to hold in the array list
    Public Class Employee
        Private myEmpID As Integer

        Public Sub New(ByVal empID As Integer)
            Me.myEmpID = empID
        End Sub 'New

        Public Overrides Function ToString() As String
            Return myEmpID.ToString()
        End Function 'ToString

        Public Property EmpID() As Integer
            Get
                Return myEmpID
            End Get
            Set(ByVal Value As Integer)
                myEmpID = Value
            End Set
        End Property
    End Class 'Employee

    Class Tester

        Public Sub Run()
            Dim intCollection As New Collection()
            Dim empCollection As New Collection()
            Dim empCollection2 As New Collection()

            'populate the Collections
            Dim i As Integer
            For i = 0 To 4
                empCollection.Add(New Employee(i + 100))
                intCollection.Add((i * 5))
            Next i

            'add key/value pairs
            empCollection2.Add(New Employee(1789), "George Washington")
            empCollection2.Add(New Employee(1797), "John Adams")
            empCollection2.Add(New Employee(1801), "Thomas Jefferson")
```

Example 9-14. Using a Collection object (continued)

```
            'print each member of the array
            For Each i In intCollection
                Console.Write("{0} ", i.ToString())
            Next i

            Console.WriteLine()
            Console.WriteLine("Employee collection...")
            Dim e As Employee
            For Each e In empCollection
                Console.Write("{0} ", e.ToString())
            Next e

            Console.WriteLine()
            Console.WriteLine("Employee collection 2...")
            For Each e In empCollection2
                Console.Write("{0} ", e.ToString())
            Next e

            Console.WriteLine()

            'retrieve an Employee by key
            Dim emp As Employee
            emp = empCollection2.Item("John Adams")
            Console.WriteLine( _
              "Key John Adams retrieved empID {0}", emp.ToString())

            'note that indexing is 1-based (rather than zero based)
            emp = empCollection2.Item(1)
            Console.WriteLine( _
              "Index(1) retrieved empID {0}", emp.ToString())

        End Sub 'Run


        Shared Sub Main()
            Dim t As New Tester()
            t.Run()
        End Sub 'Main
    End Class 'Tester
End Namespace 'CollectionDemo
```

```
Output:
0 5 10 15 20
Employee collection...
100 101 102 103 104
Employee collection 2...
1789 1797 1801
Key John Adams retrieved empID 1797
Index(1) retrieved empID 1789
```

Example 9-14 creates three Collection objects (intCollection, empCollection, and empCollection2):

```
Dim intCollection As New Collection()
Dim empCollection As New Collection()
Dim empCollection2 As New Collection()
```

The first two objects are populated in For loops, just as the ArrayList was created in Example 9-13:

```
Dim i As Integer
For i = 0 To 4
    empCollection.Add(New Employee(i + 100))
    intCollection.Add((i * 5))
Next i
```

The third Collection object, empCollection2, is populated using key values. Each new Employee is associated with a string, representing the name of the Employee:

```
empCollection2.Add(New Employee(1789), "George Washington")
empCollection2.Add(New Employee(1797), "John Adams")
empCollection2.Add(New Employee(1801), "Thomas Jefferson")
```

You retrieve objects from the collection much as you did from the ArrayLists:

```
For Each i In intCollection
    Console.Write("{0} ", i.ToString())
Next i

Dim e As Employee
For Each e In empCollection
    Console.Write("{0} ", e.ToString())
Next e

For Each e In empCollection2
    Console.Write("{0} ", e.ToString())
Next e
```

You can, however, retrieve objects from the collection using either the key value or an index value (one-based):

```
Dim emp As Employee
emp = empCollection2.Item("John Adams")
Console.WriteLine("Key John Adams retrieved empID {0}", emp.ToString())

emp = empCollection2.Item(1)
Console.WriteLine("Index(1) retrieved empID {0}", emp.ToString())
```

Queues

A *queue* represents a first-in, first-out (FIFO) collection. The classic analogy is a line (or queue if you are British) at a ticket window. The first person in line ought to be the first person to come off the line to buy a ticket.

The Queue class is a good collection to use when you are managing a limited resource. For example, you might want to send messages to a resource that can handle only one message at a time. You would then create a message queue so that you can say to your clients: "Your message is important to us. Messages are handled in the order in which they are received."

The Queue class has a number of member methods and properties, the most important of which are shown in Table 9-5.

Table 9-5. Queue members

Method or property	Purpose
Count	Public property that gets the number of elements in the Queue
Clear( )	Method that removes all objects from the Queue
Contains( )	Method that determines if an element is in the Queue
CopyTo( )	Method that copies the Queue elements to an existing one-dimensional array
Dequeue( )	Method that removes and returns the object at the beginning of the Queue
Enqueue( )	Method that adds an object to the end of the Queue
GetEnumerator( )	Method that returns an enumerator for the Queue
Peek( )	Method that returns the object at the beginning of the Queue without removing it
ToArray( )	Method that copies the elements to a new array

You add elements to your queue with the Enqueue( ) method, and you take them off the queue with Dequeue( ) or by using an enumerator. Example 9-15 shows how to use a Queue, followed by the output and a complete analysis.

Example 9-15. Implementing the Queue class

```
Option Strict On
Imports System

Namespace QueueDemo
    Class Tester
        Public Sub Run( )
            Dim intQueue As New Queue( )

            'populate the array
            Dim i As Integer
            For i = 0 To 4
                intQueue.Enqueue((i * 5))
            Next i

            'display the Queue
            Console.WriteLine("intQueue values:")
            DisplayValues(intQueue)

            'remove an element from the Queue
            Console.WriteLine("(Dequeue) {0}", intQueue.Dequeue( ))
```

Example 9-15. Implementing the Queue class (continued)

```
            'display the Queue
            Console.WriteLine("intQueue values:")
            DisplayValues(intQueue)

            'remove another element from the Queue
            Console.WriteLine("(Dequeue) {0}", intQueue.Dequeue())

            'display the Queue
            Console.WriteLine("intQueue values:")
            DisplayValues(intQueue)

            'view the first element in the Queue but do not remove
            Console.WriteLine("(Peek)   {0}", intQueue.Peek())

            'display the Queue
            Console.WriteLine("intQueue values:")
            DisplayValues(intQueue)
        End Sub 'Run

        Public Shared Sub DisplayValues(ByVal myCollection As IEnumerable)
            Dim myEnumerator As IEnumerator = myCollection.GetEnumerator()
            While myEnumerator.MoveNext()
                Console.WriteLine("{0} ", myEnumerator.Current)
            End While
            Console.WriteLine()
        End Sub 'DisplayValues

        Shared Sub Main()
            Dim t As New Tester()
            t.Run()
        End Sub 'Main
    End Class 'Tester

End Namespace 'QueueDemo

Output:
intQueue values:
0
5
10
15
20

(Dequeue) 0
intQueue values:
5
10
15
20

(Dequeue) 5
intQueue values:
```

Example 9-15. Implementing the Queue class (continued)

```
10
15
20

(Peek)    10
intQueue values:
10
15
20
```

In Example 9-15, the ArrayList from Example 9-13 is replaced by a Queue. I've dispensed with the Employee class and enqueued integers to save room in the book, but of course you can enqueue user-defined objects as well.

The program begins by creating an instance of a Queue, called intQueue:

```
Dim intQueue As New Queue( )
```

The queue is populated with integers:

```
For i = 0 To 4
    intQueue.Enqueue((i * 5))
Next i
```

The contents of the queue are then displayed using the DisplayValues() method. This method takes a collection that implements the IEnumerable interface (as does each of the collections provided by the .NET Framework) and asks that collection for its enumerator. It then explicitly iterates over the collection, displaying each element in turn:

```
Public Shared Sub DisplayValues(ByVal myCollection As IEnumerable)
    Dim myEnumerator As IEnumerator = myCollection.GetEnumerator( )
    While myEnumerator.MoveNext( )
        Console.Write("{0} ", myEnumerator.Current)
    End While
    Console.WriteLine( )
End Sub 'DisplayValues
```

You can avoid all the details of the Enumerator by using the For Each loop instead:

```
Public Shared Sub DisplayValues( _
        ByVal myCollection As IEnumerable)
    Dim o As Object
    For Each o In myCollection
        Console.WriteLine(o)
    Next
End Sub 'DisplayValues
```

Either version of DisplayValues() will work equally well.

You can display the first value in the queue without removing it by calling the Peek() method:

```
Console.WriteLine("(Peek) {0}", intQueue.Peek( ))
```

Or, having displayed the values in the For Each loop, you can remove the current value by calling the Dequeue() method:

```
Console.WriteLine("(Dequeue) {0}", intQueue.Dequeue())
```

Stacks

A *stack* is a last-in, first-out (LIFO) collection, like a stack of dishes at a buffet table or a stack of coins on your desk. You add a dish on top, and it is the first dish you take off the stack.

 The classic example of a stack is *the* stack, the portion of memory on which parameters and local variables are stored. See Chapter 5 for more about the stack.

The principal methods for adding to and removing from an instance of the Stack class are Push() and Pop(); Stack also offers a Peek() method, very much like Queue. Table 9-6 shows the most important methods and properties for Stack.

Table 9-6. Stack members

Method or property	Purpose
Clear()	Method that removes all objects from the Stack
Contains()	Method that determines if an element is in the Stack
CopyTo()	Method that copies the Stack elements to an existing one-dimensional array
Count	Public property that gets the number of elements in the Stack
GetEnumerator()	Method that returns an enumerator for the Stack
Peek()	Method that returns the object at the top of the Stack without removing it
Pop()	Method that removes and returns the object at the top of the Stack
Push()	Method that inserts an object at the top of the Stack
ToArray()	Method that copies the elements to a new array

In Example 9-16, you rewrite Example 9-15 to use a Stack rather than a Queue. The logic is almost identical. The key difference is that a Stack is Last In, First Out, while a Queue is First In, First Out.

Example 9-16. Using a Stack

```
Option Strict On
Imports System

Namespace StackDemo
    Class Tester
        Public Sub Run()
            Dim intStack As New Stack()
```

Example 9-16. Using a Stack (continued)

```
            'populate the stack
            Dim i As Integer
            For i = 0 To 7
                intStack.Push((i * 5))
            Next i

            'display the Stack
            Console.WriteLine("intStack values:")
            DisplayValues(intStack)

            'remove an element from the stack
            Console.WriteLine("(Pop){0}", intStack.Pop())

            'display the Stack
            Console.WriteLine("intStack values:")
            DisplayValues(intStack)

            'remove another element from the stack
            Console.WriteLine("(Pop){0}", intStack.Pop())

            'display the Stack
            Console.WriteLine("intStack values:")
            DisplayValues(intStack)

            'view the first element in the
            ' Stack but do not remove
            Console.WriteLine("(Peek)   {0}", intStack.Peek())

            'display the Stack
            Console.WriteLine("intStack values:")
            DisplayValues(intStack)
        End Sub 'Run

        Public Shared Sub DisplayValues(ByVal myCollection As IEnumerable)
            Dim o As Object
            For Each o In myCollection
                Console.WriteLine(o)
            Next o
        End Sub 'DisplayValues

        Shared Sub Main()
            Dim t As New Tester()
            t.Run()
        End Sub 'Main
    End Class 'Tester

End Namespace 'StackDemo

Output:
intStack values:
35
30
```

Example 9-16. Using a Stack (continued)

```
25
20
15
10
5
0
(Pop)35
intStack values:
30
25
20
15
10
5
0
(Pop)30
intStack values:
25
20
15
10
5
0
(Peek)   25
intStack values:
25
20
15
10
5
0
```

You start Example 9-16 by creating a Stack object called intStack:

```
Dim intStack As New Stack( )
```

You populate the stack with integers by calling the Push( ) method, which pushes each integer object onto the stack (i.e., adds it to the top of the Stack):

```
For i = 0 To 7
    intStack.Push((i * 5))
Next i
```

You remove an object from the stack by popping it off the stack with the Pop( ) method:

```
Console.WriteLine("(Pop){0}", intStack.Pop( ))
```

Just as you could peek at the object at the beginning of the Queue without dequeing it, you can Peek( ) at the object on top of the stack without popping it:

```
Console.WriteLine("(Peek)   {0}", intStack.Peek( ))
```

Copying from a Collection Type to an Array

The ArrayList, Queue, and Stack types contain overloaded CopyTo() and ToArray() methods for copying their elements to an array. The CopyTo() method copies its elements to an existing one-dimensional array, overwriting the contents of the array beginning at the index you specify. The ToArray() method returns a new array with the contents of the type's elements.

In the case of a Stack, ToArray() would return a new array containing the elements in the Stack. CopyTo() would copy the Stack over a pre-existing array. Example 9-17 modifies Example 9-16 to demonstrate both methods. The listing is followed by a complete analysis.

Example 9-17. Copying from a Stack to an array

```
Option Strict On
Imports System

Namespace StackDemo
    Class Tester

        Public Sub Run()
            Dim intStack As New Stack()

            'populate the array
            Dim i As Integer
            For i = 1 To 4
                intStack.Push((i * 5))
            Next i

            'display the Stack
            Console.WriteLine("intStack values:")
            DisplayValues(intStack)

            Const arraySize As Integer = 10
            Dim testArray(arraySize) As Integer

            'populate the array
            For i = 1 To arraySize - 1
                testArray(i) = i * 100
            Next i
            Console.WriteLine("Contents of the test array")
            DisplayValues(testArray)

            'copy the intStack into the new array, start offset 3
            intStack.CopyTo(testArray, 3)
            Console.WriteLine("TestArray after copy:   ")
            DisplayValues(testArray)

            'copy the entire source Stack
            ' to a new standard array
            Dim myArray As Object() = intStack.ToArray()
```

Example 9-17. Copying from a Stack to an array (continued)

```
            'display the values of the new standard array.
            Console.WriteLine("The new array:")
            DisplayValues(myArray)
        End Sub 'Run

        Public Shared Sub DisplayValues(ByVal myCollection As IEnumerable)
            Dim o As Object
            For Each o In myCollection
                Console.WriteLine(o)
            Next o
        End Sub 'DisplayValues

        Shared Sub Main()
            Dim t As New Tester()
            t.Run()
        End Sub 'Main
    End Class 'Tester

End Namespace 'StackDemo

Output:
intStack values:
20
15
10
5
Contents of the test array
0
100
200
300
400
500
600
700
800
900
0
TestArray after copy:
0
100
200
20
15
10
5
700
800
900
0
The new array:
20
```

Example 9-17. Copying from a Stack to an array (continued)

```
15
10
5
```

You begin again by creating the Stack (intStack), populating it with integers, and displaying its contents using WriteLine():

```
Dim intStack As New Stack()

'populate the array
Dim i As Integer
For i = 1 To 4
    intStack.Push((i * 5))
Next i

'display the Stack
Console.WriteLine("intStack values:")
DisplayValues(intStack)
```

You next create an array, populate it, and display its values:

```
Const arraySize As Integer = 10
Dim testArray(arraySize) As Integer

'populate the array
For i = 1 To arraySize - 1
    testArray(i) = i * 100
Next i
Console.WriteLine("Contents of the test array")
DisplayValues(testArray)
```

You are ready to copy the stack over the array. You do so with the CopyTo() method, passing in the array name, and the offset at which to begin the copy:

```
intStack.CopyTo( testArray, 3 )
```

This copies the four values from the stack over the array, starting at offset 3 (the fourth element in the array):

```
0
100
200
20
15
10
5
700
800
900
```

Rather than copying to an existing array, you are free to copy to a new array. You do this with the ToArray() method, which generates a properly sized new array to hold the contents of the stack:

```
Dim myArray As Object() = intStack.ToArray()
```

CHAPTER 10

Strings

There was a time when people thought of computers as manipulating numeric values exclusively. Early computers were first used to calculate missile trajectories, and programming was taught in the math department of major universities.

Today, most programs are concerned more with strings of characters than with numbers. Typically these strings are used for word processing, document manipulation, and creation of web pages.

VB.NET provides built-in support for a fully-functional String type. More importantly, VB.NET treats strings as objects that encapsulate all the manipulation, sorting, and searching methods normally applied to strings of characters.

Complex string manipulation and pattern matching are aided by the use of *regular expressions*. VB.NET combines the power and complexity of regular expression syntax, originally found only in string manipulation languages such as awk and Perl, with a fully object-oriented design.

In this chapter, you will learn to work with the VB.NET String type and the .NET Framework System.String class that it aliases. You will see how to extract substrings, manipulate and concatenate strings, and build new strings with the StringBuilder class. In addition, you will find a short introduction to the RegEx class used to match strings based on regular expressions.

Creating Strings

VB.NET treats strings as if they were built-in types. When you declare a VB.NET String using the String keyword, you are in fact declaring the object to be of the type System. String, one of the built-in types provided by the .NET Framework Class Library.

In .NET, each String object is an *immutable* sequence of Unicode characters. In other words, methods that appear to change the String actually return a modified copy; the original String remains intact.

The declaration of the System.String class is:

```
NotInheritable Public Class String
    Implements IComparable, ICloneable, IConvertible, IEnumerable
```

This declaration reveals that the class is NotInheritable, meaning that it is not possible to derive from the String class. The class also implements four system interfaces—IComparable, ICloneable, IConvertible, and IEnumerable—which dictate functionality that System.String shares with other classes in the .NET Framework.

The IComparable interface is implemented by types that can be sorted. Strings, for example, can be alphabetized; any given string can be compared with another string to determine which should come first in an ordered list. IComparable classes implement the CompareTo() method.

ICloneable objects can create new instances with the same value as the original instance. In this case, it is possible to clone a String object to produce a new String object with the same values (characters) as the original. ICloneable classes implement the Clone() method.

IConvertible classes provide methods to facilitate conversion to other primitive types; these methods include ToInt32(), ToDouble(), and ToDecimal().

IEnumerable, discussed in Chapter 9, lets you use the For Each construct to enumerate a String as a collection of Chars.

String Literals

The most common way to create a string is to assign a quoted string of characters, known as a *string literal*, to a user-defined variable of type String. The following code declares a string called newString that contains the phrase "This is a string literal":

```
Dim newString As String = "This is a string literal"
```

The ToString( ) Method

Another common way to create a string is to call the ToString() method on an object and assign the result to a string variable. All the built-in types override this method to simplify the task of converting a value (often a numeric value) to a string representation of that value. In the following example, the ToString() method of an Integer type is called to store its value in a string:

```
Dim myInteger As Integer = 5
Dim integerString As String = myInteger.ToString( )
```

The call to myInteger.ToString() returns a String object, which is then assigned to the string variable, integerString.

Strings Are Immutable

While Strings are considered to be reference types, the String objects themselves are immutable. They cannot be changed once created. When you appear to be changing a String, what is actually happening is that a new String is being created and the old String destroyed. Thus, suppose you write:

```
Dim myString As String = "Hello"
myString = "GoodBye"
```

The first line creates a String object on the heap with the characters *Hello* and assigns a reference to that string to the variable myString. The second line creates a new String object with the characters *GoodBye* and assigns a reference to that new string to the reference myString. The original String object is then cleaned up by the garbage collector.

Manipulating Strings

The String class provides a host of methods for comparing, searching, and manipulating strings, the most important of which are shown in Table 10-1.

Table 10-1. String class methods

Method or field	Explanation
Chars	The string indexer
Compare( )	Overloaded public shared method that compares two strings
Copy( )	Public shared method that creates a new string by copying another
Equals( )	Overloaded public shared and instance method that determines if two strings have the same value
Format( )	Overloaded public shared method that formats a string using a format specification
Length	The number of characters in the instance
PadLeft( )	Right-aligns the characters in the string, padding to the left with spaces or a specified character
PadRight( )	Left-aligns the characters in the string, padding to the right with spaces or a specified character
Remove( )	Deletes the specified number of characters
Split( )	Divides a string, returning the substrings delimited by the specified characters
StartsWith( )	Indicates if the string starts with the specified characters
SubString( )	Retrieves a substring
ToCharArray( )	Copies the characters from the string to a character array
ToLower( )	Returns a copy of the string in lowercase
ToUpper( )	Returns a copy of the string in uppercase
Trim( )	Removes all occurrences of a set of specified characters from beginning and end of the string
TrimEnd( )	Behaves like Trim( ), but only at the end
TrimStart( )	Behaves like Trim( ), but only at the start

Comparing Strings

The Compare() method is overloaded. The first version takes two strings and returns a negative number if the first string is alphabetically before the second, a positive number if the first string is alphabetically after the second, and zero if they are equal. The second version works just like the first but is case insensitive. Example 10-1 illustrates the use of Compare().

Example 10-1. Compare() method

```
Namespace StringManipulation
    Class Tester

        Public Sub Run( )
            ' create some Strings to work with
            Dim s1 As String = "abcd"
            Dim s2 As String = "ABCD"
            Dim result As Integer ' hold the results of comparisons
            ' compare two Strings, case sensitive
            result = String.Compare(s1, s2)
            Console.WriteLine( _
                "compare s1: {0}, s2: {1}, result: {2}" _
                & Environment.NewLine, s1, s2, result)

            ' overloaded compare, takes boolean "ignore case"
            '(True = ignore case)
            result = String.Compare(s1, s2, True)
            Console.WriteLine("Compare insensitive. result: {0}" _
                & Environment.NewLine, result)
        End Sub 'Run

        Shared Sub Main( )
            Dim t As New Tester( )
            t.Run( )
        End Sub 'Main
    End Class 'Tester
End Namespace 'StringManipulation
```

```
Output:
compare s1: abcd, s2: ABCD, result: -1
Compare insensitive. result: 0
```

This code uses the shared NewLine property of the Environment class to create a new line in the output. This is a very general way to ensure that the correct code sequence is sent to create the newline on the current operating system. As an alternative you can use vbNewLine from the Microsoft.VisualBasic namespace.

Example 10-1 begins by declaring two strings, s1 and s2, initialized with string literals:

```
Dim s1 As String = "abcd"
Dim s2 As String = "ABCD"
```

Compare( ) is used with many types. A negative return value indicates that the first parameter is less than the second, a positive result indicates the first parameter is greater than the second, and a zero indicates they are equal.

In Unicode (as in ASCII), a lowercase letter has a smaller value than an uppercase letter. Thus, the output properly indicates that s1 (abcd) is "less than" s2 (ABCD):

```
Compare s1: abcd, s2: ABCD, result: -1
```

The second comparison uses an overloaded version of Compare( ) that takes a third Boolean parameter, the value of which determines whether case should be ignored in the comparison. If the value of this "ignore case" parameter is true, the comparison is made without regard to case. This time the result is 0, indicating that the two strings are identical (without regard to case):

```
Compare insensitive. result: 0
```

Concatenating Strings

There are a couple ways to concatenate strings in VB.NET. You can use the Concat( ) method, which is a shared public method of the String class:

```
Dim s3 As String = String.Concat(s1, s2)
```

Or you can simply use the concatenation (&) operator:

```
Dim s4 As String = s1 & s2
```

These two methods are demonstrated in Example 10-2.

Example 10-2. Concatenation

```
Option Strict On
Imports System
Namespace StringManipulation
    Class Tester

        Public Sub Run( )
            Dim s1 As String = "abcd"
            Dim s2 As String = "ABCD"

            ' concatenation method
            Dim s3 As String = String.Concat(s1, s2)
            Console.WriteLine("s3 concatenated from s1 and s2: {0}", s3)

            ' use the overloaded operator
            Dim s4 As String = s1 & s2
            Console.WriteLine("s4 concatenated from s1 & s2: {0}", s4)
        End Sub 'Run

        Public Shared Sub Main( )
            Dim t As New Tester( )
            t.Run( )
        End Sub 'Main
```

Example 10-2. Concatenation (continued)

```
    End Class 'Tester
End Namespace 'StringManipulation
```

```
Output:
s3 concatenated from s1 and s2: abcdABCD
s4 concatenated from s1 & s2: abcdABCD
```

In Example 10-2, the new string s3 is created by calling the shared Concat( ) method and passing in s1 and s2, while the string s4 is created by using the overloaded concatenation (&) operator that concatenates two strings and returns a string as a result.

 Visual Basic .NET supports two concatenation operators (+ and &); however, the plus sign (+) is also used for adding numeric values, and the Microsoft documentation suggests using the & operator to reduce ambiguity.

Copying Strings

Creating a new copy of a string can be accomplished in two ways. First, you can use the shared Copy( ) method:

```
    Dim s5 As String = String.Copy(s2)
```

Or for convenience, you might simply use the assignment operator (=), which will implicitly make a copy:

```
    Dim s6 As String = s5
```

 When you assign one string to another, the two reference types refer to the same String in memory. This implies that altering one would alter the other because they refer to the same String object. However, this is not the case. The String type is immutable. Thus, if after assigning s5 to s6, you alter s6, the two Strings will actually be different.

Example 10-3 illustrates how to copy strings.

Example 10-3. Copying strings

```
Option Strict On
Imports System
Namespace StringManipulation

    Class Tester

        Public Sub Run( )
            Dim s1 As String = "abcd"
            Dim s2 As String = "ABCD"

            ' the String copy method
```

Example 10-3. Copying strings (continued)

```
        Dim s5 As String = String.Copy(s2)
        Console.WriteLine("s5 copied from s2: {0}", s5)

        ' use the overloaded operator
        Dim s6 As String = s5
        Console.WriteLine("s6 = s5: {0}", s6)
    End Sub 'Run

    Public Shared Sub Main()
        Dim t As New Tester()
        t.Run()
    End Sub 'Main
  End Class 'Tester
End Namespace 'StringManipulation
```

```
output:
s5 copied from s2: ABCD
s6 = s5: ABCD
```

Testing for Equality

The .NET String class provides two ways to test for the equality of two strings. First, you can use the overloaded Equals() method and ask one string (say, s6) directly whether another string (s5) is of equal value:

```
Console.WriteLine("Does s6.Equals(s5)?: {0}", s6.Equals(s5))
```

A second technique is to pass both strings to the String class's shared method Equals():

```
Console.WriteLine("Does Equals(s6,s5)?: {0}", _
    String.Equals(s6, s5))
```

In each of these cases, the returned result is a Boolean value (True for equal and False for not equal). These techniques are demonstrated in Example 10-4.

Example 10-4. Are all strings created equal?

```
Option Strict On
Imports System
Namespace StringManipulation

    Class Tester

        Public Sub Run()
            Dim s1 As String = "abcd"
            Dim s2 As String = "ABCD"

            ' the String copy method
            Dim s5 As String = String.Copy(s2)
            Console.WriteLine("s5 copied from s2: {0}", s5)
```

Example 10-4. Are all strings created equal? (continued)

```
            ' copy with the overloaded operator
            Dim s6 As String = s5
            Console.WriteLine("s6 = s5: {0}", s6)

            ' member method
            Console.WriteLine("Does s6.Equals(s5)?: {0}", s6.Equals(s5))

            ' shared method
            Console.WriteLine("Does Equals(s6,s5)?: {0}", _
                String.Equals(s6, s5))

        End Sub 'Run

        Public Shared Sub Main( )
            Dim t As New Tester( )
            t.Run( )
        End Sub 'Main
    End Class 'Tester
End Namespace 'StringManipulation

Output:
s5 copied from s2: ABCD
s6 = s5: ABCD

Does s6.Equals(s5)?: True
Does Equals(s6,s5)?: True
```

Other Useful String Methods

The String class includes a number of useful methods and properties for finding specific characters or substrings within a string, as well as for manipulating the contents of the string. A few such methods are demonstrated in Example 10-5. Following the output is a complete analysis.

Example 10-5. Useful string methods

```
Option Strict On
Imports System
Namespace StringManipulation

    Class Tester

        Public Sub Run( )
            Dim s1 As String = "abcd"
            Dim s2 As String = "ABCD"
            Dim s3 As String = "Liberty Associates, Inc. provides "
            s3 = s3 & "custom .NET development"

            ' the String copy method
            Dim s5 As String = String.Copy(s2)
            Console.WriteLine("s5 copied from s2: {0}", s5)
```

Example 10-5. Useful string methods (continued)

```vb
        ' The length
        Console.WriteLine("String s3 is {0} characters long. ", _
            s3.Length)

        Console.WriteLine()
        Console.WriteLine("s3: {0}", s3)

        ' test whether a String ends with a set of characters
        Console.WriteLine("s3: ends with Training?: {0}", _
            s3.EndsWith("Training"))
        Console.WriteLine("Ends with development?: {0}", _
            s3.EndsWith("development"))

        Console.WriteLine()
        ' return the index of the string
        Console.Write("The first occurrence of provides ")
        Console.WriteLine("in s3 is {0}", s3.IndexOf("provides"))

        ' hold the location of provides as an integer
        Dim location As Integer = s3.IndexOf("provides")

        ' insert the word usually before "provides"
        Dim s10 As String = s3.Insert(location, "usually ")
        Console.WriteLine("s10: {0}", s10)

        ' you can combine the two as follows:
        Dim s11 As String = _
            s3.Insert(s3.IndexOf("provides"), "usually ")
        Console.WriteLine("s11: {0}", s11)

        Console.WriteLine()
        'use the Mid function to replace within the string
        Mid(s11, s11.IndexOf("usually") + 1, 9) = "always!"
        Console.WriteLine("s11 now: {0}", s11)

    End Sub 'Run

    Public Shared Sub Main()
        Dim t As New Tester()
        t.Run()
    End Sub 'Main
    End Class 'Tester
End Namespace 'StringManipulation
```

Output:
```
s5 copied from s2: ABCD
String s3 is 4 characters long.

s3: Liberty Associates, Inc. provides custom .NET development
s3: ends with Training?: False
Ends with development?: True
```

Example 10-5. Useful string methods (continued)

```
The first occurrence of provides in s3 is 25
s10: Liberty Associates, Inc. usually provides custom .NET development
s11: Liberty Associates, Inc. usually provides custom .NET development

s11 now: Liberty Associates, Inc. always! provides custom .NET development
```

The Length property returns the length of the entire string:

```
Console.WriteLine("String s3 is {0} characters long. ", _
    s3.Length)
```

Here's the output:

```
String s3 is 4 characters long.
```

The EndsWith( ) method asks a string whether a substring is found at the end of the string. Thus, you might ask s3 first if it ends with "Training" (which it does not) and then if it ends with "Consulting" (which it does):

```
Console.WriteLine("s3: ends with Training?: {0}", _
    s3.EndsWith("Training"))
Console.WriteLine("Ends with development?: {0}", _
    s3.EndsWith("development"))
```

The output reflects that the first test fails and the second succeeds:

```
s3: ends with Training?: False
Ends with development?: True
```

The IndexOf( ) method locates a substring within our string, and the Insert( ) method inserts a new substring into a copy of the original string. The following code locates the first occurrence of "provides" in s3:

```
Console.Write("The first occurrence of provides ")
Console.WriteLine("in s3 is {0}", s3.IndexOf("provides"))
```

The output indicates that the offset is 25:

```
The first occurrence of provides in s3 is 25
```

You can then use that value to insert the word "usually," followed by a space, into that string. Actually the insertion is into a copy of the string returned by the Insert( ) method and assigned to s10:

```
Dim s10 As String = s3.Insert(location, "usually ")
Console.WriteLine("s10: {0}", s10)
```

Here's the output:

```
s10: Liberty Associates, Inc. usually provides custom .NET development
```

Finally, you can combine these operations to make a more efficient insertion statement:

```
Dim s11 As String = s3.Insert(s3.IndexOf("provides"), "usually ")
```

Finding Substrings

The String class has methods for finding and extracting substrings. For example, the IndexOf( ) method returns the index of the first occurrence1fc of a string (or one or more characters) within a target string.

For example, given the definition of the string s1 as:

```
Dim s1 As String = "One Two Three Four"
```

you can find the first instance of the characters "hre" by writing:

```
Dim index As Integer = s1.IndexOf("hre")
```

This code will set the integer variable index to 9, which is the offset of the letters "hre" in the string s1.

Similarly, the LastIndexOf( ) method returns the index of the *last* occurrence of a string or substring. While the following code:

```
s1.IndexOf("o")
```

will return the value 6 (the first occurrence of the lowercase letter "o" is at the end of the word Two), the method call:

```
s1.LastIndexOf("o")
```

will return the value 15, the last occurrence of "o" is in the word Four.

The Substring( ) method returns a series of characters. You can ask it for all the characters starting at a particular offset, and ending either with the end of the string or with an offset you (optionally) provide.

The Substring( ) method is illustrated in Example 10-6.

Example 10-6. Finding substrings by index

```
Option Strict On
Imports System
Namespace StringSearch

    Class Tester

        Public Sub Run( )
            ' create some strings to work with
            Dim s1 As String = "One Two Three Four"

            Dim index As Integer

            ' get the index of the last space
            index = s1.LastIndexOf(" ")

            ' get the last word
            Dim s2 As String = s1.Substring(index + 1)

            ' set s1 to the substring starting at 0
```

Example 10-6. Finding substrings by index (continued)

```
            ' and ending at index (the start of the last word
            ' thus s1 has One Two Three
            s1 = s1.Substring(0, index)

            ' find the last space in s1 (after "Two")
            index = s1.LastIndexOf(" ")

            ' set s3 to the substring starting at
            ' index, the space after "Two" plus one more
            ' thus s3 = "three"
            Dim s3 As String = s1.Substring(index + 1)

            ' reset s1 to the substring starting at 0
            ' and ending at index, thus the String "One Two"
            s1 = s1.Substring(0, index)

            ' reset index to the space between
            ' "One" and "Two"
            index = s1.LastIndexOf(" ")

            ' set s4 to the substring starting one
            ' space after index, thus the substring "Two"
            Dim s4 As String = s1.Substring(index + 1)

            ' reset s1 to the substring starting at 0
            ' and ending at index, thus "One"
            s1 = s1.Substring(0, index)

            ' set index to the last space, but there is
            ' none so index now = -1
            index = s1.LastIndexOf(" ")

            ' set s5 to the substring at one past
            ' the last space. there was no last space
            ' so this sets s5 to the substring starting
            ' at zero
            Dim s5 As String = s1.Substring(index + 1)

            Console.WriteLine("s1: {0}", s1)
            Console.WriteLine("s2: {0}", s2)
            Console.WriteLine("s3: {0}", s3)
            Console.WriteLine("s4: {0}", s4)
            Console.WriteLine("s5: {0}", s5)
        End Sub 'Run


        Public Shared Sub Main( )
            Dim t As New Tester( )
            t.Run( )
        End Sub 'Main
    End Class 'Tester
End Namespace 'StringSearch
```

Example 10-6. Finding substrings by index (continued)

```
Output:
s1: One
s2: Four
s3: Three
s4: Two
s5: One
```

Example 10-6 is not the most elegant solution possible to the problem of extracting words from a string, but it is a good first approximation and it illustrates a useful technique. The example begins by creating a string, s1:

```
Dim s1 As String = "One Two Three Four"
```

The local variable index is assigned the value of the *last* space in the string (which comes before the word Four):

```
index = s1.LastIndexOf(" ")
```

The substring that begins one space later is assigned to the new string, s2:

```
Dim s2 As String = s1.Substring(index + 1)
```

This extracts the characters from index +1 to the end of the line (i.e., the string "Four"), assigning the value "Four" to s2.

The next step is to remove the word Four from s1. You can do this by assigning to s1 the substring of s1 that begins at 0 and ends at the index:

```
s1 = s1.SubString(0,index);
```

You reassign index to the last (remaining) space, which points you to the beginning of the word Three. You then extract the characters "Three" into string s3. You can continue like this until you've populated s4 and s5. Finally, you display the results:

```
s1: One
s2: Four
s3: Three
s4: Two
s5: One
```

Splitting Strings

A more effective solution to the problem illustrated in Example 10-6 would be to use the Split( ) method of String, which parses a string into substrings. To use Split( ), you pass in an array of delimiters (characters that will indicate where to divide the words). The method returns an array of substrings. Example 10-7 illustrates. The complete analysis follows the code.

Example 10-7. The Split( ) method

```
Option Strict On
Imports System
```

Example 10-7. The Split() method (continued)

```vb
Namespace StringSearch

    Class Tester

        Public Sub Run()
            ' create some Strings to work with
            Dim s1 As String = "One,Two,Three Liberty Associates, Inc."

            ' constants for the space and comma characters
            Const Space As Char = " "c
            Const Comma As Char = ","c

            ' array of delimiters to split the sentence with
            Dim delimiters() As Char = {Space, Comma}

            Dim output As String = ""
            Dim ctr As Integer = 0

            ' split the String and then iterate over the
            ' resulting array of strings
            Dim resultArray As String() = s1.Split(delimiters)

            Dim subString As String
            For Each subString In resultArray
                ctr = ctr + 1
                output &= ctr.ToString()
                output &= ": "
                output &= subString
                output &= Environment.NewLine
            Next subString
            Console.WriteLine(output)
        End Sub 'Run

        Public Shared Sub Main()
            Dim t As New Tester()
            t.Run()
        End Sub 'Main
    End Class 'Tester
End Namespace 'StringSearch
```

Output:
1: One
2: Two
3: Three
4: Liberty
5: Associates
6:
7: Inc.

Example 10-7 starts by creating a string to parse:

```vb
Dim s1 As String = "One,Two,Three Liberty Associates, Inc."
```

The delimiters are set to the space and comma characters:

```
Const Space As Char = " "c
Const Comma As Char = ","c
Dim delimiters( ) As Char = {Space, Comma}
```

 Double quotes are used in VB.NET to signal a string constant. The c after the string literals establishes that these are characters, not strings.

You then call Split( ) on the string, passing in the delimiters:

```
Dim resultArray As String( ) = s1.Split(delimiters)
```

Split( ) returns an array of the substrings that you can then iterate over using the For Each loop, as explained in Chapter 9:

```
Dim subString As String
For Each subString In resultArray
    ctr = ctr + 1
    output &= ctr.ToString( )
    output &= ": "
    output &= subString
    output &= Environment.NewLine
Next subString
```

You increment the counter variable, ctr. Then you build up the output string in four steps. You concatenate the string value of ctr. Next you add the colon, then the substring returned by Split( ), then the newline:

```
ctr = ctr + 1
output &= ctr.ToString( )
output &= ": "
output &= subString
output &= Environment.NewLine
```

With each concatenation, a new copy of the string is made, and all four steps are repeated for each substring found by Split( ). This repeated copying of the string is terribly inefficient.

The problem is that the String type is not designed for this kind of operation. What you want is to create a new string by appending a formatted string each time through the loop. The class you need is StringBuilder.

The StringBuilder Class

The System.Text.StringBuilder class is used for creating and modifying strings. Unlike the String class, StringBuilder is mutable; when you modify an instance of the StringBuilder class, you modify the actual string, not a copy. Semantically, String-Builder is the encapsulation of a constructor for a string. The important members of StringBuilder are summarized in Table 10-2.

Table 10-2. StringBuilder members

Method or property	Explanation
Append( )	Overloaded public method that appends a typed object to the end of the current StringBuilder
AppendFormat( )	Overloaded public method that replaces format specifiers with the formatted value of an object
Capacity	Property that retrieves or assigns the number of characters the StringBuilder is capable of holding
Chars	Property that contains the indexer
EnsureCapacity( )	Ensures that the current StringBuilder has a capacity at least as large as the specified value
Insert( )	Overloaded public method that inserts an object at the specified position
Length	Property that retrieves or assigns the length of the StringBuilder
MaxCapacity	Property that retrieves the maximum capacity of the StringBuilder
Remove( )	Removes the specified characters
Replace( )	Overloaded public method that replaces all instances of specified characters with new characters

Example 10-8 replaces the String object in Example 10-7 with a StringBuilder object.

Example 10-8. The StringBuilder class

```
Option Strict On
Imports System
Imports System.Text
Namespace StringSearch

    Class Tester

        Public Sub Run( )
            ' create some Strings to work with
            Dim s1 As String = "One,Two,Three Liberty Associates, Inc."

            ' constants for the space and comma characters
            Const Space As Char = " "c
            Const Comma As Char = ","c

            ' array of delimiters to split the sentence with
            Dim delimiters( ) As Char = {Space, Comma}

            Dim ctr As Integer = 0

            ' split the String and then iterate over the
            ' resulting array of Strings
            Dim resultArray As String( ) = s1.Split(delimiters)

            Dim output As New StringBuilder( )
            Dim subString As String
            For Each subString In resultArray
                ctr = ctr + 1
                output.AppendFormat("{0} : {1}" & _
                    Environment.NewLine, ctr, subString)
            Next subString
            Console.WriteLine(output.ToString( ))
```

Example 10-8. The StringBuilder class (continued)

```
        End Sub 'Run

        Public Shared Sub Main( )
            Dim t As New Tester( )
            t.Run( )
        End Sub 'Main
    End Class 'Tester
End Namespace 'StringSearch
```

Only the last part of the program is modified from the previous example. Rather than using the concatenation operator to modify the string, you use the AppendFormat( ) method of StringBuilder to append new, formatted strings as you create them. This is much easier and far more efficient. The output is identical:

```
1: One
2: Two
3: Three
4: Liberty
5: Associates
6:
7: Inc.
```

Delimiter Limitations

Because you passed in delimiters of both comma and space, the space after the comma between "Associates" and "Inc." is returned as a word, numbered 6 previously. That is not what you want. To eliminate this, you need to tell Split( ) to match a comma (as between "One", "Two", and "Three") or a space (as between "Liberty" and "Associates") or a comma followed by a space. It is that last bit that is tricky and requires that you use a regular expression.

Regular Expressions

Regular expressions are a powerful language for describing and manipulating text. Underlying regular expressions is a technique called *pattern matching*, which involves comparing one string to another, or comparing a series of wildcards that represent a type of string to a literal string. A regular expression is *applied* to a string—that is, to a set of characters. Often that string is an entire text document.

The result of applying a regular expression to a string is either to return a substring or to return a new string representing a modification of some part of the original string. (Remember that strings are immutable and so cannot be changed by the regular expression.)

By applying a properly constructed regular expression to the following string:

```
One,Two,Three Liberty Associates, Inc.
```

you can return any or all of its substrings (e.g., Liberty or One), or modified versions of its substrings (e.g., LIBeRtY or OnE). What the regular expression *does* is determined by the syntax of the regular expression itself.

A regular expression consists of two types of characters: *literals* and *metacharacters*. A literal is just a character you want to match in the target string. A metacharacter is a special symbol that acts as a command to the regular expression parser. The parser is the engine responsible for understanding the regular expression. For example, if you create a regular expression:

```
^(From|To|Subject|Date):
```

this will match any substring with the letters "From" or the letters "To" or the letters "Subject" or the letters "Date" so long as those letters start a new line (^) and end with a colon (:).

The caret (^) in this case indicates to the regular expression parser that the string you're searching for must begin a new line. The letters "From" and "To" are literals, and the metacharacters left and right parentheses ((,)) and vertical bar (|) are all used to group sets of literals and indicate that any of the choices should match. Thus you would read the following line as, "Match any string that begins a new line followed by any of the four literal strings From, To, Subject, or Date followed by a colon":

```
^(From|To|Subject|Date):
```

 A full explanation of regular expressions is beyond the scope of this book, but all the regular expressions used in the examples are explained. For a complete understanding of regular expressions, I highly recommend *Mastering Regular Expressions,* by Jeffrey E. F. Friedl (O'Reilly).

The Regex Class

The .NET Framework provides an object-oriented approach to regular expression matching and replacement.

The Framework Class Library namespace System.Text.RegularExpressions is the home to all the .NET Framework objects associated with regular expressions. The central class for regular expression support is Regex, which represents an immutable, compiled regular expression. Example 10-9 rewrites Example 10-8 to use regular expressions and thus solve the problem of searching for more than one type of delimiter.

Example 10-9. Using the Regex class for regular expressions

```
Option Strict On
Imports System
Imports System.Text
Imports System.Text.RegularExpressions

Namespace RegularExpressions

    Class Tester

        Public Sub Run( )
            Dim s1 As String = "One,Two,Three Liberty Associates, Inc."
            Dim theRegex As New Regex(" |, |,")
            Dim sBuilder As New StringBuilder( )
            Dim id As Integer = 1

            Dim subString As String
            For Each subString In theRegex.Split(s1)
                id = id + 1
                sBuilder.AppendFormat("{0}: {1}" _
                    & Environment.NewLine, id, subString)
            Next subString
            Console.WriteLine("{0}", sBuilder.ToString( ))
        End Sub 'Run

        Public Shared Sub Main( )
            Dim t As New Tester( )
            t.Run( )
        End Sub 'Main
    End Class 'Tester
End Namespace 'RegularExpressions
```

```
Output:
1: One
2: Two
3: Three
4: Liberty
5: Associates
6: Inc.
```

Example 10-9 begins by creating a string, s1, identical to the string used in Example 10-8:

```
Dim s1 As String = "One,Two,Three Liberty Associates, Inc."
```

and a regular expression that will be used to search that string:

```
Dim theRegex As New Regex(" |, |,")
```

One of the overloaded constructors for Regex takes a regular expression string as its parameter.

This can be a bit confusing. In the context of a VB.NET program, which is the regular expression: the text passed in to the constructor or the Regex object itself? It is true that the text string passed to the constructor is a regular expression in the traditional sense of the term. From an object-oriented VB.NET point of view, however, the argument to the constructor is just a string of characters; it is the Regex object that is the regular expression object.

The rest of the program proceeds like Example 10-8 except that rather than calling Split() on string s1, the Split() method of Regex is called. Regex.Split() acts in much the same way as String.Split(), returning an array of strings as a result of matching the regular expression pattern within theRegex.

Regex.Split() is overloaded. The simplest version is called on an instance of Regex as shown in Example 10-9. There is also a shared version of this method, which takes a string to search and the pattern to search with, as illustrated in Example 10-10.

Example 10-10. Using the shared Split() method

```
Option Strict On
Imports System
Imports System.Text
Imports System.Text.RegularExpressions


Namespace RegularExpressions

    Class Tester

        Public Sub Run()
            Dim s1 As String = "One,Two,Three Liberty Associates, Inc."
            Dim sBuilder As New StringBuilder()
            Dim id As Integer = 1

            Dim subString As String
            For Each subString In Regex.Split(s1, " |, |,")
                id = id + 1
                sBuilder.AppendFormat("{0}: {1}" _
                    & Environment.NewLine, id, subString)
            Next subString
            Console.WriteLine("{0}", sBuilder.ToString())
        End Sub 'Run


        Public Shared Sub Main()
            Dim t As New Tester()
            t.Run()
        End Sub 'Main
    End Class 'Tester
End Namespace 'RegularExpressions
```

Example 10-10 is identical to Example 10-9 except that the latter example does not instantiate an object of type Regex. Instead, Example 10-10 uses the shared version of Split(), which takes two arguments: a string to be searched and a regular expression string that represents the pattern to match.

The instance method of Split() is also overloaded with versions that limit the number of times the split will occur and also that determine the position within the target string where the search will begin.

Using Match and MatchCollection

Two additional classes in the .NET RegularExpressions namespace allow you to search a string repeatedly and to return the results in a collection. The collection returned is of type MatchCollection, which consists of zero or more Match objects. Two important properties of a Match object are its length and its value, each of which can be read, as illustrated in Example 10-11.

Example 10-11. Using MatchCollection and Match

```
Option Strict On
Imports System
Imports System.Text
Imports System.Text.RegularExpressions

Namespace RegularExpressions

    Class Tester

        Public Sub Run()
            Dim string1 As String = "This is a test string"
            Dim theReg As New Regex("(\S+)\s")

            Dim theMatches As MatchCollection = theReg.Matches(string1)

            Dim theMatch As Match
            For Each theMatch In theMatches

                Console.WriteLine("theMatch.Length: {0}", _
                    theMatch.Length)

                If theMatch.Length <> 0 Then
                    Console.WriteLine("theMatch: {0}", _
                        theMatch.ToString())
                End If

            Next theMatch

        End Sub 'Run

        Public Shared Sub Main()
            Dim t As New Tester()
```

Example 10-11. Using MatchCollection and Match (continued)

```
            t.Run( )
        End Sub 'Main
    End Class 'Tester
End Namespace 'RegularExpressions
```

```
Output:
theMatch.Length: 5
theMatch: This
theMatch.Length: 3
theMatch: is
theMatch.Length: 2
theMatch: a
theMatch.Length: 5
theMatch: test
```

Example 10-11 creates a simple string to search:

```
Dim string1 As String = "This is a test string"
```

and a trivial regular expression to search it:

```
Dim theReg As New Regex("(\S+)\s")
```

The string \S finds nonwhitespace, and the plus sign indicates one or more. The string \s (note lowercase) indicates whitespace. Thus, together, this string looks for any nonwhitespace characters followed by whitespace.

The output shows that the first four words were found. The final word was not found because it is not followed by a space. If you insert a space after the word string and before the closing quote marks, this program will find that word as well.

The Length property is the length of the captured substring and will be discussed in the section "Using CaptureCollection," later in this chapter.

Using Regex Groups

It is often convenient to group subexpression matches together so that you can parse out pieces of the matching string. For example, you might want to match on IP addresses and group all IP addresses found anywhere within the string.

 IP addresses are used to locate computers on a network, and typically have the form nnn.nnn.nnn.nnn (such as 209.204.146.22).

The Group class allows you to create groups of matches based on regular expression syntax, and represents the results from a single grouping expression.

A grouping expression names a group and provides a regular expression; any substring matching the regular expression will be added to the group. For example, to create an ip group you might write:

```
"(?<ip>(\d|\.)+)\s"
```

The Match class derives from Group and has a collection called "Groups," which contains all the groups your Match finds.

Example 10-12 illustrates the creation and use of the Groups collection and Group classes.

Example 10-12. Using the Group class

```
Option Strict On
Imports System
Imports System.Text
Imports System.Text.RegularExpressions

Namespace RegularExpressions

    Class Tester

        Public Sub Run()
            Dim string1 As String = _
              "04:03:27 127.0.0.0 LibertyAssociates.com"

            ' time = one or more digits or colons
            ' followed by a space
            ' ip address = one or more digits or dots
            ' followed by space
            ' site = one or more characters
            Dim regString As String = "(?<time>(\d|\:)+)\s" & _
            "(?<ip>(\d|\.)+)\s" & _
            "(?<site>\S+)"

            Dim theReg As New Regex(regString)
            Dim theMatches As MatchCollection = theReg.Matches(string1)

            Dim theMatch As Match
            For Each theMatch In theMatches
                If theMatch.Length <> 0 Then
                    Console.WriteLine( _
                        "theMatch: {0}", _
                        theMatch.ToString())
                    Console.WriteLine( _
                        "time: {0}", _
                        theMatch.Groups("time"))
                    Console.WriteLine( _
                         "ip: {0}", _
                        theMatch.Groups("ip"))
                    Console.WriteLine( _
                         "site: {0}", _
                        theMatch.Groups("site"))
                End If
```

Example 10-12. Using the Group class (continued)

```
            Next theMatch

        End Sub 'Run

        Public Shared Sub Main( )
            Dim t As New Tester( )
            t.Run( )
        End Sub 'Main
    End Class 'Tester
End Namespace 'RegularExpressions
```

```
Output:
theMatch: 04:03:27 127.0.0.0 LibertyAssociates.com
time: 04:03:27
ip: 127.0.0.0
site: LibertyAssociates.com
```

Again, Example 10-12 begins by creating a string to search:

```
Dim string1 As String = _
            "04:03:27 127.0.0.0 LibertyAssociates.com"
```

This string might be one of many recorded in a web server log file or produced as the result of a search of the database. In this simple example there are three columns: one for the time of the log entry, one for an IP address, and one for the site, each separated by spaces; of course, in a real example solving a real-life problem, you might need to do more complex searches and choose to use other delimiters and more complex searches.

In Example 10-12, you create a single Regex object to search strings of this type and break them into three groups: time, ip address, and site. The regular expression string is fairly simple (as regular expressions go), so the example is easy to understand (however, keep in mind that in a real search, you would probably only use a part of the source string rather than the entire source string, as shown here):

```
Dim regString As String = "(?<time>(\d|\:)+)\s" & _
"(?<ip>(\d|\.)+)\s" & _
"(?<site>\S+)"
```

Let's focus on the characters that create the group:

```
(?<time>
```

The parentheses create a group. Everything between the opening parenthesis (just before the question mark) and the closing parenthesis (in this case, after the plus sign) is a single unnamed group.

```
("(?<time>(\d|\:)+)
```

The string ?<time> names that group time, and the group is associated with the matching text, the regular expression (\d|\:)+)\s". This regular expression can be interpreted as "one or more digits or colons followed by a space."

Similarly, the string ?<ip> names the ip group, and ?<site> names the site group. As Example 10-11 does, Example 10-12 asks for a collection of all the matches:

```
Dim theMatches As MatchCollection = theReg.Matches(string1)
```

Example 10-12 iterates through the Matches collection, finding each Match object.

If the Length of theMatch is greater than 0, a Match was found; then it prints the entire match:

```
If theMatch.Length <> 0 Then
    Console.WriteLine( _
        "theMatch: {0}", _
        theMatch.ToString( ))
```

Here's the output:

```
theMatch: 04:03:27 127.0.0.0 LibertyAssociates.com
```

It then gets the "time" group from theMatch.Groups collection and prints that value:

```
Console.WriteLine( _
    "time: {0}", _
    theMatch.Groups("time"))
```

This produces the output:

```
time: 04:03:27
```

The code then obtains ip and site groups:

```
Console.WriteLine( _
    "ip: {0}", _
    theMatch.Groups("ip"))
Console.WriteLine( _
    "site: {0}", _
    theMatch.Groups("site"))
```

This produces the output:

```
ip: 127.0.0.0
site: LibertyAssociates.com
```

In Example 10-12, the Matches collection has only one Match. It is possible, however, to match more than one expression within a string. To see this, modify string1 in Example 10-12 to provide several logFile entries instead of one, as follows:

```
Dim string1 As String = "04:03:27 127.0.0.0 LibertyAssociates.com " +
"04:03:28 127.0.0.0 foo.com " +
"04:03:29 127.0.0.0 bar.com " ;
```

This creates three matches in the MatchCollection, theMatches. Here's the resulting output:

```
theMatch: 04:03:27 127.0.0.0 LibertyAssociates.com
time: 04:03:27
ip: 127.0.0.0
site: LibertyAssociates.com
theMatch: 04:03:28 127.0.0.0 foo.com
```

```
time: 04:03:28
ip: 127.0.0.0
site: foo.com
theMatch: 04:03:29 127.0.0.0 bar.com
time: 04:03:29
ip: 127.0.0.0
site: bar.com
```

In this example, theMatches contains three Match objects. Each time through the outer For Each loop we find the next Match in the collection and display its contents:

```
For Each theMatch In theMatches
```

For each of the Match items found, you can print out the entire match, various groups, or both.

Using CaptureCollection

Each time a Regex object matches a subexpression, a Capture instance is created and added to a CaptureCollection collection. Each capture object represents a single capture. Each group has its own capture collection of the matches for the subexpression associated with the group.

A key property of the Capture object is its length, which is the length of the captured sub-string. When you ask Match for its length, it is Capture.Length that you retrieve because Match derives from Group, which in turn derives from Capture.

> The regular expression inheritance scheme in .NET allows Match to include in its interface the methods and properties of these parent classes. In a sense, a Group *is-a* capture—it is a capture that encapsulates the idea of grouping subexpressions. A Match, in turn, *is-a* Group—it is the encapsulation of all the groups of subexpressions making up the entire match for this regular expression. (See Chapter 5 for more about the *is-a* relationship and other relationships.)

Typically, you will find only a single Capture in a CaptureCollection; but that need not be so. Consider what would happen if you were parsing a string in which the company name might occur in either of two positions. To group these together in a single match you create the ?<company> group in two places in your regular expression pattern:

```
Dim regString As String = "(?<time>(\d|\:)+)\s" & _
"(?<company>\S+)\s" & _
"(?<ip>(\d|\.)+)\s" & _
"(?<company>\S+)\s"
```

This regular expression group captures any matching string of characters that follows time, and also any matching string of characters that follows ip. Given this regular expression, you are ready to parse the following string:

```
Dim string1 As String = "04:03:27 Jesse 0.0.0.127 Liberty "
```

The string includes names in both the positions specified. Here is the result:

```
theMatch: 04:03:27 Jesse 0.0.0.127 Liberty
time: 04:03:27
ip: 0.0.0.127
Company: Liberty
```

What happened? Why is the Company group showing Liberty? Where is the first term, which also matched? The answer is that the second term overwrote the first. The group, however, has captured both; its Captures collection can show that to you, as illustrated in Example 10-13.

Example 10-13. Captures collection

```
Imports System
Imports System.Text
Imports System.Text.RegularExpressions

Namespace RegularExpressions

    Class Tester

        Public Sub Run( )
            Dim string1 As String = _
            "04:03:27 Jesse 0.0.0.127 Liberty   "

            ' time = one or more digits or colons
            ' followed by a space
            ' ip address = on ore more digits or dots
            ' followed by space
            ' site = one or more characters
            Dim regString As String = "(?<time>(\d|\:)+)\s" & _
            "(?<company>\S+)\s" & _
            "(?<ip>(\d|\.)+)\s" & _
            "(?<company>\S+)\s"

            Dim theReg As New Regex(regString)
            Dim theMatches As MatchCollection = theReg.Matches(string1)

            Dim theMatch As Match
            For Each theMatch In theMatches
                If theMatch.Length <> 0 Then
                    Console.WriteLine( _
                        "theMatch: {0}", _
                        theMatch.ToString( ))
                    Console.WriteLine( _
                        "time: {0}", _
                        theMatch.Groups("time"))
                    Console.WriteLine( _
                        "ip: {0}", _
                        theMatch.Groups("ip"))
                    Console.WriteLine( _
                        "Company: {0}", _
                        theMatch.Groups("company"))
```

Example 10-13. Captures collection (continued)

```
                    Dim cap As Capture
                    For Each cap In _
                        theMatch.Groups("company").Captures
                        Console.WriteLine( _
                            "cap: {0}", cap.ToString())
                    Next
                End If
            Next theMatch

        End Sub 'Run

        Public Shared Sub Main()
            Dim t As New Tester()
            t.Run()
        End Sub 'Main
    End Class 'Tester
End Namespace 'RegularExpressions
```

```
Output:
theMatch: 04:03:27 Jesse 0.0.0.127 Liberty
time: 04:03:27
ip: 0.0.0.127
Company: Liberty
cap: Jesse
cap: Liberty
```

The code in bold iterates through the Captures collection for the Company group.

```
Dim cap As Capture
For Each cap In _
    theMatch.Groups("company").Captures
```

Let's review how this line is parsed. The compiler begins by finding the collection that it will iterate. theMatch is an object that has a collection named Groups. The Groups collection has a default property (as explained in the previous chapter) that takes a string and returns a single Group object. Thus, the following line returns a single Group object:

```
theMatch.Groups("company")
```

The Group object has a collection named Captures. Thus, the following line returns a Captures collection for the Group stored at Groups["company"] within the theMatch object:

```
theMatch.Groups("company").Captures
```

The For Each loop iterates over the Captures collection, extracting each element in turn and assigning it to the local variable cap, which is of type Capture. You can see from the output that there are two capture elements: Jesse and Liberty. The second one overwrites the first in the group, and so the displayed value is just Liberty, but by examining the Captures collection you can find both values that were captured.

CHAPTER 11

Exceptions

VB.NET handles errors and abnormal conditions with *exceptions*. An exception is an object that encapsulates information about an unusual program occurrence, such as running out of memory or losing a network connection.

It is important to distinguish exceptions from bugs and errors. A *bug* is a programmer mistake that should be fixed before the code is shipped. An exception is not the result of a programmer mistake (though such mistakes can also raise exceptions). Rather, exceptions are raised as a result of predictable but unpreventable problems that arise while your program is running (e.g., a network connection is dropped or you run out of disk space).

An *error* is caused by user action. For example, the user might enter a number where a letter is expected. Once again, an error might cause an exception, but you can prevent that by implementing code to validate user input. Whenever possible, user errors should be anticipated and prevented.

Even if you remove all bugs and anticipate all user errors, you will still run into unavoidable problems, such as running out of memory or attempting to open a file that no longer exists. These are exceptions. You cannot prevent exceptions, but you can handle them so that they do not bring down your program.

When your program encounters an exceptional circumstance, such as running out of memory, it *throws* (or "raises") an exception. You might throw an exception in your own methods (for example, if you realize that an invalid parameter has been provided) or an exception might be thrown in a class provided by the Framework Class Library (for example, if you try to write to a read-only file). Many exceptions are thrown at runtime when the program can no longer continue due to an operating system problem (such as a security violation). Exceptions must be *handled* before the program can continue.

You provide for the possibility of exceptions by adding try/catch blocks in your program. The catch blocks are also called *exception handlers*. The idea is that you *try* potentially dangerous code, and if an exception is thrown you *catch* (or *handle*) the exception in your catch block.

VB.NET also provides unstructured exception handling through the use of Error, On Error, and Resume statements. This approach is not object-oriented, and not consistent with how exceptions are handled in other .NET languages. Thus it is discouraged and not shown in this book.

Ideally, if the exception is caught and handled, the program can fix the problem and continue. Even if your program can't continue, by catching the exception you have an opportunity to print a meaningful error message and terminate gracefully.

When an exception is thrown, execution of the current function halts and the Common Language Runtime (CLR) searches back through the stack until an appropriate exception handler is found. The search for an exception handler can "unwind the stack." This means that if the currently running function does not handle the exception, the current function will terminate and the calling function will get a chance to handle the exception. If none of the calling functions handles it, the exception will ultimately be handled by the CLR, which will abruptly terminate your program.

If Function A calls Function B and Function B calls Function C, these function calls are all placed on the stack (an area of memory set aside for local variables). When a programmer talks about "unwinding the stack," what is meant is that you back up from C to B to A, as illustrated in Figure 11-1.

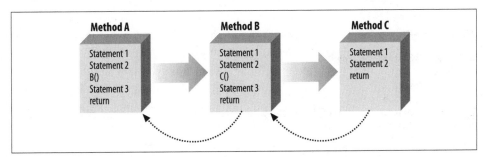

Figure 11-1. Unwinding the stack

If you must unwind the stack from C to B to A to handle the exception, when you are done you are in A; there is no automatic return to C.

If you return all the way to the first method and no exception handler is found, the *default* exception handler (provided by the compiler) just terminates the program.

Throwing and Catching Exceptions

In VB.NET, all exceptions will be either of type System.Exception or of types derived from System.Exception. The CLR System namespace includes a number of exception types that can be used by your program. These exception types include

ArgumentNullException, InvalidCastException, and OverflowException, as well as many others. You can guess their use based on their name. For example, Argument-NullException is thrown when an argument to a method is Nothing (null) and that is not an expected (or acceptable) value.

This chapter describes how to write your programs to catch and handle exceptions. This chapter will also show you how to use the properties of the Exception class to provide information to the user about what went wrong, and it will show you how to create and use your own custom exception types.

The Throw Statement

To signal an abnormal condition in a VB.NET program, you throw an exception. To do this, you use the keyword Throw. The following line of code creates a new instance of System.Exception and then throws it:

```
Throw New System.Exception()
```

Example 11-1 illustrates what happens if you throw an exception and there is no try/catch block to catch and handle the exception. In this example, you'll throw an exception even though nothing has actually gone wrong, just to illustrate how an exception can bring your program to a halt.

Example 11-1. Unhandled exception

```
Option Strict On
Imports System

Namespace ExceptionHandling

    Class Tester
        Shared Sub Main()
            Console.WriteLine("Enter Main...")
            Dim t As New Tester()
            t.Run()
            Console.WriteLine("Exit Main...")
        End Sub 'Main

        Public Sub Run()
            Console.WriteLine("Enter Run...")
            Func1()
            Console.WriteLine("Exit Run...")
        End Sub 'Run

        Public Sub Func1()
            Console.WriteLine("Enter Func1...")
            Func2()
            Console.WriteLine("Exit Func1...")
        End Sub 'Func1
```

Example 11-1. Unhandled exception (continued)

```
    Public Sub Func2( )
        Console.WriteLine("Enter Func2...")
        Throw New System.Exception( )
        Console.WriteLine("Exit Func2...")
    End Sub 'Func2

  End Class 'Tester
End Namespace 'ExceptionHandling


Enter Main...
Enter Run...
Enter Func1...
Enter Func2...

Unhandled Exception: System.Exception: Exception of type System.Exception was thrown.
 at DebuggingVB.ExceptionHandling.Tester.Func2( ) in C:...\Module1.vb:line 27
   at DebuggingVB.ExceptionHandling.Tester.Func1( )
   in C:...\Module1.vb:line 21
   at DebuggingVB.ExceptionHandling.Tester.Run( )
   in C:...\Module1.vb:line 14
   at DebuggingVB.ExceptionHandling.Tester.Main( )
   in C:...\Module1.vb:line 8
```

This simple example writes to the console as it enters and exits each method. Main( ) calls Run, which in turn calls Func1( ). After printing out the Enter Func1 message, Func1( ) immediately calls Func2( ). Func2( ) prints out the first message and throws an object of type System.Exception.

Execution immediately stops, and the CLR looks to see if there is a handler in Func2( ). There is not, and so the runtime unwinds the stack (never printing the exit statement) to Func1( ). Again, there is no handler, and the runtime unwinds the stack back to Main( ). With no exception handler there, the default handler is called, which prints the error message.

The Try and Catch Statements

To handle exceptions you take the following steps:

1. Execute any code that you suspect might throw an exception (such as code that opens a file or allocates memory) in a try block.

2. Catch any exceptions that are thrown in a catch block.

A try block is created with the keyword Try, and is ended with the keywords End Try. A catch block is created using the keyword Catch. A catch block can be terminated either by the next use of the Catch keyword or by the End Try statement. Example 11-2 illustrates these constructs. Note that Example 11-2 is the same as Example 11-1 except that a try/catch block has been added.

Example 11-2. Try and catch blocks

```
Option Strict On
Imports System
Namespace ExceptionHandling

    Class Tester

        Shared Sub Main( )
            Console.WriteLine("Enter Main...")
            Dim t As New Tester( )
            t.Run( )
            Console.WriteLine("Exit Main...")
        End Sub 'Main

        Public Sub Run( )
            Console.WriteLine("Enter Run...")
            Func1( )
            Console.WriteLine("Exit Run...")
        End Sub 'Run


        Public Sub Func1( )
            Console.WriteLine("Enter Func1...")
            Func2( )
            Console.WriteLine("Exit Func1...")
        End Sub 'Func1

        Public Sub Func2( )
            Console.WriteLine("Enter Func2...")
            Try
                Console.WriteLine("Entering Try block...")
                Throw New System.Exception( )
                Console.WriteLine("Exititg Try block...")
            Catch
                Console.WriteLine("Exception caught and handled")
            End Try
            Console.WriteLine("Exit func2...")
        End Sub 'Func2

    End Class 'Tester

End Namespace 'ExceptionHandling

Output:
Enter Main...
Enter Run...
Enter Func1...
Enter Func2...
Entering try block...
Exception caught and handled!
Exit Func2...
Exit Func1...
Exit Run...
Exit Main...
```

Following the Try statement in Example 11-2 is a generic Catch statement. The Catch statement is generic because you haven't specified what kind of exceptions to catch. If you don't specify a particular exception type, the catch block will catch any exceptions that are thrown. Using Catch statements to catch specific types of exceptions is discussed later in this chapter.

Notice that the Exit Func* statements are now written. With the exception handled, execution resumes immediately after the catch statement.

In Example 11-2, the Catch statement simply reports that the exception has been caught and handled. In a real Catch statement, you might take corrective action to fix the problem that caused an exception to be thrown. For example, if the user is trying to open a read-only file, you might invoke a method that allows the user to change the attributes of the file. If the program has run out of memory, you might give the user an opportunity to close other applications. If all else fails, the catch block can print an error message so that the user knows what went wrong.

How the Call Stack Works

Examine the output of Example 11-2 carefully. You see the code enter Main(), Func1(), Func2(), and the try block. You never see it exit the try block, though it does exit Func2(), Func1(), and Main(). What happened?

When the exception is thrown, execution halts immediately and is handed to the catch block. It *never* returns to the original code path. It never gets to the line that prints the Exit statement for the try block. The catch block handles the error, and then execution falls through to the code following the catch block.

Because there is a catch block, the stack does not need to unwind. The exception is now handled; there are no more problems, and the program continues. This becomes a bit clearer if you move the try/catch blocks up to Func1(), as shown in Example 11-3.

Example 11-3. Unwinding the stack one level

```
Option Strict On
Imports System

Namespace ExceptionHandling

    Class Tester

        Shared Sub Main( )
            Console.WriteLine("Enter Main...")
            Dim t As New Tester( )
            t.Run( )
            Console.WriteLine("Exit Main...")
        End Sub 'Main
```

Example 11-3. Unwinding the stack one level (continued)

```
Public Sub Run()
    Console.WriteLine("Enter Run...")
    Func1()
    Console.WriteLine("Exit Run...")
End Sub 'Run


Public Sub Func1()
    Console.WriteLine("Enter func1...")
    Try
        Console.WriteLine("Entering Try block...")
        Func2()
        Console.WriteLine("Exiting Try block...")
    Catch
        Console.WriteLine("Exception caught and handled")
    End Try
    Console.WriteLine("Exit func1...")
End Sub 'Func1

Public Sub Func2()
    Console.WriteLine("Enter Func2...")
    Throw New System.Exception()
    Console.WriteLine("Exit Func2...")
End Sub 'Func2

    End Class 'Tester
End Namespace 'ExceptionHandling

Output:
Enter Main...
Enter Run...
Enter Func1...
Entering try block...
Enter Func2...
Exception caught and handled!
Exit Func1...
Exit Run...
Exit Main...
```

This time the exception is not handled in Func2(); it is handled in Func1(). When Func2() is called, it uses Console.WriteLine() to display its first milestone:

```
Enter Func2...
```

Then Func2() throws an exception and execution halts. The runtime looks for a handler in Func2(), but there isn't one. Then the stack begins to unwind, and the runtime looks for a handler in the calling function, Func1(). There is a catch block in Func1() so its code is executed; then execution resumes immediately following the Catch statement, printing the Exit statement for Func1() and then for Main().

If you're not entirely sure with why the Exiting Try Block statement and the Exit Func2 statement are not printed, try putting the code into a debugger and then stepping through it.

Creating Dedicated Catch Statements

So far, you've been working only with generic Catch statements. You can create dedicated Catch statements that handle only some exceptions and not others, based on the type of exception thrown. Example 11-4 illustrates how to specify which exception you'd like to handle.

Example 11-4. Dedicated Catch statements

```
Option Strict On
Imports System

Namespace ExceptionHandling

    Class Tester

        Public Sub Run( )
            Try
                Dim a As Double = 5
                Dim b As Double = 0
                Console.WriteLine("Dividing {0} by {1}...", a, b)
                Console.WriteLine("{0} / {1} = {2}", _
                    a, b, DoDivide(a, b))

            ' most derived exception type first
            Catch e As System.DivideByZeroException
                Console.WriteLine("DivideByZeroException caught!")

            Catch e As System.ArithmeticException
                Console.WriteLine("ArithmeticException caught!")

            ' generic exception type last
            Catch
                Console.WriteLine("Unknown exception caught")
            End Try
        End Sub

        ' do the division if legal
        Public Function DoDivide(ByVal a As Double, ByVal b As Double) As Double
            If b = 0 Then
                Throw New System.DivideByZeroException( )
            End If
            If a = 0 Then
                Throw New System.ArithmeticException( )
            End If
            Return a / b
        End Function
```

Example 11-4. Dedicated Catch statements (continued)

```
        Public Shared Sub Main( )
            Console.WriteLine("Enter Main...")
            Dim t As Tester = New Tester( )
            t.Run( )
            Console.WriteLine("Exit Main...")
        End Sub

    End Class
End Namespace
```

```
Output:
Enter Main...
Dividing 5 by 0...
DivideByZeroException caught!
Exit Main...
```

In Example 11-4, the DoDivide( ) method will not let you divide zero by another number, nor will it let you divide a number by zero. If you try to divide by zero, it throws an instance of DivideByZeroException. If you try to divide zero by another number, there is no appropriate exception: dividing zero by another number is a legal mathematical operation and shouldn't throw an exception at all. However, for the sake of this example, assume you don't want to allow division of zero by any number; you will throw an ArithmeticException.

When the exception is thrown, the runtime examines each exception handler in the order in which they appear in the code and matches the first one it can. When you run this with a=5 and b=7, the output is:

```
    5 / 7 = 0.7142857142857143
```

As you'd expect, no exception is thrown. However, when you change the value of a to 0, the output is:

```
    ArithmeticException caught!
```

The exception is thrown, and the runtime examines the first exception, Divide-ByZeroException. Because this does not match, it goes on to the next handler, ArithmeticException, which does match.

In a final pass through, suppose you change a to 7 and b to 0. This throws the DivideByZeroException.

 You have to be particularly careful with the order of the Catch statements because the DivideByZeroException is derived from ArithmeticException. If you reverse the catch statements, the DivideByZeroException will match the ArithmeticException handler, and the exception will never get to the DivideByZeroException handler. In fact, if their order is reversed, it will be impossible for *any* exception to reach the DivideByZeroException handler.

Typically, a method will catch every exception it can anticipate for the code it is running. However, it is possible to distribute your try/catch statements, catching some specific exceptions in one function and more generic exceptions in higher, calling functions. Your design goals should dictate the exact design.

Assume you have a Method A that calls another Method B, which in turn calls Method C, which calls Method D, which then calls Method E. Method E is deep in your code, while Methods B and A are higher up. If you anticipate that Method E might throw an exception, you should create a try/catch block deep in your code to catch that exception as close as possible to the place where the problem arises. You might also want to create more general exception handlers higher up in the code in case unanticipated exceptions slip by.

The Finally Statement

In some instances, throwing an exception and unwinding the stack can create a problem. For example, if you have opened a file or otherwise committed a resource, you might need an opportunity to close the file or flush the buffer.

If you *must* take some action, such as closing a file, regardless of whether an exception is thrown, you have two strategies to choose from. One approach is to enclose the dangerous action in a try block and then to close the file in both the catch and try blocks. However, this is an ugly duplication of code, and it's error prone. VB.NET provides a better alternative in the finally block.

The code in the finally block is guaranteed to be executed regardless of whether an exception is thrown. You begin a finally block with the keyword Finally and end it with the End Try statement.

A finally block can be created with or without catch blocks, but a finally block requires a try block to execute. It is an error to exit a finally block with Exit, Throw, Return, or Goto. The TestFunc() method in Example 11-5 simulates opening a file as its first action. The method then undertakes some mathematical operations, and then the file is closed.

It is possible that some time between opening and closing the file an exception will be thrown. If this were to occur, it would be possible for the file to remain open. The developer knows that no matter what happens, at the end of this method the file should be closed, so the file close function call is moved to a finally block, where it will be executed regardless of whether an exception is thrown. Example 11-5 uses a finally block.

Example 11-5. Finally block

```
Option Strict On
Imports System

Namespace ExceptionHandling
```

Example 11-5. Finally block (continued)

```
Class Tester

    Public Sub Run()
        Try
            Console.WriteLine("Open file here")
            Dim a As Double = 5
            Dim b As Double = 0
            Console.WriteLine("{0} / {1} = {2}", a, b, DoDivide(a, b))
            Console.WriteLine("This line may or may not print")

            ' most derived exception type first
        Catch e As System.DivideByZeroException
            Console.WriteLine("DivideByZeroException caught!")

        Catch
            Console.WriteLine("Unknown exception caught!")

        Finally
            Console.WriteLine("Close file here.")

        End Try
    End Sub 'Run

    ' do the division if legal
    Public Function DoDivide( _
        ByVal a As Double, ByVal b As Double) As Double

        If b = 0 Then
            Throw New System.DivideByZeroException()
        End If

        If a = 0 Then
            Throw New System.ArithmeticException()
        End If

        Return a / b
    End Function 'DoDivide

    Shared Sub Main()
        Console.WriteLine("Enter Main...")
        Dim t As New Tester()
        t.Run()
        Console.WriteLine("Exit Main...")
    End Sub 'Main
End Class 'Tester
End Namespace 'ExceptionHandling

Output:
Enter Main...
Open file here
DivideByZeroException caught!
Close file here.
Exit Main...
```

In Example 11-5, one of the catch blocks from Example 11-4 has been eliminated to save space, and a finally block has been added. Whether or not an exception is thrown, the finally block is executed; thus in both examples the following message is output:

```
Close file here.
```

Exception Class Methods and Properties

So far you've been using the exception as a sentinel—that is, the presence of the exception signals the errors—but you haven't touched or examined the Exception object itself. The System.Exception object provides a number of useful methods and properties.

The Message property provides information about the exception, such as why it was thrown. The Message property is read-only; the code throwing the exception can pass in the message as an argument to the exception constructor, but it cannot be modified by any method once set in the constructor.

The HelpLink property provides a link to the help file associated with the exception. This property is read/write. In Example 11-6, the Exception.HelpLink property is set and retrieved to provide information to the user about the DivideByZeroException. It is generally a good idea to provide a help link file for any exceptions you create, so that the user can learn how to correct the exceptional circumstance.

The read-only StackTrace property is set by the runtime. This property is used to provide a stack trace for the error statement. A stack trace displays the call stack: the series of method calls that lead to the method in which the exception was thrown.

Example 11-6. Inside the Exception class

```
Option Strict On
Imports System

Namespace ExceptionHandling
    Class Tester

        Public Sub Run()
            Try
                Console.WriteLine("Open file here")
                Dim a As Double = 5
                Dim b As Double = 0
                Console.WriteLine("{0} / {1} = {2}", a, b, DoDivide(a, b))
                Console.WriteLine("This line may or may not print")

            ' most derived exception type first
            Catch e As System.DivideByZeroException
                Console.WriteLine( _
                    "DivideByZeroException! Msg: {0}", e.Message)
                Console.WriteLine( _
```

Example 11-6. Inside the Exception class (continued)

```vbnet
                    "Helplink: {0}", e.HelpLink)
                Console.WriteLine( _
                    "Stack trace: {0}", e.StackTrace)

            Catch
                Console.WriteLine("Unknown exception caught!")

            Finally
                Console.WriteLine("Close file here.")

            End Try
        End Sub 'Run

        ' do the division if legal
        Public Function DoDivide( _
            ByVal a As Double, ByVal b As Double) As Double
            If b = 0 Then
                Dim e as new System.DivideByZeroException()
               e.HelpLink = "http://www.LibertyAssociates.com"
                Throw e
            End If
            If a = 0 Then
                Throw New System.ArithmeticException()
            End If
            Return a / b
        End Function 'DoDivide

        Shared Sub Main()
            Console.WriteLine("Enter Main...")
            Dim t As New Tester()
            t.Run()
            Console.WriteLine("Exit Main...")
        End Sub 'Main
    End Class 'Tester
End Namespace 'ExceptionHandling
```

```
Output:
Enter Main...
Open file here

DivideByZeroException! Msg: Attempted to divide by zero.

HelpLink: http://www.libertyassociates.com

Stack trace:
at ExceptionHandling.Tester.DoDivide(Double a, Double b) in ...Module1.vb:line 38
   at ExceptionHandling.Tester.Run() in ...Module1.vb:line 10

Close file here.
Exit Main...
```

In the output of Example 11-6, the stack trace lists the methods in the reverse order in which they were called; by reviewing this order, you can infer that the error occurred in DoDivide(), which was called by Run(). When methods are deeply nested, the stack trace can help you understand the order of method calls and thus track down the point at which the exception occurred.

In this example, rather than simply throwing a DivideByZeroException, you create a new instance of the exception:

```
Dim e As New System.DivideByZeroException( )
Throw e
```

You do not pass in a custom message, and so the default message will be printed:

DivideByZeroException! Msg: **Attempted to divide by zero.**

If you want, you can modify this line of code to pass in a custom message:

```
Dim e As New System.DivideByZeroException( _
   "You tried to divide by zero which is not meaningful")
```

In this case, the output message will reflect the custom message:

```
DivideByZeroException! Msg:
You tried to divide by zero which is not
meaningful
```

Before throwing the exception, you set the HelpLink property:

```
e.HelpLink = "http://www.libertyassociates.com"
```

When this exception is caught, the program prints both the message and the Help-Link:

```
Catch e As System.DivideByZeroException
    Console.WriteLine( _
       "DivideByZeroException! Msg: {0}", e.Message)
    Console.WriteLine( _
        "Helplink: {0}", e.HelpLink)
```

The Message and HelpLink properties allow you to provide useful information to the user. The exception handler also prints the StackTrace by getting the StackTrace property of the exception object:

```
Console.WriteLine( _
    "Stack trace: {0}", e.StackTrace)
```

The output of this call reflects a full StackTrace leading to the moment the exception was thrown. In this case, only two methods were executed before the exception, DoDivide() and Run():

```
Stack trace:
  at ExceptionHandling.Tester.DoDivide(Double a, Double b) in Module1.vb:line 38
   at ExceptionHandling.Tester.Run( ) in Module1.vb:line 10
```

Note that I've shortened the pathnames; your printout might look a little different.

Custom Exceptions

The intrinsic exception types the CLR provides, coupled with the custom messages shown in the previous example, will often be all you need to provide extensive information to a catch block when an exception is thrown.

There will be times, however, when you want to provide more extensive information to or need special capabilities in your exception. It is a trivial matter to create your own *custom exception* class; the only restriction is that it must derive (directly or indirectly) from System.ApplicationException. Example 11-7 illustrates the creation of a custom exception.

Example 11-7. Custom exceptions

```
Option Strict On
Imports System

Namespace ExceptionHandling
    ' custom exception class

    Public Class MyCustomException
        Inherits System.ApplicationException

        Public Sub New(ByVal message As String)
            ' pass the message up to the base class
            MyBase.New(message)
        End Sub 'New

    End Class 'MyCustomException


    Class Tester

        Public Sub Run()
            Try
                Console.WriteLine("Open file here")
                Dim a As Double = 0
                Dim b As Double = 5
                Console.WriteLine("{0} / {1} = {2}", a, b, DoDivide(a, b))
                Console.WriteLine("This line may or may not print")

            ' most derived exception type first
            Catch e As System.DivideByZeroException
                Console.WriteLine( _
                    "DivideByZeroException! Msg: {0}", e.Message)
                Console.WriteLine("HelpLink: {0}", e.HelpLink)

            ' catch custom exception
            Catch e As MyCustomException
                Console.WriteLine( _
                    "MyCustomException! Msg: {0}", e.Message)
                Console.WriteLine("HelpLink: {0}", e.HelpLink)
```

Example 11-7. Custom exceptions (continued)

```
                Catch ' catch any uncaught exceptions
                    Console.WriteLine("Unknown exception caught")
                Finally
                    Console.WriteLine("Close file here.")
                End Try
            End Sub 'Run


        ' do the division if legal
        Public Function DoDivide( _
            ByVal a As Double, ByVal b As Double) As Double
            If b = 0 Then
                Dim e As New DivideByZeroException( )
                e.HelpLink = "http://www.libertyassociates.com"
                Throw e
            End If
            If a = 0 Then
                ' create a custom exception instance
                Dim e As New _
                    MyCustomException("Can't have zero divisor")
                e.HelpLink = _
                    "http://www.libertyassociates.com/NoZeroDivisor.htm"
                Throw e
            End If
            Return a / b
        End Function 'DoDivide

        Shared Sub Main( )
            Console.WriteLine("Enter Main...")
            Dim t As New Tester( )
            t.Run( )
            Console.WriteLine("Exit Main...")
        End Sub 'Main

    End Class 'Tester

End Namespace 'ExceptionHandling

Output:
Enter Main...
Open file here
MyCustomException! Msg: Can't have zero divisor
HelpLink: http://www.libertyassociates.com/NoZeroDivisor.htm
Close file here.
Exit Main...
```

MyCustomException is derived from System.ApplicationException and consists of nothing more than a constructor that takes a string message that it passes to its base class.

Remember that constructors can not be inherited, so every derived class must have its own constructor.

The advantage of creating this custom exception class is that it better reflects the particular design of the Test class, in which it is not legal to have a zero divisor. Using the ArithmeticException rather than a custom exception would work as well, but it might confuse other programmers because a zero divisor wouldn't normally be considered an arithmetic error.

Rethrowing Exceptions

You might want your catch block to take some initial corrective action and then rethrow the exception to an outer try block (in a calling function). It might rethrow the *same* exception, or it might throw a different one. If it throws a different one, it may want to embed the original exception inside the new one so that the calling method can understand the exception history. The InnerException property of the new exception retrieves the original exception.

Because the InnerException is also an exception, it too might have an inner exception. Thus, an entire chain of exceptions can be nested one within the other, much like Ukrainian dolls are contained one within the other. Example 11-8 illustrates.

Example 11-8. Rethrowing and inner exceptions

```
Option Strict On
Imports System

Namespace Programming_VBNET
    Public Class MyCustomException
        Inherits System.ApplicationException

        Public Sub New(ByVal message As String, ByVal inner As Exception)
            MyBase.New(message, inner)
        End Sub 'New
    End Class 'MyCustomException

    Public Class Test

        Public Shared Sub Main()
            Dim t As New Test()
            t.TestFunc()
        End Sub 'Main

        Public Sub TestFunc()
            Try
                DangerousFunc1()
```

Example 11-8. Rethrowing and inner exceptions (continued)

```
                  ' if you catch a custom exception
                  ' print the exception history
          Catch e As MyCustomException
              Console.WriteLine(ControlChars.Lf + "{0}", e.Message)
              Console.WriteLine("Retrieving exception history...")
              Dim inner As Exception = e.InnerException
              While Not (inner Is Nothing)
                  Console.WriteLine("{0}", inner.Message)
                  inner = inner.InnerException
              End While
          End Try
      End Sub 'TestFunc

      Public Sub DangerousFunc1( )
          Try
              DangerousFunc2( )

              ' if you catch any exception here
              ' throw a custom exception
          Catch e As System.Exception
              Dim ex As New MyCustomException( _
              "E3 - Custom Exception Situation!", e)
              Throw ex
          End Try
      End Sub 'DangerousFunc1

      Public Sub DangerousFunc2( )
          Try
              DangerousFunc3( )

              ' if you catch a DivideByZeroException take some
              ' corrective action and then throw a general exception
          Catch e As System.DivideByZeroException
              Dim ex As New Exception( _
                  "E2 - Func2 caught divide by zero", e)
              Throw ex
          End Try
      End Sub 'DangerousFunc2

      Public Sub DangerousFunc3( )
          Try
              DangerousFunc4( )
          Catch e As System.ArithmeticException
              Throw e

          Catch e As System.Exception
              Console.WriteLine("Exception handled here!")

          End Try
      End Sub 'DangerousFunc3

      Public Sub DangerousFunc4( )
```

Example 11-8. Rethrowing and inner exceptions (continued)

```
            Throw New DivideByZeroException("E1 - DivideByZero Exception")
        End Sub 'DangerousFunc4
    End Class 'Test
End Namespace 'Programming_VBNET
Output:
E3 - Custom Exception Situation!
Retrieving exception history...
E2 - Func2 caught divide by zero
E1 - DivideByZeroException
```

Because the code in Example 11-8 has been stripped to the essentials, the output might leave you scratching your head. The best way to see how this code works is to use the debugger to step through it.

You begin by calling DangerousFunc1() in a try block:

```
Public Sub TestFunc()
    Try
        DangerousFunc1()
```

DangerousFunc1() calls DangerousFunc2(), which calls DangerousFunc3(), which in turn calls DangerousFunc4(). All these calls are in their own try blocks. At the end, DangerousFunc4() throws a DivideByZeroException. System.DivideByZeroException normally has its own error message, but you are free to pass in a custom message. Here, to make it easier to identify the sequence of events, you pass in the custom message *E1 - DivideByZeroException.*

The exception thrown in DangerousFunc4() is caught in the catch block in DangerousFunc3(). The logic in DangerousFunc3() is that if any ArithmeticException is caught (such as DivideByZeroException), it takes no action; it just rethrows the exception:

```
Public Sub DangerousFunc3()
    Try
        DangerousFunc4()
    Catch e As System.ArithmeticException
        Throw e
```

The syntax to rethrow the exact same exception (without modifying it) is just the word Throw.

The exception is thus rethrown to DangerousFunc2(), which catches it, takes some corrective action, and throws a new exception of type Exception. In the constructor to that new exception, DangerousFunc2() passes in a custom message (*E2 - Func2 caught divide by zero*) and the original exception. Thus, the original exception (E1) becomes the InnerException for the new exception (E2). DangerousFunc2() then throws this new E2 exception to DangerousFunc1().

DangerousFunc1() catches the exception, does some work, and creates a new exception of type MyCustomException, passing to the constructor a new string (*E3 - Custom Exception Situation!*) and the exception it just caught (E2). Remember, the exception it just caught is the exception with a DivideByZeroException (E1) as its inner exception. At this point, you have an exception of type MyCustomException (E3), with an inner exception of type Exception (E2), which in turn has an inner exception of type DivideByZeroException (E1). All this is then thrown to the test function, where it is caught.

When the catch function runs, it prints the message:

```
E3 - Custom Exception Situation!
```

and then drills down through the layers of inner exceptions, printing their messages:

```
Catch e As MyCustomException
    Console.WriteLine(ControlChars.Lf + "{0}", e.Message)
    Console.WriteLine("Retrieving exception history...")
    Dim inner As Exception = e.InnerException
    While Not (inner Is Nothing)
        Console.WriteLine("{0}", inner.Message)
        inner = inner.InnerException
    End While
End Try
```

The output reflects the chain of exceptions thrown and caught:

```
Retrieving exception history...
E2 - Func2 caught divide by zero
E1 - DivideByZero Exception
```

CHAPTER 12

Delegates and Events

When a head of state dies, the president of the United States typically does not have time to attend the funeral personally. Instead, he dispatches a delegate. Often this delegate is the vice president, but sometimes the VP is unavailable and the president must send someone else, such as the secretary of state or even the first lady. He does not want to "hardwire" his delegated authority to a single person; he might delegate this responsibility to anyone who is able to execute the correct international protocol.

The president defines in advance what authority will be delegated (attend the funeral), what parameters will be passed (condolences, kind words), and what value he hopes to get back (good will). He then assigns a particular person to that delegated responsibility at "runtime" as the course of his presidency progresses.

In programming, you are often faced with situations where you need to execute a particular action, but you don't know in advance which method, or even which object, you'll want to call upon to execute that action. For example, a button might know that it must notify *some* object when it is pushed, but it might not know which object or objects need to be notified. Rather than wiring the button to a particular object, you will connect the button to a *delegate* and then resolve that delegate to a particular method when the program executes.

In the early, dark and primitive days of computing, a program would begin execution and then proceed through its steps until it completed. If the user was involved, the interaction was strictly controlled and limited to filling in fields.

Today's Graphical User Interface (GUI) programming model requires a different approach, known as *event-driven programming*. A modern program presents the user interface and waits for the user to take an action. The user might take many different actions, such as choosing among menu selections, pushing buttons, updating text fields, clicking icons, and so forth. Each user action causes an event to be raised. Other events can be raised without direct user action, such as events that correspond to timer ticks of the internal clock, email being received, file-copy operations completing, etc.

An event is the encapsulation of the idea that "something happened" to which the program must respond. Events and delegates are tightly coupled concepts because flexible event handling requires that the response to the event be dispatched to the appropriate event handler. An event handler is typically implemented in Visual Basic .NET as a delegate, though this may be hidden from you by the Visual Basic .NET runtime.

In addition, delegates can be used as callbacks so that one class can say to another "do this work and when you're done, let me know." Delegates can also be used to specify methods that will only become known at runtime.

Delegates

In VB.NET, a delegate is a reference type that represents a method with a specific signature and return type. You can encapsulate any matching method in that delegate. A delegate is created with the keyword Delegate, followed by a return type and the signature of the methods that can be delegated to it, as in the following:

```
Public Delegate Function WhichIsSmaller( _
    ByVal obj1 As Object, ByVal obj2 As Object) As Comparison
```

The keyword Public declares the delegate to be a public member of the class. The keyword Function indicates that the delegate will be used to encapsulate a method that returns a value. The identifier WhichIsSmaller is the name of this delegate.

The values within the parentheses are the parameters of the methods this delegate will encapsulate, or represent. That is, this delegate may encapsulate any method that takes two objects as parameters.

The final keywords As Comparison specify the return type of the methods that can be encapsulated by this delegate, in this case an enumeration. Comparison is the identifier of the enumeration you'll define:

```
Public Enum Comparison
    theFirst = 1
    theSecond = 2
End Enum
```

The method you encapsulate with this delegate must return either Comparison.the-First or Comparison.theSecond.

In total, the statement shown previously defines a public delegate named WhichIsSmaller that encapsulates functions that take two objects as parameters, and that return an instance of the enumerated type Comparison. You can encapsulate any matching method in an instance of this delegate.

Once the delegate is defined, you can encapsulate a member method with that delegate by instantiating the delegate, passing in as a parameter the name of a method that matches the return type and signature.

Using Delegates to Specify Methods at Runtime

Suppose, for example, that you want to create a simple container class called a Pair that can hold and sort any two objects passed to it. You can't know in advance what kind of objects a Pair will hold, but by creating methods within those objects to which the sorting task can be delegated, you can delegate responsibility for determining their order to the objects themselves.

Different objects will sort differently; for example, a Pair of counter objects might sort in numeric order, while a Pair of Buttons might sort alphabetically by their name.

What a nightmare this will be for the creator of the Pair class. The class must know how each type of object sorts. If you add a Button, the Pair class must know to ask the Buttons for their names and sort them alphabetically. If you then add a pair of Employees, the Pair class must know to ask the Employees for their date of hire, and sort by date. There must be a better way!

The answer is to delegate this responsibility to the objects themselves. If the Button objects know which Button comes first and the Employee objects know which Employee comes first, then the Pair class becomes *much* more flexible. This is the essence of good object-oriented design: delegate responsibility to the class that is in the best position to have the knowledge required.

Delegating the responsibility for knowing how the objects are sorted to the objects themselves decouples the Pair class from the types contained in the Pair. The Pair no longer needs to know how the objects are sorted; it just needs to know that they *can* be sorted.

Of course, the objects you put in the Pair container must know how to tell the Pair which object comes first. The Pair container needs to specify the method these objects must implement. Rather than specifying a particular method, however, the Pair will just specify the signature and return type of the method. That is, the Pair will say, in essence, "I can hold any type of object that offers a method that takes two objects and returns an enumerated value, signifying which comes first."

You create a delegate that defines the signature and return type for the object's method. The object (e.g., Button) must provide this method with this signature in order to allow the Pair to determine which object should be first and which should be second.

In the case of our example, the Pair class defines a delegate, WhichIsSmaller. The Sort() method will take as a parameter an instance of the WhichIsSmaller delegate. When the Pair needs to know how to order its objects it will invoke the delegate, passing in its two objects as parameters. The responsibility for deciding which of the two objects is smaller (and thus comes first) to the method encapsulated by the delegate.

To test the delegate, create two classes: a Dog class and a Student class. Dogs and Students have little in common, except that they both implement methods that can be encapsulated by WhichIsSmaller; thus both Dog objects and Student objects are eligible to be held within Pair objects.

In the test program, you will create a couple of Students and a couple of Dogs, and store them in Pairs. You will then create delegate objects to encapsulate their respective methods that match the delegate signature and return type, and you'll ask the Pair objects to sort the Dog and Student objects. Example 12-1 shows a complete program illustrating the use of delegates. This is a long and somewhat complicated program that will be analyzed in detail following the output.

Example 12-1. Delegates

```
Option Strict On
Imports System

Namespace DelegatesAndEvents

    Public Enum Comparison
        theFirst = 1
        theSecond = 2
    End Enum

    ' a simple collection to hold 2 items
    Public Class Pair

        ' private array to hold the two objects
        Private thePair(2) As Object

        ' the delegate declaration
        Public Delegate Function WhichIsSmaller( _
          ByVal obj1 As Object, ByVal obj2 As Object) As Comparison

        ' passed in constructor take two objects,
        ' added in order received
        Public Sub New( _
          ByVal firstObject As Object, _
          ByVal secondObject As Object)
            thePair(0) = firstObject
            thePair(1) = secondObject
        End Sub

        ' public method which orders the two objects
        ' by whatever criteria the object likes!
        Public Sub Sort(ByVal theDelegatedFunc As WhichIsSmaller)
            If theDelegatedFunc(thePair(0), thePair(1)) = _
              Comparison.theSecond Then
                Dim temp As Object = thePair(0)
                thePair(0) = thePair(1)
                thePair(1) = temp
            End If
```

Example 12-1. Delegates (continued)

```
            End Sub

            ' public method which orders the two objects
            ' by the reverse of whatever criteria the object likes!
            Public Sub ReverseSort(ByVal theDelegatedFunc As WhichIsSmaller)
                If theDelegatedFunc(thePair(0), thePair(1)) = _
                        Comparison.theFirst Then
                    Dim temp As Object = thePair(0)
                    thePair(0) = thePair(1)
                    thePair(1) = temp
                End If
            End Sub

            ' ask the two objects to give their string value
            Public Overrides Function ToString() As String
                Return thePair(0).ToString() & ", " & thePair(1).ToString()
            End Function
        End Class

        Public Class Dog

            Private weight As Integer

            Public Sub New(ByVal weight As Integer)
                Me.weight = weight
            End Sub

            ' dogs are ordered by weight
            Public Shared Function WhichDogIsSmaller( _
              ByVal o1 As Object, ByVal o2 As Object) As Comparison
                Dim d1 As Dog = DirectCast(o1, Dog)
                Dim d2 As Dog = DirectCast(o2, Dog)
                If d1.weight > d2.weight Then
                    Return Comparison.theSecond
                Else
                    Return Comparison.theFirst
                End If
            End Function

            Public Overrides Function ToString() As String
                Return weight.ToString()
            End Function
        End Class

        Public Class Student

            Private name As String

            Public Sub New(ByVal name As String)
                Me.name = name
            End Sub
```

Example 12-1. Delegates (continued)

```
        ' students are ordered alphabetically
        Public Shared Function WhichStudentIsSmaller( _
          ByVal o1 As Object, ByVal o2 As Object) As Comparison
            Dim s1 As Student = DirectCast(o1, Student)
            Dim s2 As Student = DirectCast(o2, Student)
            If String.Compare(s1.name, s2.name) < 0 Then
                Return Comparison.theFirst
            Else
                Return Comparison.theSecond
            End If
        End Function

        Public Overrides Function ToString() As String
            Return name
        End Function
    End Class

Class Tester

    Public Sub Run()
            ' create two students and two dogs
            ' and add them to Pair objects
            Dim Jesse As New Student("Jesse")
            Dim Stacey As New Student("Stacey")
            Dim Milo As New Dog(65)
            Dim Fred As New Dog(12)

            Dim studentPair As New Pair(Jesse, Stacey)
            Dim dogPair As New Pair(Milo, Fred)
            Console.WriteLine("studentPair: {0}", _
                studentPair.ToString())
            Console.WriteLine("dogPair: {0}", _
                dogPair.ToString())

            ' Instantiate  the delegates
            Dim theStudentDelegate As New _
              Pair.WhichIsSmaller(AddressOf Student.WhichStudentIsSmaller)
            Dim theDogDelegate As New _
              Pair.WhichIsSmaller(AddressOf Dog.WhichDogIsSmaller)

            ' sort using the delegates
            studentPair.Sort(theStudentDelegate)
            Console.WriteLine("After Sort studentPair: {0}", _
                studentPair.ToString())
            studentPair.ReverseSort(theStudentDelegate)
            Console.WriteLine("After ReverseSort studentPair: {0}", _
                studentPair.ToString())

            dogPair.Sort(theDogDelegate)
            Console.WriteLine("After Sort dogPair: {0}", _
                dogPair.ToString())
            dogPair.ReverseSort(theDogDelegate)
```

Example 12-1. Delegates (continued)

```
            Console.WriteLine("After ReverseSort dogPair: {0}", _
                dogPair.ToString())
        End Sub

        Public Shared Sub Main()
            Dim t As New Tester()
            t.Run()
        End Sub
    End Class
End Namespace
```

Output:
```
studentPair: Jesse, Stacey
dogPair: 65, 12
After Sort studentPair: Jesse, Stacey
After ReverseSort studentPair: Stacey, Jesse
After Sort dogPair: 12, 65
After ReverseSort dogPair: 65, 12
```

Example 12-1 begins by creating a Pair constructor that takes two objects and stashes them away in a private array:

```
Public Class Pair

    Private thePair(2) As Object

    Public Sub New( _
        ByVal firstObject As Object, _
        ByVal secondObject As Object)
        thePair(0) = firstObject
        thePair(1) = secondObject
    End Sub
```

You override ToString() to obtain the string value of the two objects:

```
Public Overrides Function ToString() As String
    Return thePair(0).ToString() & ", " & thePair(1).ToString()
End Function
```

You now have two objects in your Pair and you can display their values. You're ready to sort them and display the results of the sort.

You create the delegate WhichIsSmaller that defines the signature for the sorting method, as described previously:

```
Public Delegate Function WhichIsSmaller( _
    ByVal obj1 As Object, ByVal obj2 As Object) As Comparison
```

The return value is of type Comparison, the enumeration defined earlier in the file:

```
Public Enum Comparison
    theFirst = 1
    theSecond = 2
End Enum
```

Any method that takes two objects and returns a comparison can be encapsulated by this delegate at runtime.

You can now define the Sort( ) method for the Pair class:

```
Public Sub Sort(ByVal theDelegatedFunc As WhichIsSmaller)
    If theDelegatedFunc(thePair(0), thePair(1)) = _
        Comparison.theSecond Then
        Dim temp As Object = thePair(0)
        thePair(0) = thePair(1)
        thePair(1) = temp
    End If
End Sub
```

This method takes a parameter: a delegate of type WhichIsSmaller named the-DelegatedFunc. The Sort( ) method delegates responsibility for deciding which of the two objects in the Pair comes first to the method encapsulated by that delegate. In the body of the Sort( ) method it invokes the delegated method and examines the return value, which will be one of the two enumerated values of comparison.

If the value returned is theSecond, the objects within the pair are swapped; otherwise no action is taken.

Notice that theDelegatedFunc is the name of the parameter to represent the method encapsulated by the delegate. You can assign any method (with the appropriate return value and signature) to this parameter. It is as if you had a method that took an integer as a parameter:

```
Public Function SomeMethod (myParam As Integer)
```

The parameter name is myParam, but you can pass in any integer value or variable. Similarly the parameter name in the delegate example is theDelegatedFunc, but you can pass in any method that meets the return value and signature defined by the delegate WhichIsSmaller.

Imagine you are sorting students by name. You write a method that returns Comparison.theFirst if the first student's name comes first and Comparison.theSecond if the second student's name does. If you pass in "Amy, Beth" the method will return Comparison.theFirst, and if you pass in "Beth, Amy" it will return Comparison.theSecond. If you get back Comparison.theSecond, the Sort( ) method reverses the items in its array, setting Amy to the first position and Beth to the second.

Now add one more method, ReverseSort( ), which will put the items into the array in reverse order:

```
Public Sub ReverseSort(ByVal theDelegatedFunc As WhichIsSmaller)
    If theDelegatedFunc(thePair(0), thePair(1)) = _
    Comparison.theFirst Then
        Dim temp As Object = thePair(0)
        thePair(0) = thePair(1)
        thePair(1) = temp
    End If
End Sub
```

The logic here is identical to the Sort(), except that this method performs the swap if the delegated method says that the first item comes first. Because the delegated function thinks the first item comes first, and this is a reverse sort, the result you want is for the second item to come first.

This time if you pass in "Amy, Beth," the delegated function returns Comparison. theFirst (i.e., Amy should come first), but because this is a *reverse* sort it swaps the values, setting Beth first. This allows you to use the same delegated function as you used with Sort(), without forcing the object to support a function that returns the reverse sorted value.

Now all you need are some objects to sort. You'll create two absurdly simple classes: Student and Dog. Assign Student objects a name at creation:

```
Public Class Student

    Private name As String

    Public Sub New(ByVal name As String)
        Me.name = name
    End Sub
```

The Student class requires two methods, one to override ToString() and the other to be encapsulated as the delegated method.

Student must override ToString() so that the ToString() method in Pair, which invokes ToString() on the contained objects, will work properly. The implementation does nothing more than return the student's name (which is already a string object):

```
Public Overrides Function ToString() As String
    Return name
End Function
```

It must also implement a method to which Pair.Sort() can delegate the responsibility of determining which of two objects comes first:

```
Public Shared Function WhichStudentIsSmaller( _
   ByVal o1 As Object, ByVal o2 As Object) As Comparison
    Dim s1 As Student = DirectCast(o1, Student)
    Dim s2 As Student = DirectCast(o2, Student)
    If String.Compare(s1.name, s2.name) < 0 Then
        Return Comparison.theFirst
    Else
        Return Comparison.theSecond
    End If
End Function
```

As you saw in Chapter 10, String.Compare() is a .NET Framework method on the String class that compares two strings and returns less than zero if the first is smaller, greater than zero if the second is smaller, and zero if they are the same.

Notice that the logic here returns Comparison.theFirst only if the first string is smaller; if they are the same or the second is larger, this method returns Comparison.theSecond.

Notice that the WhichStudentIsSmaller( ) method takes two objects as parameters and returns a comparison. This qualifies it to be a Pair.WhichIsSmaller delegated method, whose signature and return value it matches.

The second class is Dog. For our purposes, Dog objects will be sorted by weight, lighter dogs before heavier. Here's the complete declaration of Dog:

```
Public Class Dog

    Private weight As Integer

    Public Sub New(ByVal weight As Integer)
        Me.weight = weight
    End Sub

    ' dogs are ordered by weight
    Public Shared Function WhichDogIsSmaller( _
      ByVal o1 As Object, ByVal o2 As Object) As Comparison
        Dim d1 As Dog = DirectCast(o1, Dog)
        Dim d2 As Dog = DirectCast(o2, Dog)
        If d1.weight > d2.weight Then
            Return Comparison.theSecond
        Else
            Return Comparison.theFirst
        End If
    End Function

    Public Overrides Function ToString( ) As String
        Return weight.ToString( )
    End Function
End Class
```

Notice that the Dog class also overrides ToString( ) and implements a shared method with the correct signature for the delegate. Notice also that the Dog and Student delegate methods do not have the same name. They do not need to have the same name, as they will be assigned to the delegate dynamically at runtime.

 You can call your delegated method names anything you like, but creating parallel names (e.g., WhichDogIsSmaller and WhichStudentIsSmaller) makes the code easier to read, understand, and maintain.

The Run( ) method creates two Student objects and two Dog objects and then adds them to Pair containers. The student constructor takes a string for the student's name and the dog constructor takes an integer for the dog's weight.

```
Public Sub Run( )
    ' create two students and two dogs
    ' and add them to Pair objects
```

```
    Dim Jesse As New Student("Jesse")
    Dim Stacey As New Student("Stacey")
    Dim Milo As New Dog(65)
    Dim Fred As New Dog(12)

Dim studentPair As New Pair(Jesse, Stacey)
Dim dogPair As New Pair(Milo, Fred)
Console.WriteLine("studentPair: {0}", _
    studentPair.ToString())
Console.WriteLine("dogPair: {0}", _
    dogPair.ToString())
```

You display the contents of the two Pair containers to see the order of the objects. The output looks like this:

```
studentPair: Jesse, Stacey
dogPair: 65, 12
```

As expected, the objects are in the order in which they were added to the Pair containers. We next instantiate two delegate objects:

```
Dim theStudentDelegate As New _
    Pair.WhichIsSmaller( _
    AddressOf Student.WhichStudentIsSmaller)
Dim theDogDelegate As New _
    Pair.WhichIsSmaller( _
    AddressOf Dog.WhichDogIsSmaller)
```

The first delegate, theStudentDelegate, is created by passing in the appropriate method from the Student class. The second delegate, theDogDelegate, is passed a method from the Dog class.

Shared Versus Instance Methods

In Example 12-1, the methods you encapsulated with the delegates were shared methods of the Student and Dog class:

```
Public Shared Function WhichStudentIsSmaller( _
    ByVal o1 As Object, ByVal o2 As Object) As Comparison
```

You could declare the WhichStudentIsSmaller method to be an instance method instead:

```
Public Function WhichStudentIsSmaller( _
    ByVal o1 As Object, ByVal o2 As Object) As Comparison
```

You can still encapsulate it as a delegate, but you must refer to it through an instance, rather than through the class:

```
Dim theStudentDelegate As New _
    Pair.WhichIsSmaller(
    AddressOf Jesse.WhichStudentIsSmaller)
```

Which you use, instance or shared methods, is entirely up to you. The advantage of shared methods is that you don't need an instance of the class to create the delegate.

The delegates are now objects that can be passed to methods. You pass the delegates first to the Sort method of the Pair object, and then to the ReverseSort method:

```
studentPair.Sort(theStudentDelegate)
studentPair.ReverseSort(theStudentDelegate)

dogPair.Sort(theDogDelegate)
dogPair.ReverseSort(theDogDelegate)
```

The results are displayed on the console:

```
After Sort studentPair: Jesse, Stacey
After ReverseSort studentPair: Stacey, Jesse
After Sort dogPair: 12, 65
After ReverseSort dogPair: 65, 12
```

Shared Delegates

A disadvantage of Example 12-1 is that it forces the calling class, in this case Tester, to instantiate the delegates it needs in order to sort the objects in a Pair. Notice that in Example 12-1, within a method of Tester, you see this code:

```
Dim theStudentDelegate As New _
    Pair.WhichIsSmaller( _
    AddressOf Student.WhichStudentIsSmaller)
```

What is going on here is that the Tester class needs to know that it must instantiate an instance of the WhichIsSmaller delegate (declared in Pair), and that it must pass in the WhichStudentIsSmaller method of the Student class. Once it has created this delegate, it can invoke the sort by passing in the delegate it just created:

```
studentPair.Sort(theStudentDelegate)
```

Tester then goes on to instantiate a second delegate, passing in the WhichDogIsSmaller( ) method to create the delegate for the Dog objects, and invoking sort with that delegate as well:

```
Dim theDogDelegate As New _
    Pair.WhichIsSmaller( _
    AddressOf Dog.WhichDogIsSmaller)

dogPair.Sort(theDogDelegate)
```

Rather than forcing Tester to know which method Student and Dog must use to accomplish the sort, it would be better to get the delegate from the Student or Dog classes themselves.

You can give the implementing classes (Student and Dog) the responsibility for instantiating the delegate by giving each implementing class its own shared delegate. In that case, rather than knowing which method implements the sort for the Student, Tester would only need to know that the Student class has a shared delegate named, for example, OrderStudents; then the author of the Tester class could write:

```
studentPair.Sort(Student.OrderStudents)
```

Thus, you can modify Student to add this:

```
Public Shared ReadOnly OrderStudents As New Pair.WhichIsSmaller( _
        AddressOf Student.WhichStudentIsSmaller)
```

This creates a shared, read-only delegate named OrderStudents.

 Marking OrderStudents with the ReadOnly keyword denotes that once this shared field is created, it will not be modified.

You can create a similar delegate within Dog:

```
Public Shared ReadOnly OrderDogs As _
  New Pair.WhichIsSmaller( _
  AddressOf Dog.WhichDogIsSmaller)
```

These are now shared fields of their respective classes. Each is pre-wired to the appropriate method within the class. You can invoke delegates without declaring a local delegate instance. You just pass in the shared delegate of the class:

```
studentPair.Sort(Student.OrderStudents)
studentPair.ReverseSort(Student.OrderStudents)
```

The complete listing is shown in Example 12-2.

Example 12-2. Shared delegate members

```
Option Strict On
Imports System

Namespace DelegatesAndEvents

    Public Enum Comparison
        theFirst = 1
        theSecond = 2
    End Enum

    ' a simple collection to hold 2 items
    Public Class Pair

        ' private array to hold the two objects
        Private thePair(2) As Object

        ' the delegate declaration
        Public Delegate Function WhichIsSmaller( _
          ByVal obj1 As Object, ByVal obj2 As Object) As Comparison

        ' passed in constructor take two objects,
        ' added in order received
        Public Sub New( _
          ByVal firstObject As Object, _
          ByVal secondObject As Object)
            thePair(0) = firstObject
```

Example 12-2. Shared delegate members (continued)

```
        thePair(1) = secondObject
    End Sub


    ' public method which orders the two objects
    ' by whatever criteria the object likes!
    Public Sub Sort(ByVal theDelegatedFunc As WhichIsSmaller)
        If theDelegatedFunc(thePair(0), thePair(1)) = _
            Comparison.theSecond Then
            Dim temp As Object = thePair(0)
            thePair(0) = thePair(1)
            thePair(1) = temp
        End If
    End Sub


    ' public method which orders the two objects
    ' by the reverse of whatever criteria the object likes!
    Public Sub ReverseSort(ByVal theDelegatedFunc As WhichIsSmaller)
        If theDelegatedFunc(thePair(0), thePair(1)) = _
        Comparison.theFirst Then
            Dim temp As Object = thePair(0)
            thePair(0) = thePair(1)
            thePair(1) = temp
        End If
    End Sub


    ' ask the two objects to give their string value
    Public Overrides Function ToString() As String
        Return thePair(0).ToString() & ", " & thePair(1).ToString()
    End Function
End Class

Public Class Dog

    Private weight As Integer
    Public Shared ReadOnly OrderDogs As _
      New Pair.WhichIsSmaller( _
      AddressOf Dog.WhichDogIsSmaller)

    Public Sub New(ByVal weight As Integer)
        Me.weight = weight
    End Sub

    ' dogs are ordered by weight
    Public Shared Function WhichDogIsSmaller( _
      ByVal o1 As Object, ByVal o2 As Object) As Comparison
        Dim d1 As Dog = DirectCast(o1, Dog)
        Dim d2 As Dog = DirectCast(o2, Dog)
        If d1.weight > d2.weight Then
            Return Comparison.theSecond
        Else
            Return Comparison.theFirst
        End If
```

Example 12-2. Shared delegate members (continued)

```
        End Function

        Public Overrides Function ToString( ) As String
            Return weight.ToString( )
        End Function
    End Class

Public Class Student

    Private name As String

    Public Shared ReadOnly OrderStudents As _
      New Pair.WhichIsSmaller( _
      AddressOf Student.WhichStudentIsSmaller)

    Public Sub New(ByVal name As String)
        Me.name = name
    End Sub

    ' students are ordered alphabetically
    Public Shared Function WhichStudentIsSmaller( _
      ByVal o1 As Object, ByVal o2 As Object) As Comparison
        Dim s1 As Student = DirectCast(o1, Student)
        Dim s2 As Student = DirectCast(o2, Student)
        If String.Compare(s1.name, s2.name) < 0 Then
            Return Comparison.theFirst
        Else
            Return Comparison.theSecond
        End If
    End Function

    Public Overrides Function ToString( ) As String
        Return name
    End Function
End Class

Class Tester

    Public Sub Run( )
        ' create two students and two dogs
        ' and add them to Pair objects
        Dim Jesse As New Student("Jesse")
        Dim Stacey As New Student("Stacey")
        Dim Milo As New Dog(65)
        Dim Fred As New Dog(12)

        Dim studentPair As New Pair(Jesse, Stacey)
        Dim dogPair As New Pair(Milo, Fred)
        Console.WriteLine("studentPair: {0}", _
            studentPair.ToString( ))
        Console.WriteLine("dogPair: {0}", _
            dogPair.ToString( ))
```

Example 12-2. Shared delegate members (continued)

```
        ' sort using the delegates
        studentPair.Sort(Student.OrderStudents)
        Console.WriteLine("After Sort studentPair: {0}", _
            studentPair.ToString())
        studentPair.ReverseSort(Student.OrderStudents)
        Console.WriteLine("After ReverseSort studentPair: {0}", _
            studentPair.ToString())

        dogPair.Sort(Dog.OrderDogs)
        Console.WriteLine("After Sort dogPair: {0}", _
            dogPair.ToString())
        dogPair.ReverseSort(Dog.OrderDogs)
        Console.WriteLine("After ReverseSort dogPair: {0}", _
            dogPair.ToString())
    End Sub

    Public Shared Sub Main()
        Dim t As New Tester()
        t.Run()
    End Sub
  End Class
End Namespace
```

The output from this modified listing (Example 12-2) is identical to the output for Example 12-1.

Delegates as Properties

The problem with shared delegates is that they must be instantiated—whether or not they are ever used—as with Student and Dog in the previous example. You can improve these classes by changing the shared delegate fields to properties.

For Student, take out the declaration:

```
Public Shared ReadOnly OrderStudents As _
    New Pair.WhichIsSmaller( _
    AddressOf Student.WhichStudentIsSmaller)
```

and replace it with the following:

```
Public Shared ReadOnly Property OrderStudents() _
    As Pair.WhichIsSmaller
    Get
        Return New Pair.WhichIsSmaller( _
            AddressOf WhichStudentIsSmaller)
    End Get
End Property
```

Similarly, you replace the Dog shared field with:

```
Public Shared ReadOnly Property OrderDogs() _
    As Pair.WhichIsSmaller
    Get
```

```
        Return New Pair.WhichIsSmaller( _
        AddressOf WhichDogIsSmaller)
    End Get
End Property
```

The assignment of the delegates is unchanged:

```
studentPair.Sort(Student.OrderStudents)
dogPair.Sort(Dog.OrderDogs)
```

When the OrderStudent property is accessed, the delegate is created:

```
Return New Pair.WhichIsSmaller( _
    AddressOf WhichStudentIsSmaller)
```

The key advantage is that the delegate is not created until it is requested. This allows the Tester class to determine when it needs a delegate but still allows the details of the creation of the delegate to be the responsibility of the Student (or Dog) class.

Multicasting

At times it is desirable to *multicast*, or call two implementing methods through a single delegate. You accomplish multicasting by encapsulating the various methods in delegates. Then you combine the delegates using the Delegate.Combine() shared method. The Combine() method takes an array of delegates as a parameter and returns a new delegate that represents the combination of all the delegates in the array.

To see how this works, create a simplistic class that declares a delegate:

```
Public Class MyClassWithDelegate
    ' the delegate declaration
    Public Delegate Sub StringDelegate(ByVal s As String)
End Class
```

Then create a class (MyImplementingClass) that implements a number of methods that match the StringDelegate:

```
Public Class MyImplementingClass

    Public Shared Sub WriteString(ByVal s As String)
        Console.WriteLine("Writing string {0}", s)
    End Sub

    Public Shared Sub LogString(ByVal s As String)
        Console.WriteLine("Logging string {0}", s)
    End Sub

    Public Shared Sub TransmitString(ByVal s As String)
        Console.WriteLine("Transmitting string {0}", s)
    End Sub
End Class
```

Within the Run() method of your Tester class, you'll instantiate three StringDelegate objects (Writer, Logger, Transmitter):

```
Dim Writer, Logger, Transmitter As MyClassWithDelegate.StringDelegate
```

You instantiate these delegates by passing in the address of the methods you wish to encapsulate:

```
Writer = New MyClassWithDelegate.StringDelegate( _
    AddressOf MyImplementingClass.WriteString)
Logger = New MyClassWithDelegate.StringDelegate( _
    AddressOf MyImplementingClass.LogString)
Transmitter = New MyClassWithDelegate.StringDelegate( _
    AddressOf MyImplementingClass.TransmitString)
```

You next instantiate a multicast delegate (myMulticastDelegate) that you'll use to combine the three other delegates:

```
Dim myMulticastDelegate As MyClassWithDelegate.StringDelegate
```

Next you create an array of the first two delegates:

```
Dim arr() As MyClassWithDelegate.StringDelegate = {Writer, Logger}
```

and use that array to instantiate the multicast delegate:

```
myMulticastDelegate = _
    DirectCast(System.Delegate.Combine(arr), _
      MyClassWithDelegate.StringDelegate)
```

DirectCast is used to cast the result of calling Combine() to the specialized type MyClassWithDelegate.StringDelegate, because Combine returns an object of the more general type Delegate.

Then you can add the third delegate to the collection by calling the overloaded Combine() method, this time passing in the existing multicast delegate and the new delegate to add:

```
myMulticastDelegate = _
    DirectCast(System.Delegate.Combine(myMulticastDelegate, Transmitter), _
    MyClassWithDelegate.StringDelegate)
```

You can remove just the Logger delegate by calling the static method Remove(), passing in the multicast delegate and the delegate you wish to remove. The return value is a Delegate, which you cast to a StringDelegate and assign back to the multicast delegate:

```
myMulticastDelegate = _
    DirectCast(System.Delegate.Remove(myMulticastDelegate, Logger), _
                  MyClassWithDelegate.StringDelegate)
```

Example 12-3 shows the complete code for this listing.

Example 12-3. Multicasting

```
Option Strict On
Imports System
```

Example 12-3. Multicasting (continued)

```
Namespace Multicasting

    Public Class MyClassWithDelegate
        ' the delegate declaration
        Public Delegate Sub StringDelegate(ByVal s As String)
    End Class

    Public Class MyImplementingClass

        Public Shared Sub WriteString(ByVal s As String)
            Console.WriteLine("Writing string {0}", s)
        End Sub

        Public Shared Sub LogString(ByVal s As String)
            Console.WriteLine("Logging string {0}", s)
        End Sub

        Public Shared Sub TransmitString(ByVal s As String)
            Console.WriteLine("Transmitting string {0}", s)
        End Sub
    End Class

    Class Tester

        Public Sub Run()
            ' define three StringDelegate objects
            Dim Writer, Logger, Transmitter As _
              MyClassWithDelegate.StringDelegate

            ' define another StringDelegate
            ' to act as the multicast delegate
            Dim myMulticastDelegate As MyClassWithDelegate.StringDelegate

            ' Instantiate the first three delegates,
            ' passing in methods to encapsulate
            Writer = New MyClassWithDelegate.StringDelegate( _
                AddressOf MyImplementingClass.WriteString)
            Logger = New MyClassWithDelegate.StringDelegate( _
                AddressOf MyImplementingClass.LogString)
            Transmitter = New MyClassWithDelegate.StringDelegate( _
                AddressOf MyImplementingClass.TransmitString)

            ' Define array of StringDelegates
            Dim arr() As MyClassWithDelegate.StringDelegate = _
              {Writer, Logger}

            ' Invoke the Writer delegate method
            ' vbCrLf is the VB equivalent of Environment.NewLine
            Writer("String passed to Writer" & vbCrLf)

            ' Invoke the Logger delegate method
            Logger("String passed to Logger" & vbCrLf)
```

Example 12-3. Multicasting (continued)

```
                   ' Invoke the Transmitter delegate method
                   Transmitter("String passed to Transmitter" & vbCrLf)

                   ' Tell the user you are about to combine
                   ' two delegates into the multicast delegate
                   Console.WriteLine(vbCrLf & "myMulticastDelegate = " + _
                       "Writer and Logger")

                   ' combine the two delegates, the result is
                   ' assigned to myMulticast Delegate
                   myMulticastDelegate = _
                       DirectCast(System.Delegate.Combine(arr), _
                         MyClassWithDelegate.StringDelegate)

                   ' Call the delegated methods, two methods
                   ' will be invoked
                   myMulticastDelegate("First string passed to Collector")

                   ' Tell the user you are about to add
                   ' a third delegate to the multicast
                   Console.WriteLine(vbCrLf & _
                       "myMulticastDelegate Adds Transmitter")

                   ' add the third delegate
                   myMulticastDelegate = _
                       DirectCast(System.Delegate.Combine(myMulticastDelegate, _
                           Transmitter), _
                           MyClassWithDelegate.StringDelegate)

                   ' invoke the three delegated methods
                   myMulticastDelegate("Second string passed to Collector")

                   ' tell the user you are about to remove
                   ' the logger delegate
                   Console.WriteLine(vbCrLf & "myMulticastDelegate -= Logger")

                   ' remove the logger delegate
                   myMulticastDelegate = _
                       DirectCast(System.Delegate.Remove(myMulticastDelegate, _
                           Logger),  MyClassWithDelegate.StringDelegate)

                   ' invoke the two remaining
                   ' delegated methods
                   myMulticastDelegate("Third string passed to Collector")
               End Sub

           Public Shared Sub Main()
               Dim t As New Tester()
               t.Run()
           End Sub
       End Class
```

Example 12-3. Multicasting (continued)

```
End Namespace ' Multicasting

Output:
Writing string String passed to Writer

Logging string String passed to Logger

Transmitting string String passed to Transmitter


myMulticastDelegate = Writer and Logger
Writing string First string passed to Collector
Logging string First string passed to Collector

myMulticastDelegate Adds Transmitter
Writing string Second string passed to Collector
Logging string Second string passed to Collector
Transmitting string Second string passed to Collector

myMulticastDelegate -= Logger
Writing string Third string passed to Collector
Transmitting string Third string passed to Collector
```

Delegates and Callback Mechanisms

There are two ways to get your laundry done. The first way is to put your laundry into the machine, put in a few quarters and then wait for the machine to run. You wait. And then you wait. About 30 minutes later the machine stops and you take your laundry back.

The second way to get your laundry done is to take it to the Laundromat and say "Here, please clean this clothing and call me back when you are done. Here's my cell number." The person in the Laundromat does the work while you go off and do something else. When your laundry is done, they call you and say "Your clothes are clean. Your pick up number is 123." When you return, you give the person at the desk the number 123, and you get back your clean clothes.

The .NET Framework supports the notion of a "callback." (Callbacks have been in use for many years, and Windows programmers have been using callbacks at least since Win 3.x.) The idea of a callback is that you say to a method, "Do this work, and call me back when you are done." It is a simple and clean mechanism for multitasking.

The .NET Framework provides a class, FileStream, which provides asynchronous reading of a file. You do not have to create the threads yourself; FileStream will read the file for you asynchronously, and callback a method you designate when it has data for you, as illustrated in Example 12-4.

Example 12-4. Using callbacks

```
Option Strict On
Imports System
Imports System.IO
Imports System.Text

    Public Class AsynchIOTester
        Private inputStream As Stream

        ' delegated method
        Private myCallBack As AsyncCallback

        ' buffer to hold the read data
        Private buffer() As Byte

        ' the size of the buffer
        Private Const BufferSize As Integer = 256

        ' constructor
        Sub New()
            ' open the input stream
            inputStream = New FileStream( _
             "C:\temp\streams.txt", _
            FileMode.Open, _
            FileAccess.Read, _
            FileShare.ReadWrite, _
            1024, _
            True)

            ' allocate a buffer
            buffer = New Byte(BufferSize) {}

            ' assign the call back
            ' myCallBack = New AsyncCallback(AddressOf OnCompletedRead)
            myCallBack = AddressOf OnCompletedRead

        End Sub 'New

        Public Shared Sub Main()
            ' create an instance of AsynchIOTester
            ' which invokes the constructor
            Dim theApp As New AsynchIOTester()

            ' call the instance method
            theApp.Run()
        End Sub 'Main

        Sub Run()
            inputStream.BeginRead( _
            buffer, _
            0, _
            buffer.Length, _
            myCallBack, _
```

Example 12-4. Using callbacks (continued)

```
            Nothing)

            Dim i As Long
            For i = 0 To 499999
                If i Mod 1000 = 0 Then
                    Console.WriteLine("i: {0}", i)
                End If
            Next i
        End Sub 'Run

        ' call back method
        Sub OnCompletedRead(ByVal asyncResult As IAsyncResult)
            Dim bytesRead As Integer = inputStream.EndRead(asyncResult)

            ' if we got bytes, make them a string
            ' and display them, then start up again.
            ' Otherwise, we're done.
            If bytesRead > 0 Then
                Dim s As String = _
                    Encoding.ASCII.GetString(buffer, 0, bytesRead)
                Console.WriteLine(s)
                inputStream.BeginRead( _
                    buffer, 0, buffer.Length, myCallBack, Nothing)
            End If
        End Sub 'OnCompletedRead
    End class
```

In Example 12-4, you open a FileStream object, passing in the (hardwired) name of
the file, the fileMode (e.g., Open), the FileAccess flag (e.g., Read), and the FileShare
mode (e.g., ReadWrite). You also pass in an integer signifying the buffer size and a
Boolean indicating whether the FileStream should be opened asynchronously:

```
inputStream = New FileStream( _
  "C:\temp\streams.txt", _
FileMode.Open, _
FileAccess.Read, _
FileShare.ReadWrite, _
1024, _
True)
```

The FileStream object provides a method, BeginRead(), to provide asynchronous
reading of the file (reading a block of text into memory while your other code does
its work). You must pass in a buffer in which it will place your data, along with the
offset into that buffer into which it will begin reading. You pass in the length of the
buffer and you must tell BeginRead() the method you want to call back to.

You designate the method you want to call back to by passing in a delegate. You'll
create that delegate in the next example as a member of your class:

```
Private myCallBack As AsyncCallback
```

The type of the delegate was determined by the author of the FileStream class, which designated that you must pass in a Delegate of type AsyncCallback. The AsyncCallback delegate is defined in the documentation as follows:

```
Public Delegate Sub AsyncCallback( _
    ByVal ar As IAsyncResult)
```

That is, it is a subroutine (and thus returns no value) and takes as its single parameter an object that implements the interface IAsyncResult. You do not have to implement that class yourself. All you need to do is create a method that declares a parameter of type IAsyncResult. Such an object will be passed to you by the FileStream's BeginRead() method, and you will use it as a token that you will return to the FileStream by calling EndRead(). Here is the declaration of the OnCompletedRead() method, which you'll encapsulate in your AsyncCallback delegate:

```
Sub OnCompletedRead(ByVal asyncResult As IAsyncResult)
    '...
End Sub 'OnCompletedRead
```

You instantiate the delegate in the constructor to your class:

```
myCallBack = New AsyncCallback(AddressOf OnCompletedRead)
```

As an alternative, you can simply write:

```
myCallBack = AddressOf OnCompletedRead
```

and the compiler will figure out that you are instantiating an AsyncCallback delegate based on the declared type of myCallBack.

You are now ready to start the callback process. You begin in your test class's Run() method by calling BeginRead():

```
Sub Run( )
    inputStream.BeginRead( _
    buffer, _
    0, _
    buffer.Length, _
    myCallBack, _
    Nothing)
```

The first parameter is a buffer, declared in this case as a member variable:

```
Private buffer( ) As Byte
```

The second parameter (0) is the offset into that buffer. By entering 0, the data read from the disk will be written to the buffer starting at offset 0. The third parameter is the length of the buffer. The fourth parameter is the one we care about: the AsyncCallBack delegate you declared and instantiated earlier. The fifth and final parameter is a state object. The state object can be any object you want; typically it is used to hold the current state of your calling object. In the case shown, you pass Nothing, a VB.NET keyword that indicates that you have no state object.

After you call BeginRead(), you go on with your other work. In Example 12-4, that work is simulated by counting to half a million:

```
Dim i As Long
For i = 0 To 499999
    If i Mod 1000 = 0 Then
        Console.WriteLine("i: {0}", i)
    End If
Next i
```

The FileStream will go off and open the file on your behalf. It will then read from the file and fill your buffer. When it is ready for you to process the data, it will interrupt your work in Run(), and will call the method you encapsulated with the delegate. You will remember that the delegated method is called OnCompletedRead():

```
Sub OnCompletedRead(ByVal asyncResult As IAsyncResult)
    Dim bytesRead As Integer = inputStream.EndRead(asyncResult)

    ' if we got bytes, make them a string
    ' and display them, then start up again.
    ' Otherwise, we're done.
    If bytesRead > 0 Then
        Dim s As String = Encoding.ASCII.GetString(buffer, 0, bytesRead)
        Console.WriteLine(s)
        inputStream.BeginRead(buffer, 0, buffer.Length, myCallBack, Nothing)
    End If
```

When the FileStream calls your method, it will pass in an instance of a class that implements the IAsyncResult interface. The first thing you do in this method is pass that IAsyncResult object to the FileStream's EndRead() method. EndRead() returns an integer indicating the number of bytes successfully read from the file. If that value is greater than zero, your buffer has data in it.

The buffer is a buffer of bytes, but you need a string to display. To convert the buffer to a string, you will call Encoding.ASCII.GetString()—a shared method that will take your buffer, an offset, and the number of bytes read and return an ASCII string. You can then display that string to the console.

Finally, you'll call BeginRead() again, passing back the buffer, the offset (again 0), the length of the buffer, and the delegate, as well as Nothing for the state object. This begins another round. Control will return to the Run() method, and you will continue counting.

The effect is that you ping-pong back and forth between the work you are doing in Run() (counting to 500,000) and the work you are doing in OnCompletedRead(). You have achieved multitasking without instantiating or managing any threads; you have only to write the callback mechanism and let the FileStream do the thread management for you.

Events

Today's Graphical User Interface programming model requires *event-driven programming*. A GUI program waits for the user to take an action, such as choosing among menu selections, pushing buttons, updating text fields, clicking icons, and so forth. Each action causes an event to be raised. Other events can be raised without direct user action, such as events that correspond to timer ticks of the internal clock, email being received, file-copy operations completing, etc.

An event is the encapsulation of the idea that "something happened" to which the program must respond.

In a GUI environment, any number of widgets can *raise* an event. For example, when you click a button, it might raise the Click event. When you add to a drop-down list, it might raise a ListChanged event.

Other classes will be interested in responding to these events. How they respond is not of interest to the class raising the event. The button says, "I was clicked," and the responding classes react appropriately.

Publishing and Subscribing

In VB.NET, any object can *publish* a set of events to which other classes can *subscribe*. When the publishing class raises an event, all the subscribed classes are notified.

> This design is similar to the Publish/Subscribe (Observer) Pattern described in the seminal work *Design Patterns* by Gamma, et al. (Addison-Wesley). Gamma describes the intent of this pattern: "Define a one to many dependency between objects so that when one object changes state, all its dependents are notified and updated automatically."

With this mechanism, your object can say, "Here are things I can notify you about," and other classes might sign up, saying, "Yes, let me know when that happens." For example, a button might notify any number of interested observers when it is clicked. The button is called the *publisher* because the button publishes the Click event and the other classes are the *subscribers* because they subscribe to the Click event.

Visual Basic .NET provides extensive support for handling events such as button clicks. The Button object is declared with the keyword WithEvents. Right-click on your form, and choose View Code. Visual Studio .NET will take you to the code view of your form, as shown in Figure 12-1.

It looks like there is not much there. Notice, however, that there is a gray box with the words "Windows Form Designer generated code," and to the left of the box is a plus sign. Click on the plus sign to expand this region of code that was created by Visual Studio .NET.

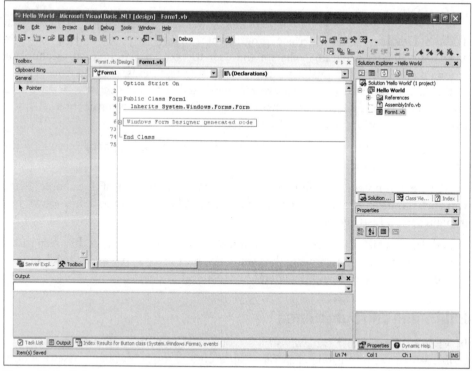

Figure 12-1. Code view

Inside this area, Visual Studio .NET has provided your class with a constructor, a Dispose() method, and various declarations. Just below the Dispose() method are the declarations of the two controls you've added to your form: the Label and the Button, as shown circled and highlighted in Figure 12-2.

Notice that the declaration of both controls includes the keyword WithEvents. This indicates that the Button will raise events. The Button class raises a number of events, as you can discover by looking up the Button class in the documentation, as shown in Figure 12-3.

The event we care about is the Click event, which is raised every time the button is clicked. Each control has a default event, and the Button's default event is Click. You can create the event handler for the default event by double-clicking on the Button from the design view.

Doing so causes Visual Studio .NET to create a skeleton event handler for you:

```
Private Sub btnChange_Click( _
     ByVal sender As System.Object, _
     ByVal e As System.EventArgs) _
         Handles btnChange.Click
End Sub
```

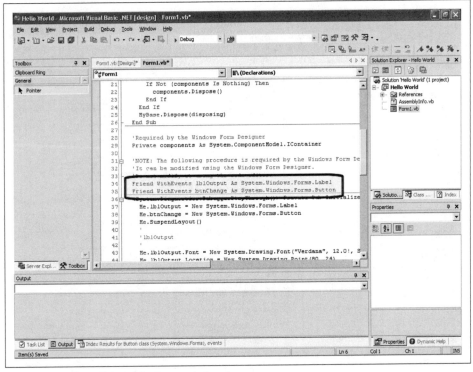

Figure 12-2. The Label and the Button declared

Every event handler takes two parameters. The first is of type Object and is called sender, by convention. This is the control that raised the event. The second is of type EventArgs (or a class derived from EventArgs) and is a class that contains information about the event. Often this class has no useful content, but for some events this class provides useful information for handling the event.

Finally, the method is appended with the keyword Handles followed by the event that the method is designed to handle. In this case, Visual Studio .NET has declared that the btnChange_Click method will handle the Click event for the control btnChange.

All you need do is write the code within the method for whatever is supposed to happen when the button is clicked. In this case, we'd like to change the contents of the label when the button is clicked. Add the following code to the event handler method:

```
Private Sub btnChange_Click( _
    ByVal sender As System.Object, _
    ByVal e As System.EventArgs) _
    Handles btnChange.Click

    lblOutput.Text = "Goodbye!"
    lblOutput.BackColor = Color.Blue
    lblOutput.ForeColor = Color.Yellow
End Sub
```

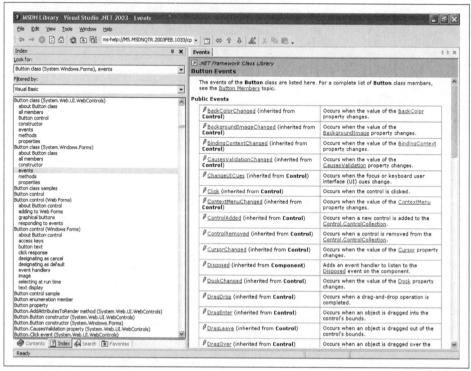

Figure 12-3. Button documentation

This code will cause the text of the label to change, along with its background color and foreground color. Run the application with Control-F5. Click on the button. Hey! Presto! The text changes, as shown in Figure 12-4.

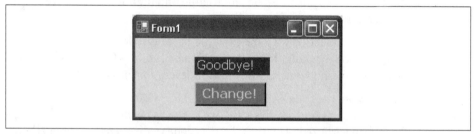

Figure 12-4. Testing the event handler

To ensure that you fully understand what is happening with this code, put a break point in the event handler and then run the program in debug mode. When you click on the button you'll see the program stop at the break point in the event handler.

Events and Delegates

An alternative to the WithEvents/Handles syntax is to add the keyword AddHandler and to use the keyword AddressOf to mark the method that handles the event.

When you write:

```
AddHandler myButton.Click, AddressOf MyButton_Click
```

what you are writing is really shorthand for:

```
AddHandler myButton.Click, New EventHandler(AddressOf MyButton_Click)
```

EventHandler is the name of the implicitly defined delegate. Every event-handling delegate in .NET is in the following form:

```
Public Delegate Event (sender as Object, e as EventArgs)
```

The first parameter, sender, represents the object raising the event, and the second parameter, e, is an EventArgs (or derived) object that may contain useful information about the event.

When you call RaiseEvent, you are calling Invoke() on EventHandler (the implicitly created delegate).

PART II

Programming with VB.NET

CHAPTER 13

Building Windows Applications

The previous chapters have used console applications to demonstrate Visual Basic .NET and the Common Language Runtime (CLR). Although console applications can be implemented simply, it is time to turn your attention to the reason you're learning the Visual Basic .NET language in the first place: building Windows and web applications.

In the early days of Windows computing, an application ran on a desktop, in splendid isolation. Over time, developers found it beneficial to spread their applications across a network, with the user interface on one computer and a database on another. This division of responsibilities or partitioning of an application came to be called two-tier or client-server application development. Later, three-tier or *n*-tier approaches emerged as developers began to use web servers to host business objects that could handle the database access on behalf of clients.

When the Web first came along, there was a clear distinction between Windows applications and web applications. Windows applications ran on the desktop or a local-area network (LAN), and web applications ran on a distant server and were accessed by a browser. This distinction is now being blurred as Windows applications reach out to the Web for services. Many new applications consist of logic running on a client, a database server, and remote third-party computers located on the Web. Traditional desktop applications such as Excel or Outlook are now able to integrate data retrieved through web connections seamlessly, and web applications can distribute some of their processing to client-side components.

The primary remaining distinction between a Windows application and a web application might be this: Who owns the user interface? Will your application use a browser to display its user interface, or will the UI be built into the executable running on the desktop?

There are enormous advantages to web applications, starting with the obvious: they can be accessed from any browser that can connect to the server. In addition, updates can be made at the server, without the need to distribute new dynamic link libraries (DLLs) to your customers.

On the other hand, if your application derives no benefit from being on the Web, you might find that you can achieve greater control over the look and feel of your application or that you can achieve better performance by building a desktop application.

.NET offers closely related, but distinguishable, suites of tools for building Windows or web applications. Both are based on forms, with the premise that many applications have user interfaces centered on interacting with the user through forms and controls such as buttons, listboxes, text, and so forth.

The tools for creating web applications are called Web Forms and are considered in Chapter 15. The tools for creating Windows applications are called Windows Forms and are the subject of this chapter.

 It is my prediction that the distinction between Web Forms and Windows Forms is temporary. There is such obvious similarity between these two approaches that I'd be very surprised if some future version of .NET didn't merge these two tools into one unified development environment.

In the following pages, you will learn how to create a simple Windows Form using either a text editor such as Notepad or the design tool in Visual Studio .NET. Next you will build a more complex Windows application using VS.NET, the Windows Forms framework, and a number of Visual Basic .NET programming techniques you learned in earlier chapters. The chapter concludes with an introduction to the deployment of .NET applications.

Creating a Simple Windows Form

A Windows Form is a tool for building a Windows application. The .NET Framework offers extensive support for Windows application development, the centerpiece of which is the Windows Forms framework. Not surprisingly, Windows Forms use the metaphor of a form. This idea was brought forward from the wildly successful Visual Basic 6 environment and supports Rapid Application Development (RAD). Visual Basic .NET marries the RAD tools of VB6 with the scalability and maintainability of a fully object-oriented language.

Using Notepad

Visual Studio .NET provides a rich set of drag-and-drop tools for working with Windows Forms. It is possible to build a Windows application without using the Visual Studio Integrated Development Environment (IDE), but it is far more painful and takes a lot longer.

However, just to prove the point, you'll use Notepad to create a simple Windows Form application: a dialog box in which you will display the words "Hello World" and a button with the text "Cancel" (see Figure 13-1). When you click on the button, the application closes.

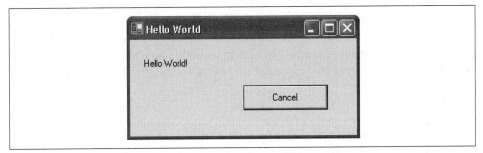

Figure 13-1. The hand-drawn Windows Form

You start by adding an `Imports` statement for the Windows Forms namespace:

```
Imports System.Windows.Forms
```

The key to creating a Windows Form application is to derive your form from System.Windows.Forms.Form:

```
Public Class HandDrawnClass
    Inherits Form
```

The Form object represents any window displayed in your application. You can use the Form class to create standard windows, as well as floating windows, tools, dialog boxes, and so forth. Microsoft apparently chose to call this a form rather than a window to emphasize that most windows now have an interactive component that includes controls for interacting with users.

All the Windows widgets you'll need (labels, buttons, list boxes, etc.) are found within the Windows.Forms namespace. In the IDE, you'll be able to drag and drop these objects onto a designer, but for now you'll declare them right in your program code.

To get started, declare the two widgets you need, a label to hold the "Hello World" text, and a button to exit the application:

```
Private lblOutput As System.Windows.Forms.Label
Private btnCancel As System.Windows.Forms.Button
```

You're now ready to instantiate these objects, which is done in the form's constructor:

```
Me.lblOutput = New System.Windows.Forms.Label( )
Me.btnCancel = New System.Windows.Forms.Button( )
```

Next you can set the form's title text to `Hello World`:

```
Me.Text = "Hello World"
```

 Note that the preceding statements appear in your form's constructor, HandDrawnClass, and so the Me keyword refers to the form itself.

Set the label's location, text, and size:

```
lblOutput.Location = New System.Drawing.Point(16, 24)
lblOutput.Text = "Hello World!"
lblOutput.Size = New System.Drawing.Size(216, 24)
```

The location is expressed as a System.Drawing.Point object, whose constructor takes a horizontal and vertical position. The size is set with a Size object, whose constructor takes a pair of integers that represent the width and height of the object.

 The .NET Framework provides the System.Drawing namespace, which encapsulates the Win32 GDI+ graphics functions. Much of the .NET Framework Class Library (FCL) consists of classes that encapsulate Win32 methods as objects.

Next, do the same for the Button object, setting its location, size, and text:

```
btnCancel.Location = New System.Drawing.Point(150, 200)
btnCancel.Size = New System.Drawing.Size(112, 32)
btnCancel.Text = "&Cancel"
```

The button also needs an event handler, which you implement with the AddHandler keyword, passing in the address of the event handling method, btnCancel_Click():

```
AddHandler btnCancel.Click, AddressOf Me.btnCancel_Click
```

This code links your event to the btnCancel_Click() method:

```
Protected Sub btnCancel_Click( _
    sender As Object, e As System.EventArgs)
    Application.Exit()
End Sub 'btnCancel_Click
```

Now you must set up the form's dimensions. The form property AutoScaleBaseSize sets the base size used at display time to compute the scaling factor for the form. The ClientSize property sets the size of the form's client area, which is the size of the form excluding borders and titlebar. (When you use the designer, these values are provided for you interactively.)

```
Me.AutoScaleBaseSize = New System.Drawing.Size(5, 13)
Me.ClientSize = New System.Drawing.Size(300, 300)
```

Finally, remember to add the widgets to the form:

```
Me.Controls.Add(Me.btnCancel)
Me.Controls.Add(Me.lblOutput)
```

That's it; you just need an entry point to invoke the constructor on the form:

```
Public Shared Sub Main()
    Application.Run(New HandDrawnClass())
End Sub 'Main
```

The complete source is shown in Example 13-1. When you run this application, the window is opened and the text is displayed. Pressing Cancel closes the application.

Example 13-1. Creating a hand-drawn Windows Form

```
Imports System.Windows.Forms

Namespace ProgVBNET
    Public Class HandDrawnClass
        Inherits Form
        ' a label to display Hello World
        Private lblOutput As System.Windows.Forms.Label

        ' a cancel button
        Private btnCancel As System.Windows.Forms.Button


        Public Sub New()
            ' create the objects
            Me.lblOutput = New System.Windows.Forms.Label()
            Me.btnCancel = New System.Windows.Forms.Button()

            ' set the form's title
            Me.Text = "Hello World"

            ' set up the output label
            lblOutput.Location = New System.Drawing.Point(16, 24)
            lblOutput.Text = "Hello World!"
            lblOutput.Size = New System.Drawing.Size(216, 24)

            ' set up the cancel button
            btnCancel.Location = New System.Drawing.Point(150, 200)
            btnCancel.Size = New System.Drawing.Size(112, 32)
            btnCancel.Text = "&Cancel"

            ' set up the event handler
            AddHandler btnCancel.Click, AddressOf Me.btnCancel_Click

            ' Add the controls and set the client area
            Me.AutoScaleBaseSize = New System.Drawing.Size(5, 13)
            Me.ClientSize = New System.Drawing.Size(300, 300)
            Me.Controls.Add(Me.btnCancel)
            Me.Controls.Add(Me.lblOutput)
        End Sub 'New


        ' handle the cancel event
        Protected Sub btnCancel_Click( _
            sender As Object, e As System.EventArgs)
            Application.Exit()
        End Sub 'btnCancel_Click


        ' Run the app
        Public Shared Sub Main()
            Application.Run(New HandDrawnClass())
        End Sub 'Main
```

Example 13-1. Creating a hand-drawn Windows Form (continued)

```
    End Class 'HandDrawnClass
End Namespace 'ProgVBNET
```

Using the Visual Studio .NET Designer

Although hand-coding is always great fun, it is also a lot of work, and the result in the previous example is not as elegant as most programmers would expect. The Visual Studio IDE provides a design tool for Windows Forms that is much easier to use.

To begin work on a new Windows application, first open Visual Studio and choose New Project. In the New Project window, create a new Visual Basic .NET Windows application and name it ProgVBNetWindowsForm, as shown in Figure 13-2.

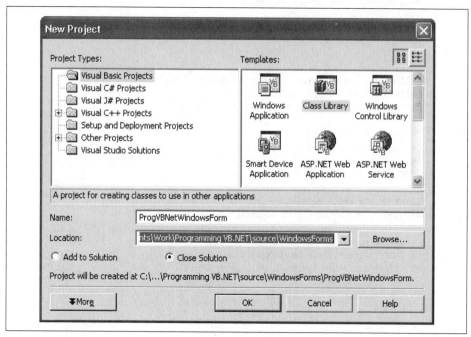

Figure 13-2. Creating a Windows Forms application

Visual Studio responds by creating a Windows Forms application and, best of all, putting you into a design environment as shown in Figure 13-3.

The Design window displays a blank Windows Form (Form1). A Toolbox window is also available, with a selection of Windows widgets and controls. If the Toolbox is not displayed, try clicking the word "Toolbox," or select View->Toolbox on the Visual Studio menu. You can also use the keyboard shortcut Ctrl-Alt-X to display the Toolbox. With the Toolbox displayed, you can drag a label and a button directly onto the form, as shown in Figure 13-4.

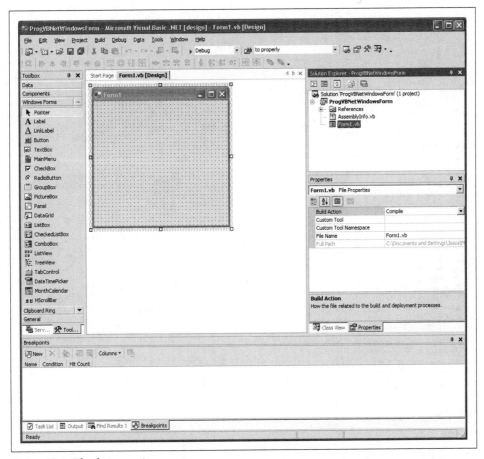

Figure 13-3. The design environment

Before proceeding, take a look around. The Toolbox is filled with controls that you can add to your Windows Forms application. In the upper-right corner you should see the Solution Explorer, a window that displays all the files in your projects. Below the Solution Explorer is the Properties window, which displays all the properties of the currently selected item. In Figure 13-4, the button (Button1) is selected, and the Properties window displays *its* properties.

You can use the Properties window to set the static properties of the various controls. For example, to add text to Label1, you can type the words "Hello World" into the box to the right of its Text property. If you want to change the font for the lettering in the "Hello World" label, you click the button on the Font property (marked with an ellipsis), as shown in Figure 13-5.

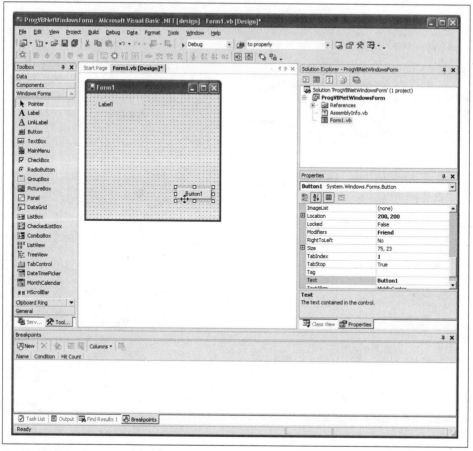

Figure 13-4. Dragging controls onto the form

Clicking the button for the Font brings up the Font dialog box, as shown in Figure 13-6.

You can provide text in the same way for your button (Button1) by selecting it in the Property window and typing the word "Change!" into its Text property. While you are at it, change the name of the button from Button1 to btnChange, as shown in Figure 13-7.

Once you have the form laid out the way you want, all that remains is to create an event handler for btnChange. Double-clicking the button will create the event handler, register it, and put you in the code editing window, where you can enter the event-handling logic, as shown in Figure 13-8. (To make it easier to read, the event handler is circled in the figure, and the very long header is broken onto multiple lines.)

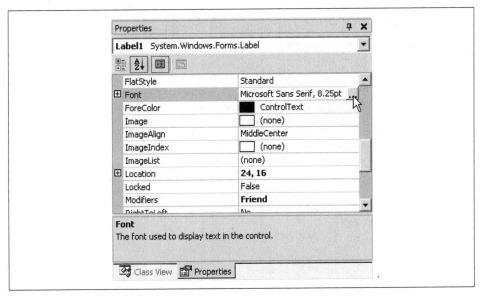

Figure 13-5. Changing the font

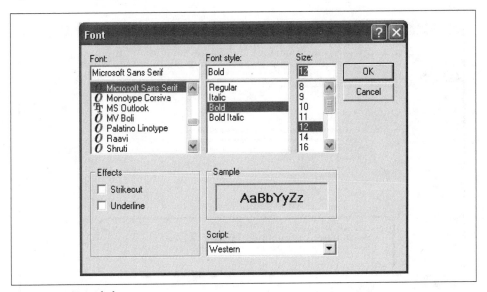

Figure 13-6. Font dialog

The cursor is already in place; you have only to enter the one line of code:

```
Label1.Text = "Goodbye!"
```

 In the IDE, the cursor flashes, making it very easy to see where the code goes. For most readers, the cursor probably will not flash in this book.

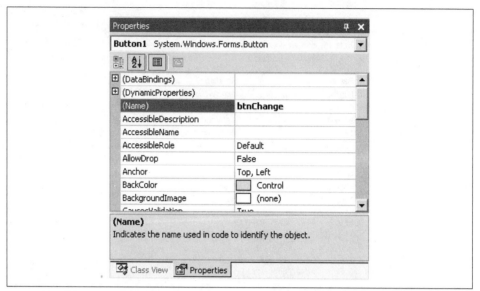

Figure 13-7. Renaming the button

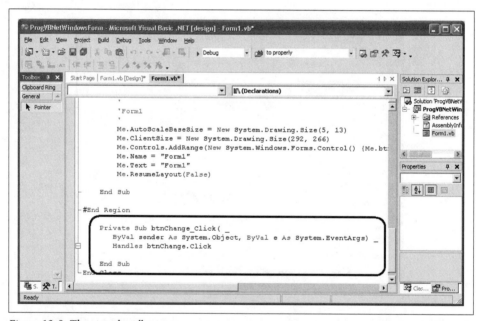

Figure 13-8. The event handler

Visual Studio .NET generates all the code necessary to create and initialize the components. The complete source code is shown in Example 13-2, including the one line of code you provided (shown in bold in this example) to handle the Change button-click event.

Example 13-2. Creating a simple windows application

```vb
Option Strict On
Imports System
Public Class Form1

Inherits System.Windows.Forms.Form

#Region " Windows Form Designer generated code "

    Public Sub New( )
        MyBase.New( )

        'This call is required by the Windows
        'Form Designer.
        InitializeComponent( )

        'Add any initialization after the
        'InitializeComponent( ) call

    End Sub

    'Form overrides dispose to clean up the
    'component list.
    Protected Overloads Overrides Sub Dispose( _
    ByVal disposing As Boolean)
        If disposing Then
            If Not (components Is Nothing) Then
                components.Dispose( )
            End If
        End If
        MyBase.Dispose(disposing)
    End Sub

    'Required by the Windows Form Designer
    Private components As System.ComponentModel.IContainer

    'NOTE: The following procedure is required by the Windows
    'Form Designer
    'It can be modified using the Windows Form Designer.
    'Do not modify it using the code editor.
    Friend WithEvents Label1 As System.Windows.Forms.Label
    Friend WithEvents btnChange As System.Windows.Forms.Button
    <System.Diagnostics.DebuggerStepThrough( )> _
    Private Sub InitializeComponent( )
        Me.Label1 = New System.Windows.Forms.Label( )
        Me.btnChange = New System.Windows.Forms.Button( )
        Me.SuspendLayout( )
        '
        'Label1
        '
        Me.Label1.Font = New System.Drawing.Font( _
        "Microsoft Sans Serif", 12.0!, System.Drawing.FontStyle.Bold, _
        System.Drawing.GraphicsUnit.Point, CType(0, Byte))
```

Example 13-2. Creating a simple windows application (continued)

```
        Me.Label1.Location = New System.Drawing.Point(24, 16)
        Me.Label1.Name = "Label1"
        Me.Label1.TabIndex = 0
        Me.Label1.Text = "Hello World"
        '
        'btnChange
        '
        Me.btnChange.Location = New System.Drawing.Point(200, 200)
        Me.btnChange.Name = "btnChange"
        Me.btnChange.TabIndex = 1
        Me.btnChange.Text = "Change!"
        '
        'Form1
        '
        Me.AutoScaleBaseSize = New System.Drawing.Size(5, 13)
        Me.ClientSize = New System.Drawing.Size(292, 266)
        Me.Controls.AddRange(New System.Windows.Forms.Control( ) _
        {Me.btnChange, Me.Label1})
        Me.Name = "Form1"
        Me.Text = "Form1"
        Me.ResumeLayout(False)

    End Sub

#End Region

    Private Sub btnChange_Click( _
        ByVal sender As System.Object, ByVal e As System.EventArgs) _
        Handles btnChange.Click
        Label1.Text = "Goodbye!"

    End Sub
End Class
```

 There is quite a bit of code in Example 13-2, though some of it is boilerplate code. Visual Studio .NET will make your life easier, but it does add quite a bit of clutter. Most of the clutter is restricted to the region marked by Visual Studio .NET as "Windows Form Designer generated code." That code will be omitted from subsequent examples to save space in the book.

Some of the code in Example 13-2 has been reformatted to fit the printed page.

The program in Example 13-2 begins by declaring a Form class, which derives from System.Windows.Forms.Form.

```
    Public Class Form1
        Inherits System.Windows.Forms.Form
```

The Form object represents any window displayed in your application. You can use the Form class to create standard windows, as well as floating windows, tools, dialog boxes, and so forth. Microsoft apparently chose to call this a form rather than a window to emphasize that most windows now have an interactive component that includes controls for interacting with users.

All the Windows widgets you'll need (labels, buttons, list boxes, etc.) are found within the Windows.Forms namespace. Visual Studio .NET declares the label and button for you:

```
Friend WithEvents Label1 As System.Windows.Forms.Label
Friend WithEvents btnChange As System.Windows.Forms.Button
```

Visual Studio .NET then goes on to initialize these objects in the InitializeComponent() method it provides, where it also sets the Location, Name, TabIndex, and Text properties of each control and the size, Name, and Text properties of the form itself:

```
Private Sub InitializeComponent()
    Me.Label1 = New System.Windows.Forms.Label()
    Me.btnChange = New System.Windows.Forms.Button()
    Me.SuspendLayout()
    '
    'Label1
    '
    Me.Label1.Font = New System.Drawing.Font( _
    "Microsoft Sans Serif", 12.0!, System.Drawing.FontStyle.Bold, _
    System.Drawing.GraphicsUnit.Point, CType(0, Byte))
    Me.Label1.Location = New System.Drawing.Point(24, 16)
    Me.Label1.Name = "Label1"
    Me.Label1.TabIndex = 0
    Me.Label1.Text = "Hello World"
    '
    'btnChange
    '
    Me.btnChange.Location = New System.Drawing.Point(200, 200)
    Me.btnChange.Name = "btnChange"
    Me.btnChange.TabIndex = 1
    Me.btnChange.Text = "Change!"
    '
    'Form1
    '
    Me.AutoScaleBaseSize = New System.Drawing.Size(5, 13)
    Me.ClientSize = New System.Drawing.Size(292, 266)
    Me.Controls.AddRange(New System.Windows.Forms.Control() _
    {Me.btnChange, Me.Label1})
    Me.Name = "Form1"
    Me.Text = "Form1"
    Me.ResumeLayout(False)

End Sub
```

The location of each control is expressed as a System.Drawing.Point object, whose constructor takes a horizontal and vertical position.

If you adjust the size of the label and button (by dragging the size handles on the form), you'll find that Visual Studio .NET will add Size properties for each control:

```
Me.Label1.Size = New System.Drawing.Size(112, 23)
Me.btnChange.Size = New System.Drawing.Size(80, 23)
```

The Size property is set with a System.Drawing.Size object, whose constructor takes a pair of integers that represent the width and height of the object.

Creating a Windows Forms Application

To see how Windows Forms can be used to create a more realistic Windows application, in this section you'll build a utility named FileCopier that copies all files from a group of directories selected by the user to a single target directory or device, such as a floppy or backup hard drive on the company network. Although you won't implement every possible feature, you can imagine programming this application so that you can mark dozens of files and have them copied to multiple disks, packing them as tightly as possible. You might even extend the application to compress the files. The true goal of this example is for you to exercise many of the Visual Basic .NET skills learned in earlier chapters and to explore the Windows.Forms namespace.

For the purposes of this example and to keep the code simple, you'll focus on the user interface and the steps needed to wire up its various controls. The final application UI is shown in Figure 13-9.

The user interface for FileCopier consists of the following controls:

- Labels: Source Files and Target Directory
- Buttons: Clear, Copy, Delete, and Cancel
- An "Overwrite if exists" checkbox
- A text box displaying the path of the selected target directory
- Two large tree view controls, one for available source directories and one for available target devices and directories

The goal is to allow the user to check files (or entire directories) in the left tree view (source). If the user presses the Copy button, the files checked on the left side will be copied to the Target Directory specified in the right-hand control. If the user presses Delete, the checked files will be deleted.

The rest of this chapter implements a number of FileCopier features in order to demonstrate the fundamental features of Windows Forms. The complete code listing is shown in Example 13-3.

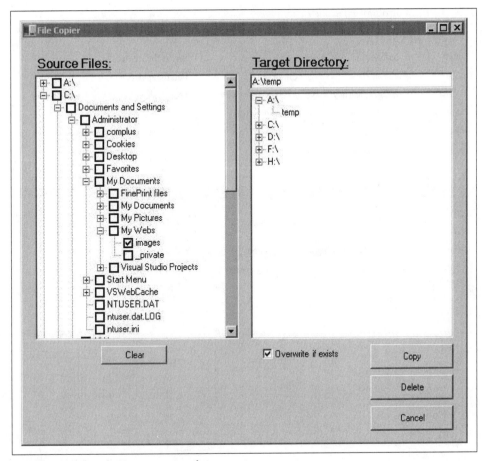

Figure 13-9. The FileCopier user interface

Creating the Basic UI Form

The first task is to open a new project named FileCopier. The IDE puts you into the Designer, where you can drag widgets onto the form. You can expand the form to the size you want. Create the controls as shown in Table 13-1 so that your form looks like Figure 13-10.

Table 13-1. Controls for FileCopier

Type	Name	Text	Notes
Label	lblSource	Source Files	Bold, underlined, 12 point font
Label	lblTarget	Target Directory	Bold, underlined, 12 point font
Label	lblStatus	<none>	Blank label, multi-line
Button	btnClear	Clear	Clears the checkboxes
Button	btnCopy	Copy	Copies from source to destination

Table 13-1. Controls for FileCopier (continued)

Type	Name	Text	Notes
Button	btnDelete	Delete	Deletes the selected files
Button	btnCancel	Cancel	Exits the application
TextBox	txtTargetDirectory	<none>	Appears above treeview for Target directory
CheckBox	chkOverwrite	Overwrite if exists	
TreeView	tvwSource		Set CheckBoxes property = True
TreeView	tvwTargetDir		Set CheckBoxes property = False

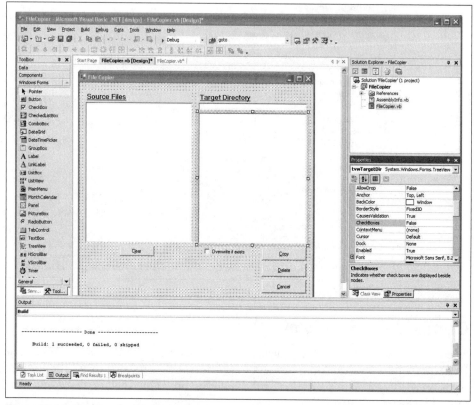

Figure 13-10. Creating the FileCopier form

Once your form is created, double-click the Cancel button to create its event handler. When you double-click a control, Visual Studio .NET creates an event handler for that object and places you at the correct location within the code editor. One particular event is the button click event, and Visual Studio .NET opens that event's event handler:

```
Private Sub btnCancelClick( _
    ByVal sender As Object, ByVal e As System.EventArgs) _
    Handles btnCancel.Click
```

```
        Application.Exit()
    End Sub 'btnCancelClick
```

You can set many different events for the TreeView control by clicking the Events button in the Properties window. From there you can create new handlers, just by filling in a new event handler method name. Visual Studio .NET will register the event handler and open the editor for the code, where it will create the header and put the cursor in an empty method body.

So much for the easy part. Visual Studio .NET will generate code to set up the form and initialize all the controls, but it won't fill the TreeView controls. That you must do by hand.

Populating the TreeView Controls

The two TreeView controls work identically, except that the left control, tvwSource, lists the directories and files, whereas the right control, tvwTargetDir, lists only directories. The CheckBoxes property on tvwSource is set to True, and on tvwTargetDir it is set to False. Also, although tvwSource will allow multiselect, which is the default for TreeView controls, you will enforce single selection for tvwTargetDir.

You'll factor the common code for both TreeView controls into a shared method, FillDirectoryTree(), and pass in the control with a flag indicating whether to get the files. You'll call this method from the constructor, once for each of the two controls:

```
    FillDirectoryTree(tvwSource, True)
    FillDirectoryTree(tvwTargetDir, False)
```

The FillDirectoryTree() implementation names the TreeView parameter tvw. This will represent the source TreeView and the destination TreeView in turn.

```
    Private Sub FillDirectoryTree( _
        ByVal tvw As TreeView, _
        ByVal isSource As Boolean)
```

TreeNode objects

The TreeView control has a property, Nodes, which gets a TreeNodeCollection object. The TreeNodeCollection is a collection of TreeNode objects, each of which represents a node in the tree. Start by emptying that collection:

```
    tvw.Nodes.Clear()
```

You are ready to fill the TreeView's Nodes collection by recursing through the directories of all the drives. First, you get all the logical drives on the system. To do so you call a shared method of the Environment object, GetLogicalDrives(). The Environment class provides information about and access to the current platform environment. You can use the Environment object to get the machine name, OS version, system directory, and so forth, from the computer on which you are running your program:

```
    Dim strDrives As String() = Environment.GetLogicalDrives()
```

GetLogicalDrives( ) returns an array of strings, each of which represents the root directory of one of the logical drives. You will iterate over that collection, adding nodes to the TreeView control as you go:

```
Dim rootDirectoryName As String
For Each rootDirectoryName In strDrives
```

You should process each drive within the For Each loop. The very first thing you need to determine is whether the drive is ready. My hack for that is to get the list of top-level directories from the drive by calling GetDirectories( ) on a DirectoryInfo object I created for the root directory:

```
Dim dir As New DirectoryInfo(rootDirectoryName)
dir.GetDirectories( )
```

The DirectoryInfo class exposes instance methods for creating, moving, and enumerating through directories, their files, and their subdirectories. The GetDirectories( ) method returns a list of directories, but you'll throw this list away. You are calling it here only to generate an exception if the drive is not ready.

You'll wrap the call in a try block and take no action in the catch block. The effect is that if an exception is thrown, the drive is skipped.

 In the code shown in Example 13-3, the catch block displays a message box with the exception. This is used for debugging purposes only.

Once you know that the drive is ready, you create a TreeNode to hold the root directory of the drive and add that node to the TreeView control:

```
Dim ndRoot As New TreeNode(rootDirectoryName)
tvw.Nodes.Add(ndRoot)
```

You now want to recurse through the directories, so you call into a new routine, GetSubDirectoryNodes( ), passing in the root node, the name of the root directory, and the flag indicating whether you want files:

```
GetSubDirectoryNodes(ndRoot, ndRoot.Text, isSource)
```

You're probably wondering why you need to pass in ndRoot.Text if you're already passing in ndRoot. Patience; you'll see why this is needed when you recurse back into GetSubDirectoryNodes.

Recursing through the subdirectories

GetSubDirectoryNodes( ) begins by once again calling GetDirectories( ), this time stashing away the resulting array of DirectoryInfo objects:

```
Private Sub GetSubDirectoryNodes( _
    ByVal parentNode As TreeNode, _
    ByVal fullName As String, _
    ByVal getFileNames As Boolean)
```

```
Dim dir As New DirectoryInfo(fullName)
Dim dirSubs As DirectoryInfo() = dir.GetDirectories()
```

Notice that the node passed in is named parentNode. The current level of nodes will be considered children to the node passed in. This is how you map the directory structure to the hierarchy of the tree view.

Iterate over each subdirectory, skipping any that are marked Hidden:

```
Dim dirSub As DirectoryInfo
For Each dirSub In dirSubs

    If (dirSub.Attributes And FileAttributes.Hidden) = 0 Then
```

FileSystemAttributes is an enum; other possible values include Archive, Compressed, Directory, Encrypted, Hidden, Normal, ReadOnly, etc.

> The property dirSub.Attributes is the bit pattern of the current attributes of the directory. If you logically AND that value with the bit pattern FileSystemAttributes.Hidden, a bit is set if the file has the hidden attribute; otherwise all the bits are cleared. You can test for any hidden bit by testing whether the resulting integer is other than zero.

You create a TreeNode with the directory name and add it to the Nodes collection of the node passed in to the method (parentNode):

```
Dim subNode As New TreeNode(dirSub.Name)
parentNode.Nodes.Add(subNode)
```

Now recurse back into the GetSubDirectoryNodes() method, passing in the node you just created as the new parent, the full path as the full name of the parent, and the flag:

```
GetSubDirectoryNodes(subNode,dirSub.FullName,getFileNames)
```

> Notice that the call to the TreeNode constructor uses the Name property of the DirectoryInfo object, while the call to GetSubDirectoryNodes() uses the FullName property. If your directory is *c:\ WinNT\Media\Sounds*, the FullName property will return the full path, while the Name property will return just *Sounds*. You pass in only the name to the node because that is what you want displayed in the tree view. You pass in the full name with path to the GetSubDirectoryNodes() method so that the method can locate all the subdirectories on the disk. This answers the question asked earlier as to why you need to pass in the root node's name the first time you call this method; what is passed in is not the name of the node, it is the full path to the directory represented by the node!

Getting the files in the directory

Once you've recursed through the subdirectories, it is time to get the files for the directory, if the getFileNames flag is true. To do so, you call the GetFiles() method on the DirectoryInfo object. What is returned is an array of FileInfo objects:

```
If getFileNames Then
    Dim files As FileInfo() = dir.GetFiles()
```

The FileInfo class provides instance methods for manipulating files.

You can now iterate over this collection, accessing the Name property of the FileInfo object and passing that name to the constructor of a TreeNode, which you then add to the parent node's Nodes collection (thus creating a child node). There is no recursion this time because files do not have subdirectories:

```
Dim file As FileInfo
For Each file In files
    Dim fileNode As New TreeNode(file.Name)
    parentNode.Nodes.Add(fileNode)
Next file
```

That's all it takes to fill the two tree views.

 If you found any of this confusing, I highly recommend putting the code into your debugger and stepping through the recursion; you can watch the TreeView build its nodes.

Begin and EndUpdate

You might be adding many nodes to the TreeView control. To enhance the performance of the program, you'll call BeginUpdate() on the TreeView before you begin looping through the entries, and EndUpdate() when you are done. The BeginUpdate() method prevents the control from painting until the EndUpdate() method is called, which greatly enhances its performance.

Handling TreeView Events

You must handle a number of events in this example. First, the user might click Cancel, Copy, Clear, or Delete. Second, the user might click one of the checkboxes in the left TreeView or one of the nodes in the right TreeView.

Let's consider the clicks on the TreeViews first, as they are more interesting, and potentially more challenging.

Clicking the source TreeView

There are two TreeView objects, each with its own event handler. Consider the source TreeView object first. The user checks the files and directories he wants to copy from. Each time the user clicks a file or directory, a number of events are raised. The event you must handle is AfterCheck.

To do so, you implement a custom event-handler method you will create and name tvwSource_AfterCheck(). The implementation of AfterCheck() delegates the work to a recursable method named SetCheck(), which you'll also write:

```
Private Sub tvwSourceAfterCheck( _
ByVal sender As Object, _
ByVal e As System.Windows.Forms.TreeViewEventArgs) _
    Handles tvwSource.AfterCheck
        SetCheck(e.Node, e.Node.Checked)
End Sub 'tvwSourceAfterCheck
```

The event handler passes in the sender object and an object of type TreeView-EventArgs. It turns out that you can get the node from this TreeViewEventArgs object (e). You call SetCheck(), passing in the node and the state of whether the node has been checked.

Each node has a Nodes property, which gets a TreeNodeCollection containing all the subnodes. SetCheck() recurses through the current node's Nodes collection, setting each subnode's checkmark to match that of the node that was checked. In other words, when you check a directory, all its files and subdirectories are checked, recursively, all the way down.

It's Turtles, All the Way Down

Steven Hawking tells one of my favorites stories on recursion in *A Brief History of Time*. A well-known scientist was lecturing on astronomy. He described the Earth's orbit around the sun, and the sun's orbit around the galactic center.

An old lady interrupted to say "Rubbish. The world is really a flat plate supported on the back of a giant tortoise."

The scientist smiled and asked "What is the tortoise standing on?"

"You're very clever, young man, very clever," the old lady replied, "but it's turtles all the way down."

For each TreeNode in the Nodes collection, you check to see if it is a leaf. A node is a leaf if its own Nodes collection has a count of zero. If so, you set its check property to whatever was passed in as a parameter. If it is not a leaf, you recurse.

```
Private Sub SetCheck( _
ByVal node As TreeNode, ByVal check As Boolean)
    Dim n As TreeNode
    For Each n In node.Nodes
        n.Checked = check
        If n.Nodes.Count <> 0 Then
            SetCheck(n, check)
        End If
    Next n
End Sub
```

This propagates the checkmark (or clears the checkmark) down through the entire structure. In this way, the user can indicate that she wants to select all the files in all the subdirectories by clicking a single directory.

Clicking the target TreeView

The event handler for the target TreeView is somewhat trickier. The event itself is AfterSelect. (Remember that the target TreeView does not have checkboxes.) This time, you want to take the one directory chosen and put its full path into the text box above the tree view.

To do so, you must work your way up through the nodes, finding the name of each parent directory and building the full path:

```
Private Sub tvwTargetDirAfterSelect( _
ByVal sender As Object, _
ByVal e As System.Windows.Forms.TreeViewEventArgs) _
  Handles tvwTargetDir.AfterSelect

    Dim theFullPath As String = GetParentString(e.Node)
```

We'll look at GetParentString( ) in just a moment. Once you have the full path, you must lop off the backslash (if any) on the end and then you can fill the text box:

```
If theFullPath.EndsWith("\") Then
    theFullPath = _
    theFullPath.Substring( _
        0, theFullPath.Length - 1)
End If
txtTargetDir.Text = theFullPath
```

The GetParentString( ) method takes a node and returns a string with the full path. To do so, it recurses upward through the path, adding the backslash after any node that is not a leaf:

```
Private Function GetParentString( _
    ByVal node As TreeNode) As String
    If node.Parent Is Nothing Then
        Return node.Text
    Else
        Dim suffix As String
        If node.Nodes.Count = 0 Then
            suffix = ""
        Else
            suffix = "\"
        End If
        Return GetParentString(node.Parent) _
            + node.Text + suffix
    End If
End Function 'GetParentString
```

The recursion stops when there is no parent; that is, when you hit the root directory.

Handling the Clear button event

Given the SetCheck()method developed earlier, handling the Clear button's click event is trivial:

```
Private Sub btnClearClick( _
ByVal sender As Object, ByVal e As System.EventArgs) _
   Handles btnClear.Click

    Dim node As TreeNode
    For Each node In tvwSource.Nodes
        SetCheck(node, False)
    Next node

End Sub 'btnClearClick
```

You just call the SetCheck() method on the root nodes and tell them to recursively uncheck all their contained nodes.

Implementing the Copy Button Event

Now that you can check the files and pick the target directory, you're ready to handle the Copy button-click event. The very first thing you need to do is to get a list of which files were selected. What you want is an array of FileInfo objects, but you have no idea how many objects will be in the list. That is a perfect job for ArrayList. You'll delegate responsibility for filling the list to a method called GetFileList():

```
Private Sub btnCopyClick( _
    ByVal sender As Object, _
    ByVal e As System.EventArgs) _
    Handles btnCopy.Click

    Dim fileList As ArrayList = GetFileList()
```

Let's pick that method apart before returning to the event handler.

Getting the selected files

You start by instantiating a new ArrayList object to hold the strings representing the names of all the files selected:

```
Private Function GetFileList() As ArrayList
    Dim fileNames As New ArrayList()
```

To get the selected filenames, you can walk through the source TreeView control:

```
Dim theNode As TreeNode
For Each theNode In tvwSource.Nodes
    GetCheckedFiles(theNode, fileNames)
Next theNode
```

To see how this works, you want to step into the GetCheckedFiles() method. This method is pretty simple: it examines the node it was handed. If that node has no children (node.Nodes.Count = 0), it is a leaf. If that leaf is checked, you want to get the full path (by calling GetParentString() on the node) and add it to the ArrayList passed in as a parameter:

```
Private Sub GetCheckedFiles( _
    ByVal node As TreeNode, _
    ByVal fileNames As ArrayList)

    If node.Nodes.Count = 0 Then
        If node.Checked Then
            Dim fullPath As String = _
                GetParentString(node)
            fileNames.Add(fullPath)
        End If
```

If the node is *not* a leaf, you want to recurse down the tree, finding the child nodes:

```
    Else
        Dim n As TreeNode
        For Each n In node.Nodes
            GetCheckedFiles(n, fileNames)
        Next n
    End If
End Sub 'GetCheckedFiles
```

This will return the ArrayList filled with all the filenames. Back in GetFileList(), you'll use this ArrayList of filenames to create a second ArrayList, this time to hold the actual FileInfo objects:

```
Dim fileList As New ArrayList()
```

Notice that once again you do not tell the ArrayList constructor what kind of object it will hold. This is one of the advantages of a rooted type-system: the collection only needs to know that it has some kind of Object; because all types are derived from Object, the list can hold FileInfo objects as easily as it can hold string objects.

You can now iterate through the filenames in ArrayList, picking out each name and instantiating a FileInfo object with it. You can detect if it is a file or a directory by calling the Exists property, which will return false if the File object you created is actually a directory. If it is a File, you can add it to the new ArrayList:

```
Dim fileName As String
For Each fileName In fileNames
    Dim file As New FileInfo(fileName)
    If file.Exists Then
        fileList.Add(file)
    End If
```

Sorting the list of selected files

You want to work your way through the list of selected files in large to small order so that you can pack the target disk as tightly as possible. You must therefore sort the ArrayList. You can call its Sort() method, but how will it know how to sort File objects? Remember, the ArrayList has no special knowledge about its contents.

To solve this, you must pass in an IComparer interface. We'll create a class called FileComparer that will implement this interface and that will know how to sort FileInfo objects:

```
Public Class FileComparer
    Implements IComparer
```

This class has only one method, Compare(), which takes two objects as arguments:

```
Public Function Compare( _
    ByVal f1 As Object, _
    ByVal f2 As Object) _
    As Integer _
    Implements IComparer.Compare
```

The normal approach is to return 1 if the first object (f1) is larger than the second (f2), to return −1 if the opposite is true, and to return 0 if they are equal. In this case, however, you want the list sorted from big to small, so you should reverse the return values.

 Since this is the only use of this Compare() method, it is reasonable to put this special knowledge that the sort is from big to small right into the Compare() method itself. The alternative is to sort small to big, and have the calling method reverse the results, as you saw in Example 13-3.

To test the length of the FileInfo object, you must cast the Object parameters to FileInfo objects (which is safe, as you know this method will never receive anything else):

```
Dim file1 As FileInfo = CType(f1, FileInfo)
Dim file2 As FileInfo = CType(f2, FileInfo)
If file1.Length > file2.Length Then
    Return -1
End If
If file1.Length < file2.Length Then
    Return 1
End If
Return 0
    End Function 'Compare
End Class 'FileComparer
```

 In a production program, you might want to test the type of the object and perhaps handle the exception if the object is not of the expected type.

Returning to GetFileList(), you were about to instantiate the IComparer reference and pass it to the Sort() method of fileList:

```
Dim comparer As IComparer = _
    CType(New FileComparer(), IComparer)
fileList.Sort(comparer)
```

That done, you can return fileList to the calling method:

```
Return fileList
```

The calling method was btnCopy_Click. Remember, you went off to GetFileList() in the first line of the event handler!

```
Private Sub btnCopyClick( _
    ByVal sender As Object, _
    ByVal e As System.EventArgs) _
    Handles btnCopy.Click
    ' get the list
    Dim fileList As ArrayList = GetFileList()
```

At this point you've returned with a sorted list of File objects, each representing a file selected in the source TreeView.

You can now iterate through the list, copying the files and updating the UI:

```
        Dim file As FileInfo
        For Each file In fileList
            Try
                lblStatus.Text = _
                  "Copying " + txtTargetDir.Text + _
                  "\" + file.Name + "..."
                Application.DoEvents()

                file.CopyTo( _
                    txtTargetDir.Text + _
                    "\" + file.Name, _
                    chkOverwrite.Checked)

            Catch ex As Exception
                MessageBox.Show(ex.Message)
            End Try
        Next file
        lblStatus.Text = "Done."
        Application.DoEvents()
    End Sub 'btnCopyClick
```

As you go, you write the progress to the lblStatus label and call Application. DoEvents() to give the UI an opportunity to redraw. You then call CopyTo() on the file, passing in the target directory, obtained from the text field, and a Boolean flag indicating whether the file should be overwritten if it already exists.

You'll notice that the flag you pass in is the value of the chkOverwrite checkbox. The Checked property evaluates true if the checkbox is checked and false if not.

The copy is wrapped in a try block because you can anticipate any number of things going wrong when copying files. For now, you handle all exceptions by popping up a dialog box with the error, but you might want to take corrective action in a commercial application.

That's it; you've implemented file copying!

Handling the Delete Button Event

The code to handle the delete event is even simpler. The very first thing you do is ask the user if she is sure she wants to delete the files:

```
Private Sub btnDeleteClick( _
ByVal sender As Object, ByVal e As System.EventArgs) _
  Handles btnDelete.Click
     ' ask them if they are sure
     Dim result As System.Windows.Forms.DialogResult = _
         MessageBox.Show( _
         "Are you quite sure?", _
            "Delete Files", _
         MessageBoxButtons.OKCancel, _
             MessageBoxIcon.Exclamation, _
             MessageBoxDefaultButton.Button2)
```

You can use the MessageBox static Show( ) method, passing:

- The message you want to display
- The title "Delete Files" as a string
- MessageBox.OKCancel, a flag indicating the message box should ask for two buttons: OK and Cancel
- MessageBox.Exclamation, a flag indicating that you want to display an exclamation mark icon
- MessageBox.DefaultButton.Button2, a flag that sets the second button (Cancel) as the default choice

When the user chooses OK or Cancel, the result is passed back as a System.Windows.Forms.DialogResult enumerated value. You can test this value to see if the user pressed OK:

```
If result = System.Windows.Forms.DialogResult.OK Then
```

If so, you can get the list of fileNames and iterate through it, deleting each as you go:

```
Dim fileNames As ArrayList = GetFileList( )

Dim file As FileInfo
For Each file In fileNames
    Try
        ' update the label to show progress
        lblStatus.Text = _
            "Deleting " + txtTargetDir.Text + _
            "\" + file.Name + "..."
        Application.DoEvents( )

        ' Danger Will Robinson!
        file.Delete( )

    Catch ex As Exception
        ' you may want to do more than
```

```
                ' just show the message
                MessageBox.Show(ex.Message)
            End Try
        Next file
        lblStatus.Text = "Done."
        Application.DoEvents()
```

This code is identical to the copy code, except that the method that is called on the file is Delete().

Example 13-3 provides the commented source code for this example.

Example 13-3. Complete FileCopier code

```
Imports System
Imports System.Drawing
Imports System.Collections
Imports System.ComponentModel
Imports System.Windows.Forms
Imports System.Data
Imports System.IO

Namespace FileCopier

    ' Form demonstrating Windows Forms implementation
    Public Class Form1
        Inherits System.Windows.Forms.Form
        'Tree view of source directories
        'includes check boxes for checking
        'chosen files or directories
        Private WithEvents tvwSource As System.Windows.Forms.TreeView

        'Tree view of potential target directories
        Private WithEvents tvwTargetDir As System.Windows.Forms.TreeView

        'When pressed, sets all check boxes
        'in source tree view to clear
        Private WithEvents btnClear As System.Windows.Forms.Button

        'If checked, when copying we'll
        'overwrite existing files
        Private WithEvents chkOverwrite As System.Windows.Forms.CheckBox

        'Shuts the application
        Private WithEvents btnCancel As System.Windows.Forms.Button

        'Copies the selected files
        'to the target directory
        Private WithEvents btnCopy As System.Windows.Forms.Button

        'Label displays progress when
        'copying or deleting files
        Private lblStatus As System.Windows.Forms.Label
```

Example 13-3. Complete FileCopier code (continued)

```vb
'Deletes the selected files
Private WithEvents btnDelete As System.Windows.Forms.Button

'Currently selected target directory
Private WithEvents txtTargetDir As System.Windows.Forms.TextBox

Private lblSource As System.Windows.Forms.Label
Private lblTarget As System.Windows.Forms.Label

' Required designer variable.
Private components As System.ComponentModel.Container = Nothing

'internal class which knows how to compare
'two files we want to sort large to small,
'so reverse the normal return values.
Public Class FileComparer
    Implements IComparer

    Public Function Compare( _
        ByVal f1 As Object, _
        ByVal f2 As Object) _
        As Integer _
        Implements IComparer.Compare

        Dim file1 As FileInfo = CType(f1, FileInfo)
        Dim file2 As FileInfo = CType(f2, FileInfo)
        If file1.Length > file2.Length Then
            Return -1
        End If
        If file1.Length < file2.Length Then
            Return 1
        End If
        Return 0
    End Function 'Compare

    Public Sub New()

    End Sub
End Class 'FileComparer

Public Sub New()
    '
    ' Required for Windows Form Designer support
    '
    InitializeComponent()

    ' fill the source and target directory trees
    FillDirectoryTree(tvwSource, True)
    FillDirectoryTree(tvwTargetDir, False)
End Sub 'New

' Fill the directory tree for either the Source or
```

Example 13-3. Complete FileCopier code (continued)

```
' Target TreeView.
Private Sub FillDirectoryTree( _
    ByVal tvw As TreeView, _
    ByVal isSource As Boolean)

    ' Populate tvwSource, the Source TreeView,
    ' with the contents of
    ' the local hard drive.
    ' First clear all the nodes.
    tvw.Nodes.Clear()

    ' Get the logical drives and put them into the
    ' root nodes. Fill an array with all the
    ' logical drives on the machine.
    Dim strDrives As String() = Environment.GetLogicalDrives()

    tvw.BeginUpdate()

    ' Iterate through the drives, adding them to the tree.
    ' Use a try/catch block, so if a drive is not ready,
    ' e.g. an empty floppy or CD,
    ' it will not be added to the tree.
    Dim rootDirectoryName As String
    For Each rootDirectoryName In strDrives
        If rootDirectoryName = "Z:\" Then
            Try

                ' Fill an array with all the first level
                ' subdirectories. If the drive is
                ' not ready, this will throw an exception.
                Dim dir As New DirectoryInfo(rootDirectoryName)
                dir.GetDirectories()

                Dim ndRoot As New TreeNode(rootDirectoryName)

                ' Add a node for each root directory.
                tvw.Nodes.Add(ndRoot)

                ' Add subdirectory nodes.
                ' If Treeview is the source,
                ' then also get the filenames.
                GetSubDirectoryNodes(ndRoot, ndRoot.Text, isSource)

                ' Catch any errors such as
                ' Drive not ready.
            Catch e As Exception
                MessageBox.Show(e.Message)
            End Try
        End If
    Next rootDirectoryName

    tvw.EndUpdate()
```

Example 13-3. Complete FileCopier code (continued)

```
    End Sub 'FillDirectoryTree

' close for FillSourceDirectoryTree
' Gets all the subdirectories below the
' passed in directory node.
' Adds to the directory tree.
' The parameters passed in at the parent node
' for this subdirectory,
' the full path name of this subdirectory,
' and a Boolean to indicate
' whether or not to get the files in the subdirectory.
Private Sub GetSubDirectoryNodes( _
    ByVal parentNode As TreeNode, _
    ByVal fullName As String, _
    ByVal getFileNames As Boolean)

    Dim dir As New DirectoryInfo(fullName)
    Dim dirSubs As DirectoryInfo() = dir.GetDirectories()

    '  Add a child node for each subdirectory.
    Dim dirSub As DirectoryInfo
    For Each dirSub In dirSubs

        ' do not show hidden folders
        If (dirSub.Attributes And FileAttributes.Hidden) = 0 Then

            ' Each directory contains the full path.
            ' We need to split it on the backslashes,
            ' and only use
            ' the last node in the tree.
            ' Need to double the backslash since it
            ' is normally
            ' an escape character
            Dim subNode As New TreeNode(dirSub.Name)
            parentNode.Nodes.Add(subNode)

            ' Call GetSubDirectoryNodes recursively.
            GetSubDirectoryNodes( _
                subNode, _
                dirSub.FullName, _
                getFileNames)
        End If ' not hidden files
    Next dirSub

    If getFileNames Then
        ' Get any files for this node.
        Dim files As FileInfo() = dir.GetFiles()

        ' After placing the nodes,
        ' now place the files in that subdirectory.
        Dim file As FileInfo
        For Each file In files
```

Example 13-3. Complete FileCopier code (continued)

```
                Dim fileNode As New TreeNode(file.Name)
                parentNode.Nodes.Add(fileNode)
            Next file
        End If
    End Sub 'GetSubDirectoryNodes

    ' Clean up any resources being used.
    Protected Overrides Sub Dispose(ByVal disposing As Boolean)
        If disposing Then
            If Not (components Is Nothing) Then
                components.Dispose()
            End If
        End If
        MyBase.Dispose(disposing)
    End Sub 'Dispose

    Private Sub InitializeComponent()
        ' contents elided to save space in the book
    End Sub 'InitializeComponent



    ' Create an ordered list of all
    ' the selected files, copy to the
    ' target directory
    Private Sub btnCopyClick( _
        ByVal sender As Object, _
        ByVal e As System.EventArgs) _
        Handles btnCopy.Click
        ' get the list
        Dim fileList As ArrayList = GetFileList()

        ' copy the files
        Dim file As FileInfo
        For Each file In fileList
            Try
                ' update the label to show progress
                lblStatus.Text = _
                  "Copying " + txtTargetDir.Text + _
                  "\" + file.Name + "..."
                Application.DoEvents()

                ' copy the file to its destination location
                file.CopyTo( _
                  txtTargetDir.Text + _
                  "\" + file.Name, _
                  chkOverwrite.Checked)

            Catch ex As Exception
                ' you may want to do more than
                ' just show the message
                MessageBox.Show(ex.Message)
```

Example 13-3. Complete FileCopier code (continued)

```
            End Try
        Next file
        lblStatus.Text = "Done."
        Application.DoEvents( )
    End Sub 'btnCopyClick


    ' on cancel, exit
    Private Sub btnCancelClick( _
        ByVal sender As Object, ByVal e As System.EventArgs) _
        Handles btnCancel.Click
        Application.Exit( )
    End Sub 'btnCancelClick


    ' Tell the root of each tree to uncheck
    ' all the nodes below
    Private Sub btnClearClick( _
    ByVal sender As Object, ByVal e As System.EventArgs) _
      Handles btnClear.Click
        ' get the top most node for each drive
        ' and tell it to clear recursively
        Dim node As TreeNode
        For Each node In tvwSource.Nodes
            SetCheck(node, False)
        Next node
    End Sub 'btnClearClick


    ' check that the user does want to delete
    ' Make a list and delete each in turn
    Private Sub btnDeleteClick( _
    ByVal sender As Object, ByVal e As System.EventArgs) _
      Handles btnDelete.Click
        ' ask them if they are sure
        Dim result As System.Windows.Forms.DialogResult = _
            MessageBox.Show("Are you quite sure?", _
                "Delete Files", MessageBoxButtons.OKCancel, _
                MessageBoxIcon.Exclamation, _
                MessageBoxDefaultButton.Button2)

        If result = System.Windows.Forms.DialogResult.OK Then
            ' iterate through the list and delete them.
            ' get the list of selected files
            Dim fileNames As ArrayList = GetFileList( )

            Dim file As FileInfo
            For Each file In fileNames
                Try
                    ' update the label to show progress
                    lblStatus.Text = _
                        "Deleting " + txtTargetDir.Text + _
                        "\" + file.Name + "..."
                    Application.DoEvents( )
```

Example 13-3. Complete FileCopier code (continued)

```
                      ' Danger Will Robinson!
                      file.Delete( )

              Catch ex As Exception
                      ' you may want to do more than
                      ' just show the message
                      MessageBox.Show(ex.Message)
              End Try
          Next file
          lblStatus.Text = "Done."
          Application.DoEvents( )
      End If
End Sub 'btnDeleteClick


' Get the full path of the chosen directory
' copy it to txtTargetDir
Private Sub tvwTargetDirAfterSelect( _
ByVal sender As Object, _
ByVal e As System.Windows.Forms.TreeViewEventArgs) _
  Handles tvwTargetDir.AfterSelect
    ' get the full path for the selected directory
    Dim theFullPath As String = GetParentString(e.Node)

    ' if it is not a leaf, it will end with a back slash
    ' remove the backslash
    If theFullPath.EndsWith("\") Then
        theFullPath = _
        theFullPath.Substring( _
            0, theFullPath.Length - 1)
    End If
    ' insert the path in the text box
    txtTargetDir.Text = theFullPath
End Sub 'tvwTargetDirAfterSelect


' Mark each node below the current
' one with the current value of checked
Private Sub tvwSourceAfterCheck( _
    ByVal sender As Object, _
    ByVal e As System.Windows.Forms.TreeViewEventArgs) _
      Handles tvwSource.AfterCheck
    ' Call a recursible method.
    ' e.node is the node which was checked by the user.
    ' The state of the check mark is already
    ' changed by the time you get here.
    ' Therefore, we want to pass along
    ' the state of e.node.Checked.
    SetCheck(e.Node, e.Node.Checked)
End Sub 'tvwSourceAfterCheck

' recursively set or clear check marks
```

Example 13-3. Complete FileCopier code (continued)

```
Private Sub SetCheck( _
ByVal node As TreeNode, ByVal check As Boolean)
    ' find all the child nodes from this node
    Dim n As TreeNode
    For Each n In node.Nodes
        n.Checked = check ' check the node
        ' if this is a node in the tree, recurse
        If n.Nodes.Count <> 0 Then
            SetCheck(n, check)
        End If
    Next n
End Sub 'SetCheck


' Given a node and an array list
' fill the list with the names of
' all the checked files
' Fill the ArrayList with the full paths of
' all the files checked
Private Sub GetCheckedFiles( _
    ByVal node As TreeNode, _
    ByVal fileNames As ArrayList)
    ' if this is a leaf...
    If node.Nodes.Count = 0 Then
        ' if the node was checked...
        If node.Checked Then
            ' get the full path and add it
            ' to the arrayList
            Dim fullPath As String = _
                GetParentString(node)
            fileNames.Add(fullPath)
        End If
        ' if this node is not a leaf
    Else
        ' if this node is not a leaf
        Dim n As TreeNode
        For Each n In node.Nodes
            GetCheckedFiles(n, fileNames)
        Next n
    End If
End Sub 'GetCheckedFiles


' Given a node, return the full path name
Private Function GetParentString( _
    ByVal node As TreeNode) As String
    ' if this is the root node (c:\) return the text
    If node.Parent Is Nothing Then
        Return node.Text
    Else
        ' recurse up and get the path then
        ' add this node and a slash
        ' if this node is the leaf, don't add the slash
        Dim suffix As String
```

Example 13-3. Complete FileCopier code (continued)

```
            If node.Nodes.Count = 0 Then
                suffix = ""
            Else
                suffix = "\"
            End If
            Return GetParentString(node.Parent) _
                + node.Text + suffix
        End If
    End Function 'GetParentString


    ' shared by delete and copy
    ' creates an ordered list of all
    ' the selected files
    Private Function GetFileList() As ArrayList
        ' create an unsorted array list of the full file names
        Dim fileNames As New ArrayList()

        ' fill the fileNames ArrayList with the
        ' full path of each file to copy
        Dim theNode As TreeNode
        For Each theNode In tvwSource.Nodes
            GetCheckedFiles(theNode, fileNames)
        Next theNode

        ' Create a list to hold the FileInfo objects
        Dim fileList As New ArrayList()

        ' for each of the file names we have in our
        ' unsorted(list)if the name corresponds to
        ' a file (and not a directory)
        ' add it to the file list
        Dim fileName As String
        For Each fileName In fileNames
            ' create a file with the name
            Dim file As New FileInfo(fileName)

            ' see if it exists on the disk
            ' this fails if it was a directory
            If file.Exists Then
                ' both the key and the value are the file
                ' would it be easier to have an empty value?
                fileList.Add(file)
            End If
        Next fileName

        ' Create an instance of the IComparer interface
        Dim comparer As IComparer = _
            CType(New FileComparer(), IComparer)

        ' pass the comparer to the sort method so that the list
        ' is sorted by the compare method of comparer.
```

Example 13-3. Complete FileCopier code (continued)

```
            fileList.Sort(comparer)
            Return fileList
        End Function 'GetFileList
    End Class 'Form1
End Namespace 'FileCopier
```

Deploying an Application

Now that the application works, how do you deploy it? The good news is that in .NET there is no Registry to fuss with; you could, in fact, just copy the assembly to a new machine.

For example, you can compile the program in Example 13-3 into an assembly named FileCopier.exe. You can then copy that file to a new machine running .NET and double-click it. Presto! It works. No muss, no fuss.

Deployment Projects

For larger commercial applications, this simple approach might not be enough; sweet as it is. Customers would like you to install the files in the appropriate directories, set up shortcuts, and so forth.

Visual Studio provides extensive help for deployment. The process is to add a Setup and Deployment project to your application project. For example, assuming you are in the FileCopier project, click Add Project and choose Setup and Deployment Projects. You should see the dialog box shown in Figure 13-11.

You have a variety of choices here. For a Windows project such as this one, your choices include:

Cab Project
> Much like a ZIP file, this compresses a number of small files into an easy-to-use (and easy-to-transport) package. This option can be combined with the others.

Merge Module Project
> If you have more than one project that use files in common, this option helps you make intermediate merge modules. You can then integrate these modules into the other deployment projects.

Setup Project
> This creates a setup file that automatically installs your files and resources.

Setup Wizard
> Helps you create one of the other types.

Web Setup Project
> Helps you deploy a web-based project.

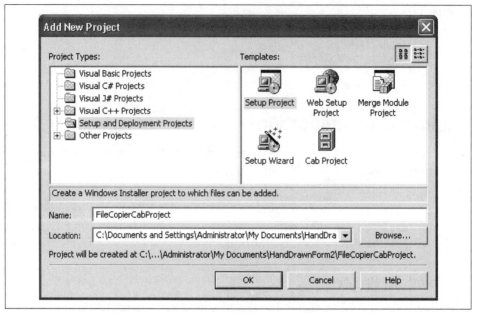

Figure 13-11. The New Project dialog box

You would create a Cab Project first if you had many small ancillary files that had to be distributed with your application (for example, if you had *.html* files, *.gif* files, or other resources included with your program).

To see how this works, use the menu choice `File->Add Project->New Project` and choose and name a Setup and Deployment Project, selecting CAB File. When you name the project (for example, FileCopierCabProject) and click OK, you'll see that the project has been added to your group, as shown in Figure 13-12.

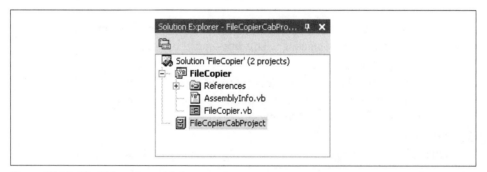

Figure 13-12. The Cab project added to your group

Right-clicking the project brings up a context menu. Choose Add, and you have two choices: Project Output... and File... The latter allows you to add *any* arbitrary file to the Cab. The former offers a dialog box of its own, as shown in Figure 13-13.

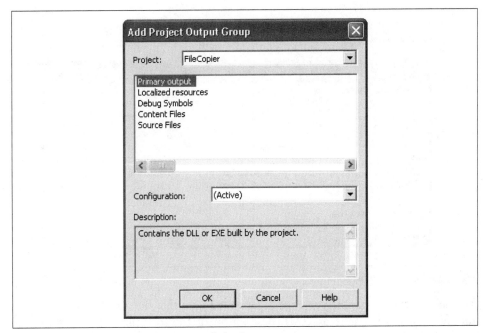

Figure 13-13. Add Project Output Group dialog box

In the Add Project...dialog box you can choose to add sets of files to your Cab collection. The Primary output is the target assembly for the selected project. The other files are optional elements of the selected project that you might or might not want to distribute.

Select Primary output. The choice is reflected in the Solution Explorer, as shown in Figure 13-14.

Figure 13-14. The modified project

You can now build this project, and the result is a *.cab* file, which you can examine with WinZip, as shown in Figure 13-15.

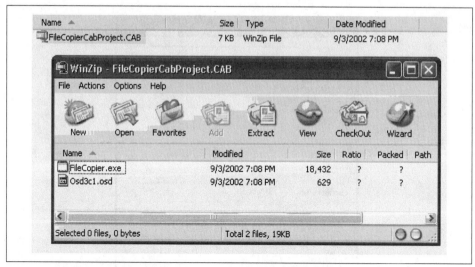

Figure 13-15. The Cab file contents

You see the executable file you expect, along with another file, *Osd3c1.osd*. Opening this file reveals that it is an XML description of the *.cab* file itself, as shown in Example 13-4.

Example 13-4. Code for the .cab file

```
<?XML version="1.0" ENCODING='UTF-8'?>
<!DOCTYPE SOFTPKG SYSTEM "http://www.microsoft.com/standards/osd/osd.dtd">
<?XML::namespace href="http://www.microsoft.com/standards/osd/msicd.dtd" as="MSICD"?>
<SOFTPKG NAME="FileCopierCabProject" VERSION="1,0,0,0">
        <TITLE> FileCopierCabProject </TITLE>
            <MSICD::NATIVECODE>
                <CODE NAME="FileCopier">
                    <IMPLEMENTATION>
                        <CODEBASE FILENAME="FileCopier.exe">
                        </CODEBASE>
                    </IMPLEMENTATION>
                </CODE>
            </MSICD::NATIVECODE>
</SOFTPKG>
```

Setup Project

To create a Setup package, add another project, this time choosing Setup Project from the New Project dialog box. This project type is very flexible; it allows all of your setup options to be bundled in an MSI installation file.

If you right-click the project and select Add, you see additional options in the pop-up menu. In addition to Project Output and File, you now find Merge Module and Assembly.

Merge modules are mix-and-match pieces that can later be added to a full Setup project. The Assembly menu option allows you to add .NET components that your distribution might need but which might not be on the target machine; just add the target executable through Project Output.

The user interface for customizing Setup consists of a split pane whose contents are determined by the View menu. You access the View menu by right-clicking the project itself, as shown in Figure 13-16.

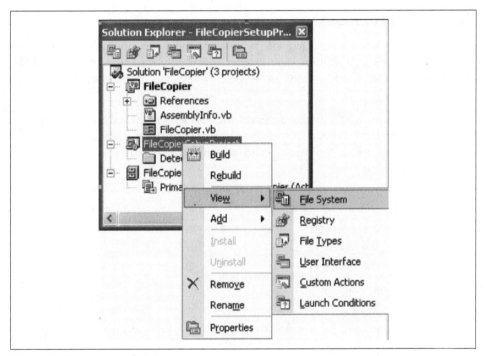

Figure 13-16. Accessing the View menu

As you make selections from the View menu, the panes in the IDE change to reflect your choices and to offer you options.

For example, if you choose File System, the IDE opens a split-pane viewer, with a directory tree on the left and the details on the right. Clicking the Application Folder shows the myriad files you've already added (the primary output and its dependencies), as shown in Figure 13-17.

You are free to add or delete files. Right-clicking in the detail window brings up a context menu. There is great flexibility to add precisely those files you want.

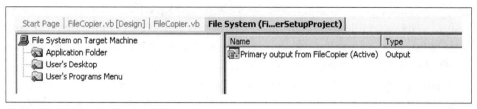

Figure 13-17. The Application folder

Deployment Locations

The folder into which your files will be loaded (the Application Folder) is determined by the Default Location. The Properties window for the Application Folder describes the Default Location as *[ProgramFilesFolder]\[Manufacturer]\[Product Name*.

ProgramFilesFolder refers to the program files folder on the target machine. The *Manufacturer* and the *Product Name* are properties of the project. If you click the Project and examine its properties, you see that the IDE has made some good guesses, as shown in Figure 13-18.

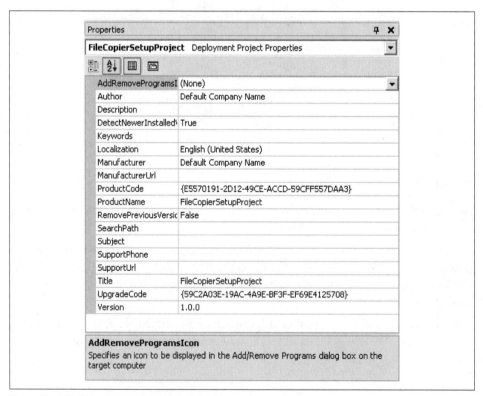

Figure 13-18. Setup project properties

You can easily modify these properties. For example, you can modify the property Manufacturer to change the folder in which the product will be stored under Program Files.

Creating a shortcut

If you want the install program to create a shortcut on the user's desktop, you can right-click the Primary Output file in the Application Folder and drag it to the user's Desktop, as shown in Figure 13-19.

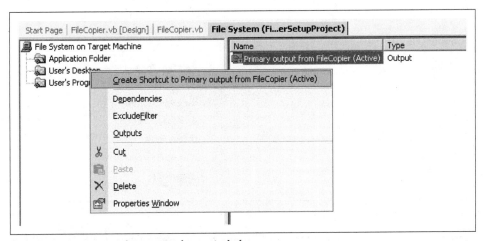

Figure 13-19. Create a shortcut on the user's desktop

Entries in My Documents

You can add items to the My Documents folder on the user's machine by placing them in the User's Personal Data Folder.

Shortcuts in the Start menu

In addition to adding a shortcut to the desktop, you might want to create a folder within the Start → Programs menu. To do so, click the User's Program Menu folder, right-click in the right pane, and choose Add Folder. Within that folder, you can add the Primary Output, either by dragging or by right-clicking and choosing Add.

Adding Special Folders

In addition to the four folders provided for you (Application Folder, User's Desktop, User's Personal Data Folder, User's Program Menu) there are a host of additional options. Right-click the File System On Target Machine folder to get the menu, as shown in Figure 13-20.

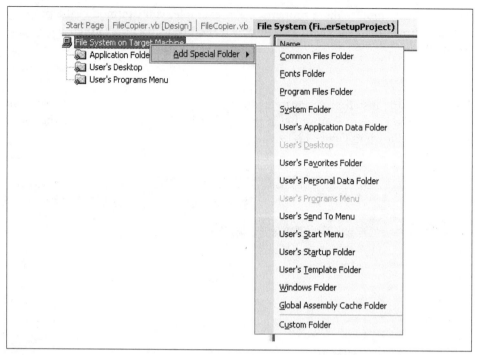

Figure 13-20. Custom folder menu

Here you can add folders for fonts, add items to the user's Favorites Folder, and so forth. Most of these are self-explanatory.

Other View Windows

So far, you've looked only at the File System folders from the original View menu (pictured in Figure 13-16).

The following sections will review how you can use the deployment process to edit the Registry, set up file types, and otherwise customize the deployment process.

Making changes to the Registry

The Registry window (right click on FileCopierSetupProject, and select Registry from the View menu) allows you to tell Setup to make adjustments to the user's Registry files, as shown in Figure 13-21. Click any folder in this list to edit the associated properties in the Properties window.

 Careful! There is nothing more dangerous than touching the Registry. In most .NET applications this will not be needed because .NET-managed applications do not use the Registry.

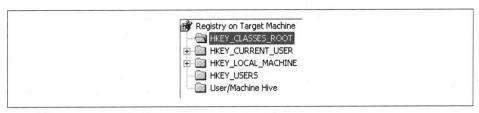

Figure 13-21. Setting up the Registry

Registering file types

The File Types choice on the View menu allows you to associate application-specific file types on the user's machine. You can also set the action to take with these files.

Managing the UI during Setup

The View/User Interface selection lets you take direct control over the text and graphics shown during each step of the Setup process. The workflow of Setup is shown as a tree, as shown in Figure 13-22.

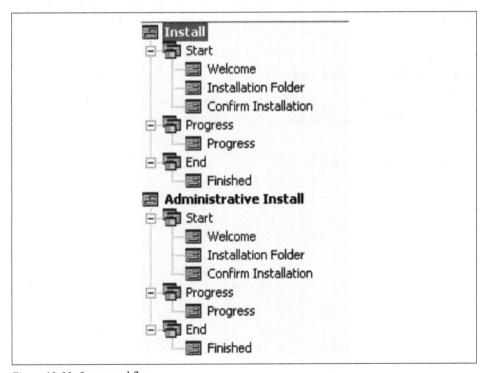

Figure 13-22. Setup workflow

When you click a step in the process, the properties for that form are displayed. For example, clicking the Welcome form under Install/Start displays the properties shown in Figure 13-23.

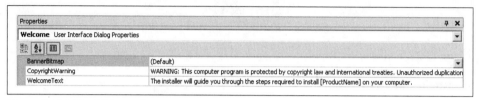

Figure 13-23. The Welcome form

The dynamic Properties window offers you the opportunity to change the Banner Bitmap and the text displayed in the opening dialog box. You can add dialog boxes that Microsoft provides, or import your own dialog boxes into the process.

Other View choices

If the workflow does not provide sufficient control, you can choose the Custom Options choice from the View menu. You can also specify Launch conditions for the Setup process itself.

Building the Setup Project

Once you've made all your choices and set all the options, you can build the Setup project. The result is a single Setup file that can be distributed to your customers.

CHAPTER 14

Accessing Data
with ADO.NET

Many real-world applications interact with a database. The .NET Framework provides a rich set of objects to manage database interaction; these classes are collectively referred to as ADO.NET.

ADO.NET looks very similar to ADO, its predecessor. The key difference is that ADO.NET is a *disconnected* data architecture. In a disconnected architecture, data is retrieved from a database and cached on your local machine. You manipulate the data on your local computer and connect to the database only when you wish to alter records or acquire new data.

There are significant advantages to disconnecting your data architecture from your database. The biggest advantage is that you avoid many of the problems associated with connected data objects that do not scale very well. Database connections are resource-intensive, and it is difficult to have thousands (or hundreds of thousands) of simultaneous continuous connections. A disconnected architecture is resource-frugal.

ADO.NET connects to the database to retrieve data, and connects again to update data when you've made changes. Most applications spend most of their time simply reading through data and displaying it; ADO.NET provides a disconnected subset of the data for your use while reading and displaying.

Disconnected data objects work in a mode similar to that of the Web. All web sessions are disconnected, and state is not preserved between web page requests. A disconnected data architecture makes for a cleaner marriage with web applications.

Relational Databases and SQL

Although one can certainly write an entire book on relational databases, and another on SQL, the essentials of these technologies are not hard to understand. A *database* is a repository of data. A *relational database* organizes your data into tables. Consider the Northwind database provided with Microsoft SQL Server 7, SQL Server 2000, and all versions of Microsoft Access.

Tables, Records, and Columns

The Northwind database describes a fictional company buying and selling food products. The data for Northwind is divided into 13 tables, including Customers, Employees, Orders, Order Details, Products, and so forth.

Every table in a relational database is organized into rows, where each row represents a single record. The rows are organized into columns. All the rows in a table have the same column structure. For example, the Orders table has these columns: OrderID, CustomerID, EmployeeID, OrderDate, etc.

For any given order, you need to know the customer's name, address, contact name, and so forth. You could store that information with each order, but that would be very inefficient. Instead, we use a second table called Customers, in which each row represents a single customer. In the Customers table is a column for the CustomerID. Each customer has a unique ID, and that field is marked as the *primary key* for that table. A primary key is the column or combination of columns that uniquely identifies a record in a given table.

The Orders table uses the CustomerID as a *foreign key*. A foreign key is a column (or combination of columns) that is a primary (or otherwise unique) key from a different table. The Orders table uses the CustomerID, which is the primary key used in the Customers table, to identify which customer has placed the order. To determine the address for the order, you can use the CustomerID to look up the customer record in the Customers table.

This use of foreign keys is particularly helpful in representing one-to-many or many-to-one relationships between tables. By separating information into tables that are linked by foreign keys, you avoid having to repeat information in records. A single customer, for example, can have multiple orders, but it is inefficient to place the same customer information (name, phone number, credit limit, and so on) in every order record. The process of removing redundant information from your records and shifting it to separate tables is called *normalization*.

Normalization

Normalization not only makes your use of the database more efficient, but also it reduces the likelihood of data corruption. If you kept the customer's name and address both in the Customers table and also in the Orders table, you would run the risk that a change in one table might not be reflected in the other. Thus, if you changed the customer's address in the Customers table, that change might not be reflected in every row in the Orders table (and a lot of work would be necessary to make sure that it was reflected). By keeping only the CustomerID in Orders, you are free to change the address in Customers, and the change is automatically reflected for each order. The CustomerID for a given customer never changes.

Just as Visual Basic .NET programmers want the compiler to catch bugs at compile time rather than at runtime, database programmers want the database to help them avoid data corruption. The compiler helps avoid bugs in Visual Basic .NET by enforcing the rules of the language. SQL Server and other modern relational databases avoid bugs by enforcing constraints that you request. For example, the Customers database marks the CustomerID as a primary key. This creates a primary key constraint in the database, which ensures that each CustomerID is unique. If you were to enter a customer named Liberty Associates, Inc. with the CustomerID of LIBE, and then tried to add Liberty Mutual Funds with a CustomerID of LIBE, the database would reject the second record because of the primary key constraint.

Declarative Referential Integrity

Relational databases use *Declarative Referential Integrity* (DRI) to establish constraints on the relationships among the various tables. For example, you might declare a constraint on the Orders table that dictates that no order can have a CustomerID unless that CustomerID represents a valid record in Customers. This helps you avoid two types of mistakes. First, you cannot enter a record with an invalid CustomerID. Second, you cannot delete a Customer record if that CustomerID is used in any order. The integrity of your data and their relationships are thus protected.

SQL

The most popular language for querying and manipulating databases is SQL, usually pronounced "sequel." SQL is a declarative language, as opposed to a procedural language, and it can take a while to get used to working with a declarative language when you are used to languages such as Visual Basic .NET.

The heart of SQL is the *query*. A query is a statement that returns a set of records from the database.

For example, you might like to see all the CompanyNames and CustomerIDs of every record in the Customers table where the customer's address is in London. To do so you would write:

```
Select CustomerID, CompanyName from Customers where city = 'London'
```

This returns the following six records as output:

```
CustomerID CompanyName
---------- ------------------------------------------
AROUT      Around the Horn
BSBEV      B's Beverages
CONSH      Consolidated Holdings
EASTC      Eastern Connection
NORTS      North/South
SEVES      Seven Seas Imports
```

SQL is capable of much more powerful queries. For example, suppose the North-winds manager would like to know what products were purchased in July of 1996 by the customer "Vins et alcools Chevalier." This turns out to be somewhat complicated. The Order Details table knows the ProductID for all the products in any given order. The Orders table knows which CustomerIDs are associated with an order. The Customers table knows the CustomerID for a customer, and the Products table knows the Product name for the ProductID. How do you tie all this together? Here's the query:

```
select  o.OrderID, productName
from [Order Details] od
join orders o on o.OrderID = od.OrderID
join products p on p.ProductID = od.ProductID
join customers c on o.CustomerID = c.CustomerID
where c.CompanyName = 'Vins et alcools Chevalier'
and orderDate >= '7/1/1996' and orderDate <= '7/31/1996'
```

This query asks the database to get the OrderID and the product name from the relevant tables: first look at Order Details (which we've called od for short), then join that with the Orders table for every record where the OrderID in the Order Details table is the same as the OrderID in the Orders table.

When you join two tables you can say either "Get every record that exists in either table" (this is called an *outer join*), or you can say, as I've done here, "Get only those records that exist in both tables" (called an *inner join*). That is, an inner join states to get only the records in Orders that match the records in Order Details by having the same value in the OrderID field (on `o.Orderid = od.Orderid`).

 SQL joins are inner joins by default. Writing "join orders" is the same as writing "inner join orders."

The SQL statement goes on to ask the database to create an inner join with Products, getting every row in which the ProductID in the Products table is the same as the ProductID in the Order Details table.

You then create an inner join with customers for those rows in which the CustomerID is the same in both the Orders table and the Customer table.

Finally, you tell the database to constrain the results to only those rows in which the CompanyName is the one you want, and the dates are in July.

The collection of constraints finds only three records that match:

```
OrderID      ProductName
----------   ------------------------------------------------
10248        Queso Cabrales
10248        Singaporean Hokkien Fried Mee
10248        Mozzarella di Giovanni
```

This output shows that there was only one order (10248) where the customer had the right ID and where the date of the order was July 1996. That order produced three records in the Order Details table, and using the product IDs in these three records, we got the product names from the Products table.

You can use SQL not only for searching for and retrieving data, but also for creating, updating, and deleting tables and generally managing and manipulating both the content and the structure of the database.

For a full explanation of SQL and tips on how to put it to best use, I recommend *Transact-SQL Programming*, by Kline, Gould, and Zanevsky (O'Reilly) and *The Guru's Guide to Transact-SQL* by Ken Henderson (Addison-Wesley).

The ADO.NET Object Model

The ADO.NET object model is rich, but at its heart it is a fairly straightforward set of classes. The most important of these is the DataSet. The DataSet represents a subset of the entire database, cached on your machine without a continuous connection to the database.

Periodically, you'll reconnect the DataSet to its parent database, update the database with changes you've made to the DataSet, and update the DataSet with changes in the database made by other processes.

This is highly efficient, but to be effective the DataSet must be a robust subset of the database, capturing not just a few rows from a single table, but a set of tables with all the metadata necessary to represent the relationships and constraints of the original database. This is, not surprisingly, what ADO.NET provides.

The DataSet is composed of DataTable objects as well as DataRelation objects. These are accessed as properties of the DataSet object. The Tables property returns a DataTableCollection, which in turn contains all the DataTable objects.

DataTables and DataColumns

The DataTable can be created programmatically or as a result of a query against the database. The DataTable has a number of public properties, including the Columns collection, which returns the DataColumnCollection object, which in turn consists of DataColumn objects. Each DataColumn object represents a column in a table.

DataRelations

In addition to the Tables collection, the DataSet has a Relations property, which returns a DataRelationCollection consisting of DataRelation objects. Each DataRelation represents a relationship between two tables, through DataColumn objects. For example, in the Northwind database the Customers table is in a relationship with the Orders table through the CustomerID column.

The nature of the relationship is one-to-many, or parent-to-child: for any given order, there will be exactly one customer, but any given customer might be represented in any number of orders.

Rows

DataTable's Rows collection returns a set of rows for any given table. Use this collection to examine the results of queries against the database, iterating through the rows to examine each record in turn. Programmers experienced with ADO are often confused by the absence of the RecordSet with its moveNext and movePrevious commands. With ADO.NET, you do not iterate through the DataSet; instead, you access the table you need, and then you can iterate through the Rows collection, typically with a For Each loop. You'll see this in the first example in this chapter.

Data Adapter

The DataSet is an abstraction of a relational database. ADO.NET uses a Data-Adapter as a bridge between the DataSet and the data source (i.e., the underlying database). DataAdapter provides the Fill( ) method to retrieve data from the database and populate the DataSet.

DBCommand and DBConnection

The DBConnection object represents a connection to a data source. This connection can be shared among different command objects. The DBCommand object allows you to send a command (typically a SQL statement or a stored procedure) to the database. Often these objects are implicitly created when you create your DataSet, but you can explicitly access these objects, as you'll see in a later example.

The DataAdapter Object

Rather than tie the DataSet object too closely to your database architecture, ADO.NET uses a DataAdapter object to mediate between the DataSet object and the database. This decouples the DataSet from the database and allows a single DataSet to represent more than one database or other data source.

Getting Started with ADO.NET

Enough theory! Let's write some code and see how this works. Working with ADO.NET can be complex, but for many queries, the model is surprisingly simple.

In this example, you'll create a simple Windows Form, with a single listbox in it called lbCustomers. You'll populate this listbox with bits of information from the Customers table in the Northwind database.

Begin by creating a DataAdapter object:

```
Dim myDataAdapter As New SqlDataAdapter( _
    commandString, connectionString)
```

The two parameters are commandString and connectionString. The commandString is the SQL statement that will generate the data you want in your DataSet:

```
Dim commandString As String = _
    "Select CompanyName, ContactName from Customers"
```

The connectionString is whatever string is needed to connect to the database. In my case, I'm running SQL Server on my development machine where I have left the system administrator (*sa*) password blank (I know, I know, not a good idea. I'll fix it by the time this book is released. Honest.):

```
Dim connectionString As String = _
    "server=localhost; uid=sa; pwd=; database=northwind"
```

With the DataAdapter in hand, you're ready to create the DataSet and fill it with the data that you obtain from the SQL select statement:

```
Dim myDataSet As New DataSet( )
myDataAdapter.Fill(myDataSet, "Customers")
```

That's it. You now have a DataSet, and you can query, manipulate, and otherwise manage the data. The DataSet has a collection of tables; you care only about the first one because you've retrieved only a single record:

```
DataTable dataTable = DataSet.Tables[0]
```

You can extract the rows you've retrieved with the SQL statement and add the data to the listbox:

```
Dim tempRow As DataRow
For Each tempRow In myDataTable.Rows
    lbCustomers.Items.Add((tempRow("CompanyName") & _
      " (" & tempRow("ContactName") & ")"))
Next
```

The listbox is filled with the company name and contact name from the table in the database, according to the SQL statement we passed in. Example 14-1 contains the complete source for this example.

Example 14-1. Working with ADO.NET

```
Option Strict On
Imports System
Imports System.Drawing
Imports System.Collections
Imports System.ComponentModel
```

Example 14-1. Working with ADO.NET (continued)

```vb
Imports System.Windows.Forms
Imports System.Data
Imports System.Data.SqlClient

Public Class ADOForm1
    Inherits System.Windows.Forms.Form

    Private components As System.ComponentModel.Container
    Private lbCustomers As System.Windows.Forms.ListBox

    Public Sub New( )
        InitializeComponent( )

        ' connect to my local server, northwind db
        Dim connectionString As String = _
            "server=localhost; " & _
            "uid=sa; " & _
            "pwd=YourPassword; " & _
            "database=northwind"

        ' get records from the customers table
        Dim commandString As String = _
            "Select CompanyName, ContactName from Customers"

        ' create the data set command object
        ' and the myDataSet
        Dim myDataAdapter As New SqlDataAdapter( _
            commandString, connectionString)

        Dim myDataSet As New DataSet( )

        ' fill the data set object
        myDataAdapter.Fill(myDataSet, "Customers")

        ' Get the one table from the myDataSet
        Dim myDataTable As DataTable = myDataSet.Tables(0)

        ' for each row in the table, display the info
        Dim tempRow As DataRow
        For Each tempRow In myDataTable.Rows
            lbCustomers.Items.Add((tempRow("CompanyName") & _
                " (" & tempRow("ContactName") & ")"))
        Next

    End Sub 'New

    Private Sub InitializeComponent( )
        Me.components = New System.ComponentModel.Container( )
        Me.lbCustomers = New System.Windows.Forms.ListBox( )
        lbCustomers.Location = New System.Drawing.Point(48, 24)
        lbCustomers.Size = New System.Drawing.Size(368, 160)
        lbCustomers.TabIndex = 0
```

Example 14-1. Working with ADO.NET (continued)

```
        Me.Text = "ADOFrm1"
        Me.AutoScaleBaseSize = New System.Drawing.Size(5, 13)
        Me.ClientSize = New System.Drawing.Size(464, 273)
        Me.Controls.Add(lbCustomers)
    End Sub 'InitializeComponent

    Public Overloads Shared Sub Main(ByVal args() As String)
        Application.Run(New ADOForm1())
    End Sub 'Main
End Class 'ADOForm1
```

With just a few lines of code, you have extracted a set of data from the database and displayed it in the listbox, as shown in Figure 14-1.

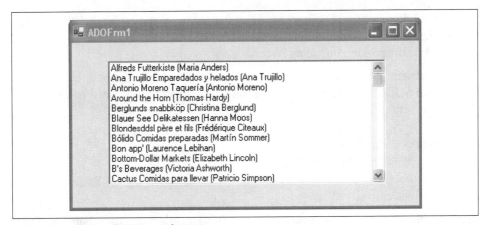

Figure 14-1. Output from Example 14-1

These lines of code accomplish the following tasks:

- Create the string for the connection:

```
Dim connectionString As String = _
    "server=localhost; uid=sa; pwd=; database=northwind"
```

- Create the string for the select statement:

```
Dim commandString As String = _
    "Select CompanyName, ContactName from Customers"
```

- Create the DataAdapter and pass in the selection and connection strings:

```
Dim myDataAdapter As New SqlDataAdapter( _
    commandString, connectionString)
```

- Create a new DataSet object:

```
Dim myDataSet As New DataSet()
```

- Fill the DataSet from the Customers table using the DataAdapter:

```
myDataAdapter.Fill(myDataSet, "Customers")
```

- Extract the DataTable from the DataSet:

```
Dim myDataTable As DataTable = myDataSet.Tables(0)
```

- Use the DataTable to fill the listbox:

```
Dim tempRow As DataRow
For Each tempRow In myDataTable.Rows
    lbCustomers.Items.Add((tempRow("CompanyName") & _
      " (" & tempRow("ContactName") & ")"))
Next
```

Using ADO Managed Providers

Example 14-1 used one of the managed providers currently available with ADO.NET: the SQL Managed Provider, the OLE DB Managed Provider, etc. The SQL Managed Provider is optimized for SQL Server and is restricted to working with SQL Server databases. The more general solution is the OLE DB Managed Provider, which will connect to any OLE DB provider, including Access.

You can rewrite Example 14-1 to work with the Northwind database using Access rather than SQL Server with just a few small changes. First, you need to change the connection string:

```
Dim connectionString As String = _
"provider=Microsoft.JET.OLEDB.4.0; " & _
"data source = c:\\nwind.mdb"
```

This query connects to the Northwind database on the C drive. (Your exact path might be different.)

Next, change the DataAdapter object to an ADODataAdapter rather than a SqlDataAdapter:

```
Dim myDataAdapter As New OleDbDataAdapter( _
    commandString, connectionString)
```

Also be sure to add an Imports statement for the OleDb namespace:

```
Imports System.Data.OleDb
```

This design pattern continues throughout the two Managed Providers; for every object whose class name begins with "Sql," there is a corresponding class beginning with "ADO." Example 14-2 illustrates the complete OLE DB version of Example 14-1.

Example 14-2. Using the OLE DB Managed Provider

```
Option Strict On
Imports System
Imports System.Drawing
Imports System.Collections
Imports System.ComponentModel
Imports System.Windows.Forms
```

Example 14-2. Using the OLE DB Managed Provider (continued)

```
Imports System.Data
Imports System.Data.OleDb

Public Class ADOForm1
    Inherits System.Windows.Forms.Form

    Private components As System.ComponentModel.Container
    Private lbCustomers As System.Windows.Forms.ListBox

    Public Sub New()
        InitializeComponent()

        ' connect to my local server, northwind db
        Dim connectionString As String = _
            "provider=Microsoft.JET.OLEDB.4.0; " & _
            "data source = c:\\nwind.mdb"

        ' get records from the customers table
        Dim commandString As String = _
          "Select CompanyName, ContactName from Customers"

        ' create the data set command object
        ' and the myDataSet
        Dim myDataAdapter As New OleDbDataAdapter( _
          commandString, connectionString)

        Dim myDataSet As New DataSet()

        ' fill the data set object
        myDataAdapter.Fill(myDataSet, "Customers")

        ' Get the one table from the myDataSet
        Dim myDataTable As DataTable = myDataSet.Tables(0)

        ' for each row in the table, display the info
        Dim tempRow As DataRow
        For Each tempRow In myDataTable.Rows
            lbCustomers.Items.Add((tempRow("CompanyName") & _
              " (" & tempRow("ContactName") & ")"))
        Next

    End Sub 'New

    Private Sub InitializeComponent()
        Me.components = New System.ComponentModel.Container()
        Me.lbCustomers = New System.Windows.Forms.ListBox()
        lbCustomers.Location = New System.Drawing.Point(48, 24)
        lbCustomers.Size = New System.Drawing.Size(368, 160)
        lbCustomers.TabIndex = 0
        Me.Text = "ADOFrm1"
        Me.AutoScaleBaseSize = New System.Drawing.Size(5, 13)
        Me.ClientSize = New System.Drawing.Size(464, 273)
```

Example 14-2. Using the OLE DB Managed Provider (continued)

```
      Me.Controls.Add(lbCustomers)
   End Sub 'InitializeComponent

   Public Overloads Shared Sub Main(ByVal args( ) As String)
      Application.Run(New ADOForm1( ))
   End Sub 'Main
End Class 'ADOForm1
```

The output from this is identical to that from the previous example, as shown in Figure 14-2.

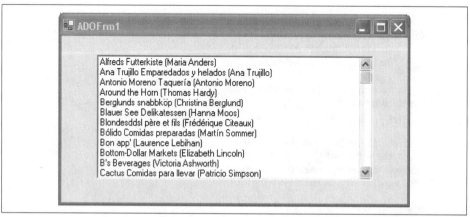

Figure 14-2. Output from Example 14-2

The ADO Managed Provider is more general than the SQL Managed Provider and can, in fact, be used to connect to SQL Server as well as to any other OLE DB object. Because the SQL Server Provider is optimized for SQL Server, it will be more efficient to use the SQL Server-specific provider when working with SQL Server. In time, any number of specialized managed providers will be available.

Working with Data-Bound Controls

ADO.NET provides good support for "data-bound" objects (that is, objects that can be tied to a particular data set, such as those retrieved from a database by ADO.NET).

A simple example of a data-bound control is the DataGrid control provided with both Windows Forms and Web Forms.

Populating a DataGrid

In its simplest use, a DataGrid is easy to implement. Once again, first create a DataSet and then fill it from the Customers table of the Northwind database, but this time, rather than iterating through the rows of the data set and writing the output to a listbox, you can simply bind the Customers table in your data set to a DataGrid control.

To illustrate, alter Example 14-1 by deleting the listbox from the form you created and replace it with a DataGrid. The default name provided by the Visual Studio design tool is DataGrid1, but let's change it to CustomerDataGrid. After the data set is created and filled, you bind the DataGrid through its DataSource property:

```
CustomerDataGrid.DataSource =
    myDataSet.Tables("Customers").DefaultView
```

Example 14-3 provides the complete source code for this example.

Example 14-3. Using a DataGrid

```
Option Strict On
Imports System
Imports System.Drawing
Imports System.Collections
Imports System.ComponentModel
Imports System.Windows.Forms
Imports System.Data
Imports System.Data.SqlClient

Public Class ADOForm3
    Inherits System.Windows.Forms.Form
    Private components As System.ComponentModel.Container
    Friend WithEvents CustomerDataGrid As _
        System.Windows.Forms.DataGrid


    Public Sub New( )
        InitializeComponent( )

        ' set up connection and command strings
        Dim connectionString As String = _
        "server=localhost; " & _
        "uid=sa; pwd=YourPassword; database=northwind"
        Dim commandString As String = _
        "Select CompanyName, ContactName, ContactTitle, " & _
        "Phone, Fax from Customers"

        ' create a data set and fill it
        Dim myDataAdapter As _
        New SqlDataAdapter(commandString, connectionString)
        Dim myDataSet As New DataSet( )
        myDataAdapter.Fill(myDataSet, "Customers")

        ' bind the DataSet to the grid
        CustomerDataGrid.DataSource = _
            myDataSet.Tables("Customers").DefaultView
    End Sub 'New

    Private Sub InitializeComponent( )
```

Example 14-3. Using a DataGrid (continued)

```
        ' Removed to save space
    End Sub 'InitializeComponent

End Class 'ADOForm3
```

The code is embarrassingly easy to implement and the results are quite impressive, as shown in Figure 14-3. Notice that every field in the record is represented by a column in the DataGrid, and that the titles of the columns are the names of the fields. All of this is the default behavior of the DataGrid.

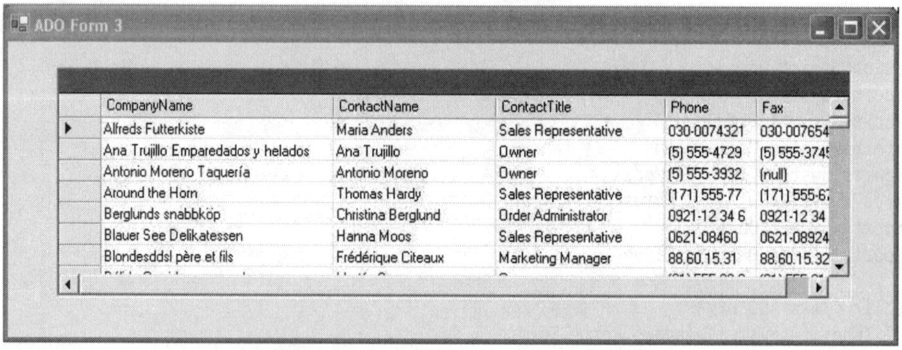

Figure 14-3. Using the DataGrid

Customizing the DataSet

It is possible to precisely control every aspect of creating the DataSet, rather than using the default settings. In the previous examples, when you created the DataSet you passed in a commandString and a connectionString:

```
Dim myDataAdapter As _
    New SqlDataAdapter(commandString, connectionString)
```

These were assigned internally to a SqlCommand object and a SqlConnection object, respectively. You can instead explicitly create these objects to gain finer control over their properties.

In this next example, you'll give the class four new class members:

```
Private myConnection As System.Data.SqlClient.SqlConnection
Private myDataSet As System.Data.DataSet
Private myCommand As System.Data.SqlClient.SqlCommand
Private myDataAdapter As System.Data.SqlClient.SqlDataAdapter
```

The connection is created by instantiating a SqlConnection object with the connection string:

```
Dim connectionString As String = _
    "server=localhost; uid=sa; " & _
```

```
"pwd=YourPassword; database=northwind"

myConnection = _
    New System.Data.SqlClient.SqlConnection(connectionString)
```

and then it is opened explicitly:

```
myConnection.Open( )
```

By hanging on to this connection, you can reuse it (as you'll see in a subsequent example) and you can also use its transaction support if needed.

Next, explicitly create the DataSet object and set one of its properties:

```
myDataSet = New System.Data.DataSet( )
myDataSet.CaseSensitive = True
```

Setting CaseSensitive to true indicates that string comparisons within DataTable objects are case-sensitive.

Next, explicitly create the SqlCommand object and give that new command object the connection object and the text for the command:

```
myCommand = New System.Data.SqlClient.SqlCommand( )
myCommand.Connection = myConnection
myCommand.CommandText = "Select * from Customers"
```

Finally, create the SqlDataAdapter object and assign to it the SqlCommand object you just established. Then tell the DataSet how to map the table columns, using the table you're searching, and instruct the SqlDataAdapter to fill the DataSet object:

```
myDataAdapter = New System.Data.SqlClient.SqlDataAdapter( )
myDataAdapter.SelectCommand = myCommand
myDataAdapter.TableMappings.Add("Table", "Customers")
myDataAdapter.Fill(myDataSet)
```

That done, you're ready to fill the DataGrid:

```
dataGrid1.DataSource = _
    myDataSet.Tables("Customers").DefaultView
```

(This time I've used the default name for the DataGrid.)

Example 14-4 provides the complete source code.

Example 14-4. Customizing a DataSet

```
Option Strict On
Imports System
Imports System.Drawing
Imports System.Collections
Imports System.ComponentModel
Imports System.Windows.Forms
Imports System.Data
Imports System.Data.SqlClient

Public Class ADOForm1
```

Example 14-4. Customizing a DataSet (continued)

```
    Inherits System.Windows.Forms.Form
    Private components As System.ComponentModel.Container
    Private dataGrid1 As System.Windows.Forms.DataGrid

    ' private System.Data.ADO.ADOConnection myConnection;
    Private myConnection As System.Data.SqlClient.SqlConnection
    Private myDataSet As System.Data.DataSet
    Private myCommand As System.Data.SqlClient.SqlCommand
    Private myDataAdapter As System.Data.SqlClient.SqlDataAdapter

    Public Sub New( )
        InitializeComponent( )

        ' create the connection object and open it
        Dim connectionString As String = _
            "server=localhost; uid=sa; " & _
            "pwd=YourPassword; database=northwind"

        myConnection = _
            New System.Data.SqlClient.SqlConnection(connectionString)
        myConnection.Open( )

        ' create the DataSet and set a property
        myDataSet = New System.Data.DataSet( )
        myDataSet.CaseSensitive = True

        ' create the SqlCommand  object and assign the
        ' connection and the select statement
        myCommand = New System.Data.SqlClient.SqlCommand( )
        myCommand.Connection = myConnection
        myCommand.CommandText = "Select * from Customers"

        ' create the myDataAdapter object and pass in the
        ' SQL Command object and establish the table mappings
        myDataAdapter = New System.Data.SqlClient.SqlDataAdapter( )
        myDataAdapter.SelectCommand = myCommand
        myDataAdapter.TableMappings.Add("Table", "Customers")

        ' Tell the myDataAdapter object to fill the DataSet
        myDataAdapter.Fill(myDataSet)

        ' display it in the grid
        dataGrid1.DataSource = _
            myDataSet.Tables("Customers").DefaultView
    End Sub 'New

    Private Sub InitializeComponent( )
        ' Removed to save space
    End Sub 'InitializeComponent

End Class 'ADOForm1
```

The result of this is shown in Figure 14-4. Now that you have this control, you are in a position to get much fancier in your use of the grid.

	CustomerID	CompanyNa	ContactName	ContactTitle	Address	City	Region	PostalCode	Cou
▶	ALFKI	Alfreds Futter	Maria Anders	Sales Repres	Obere Str. 57	Berlin	(null)	12209	Gern
	ANATR	Ana Trujillo E	Ana Trujillo	Owner	Avda. de la C	México D.F.	(null)	05021	Mexi
	ANTON	Antonio More	Antonio More	Owner	Mataderos 2	México D.F.	(null)	05023	Mexi
	AROUT	Around the H	Thomas Hard	Sales Repres	120 Hanover	London	(null)	WA1 1DP	UK
	BERGS	Berglunds sn	Christina Ber	Order Admini	Berguvsväge	Luleå	(null)	S-958 22	Swe
	BLAUS	Blauer See D	Hanna Moos	Sales Repres	Forsterstr. 57	Mannheim	(null)	68306	Gern
	BLONP	Blondesddsl	Frédérique Ci	Marketing Ma	24, place Klé	Strasbourg	(null)	67000	Fran
	BOLID	Bólido Comid	Martín Somm	Owner	C/ Araquil, 67	Madrid	(null)	28023	Spai
	BONAP	Bon app'	Laurence Leb	Owner	12, rue des B	Marseille	(null)	13008	Fran
	BOTTM	Bottom-Dollar	Elizabeth Lin	Accounting M	23 Tsawasse	Tsawassen	BC	T2F 8M4	Cana
	BSBEV	B's Beverage	Victoria Ashw	Sales Repres	Fauntleroy Ci	London	(null)	EC2 5NT	UK

Figure 14-4. Taking direct control of the DataGrid

Combining Data Tables

With the work you've done so far, it is easy now to build a grid that reflects the relationship between two or more tables. For example, you might like to examine all the orders that each customer has placed over some period of time.

Relational databases are built on the idea that one table relates to other tables. The relationship between Orders and Customers is that every order includes a CustomerID, which is a *foreign key* in Orders and a *primary key* in Customers. Thus, you have a one-to-many relationship, in which one customer can have many orders, but each order has exactly one customer. You'd like to be able to display this relationship in the grid.

ADO.NET makes this fairly easy, and you can build on the previous example. This time, you want to represent two tables, Customers and Orders, rather than just the Customers table. To do so, you need only a single DataSet object and a single Connection object, but you need two SqlCommand objects and two SqlDataAdapter objects.

After you create the SqlDataAdapter for Customers, just as you did in the previous example, go on to create a second command for Orders:

```
myCommand2 = New System.Data.SqlClient.SqlCommand( )
myCommand2.Connection = myConnection
myCommand2.CommandText = "Select * from Orders"
```

Notice that DataAdapter2 can reuse the same connection as used by the earlier DataAdapter object. The new CommandText is different, of course, because you are searching a different table.

Next, instantiate a second SqlDataAdapter object with this new command and map its table to Orders. You can then fill the DataSet with the second table:

```
myDataAdapter2 = New System.Data.SqlClient.SqlDataAdapter()
myDataAdapter2.SelectCommand = myCommand2
myDataAdapter2.TableMappings.Add("Table", "Orders")
```

You now have a single DataSet with two tables. You can display either one or both of the tables, but in this example you'll do more. There is a relationship between these tables, and you want to display that relationship. Unfortunately, the DataSet is ignorant of the relationship, unless you explicitly create a DataRelation object and add it to the DataSet.

Start by declaring an object of type DataRelation:

```
Dim myDataRelation As System.Data.DataRelation
```

This relation will represent the relationship in the database between Customers.CustomerID and Orders.CustomerID. To model this, you need a pair of DataColumn objects:

```
Dim dataColumn1 As System.Data.DataColumn
Dim dataColumn2 As System.Data.DataColumn
```

Each DataColumn must be assigned a column in the table within the DataSet:

```
dataColumn1 = _
    myDataSet.Tables("Customers").Columns("CustomerID")
dataColumn2 = _
    myDataSet.Tables("Orders").Columns("CustomerID")
```

You're now ready to create the DataRelation object, passing into the constructor the name of the relationship and the two DataColumn objects:

```
myDataRelation = New System.Data.DataRelation( _
    "CustomersToOrders", dataColumn1, dataColumn2)
```

You can now add that relation to the DataSet:

```
myDataSet.Relations.Add(myDataRelation)
```

Next, create a DataViewManager object that provides a view of the DataSet for the DataGrid, and set the DataGrid.DataSource property to that view:

```
Dim dataSetView As DataViewManager = _
    myDataSet.DefaultViewManager
DataGrid1.DataSource = _
    dataSetView
```

Finally, because the DataGrid now has more than one table, you must tell the grid which table is the "parent" table, or the one table to which many other tables can relate. Do this by setting the DataMember property as shown:

```
DataGrid1.DataMember= "Customers"
```

Example 14-5 provides the complete source for this program.

Example 14-5. Using a DataGrid with two tables

```
Option Strict On
Imports System
Imports System.Drawing
Imports System.Collections
Imports System.ComponentModel
Imports System.Windows.Forms
Imports System.Data
Imports System.Data.SqlClient

Public Class ADOForm1
    Inherits System.Windows.Forms.Form
    Private components As System.ComponentModel.Container

    ' private System.Data.ADO.ADOConnection myConnection;
    Private myConnection As System.Data.SqlClient.SqlConnection
    Private myDataSet As System.Data.DataSet
    Private myCommand As System.Data.SqlClient.SqlCommand
    Private myCommand2 As System.Data.SqlClient.SqlCommand
    Private myDataAdapter As System.Data.SqlClient.SqlDataAdapter
    Private myDataAdapter2 As System.Data.SqlClient.SqlDataAdapter

    Public Sub New()
        InitializeComponent()

        ' create the connection object and open it
        Dim connectionString As String = _
            "server=localhost; uid=sa; " & _
            "pwd=YourPassword; database=northwind"

        myConnection = _
        New System.Data.SqlClient.SqlConnection(connectionString)
        myConnection.Open()

        ' create the DataSet and set a property
        myDataSet = New System.Data.DataSet()
        myDataSet.CaseSensitive = True

        ' create the SqlCommand  object and assign the
        ' connection and the select statement
        myCommand = New System.Data.SqlClient.SqlCommand()
        myCommand.Connection = myConnection
        myCommand.CommandText = "Select * from Customers"

        myCommand2 = New System.Data.SqlClient.SqlCommand()
        myCommand2.Connection = myConnection
        myCommand2.CommandText = "Select * from Orders"

        ' create the myDataAdapter object and pass in the
        ' SQL Command object and establish the table mappings
        myDataAdapter = New System.Data.SqlClient.SqlDataAdapter()
        myDataAdapter2 = New System.Data.SqlClient.SqlDataAdapter()
```

Example 14-5. Using a DataGrid with two tables (continued)

```
        myDataAdapter.SelectCommand = myCommand
        myDataAdapter2.SelectCommand = myCommand2
        myDataAdapter.TableMappings.Add("Table", "Customers")
        myDataAdapter2.TableMappings.Add("Table", "Orders")

        ' Tell the myDataAdapter object to fill the DataSet
        myDataAdapter.Fill(myDataSet)
        myDataAdapter2.Fill(myDataSet)

        Dim myDataRelation As System.Data.DataRelation
        Dim dataColumn1 As System.Data.DataColumn
        Dim dataColumn2 As System.Data.DataColumn
        dataColumn1 = _
            myDataSet.Tables("Customers").Columns("CustomerID")
        dataColumn2 = _
            myDataSet.Tables("Orders").Columns("CustomerID")

        myDataRelation = New System.Data.DataRelation( _
            "CustomersToOrders", dataColumn1, dataColumn2)

        myDataSet.Relations.Add(myDataRelation)

        Dim dataSetView As DataViewManager = _
            myDataSet.DefaultViewManager

        ' display it in the grid
        DataGrid1.DataSource = _
            dataSetView
        DataGrid1.DataMember = "Customers"

    End Sub 'New
    Friend WithEvents DataGrid1 As System.Windows.Forms.DataGrid

    Private Sub InitializeComponent()
        ' Removed to save space
    End Sub 'InitializeComponent

End Class 'ADOForm1
```

The result is impressive. Figure 14-5 shows the grid with one customer chosen. The CustomersToOrders link is open under customer ID CACTU.

Clicking the link opens all the orders for that customer, as shown in Figure 14-6.

Changing Database Records

So far, you've retrieved data from a database, but you haven't manipulated its records in any way. Using ADO.NET, it is of course possible to add records, change an existing record, or delete a record altogether.

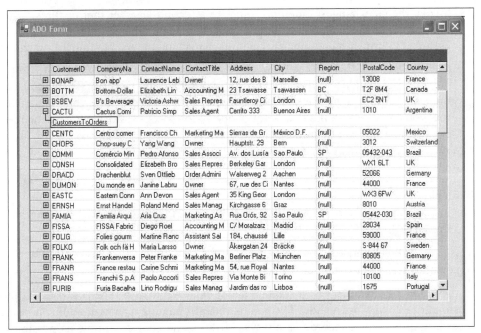

Figure 14-5. All the customers, with a CustomersToOrders link open

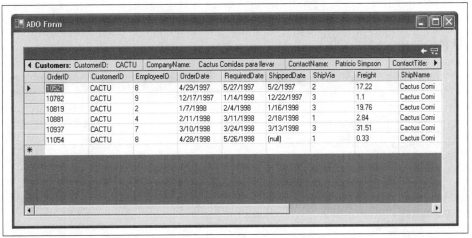

Figure 14-6. All the orders for the chosen customer

In a typical implementation, you might work your way through the following steps:

1. Fill the tables for your DataSet using a stored procedure or SQL.

2. Display the data in various DataTable objects within your DataSet by either binding to a control or looping through the rows in the tables.

3. Change data in individual DataTable objects by adding, modifying, or deleting DataRow objects.

4. Invoke the GetChanges() method to create a second DataSet that features only the changes to the data.

5. Check for errors in the second newly created DataSet by examining the HasErrors property. If there are errors, check the HasErrors property of each DataTable in the DataSet. If the table has errors, invoke the GetErrors() method of the DataTable and get back an array of DataRow objects with errors. On each row you can examine the RowError property for specific information about the error, which you can then resolve.

6. Merge the second DataSet with the first.

7. Call the Update() method on the DataAdapter object and pass in the merged DataSet.

8. Invoke the AcceptChanges() method on the DataSet, or invoke RejectChanges() to cancel the changes.

This process gives you very fine control over the update to your data as well as an opportunity to fix any data that would otherwise cause an error.

In the following example, you'll create a dialog box that displays the contents of the Customer table in Northwinds. The goal is to test updating a record, adding a new record, and deleting a record. As always, I'll keep the code as simple as possible, which means eliminating many of the error-checking and exception-handling routines you might expect in a production program.

Figure 14-7 shows the somewhat crude but useful form I've built to experiment with these features of ADO.NET.

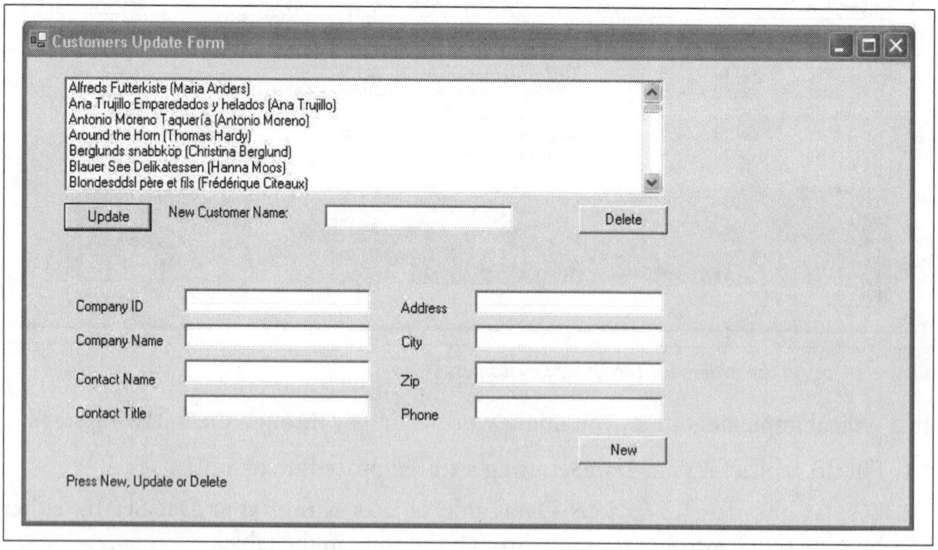

Figure 14-7. The ADO Update form

This form consists of a listbox (lbCustomers), a button for Update (btnUpdate), an associated text box (txtCustomerName), and a Delete button (btnDelete). There is also a set of eight text fields that are used in conjunction with the New button (btnNew). These text fields represent eight of the fields in the Customers table in the Northwind database. There is also a label (lblMessage) that you can use for writing messages to the user (it currently says "Press New, Update or Delete").

Accessing the Data

First, create the DataAdapter object and the DataSet as private member variables, along with the DataTable:

```
Private myDataAdapter As SqlDataAdapter
Private myDataSet As DataSet
Private myDataTable As DataTable
```

This enables you to refer to these objects from various member methods. You start by creating strings for the connection and the command that will get you the table you need:

```
Dim connectionString As String = _
    "server=localhost; uid=sa; " & _
    "pwd=YourPassword; database=northwind"

Dim commandString As String = _
    "Select * from Customers"
```

These strings are passed as parameters to the SqlDataAdapter constructor:

```
myDataAdapter = New SqlDataAdapter( _
    commandString, connectionString)
```

A DataAdapter may have four SQL commands associated with it. Right now, we have only one: myDataAdapter.SelectCommand. The InitializeCommands() method creates the remaining three: InsertCommand, UpdateCommand, and DeleteCommand. InitializeCommands() uses the AddParams() method to associate a column in each SQL command with the columns in the modified rows:

```
Private Sub AddParms( _
    ByVal cmd As SqlCommand, _
    ByVal ParamArray cols( ) As String)
    ' Add each parameter
    Dim column As [String]
    For Each column In cols
        cmd.Parameters.Add("@" & column, SqlDbType.Char, 0, column)
    Next column
End Sub 'AddParms
```

InitializeCommands() creates each SQL command in turn, using placeholders that correspond to the column argument passed to AddParm():

```
Private Sub InitializeCommands( )

    ' Reuse the SelectCommand's Connection.
```

```
        Dim connection As SqlConnection = _
            CType(myDataAdapter.SelectCommand.Connection, _
            SqlConnection)

        ' Create an explicit, reusable insert command
        myDataAdapter.InsertCommand = connection.CreateCommand( )
        myDataAdapter.InsertCommand.CommandText = _
            "Insert into customers " & _
            "(CustomerId, CompanyName, ContactName, ContactTitle, " & _
            " Address, City, PostalCode, Phone) " & _
            "values(@CustomerId, @CompanyName, @ContactName, " & _
            "  @ContactTitle, @Address, @City, @PostalCode, @Phone)"

        AddParms(myDataAdapter.InsertCommand, _
            "CustomerId", "CompanyName", "ContactName", _
            "ContactTitle", "Address", "City", "PostalCode", "Phone")

        ' Create an explicit update command
        myDataAdapter.UpdateCommand = _
            connection.CreateCommand( )
        myDataAdapter.UpdateCommand.CommandText = _
            "update Customers " & _
            "set CompanyName = _"
            @CompanyName where CustomerID = @CustomerId"
        AddParms(myDataAdapter.UpdateCommand, _
            "CompanyName", "CustomerID")

        ' Create an explicit delete command
        myDataAdapter.DeleteCommand = _
            connection.CreateCommand( )
        myDataAdapter.DeleteCommand.CommandText = _
            "delete from customers where customerID = @CustomerId"
        AddParms(myDataAdapter.DeleteCommand, "CustomerID")
    End Sub 'InitializeCommands
```

The DataAdapter uses these three commands to modify the table when you invoke Update().

Back in the constructor, you can now create the DataSet and fill it with the SqlData-Adapter object you've just created:

```
    myDataSet = New DataSet( )
    myDataAdapter.Fill(myDataSet, "Customers")
```

Display the table contents by calling the PopulateLB() method, which is a private method that fills the listbox from the contents of the single table in the DataSet:

```
    Private Sub PopulateLB( )
        myDataTable = myDataSet.Tables(0)
        lbCustomers.Items.Clear( )
        Dim dr As DataRow
        For Each dr In myDataTable.Rows
            lbCustomers.Items.Add(dr("CompanyName") & _
                " (" & dr("ContactName") & ")")
        Next
    End Sub 'PopulateLB
```

Updating a Record

The form is now displayed, and you're ready to update a record. Highlight a record and fill in a new customer name in the topmost text field. When you press Update, read the resulting name and put it into the chosen record.

The first task is to get the specific row the user wants to change:

```
Protected Sub btnUpdate_Click( _
    ByVal sender As Object, _
    ByVal e As System.EventArgs) _
    Handles btnUpdate.Click

    Dim targetRow As DataRow = _
        myDataTable.Rows(lbCustomers.SelectedIndex)
```

You declare a new object of type DataRow and initialize it with a reference to the specific row in the DataTable's Rows collection that corresponds to the selected item in the listbox. Remember that DataTable was declared as a member variable and initialized in the PopulateLB() method shown in the previous section.

You can now display the name of the company you're going to update:

```
lblMessage.Text = "Updating " & _
    targetRow("CompanyName")
Application.DoEvents()
```

 The call to the static method DoEvents() of the Application class causes the application to process Windows messages and paint the screen with the message. If you were to leave this line out, the current thread would dominate the processor and the messages would not be printed until the button handler completes its work.

Call BeginEdit() on the DataRow to put the row into editing mode. This suspends events on the row so that you could, if you chose, edit a number of rows at once without triggering validation rules (there are no validation rules in this example). It is good form to bracket changes on DataRows with calls to BeginEdit() and EndEdit():

```
targetRow.BeginEdit()
targetRow("CompanyName") = txtCustomerName.Text
targetRow.EndEdit()
```

The actual edit is to the column CompanyName within the targetRow object, which is set to the text value of the text control txtCustomerName. The net effect is that the CompanyName field in the row is set to whatever the user put into that text box.

Notice that the column you want is indexed within the row by the name of that column. In this case, the name will match the name that is used in the database, but this is not required. When you created the DataSet, you could have used the TableMappings() method to change the names of the columns.

Having edited the column, you are ready to check to make sure there are no errors. First, extract all the changes made to the DataSet (in this case, there will be only one change) using the GetChanges() method, passing in a DataRowState enumeration to indicate that you want only those rows that have been modified. GetChanges() returns a new DataSet object:

```
Dim dataSetChanged As DataSet = _
    myDataSet.GetChanges(DataRowState.Modified)
```

Now you can check for errors. To simplify the code, I've included a flag to indicate that all is OK. If you find any errors, rather than trying to fix them you can just set the flag to false and not make the updates:

```
Dim okayFlag As Boolean = True
If dataSetChanged.HasErrors Then
    okayFlag = False
    Dim msg As String = "Error in row with customer ID "

    Dim theTable As DataTable
    For Each theTable In dataSetChanged.Tables
        If theTable.HasErrors Then
            Dim errorRows As DataRow() = theTable.GetErrors()
            Dim errorRow As DataRow
            For Each errorRow In errorRows
                msg = msg & errorRow("CustomerID")
            Next
        End If
    Next
    lblMessage.Text = msg
End If
```

You first test to see whether the new data record set has any errors by checking the HasErrors property. If HasErrors is true, there are errors; set the Boolean okayFlag to false, and then go on to discover where the error lies. To do so, iterate through all the tables in the new database (in this case, there is only one), and if a table has errors you'll get an array of all the rows in that table with errors (shown here as the error-Rows array).

Then iterate through the array of rows with errors, handling each in turn. In this case, you just update the message on the dialog box, but in a production environment you might interact with the user to fix the problem.

If the okayFlag is still true after testing HasErrors, there were no errors and you are ready to update the database. First, merge the new DataSet back in with the original (presumably, in a production program you'd be merging the fixed tables back in with the original):

```
If okayFlag Then
    myDataSet.Merge(dataSetChanged)
```

You can now update the DataSet:

```
myDataAdapter.Update(myDataSet, "Customers")
```

This causes the DataAdapter object to create the necessary command text to update the database. You can actually see that text by accessing the CommandText property of the DataAdapter object. You can display the command in the message text:

```
lblMessage.Text = myDataAdapter.UpdateCommand.CommandText
Application.DoEvents( )
```

You now must tell the DataSet to accept the changes and then repopulate the listbox from the DataSet:

```
myDataSet.AcceptChanges( )
PopulateLB( )
```

If okayFlag were false, there would have been errors; in this example, we'd just reject the changes:

```
Else
    myDataSet.RejectChanges( )
End If
```

Deleting a Record

The code for handling the Delete button is even simpler. First, get the target row:

```
Protected Sub btnDelete_Click( _
    ByVal sender As Object, _
    ByVal e As System.EventArgs) _
    Handles btnDelete.Click
    ' get the selected row
    Dim targetRow As DataRow = _
        myDataTable.Rows(lbCustomers.SelectedIndex)
```

and form the delete message:

```
Dim msg As String = _
    targetRow("CompanyName") & " deleted. "
```

You don't want to show the message until the row is deleted, but you need to get it now because after you delete the row it will be too late!

You're now ready to mark the row for deletion:

```
targetRow.Delete( )
```

 Calling AcceptChanges( ) on the DataSet causes AcceptChanges( ) to be called on each table within the DataSet. This in turn causes AcceptChanges( ) to be called on each row in those tables. Thus the one call to DataSet.AcceptChanges( ) cascades down through all the contained tables and rows.

Next, you need to call Update( ) and AcceptChanges( ), and then refresh the listbox. However, if this operation fails, the row will still be marked for deletion. If you then try to issue a legitimate command, such as an insertion, update or another deletion, the DataAdapter will try to commit the erroneous deletion again, and the whole batch will fail because of the delete. In order to avert this situation, wrap the remaining operations in a try block, and call RejectChanges( ) if they fail:

```
Try
    myDataAdapter.Update(myDataSet, "Customers")
    myDataSet.AcceptChanges( )
    PopulateLB( )
    lblMessage.Text = msg
    Application.DoEvents( )
Catch ex As SqlException
    myDataSet.RejectChanges( )
    MessageBox.Show(ex.Message)
End Try
```

 Deleting records from the Customers database might cause an exception if the record deleted is constrained by database integrity rules. For example, if a customer has orders in the Orders table, you cannot delete the customer until you delete the orders. To solve this, Example 14-6 will create new Customer records that you can then delete at will.

Creating New Records

To create a new record, the user will fill in the fields and press the New button. This will fire the btnNew.Click event, which invokes the btnNew_Click( ) event handling method:

```
Protected Sub btnNew_Click( _
    ByVal sender As Object, _
    ByVal e As System.EventArgs) _
    Handles btnNew.Click
```

In the event handler, you call DataTable.NewRow( ), which asks the table for a new DataRow object:

```
Dim newRow As DataRow = myDataTable.NewRow( )
```

This is very elegant because the new row that the DataTable produces has all the necessary DataColumns for this table. You can just fill in the columns you care about, taking the text from the user interface (UI):

```
newRow("CustomerID") = txtCompanyID.Text
newRow("CompanyName") = txtCompanyName.Text
newRow("ContactName") = txtContactName.Text
newRow("ContactTitle") = txtContactTitle.Text
newRow("Address") = txtAddress.Text
newRow("City") = txtCity.Text
newRow("PostalCode") = txtZip.Text
newRow("Phone") = txtPhone.Text
```

Now that the row is fully populated, just add it back to the table:

```
myDataTable.Rows.Add(newRow)
```

The table resides within the DataSet, so all you have to do is tell the DataAdapter object to update the database with the DataSet and accept the changes:

```
myDataAdapter.Update(myDataSet, "Customers")
myDataSet.AcceptChanges()
```

Next, update the user interface:

```
lblMessage.Text = _
    myDataAdapter.UpdateCommand.CommandText
Application.DoEvents()
```

You can now repopulate the listbox with your new added row and clear the text fields so that you're ready for another new record:

```
PopulateLB()
ClearFields()
```

ClearFields() is a private method that simply sets all the text fields to empty strings. That method and the entire program are shown in Example 14-6.

Example 14-6. Updating, deleting, and adding records

```
Option Strict On
Imports System
Imports System.Drawing
Imports System.Collections
Imports System.ComponentModel
Imports System.Windows.Forms
Imports System.Data
Imports System.Data.SqlClient

Public Class ADOForm1
    Inherits System.Windows.Forms.Form
    Private components As System.ComponentModel.Container
    Private label9 As System.Windows.Forms.Label
    Private txtPhone As System.Windows.Forms.TextBox
    Private label8 As System.Windows.Forms.Label
    Private txtContactTitle As System.Windows.Forms.TextBox
    Private label7 As System.Windows.Forms.Label
    Private txtZip As System.Windows.Forms.TextBox
    Private label6 As System.Windows.Forms.Label
    Private txtCity As System.Windows.Forms.TextBox
    Private label5 As System.Windows.Forms.Label
    Private txtAddress As System.Windows.Forms.TextBox
    Private label4 As System.Windows.Forms.Label
    Private txtContactName As System.Windows.Forms.TextBox
    Private label3 As System.Windows.Forms.Label
    Private txtCompanyName As System.Windows.Forms.TextBox
    Private label2 As System.Windows.Forms.Label
    Private txtCompanyID As System.Windows.Forms.TextBox
    Private label1 As System.Windows.Forms.Label
    Private WithEvents btnNew As System.Windows.Forms.Button
    Private txtCustomerName As System.Windows.Forms.TextBox
    Private WithEvents btnUpdate As System.Windows.Forms.Button
```

Example 14-6. Updating, deleting, and adding records (continued)

```
    Private lblMessage As System.Windows.Forms.Label
    Private WithEvents btnDelete As System.Windows.Forms.Button
    Private lbCustomers As System.Windows.Forms.ListBox

    ' the myDataSet, myDataAdapter, and myDataTable are members
    ' so that we can access them from any member method.
    Private myDataAdapter As SqlDataAdapter
    Private myDataSet As DataSet
    Private myDataTable As DataTable


    Public Sub New( )
        InitializeComponent( )

        Dim connectionString As String = _
            "server=localhost; uid=sa; " & _
            "pwd=YourPassword; database=northwind"

        Dim commandString As String = _
            "Select * from Customers"
        myDataAdapter = _
            New SqlDataAdapter( _
                commandString, connectionString)

        InitializeCommands( )

        myDataSet = New DataSet( )
        myDataAdapter.Fill(myDataSet, "Customers")
        PopulateLB( )
    End Sub 'New

    Private Sub AddParms( _
        ByVal cmd As SqlCommand, _
        ByVal ParamArray cols( ) As String)
        ' Add each parameter
        Dim column As [String]
        For Each column In cols
            cmd.Parameters.Add("@" & column, SqlDbType.Char, 0, column)
        Next column
    End Sub 'AddParms

    Private Sub InitializeCommands( )

        ' Reuse the SelectCommand's Connection.
        Dim connection As SqlConnection = _
            CType(myDataAdapter.SelectCommand.Connection, _
            SqlConnection)

        ' Create an explicit, reusable insert command
        myDataAdapter.InsertCommand = connection.CreateCommand( )
        myDataAdapter.InsertCommand.CommandText = _
            "Insert into customers " & _
```

Example 14-6. Updating, deleting, and adding records (continued)

```
            "(CustomerId, CompanyName, ContactName, ContactTitle, " & _
            " Address, City, PostalCode, Phone) " & _
            "values(@CustomerId, @CompanyName, @ContactName, " & _
            "   @ContactTitle, @Address, @City, @PostalCode, @Phone)"

        AddParms(myDataAdapter.InsertCommand, _
            "CustomerId", "CompanyName", "ContactName", _
            "ContactTitle", "Address", "City", "PostalCode", "Phone")

        ' Create an explicit update command
        myDataAdapter.UpdateCommand = _
            connection.CreateCommand()
        myDataAdapter.UpdateCommand.CommandText = _
            "update Customers " & _
            "set CompanyName = _"
            @CompanyName where CustomerID = @CustomerId"
        AddParms(myDataAdapter.UpdateCommand, _
            "CompanyName", "CustomerID")

        ' Create an explicit delete command
        myDataAdapter.DeleteCommand = _
            connection.CreateCommand()
        myDataAdapter.DeleteCommand.CommandText = _
            "delete from customers where customerID = @CustomerId"
        AddParms(myDataAdapter.DeleteCommand, "CustomerID")
    End Sub 'InitializeCommands

    ' fill the listbox with columns from the Customers table
    Private Sub PopulateLB()
        myDataTable = myDataSet.Tables(0)
        lbCustomers.Items.Clear()
        Dim dataRow As DataRow
        For Each dataRow In myDataTable.Rows
            lbCustomers.Items.Add((dataRow("CompanyName") & _
                " (" & dataRow("ContactName") & ")"))
        Next dataRow
    End Sub 'PopulateLB

    Private Sub InitializeComponent()
        ' Removed to save space
    End Sub 'InitializeComponent

    ' handle the new button click
    Protected Sub btnNew_Click( _
        ByVal sender As Object, _
        ByVal e As System.EventArgs) _
        Handles btnNew.Click
        ' create a new row, populate it
        Dim newRow As DataRow = myDataTable.NewRow()
        newRow("CustomerID") = txtCompanyID.Text
        newRow("CompanyName") = txtCompanyName.Text
        newRow("ContactName") = txtContactName.Text
```

Example 14-6. Updating, deleting, and adding records (continued)

```
    newRow("ContactTitle") = txtContactTitle.Text
    newRow("Address") = txtAddress.Text
    newRow("City") = txtCity.Text
    newRow("PostalCode") = txtZip.Text
    newRow("Phone") = txtPhone.Text

    ' add the new row to the table
    myDataTable.Rows.Add(newRow)

    ' update the database
    Try
        myDataAdapter.Update(myDataSet, "Customers")
        myDataSet.AcceptChanges( )

        ' inform the user
        lblMessage.Text = "Updated!"
        Application.DoEvents( )

        ' repopulate the listbox
        PopulateLB( )
        ' clear all the text fields
        ClearFields( )
    Catch ex As SqlException
        myDataSet.RejectChanges( )
        MessageBox.Show(ex.Message)
    End Try
End Sub 'btnNew_Click

' set all the text fields to empty strings
Private Sub ClearFields( )
    txtCompanyID.Text = ""
    txtCompanyName.Text = ""
    txtContactName.Text = ""
    txtContactTitle.Text = ""
    txtAddress.Text = ""
    txtCity.Text = ""
    txtZip.Text = ""
    txtPhone.Text = ""
End Sub 'ClearFields

' handle the update button click
Protected Sub btnUpdate_Click( _
    ByVal sender As Object, _
    ByVal e As System.EventArgs) _
    Handles btnUpdate.Click

    ' get the selected row
    Dim targetRow As DataRow = _
        myDataTable.Rows(lbCustomers.SelectedIndex)

    ' inform the user
    lblMessage.Text = "Updating " & targetRow("CompanyName")
```

Example 14-6. Updating, deleting, and adding records (continued)

```
Application.DoEvents( )

' edit the row
targetRow.BeginEdit( )
targetRow("CompanyName") = txtCustomerName.Text
targetRow.EndEdit( )

' get each row that changed
Dim myDataSetChanged As DataSet = _
    myDataSet.GetChanges(DataRowState.Modified)

' test to make sure all the changed rows are without errors
Dim okayFlag As Boolean = True
If myDataSetChanged.HasErrors Then
    okayFlag = False
    Dim msg As String = "Error in row with customer ID "

    ' examine each table in the changed myDataSet
    Dim theTable As DataTable
    For Each theTable In myDataSetChanged.Tables
        ' if any table has errors, find out which rows
        If theTable.HasErrors Then
            ' get the rows with errors
            Dim errorRows As DataRow( ) = theTable.GetErrors( )

            ' iterate through the errors and correct
            ' (in our case, just identify)
            Dim theRow As DataRow
            For Each theRow In errorRows
                msg = msg & theRow("CustomerID")
            Next theRow
        End If
    Next theTable
    lblMessage.Text = msg
End If
' if we have no errors
If okayFlag Then

    ' update the database
    myDataAdapter.Update(myDataSetChanged, "Customers")

    ' inform the user
    lblMessage.Text = "Updated " & targetRow("CompanyName")
    Application.DoEvents( )

    ' accept the changes and repopulate the listbox
    myDataSet.AcceptChanges( )
    PopulateLB( )
    ' if we had errors, reject the changes
Else
    myDataSet.RejectChanges( )
End If
```

Example 14-6. Updating, deleting, and adding records (continued)

```
    End Sub 'btnUpdate_Click

    ' handle the delete button click
    Protected Sub btnDelete_Click( _
        ByVal sender As Object, _
        ByVal e As System.EventArgs) _
        Handles btnDelete.Click
        ' get the selected row
        Dim targetRow As DataRow = _
            myDataTable.Rows(lbCustomers.SelectedIndex)

        ' prepare message for user
        Dim msg As String = targetRow("CompanyName") & " deleted. "

        ' delete the selected row
        targetRow.Delete( )

        ' update the database
        Try
            myDataAdapter.Update(myDataSet, "Customers")
            myDataSet.AcceptChanges( )
            ' repopulate the listbox without the deleted record
            PopulateLB( )

            ' inform the user
            lblMessage.Text = msg
            Application.DoEvents( )
        Catch ex As SqlException
            myDataSet.RejectChanges( )
            MessageBox.Show(ex.Message)
        End Try
    End Sub 'btnDelete_Click

End Class 'ADOForm1
```

Figure 14-8 shows the filled-out form just before the New button is pressed.

Figure 14-9 shows the form immediately after the new record is added. Note that the new record is appended to the end of the list and the text fields are cleared.

ADO.NET and XML

In this chapter, I have demonstrated the kinds of data access that users have come to expect from ADO and shown how the new ADO.NET data access framework provides such support through its class libraries. I would be remiss, however, if I failed to mention that ADO.NET also provides complete support for XML. Most interesting is its support for presenting the contents of a data set as either a collection of tables, as we have explored in this chapter, or as an XML document. The tight integration of ADO.NET and XML and its applications are beyond the scope of this book.

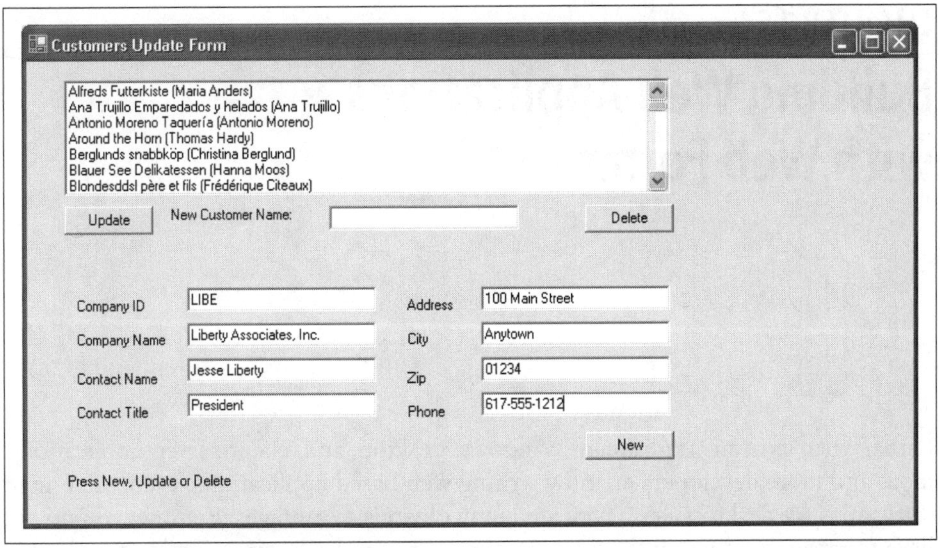

Figure 14-8. Ready to add a new record

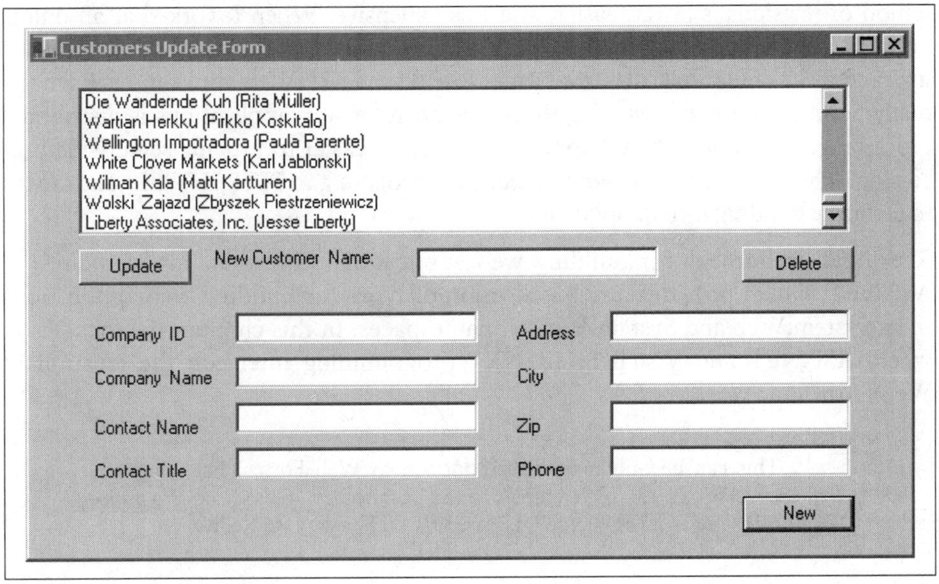

Figure 14-9. After adding the new record

CHAPTER 15

Building Web Applications with Web Forms

Rather than writing traditional Windows desktop and client-server applications, more and more developers are now writing web-based applications, even when their software is for desktop use. There are many obvious advantages. For one, you do not have to create as much of the user interface; you can let Internet Explorer and other browsers handle a lot of it for you. Another, perhaps bigger advantage is that distribution of revisions is faster, easier, and less expensive. When I worked at an online network that predated the Web, we estimated our cost of distribution for each upgrade at $1 million per diskette (remember diskettes?). Web applications have virtually zero distribution cost. The third advantage of web applications is distributed processing. With a web-based application, it is far easier to provide server-side processing. The Web provides standardized protocols (e.g., HTTP, HTML, and XML) to facilitate building *n*-tier applications.

The .NET technology for building web applications (and dynamic web sites) is ASP.NET, which provides a rich collection of types for building web applications in its System.Web and System.Web.UI namespaces. In this chapter, the focus is on where ASP.NET and Visual Basic .NET programming intersect: the creation of Web Forms.

 This can be only a brief introduction to Web Forms. For complete coverage of this rich and powerful technology, please see *Programming ASP.NET*, by Jesse Liberty and Dan Hurwitz (O'Reilly).

Web Forms bring Rapid Application Development (RAD) techniques (such as those used in Windows Forms) to the development of web applications. As with Windows Forms, you can drag and drop controls onto a form and write the supporting code either inline or in code-behind pages. With Web Forms, however, the application is deployed to a web server, and users interact with the application through a standard browser.

Understanding Web Forms

Web Forms implement a programming model in which web pages are dynamically generated on a web server for delivery to a browser over the Internet. They are, in some ways, the successor to ASP pages, and they marry ASP technology with traditional programming.

With Web Forms, you create an HTML page with static content, and you write Visual Basic .NET code to generate dynamic content. The VB.NET code runs on the server, and the data produced is integrated with your static HTML to create the web page. What is sent to the browser is standard HTML.

Web Forms are designed to run on any browser, with the server rendering the correct browser-compliant HTML. You can do the programming for the logic of the Web Form in any .NET language.

Just as with Windows Forms, you *can* create Web Forms in Notepad (or another editor of your choice) rather than in Visual Studio. Many developers will choose to do so, but Visual Studio makes the process of designing and testing Web Forms *much* easier.

Web Forms divide the user interface into two parts: the visual part or user interface (UI), and the logic that lies behind it. This is very similar to developing Windows Forms as shown in Chapter 13, but with Web Forms the UI page and the code are in separate files.

The UI page is stored in a file with the extension *.aspx*. The logic (code) for that page can be stored in a separate code-behind Visual Basic .NET source file. When you run the form, the code-behind class file runs and dynamically creates the HTML sent to the client browser. This code makes use of the rich Web Forms types found in the System.Web and System.Web.UI namespaces of the .NET Framework Class Library (FCL).

With Visual Studio, Web Forms programming couldn't be simpler: open a form, drag some controls onto it, and write the code to handle events. Presto! You've written a web application.

On the other hand, even with Visual Studio, writing a robust and complete web application can be a daunting task. Web Forms offer a very rich UI; the number and complexity of web controls have greatly multiplied in recent years, and user expectations about the look and feel of web applications have risen accordingly.

In addition, web applications are inherently distributed. Typically, the client will not be in the same building as the server. For most web applications, you must take network latency, bandwidth, and network server performance into account when creating the UI; a round trip from client to host might take a few seconds.

Web Form Events

Web Forms are event-driven. An *event* is an object that encapsulates the idea that "something happened." An event is generated (or *raised*) when the user presses a button, selects from a listbox, or otherwise interacts with the UI. Events can also be generated by the system starting or finishing work. For example, open a file for reading, and the system raises an event when the file has been read into memory.

The method that responds to the event is called the *event handler*. Event handlers are written in Visual Basic .NET in the code-behind page and are associated with controls in the HTML page through control attributes.

Event handlers are delegates (see Chapter 12). By convention, ASP.NET event handlers return void and take two parameters. The first parameter represents the object raising the event. The second, called the *event argument*, contains information specific to the event, if any. For most events, the event argument is of type EventArgs, which does not expose any properties. For some controls, the event argument might be of a type derived from EventArgs that can expose properties specific to that event type.

In web applications, most events are typically handled on the server and, therefore, require a round trip. ASP.NET supports only a limited set of events, such as button clicks and text changes. These are events that the user might expect to cause a significant change, as opposed to Windows events (such as mouse-over) that might happen many times during a single user-driven task.

Postback versus non-postback events

Postback events are those that cause the form to be posted back to the server immediately. These include click type events, such as the Button Click event. In contrast, many events (typically change events) are considered *non-postback* in that the form is not posted back to the server immediately. Instead, these events are cached by the control until the next time a postback event occurs. You can force controls with non-postback events to behave in a postback manner by setting their AutoPostBack property to True.

State

A web application's *state* is the current value of all the controls and variables for the current user in the current session. The Web is inherently a "stateless" environment. This means that every post to the server loses the state from previous posts, unless the developer takes great pains to preserve this session knowledge. ASP.NET, however, provides support for maintaining the state of a user's session.

Whenever a page is posted to the server, it is re-created by the server from scratch before it is returned to the browser. ASP.NET provides a mechanism that automatically maintains state for server controls. Thus, if you provide a list and the user has

---

made a selection, that selection is preserved after the page is posted back to the server and redrawn on the client.

Web Form Life Cycle

Every request for a page made from a web server causes a chain of events at the server. These events, from beginning to end, constitute the *life cycle* of the page and all its components. The life cycle begins with a request for the page, which causes the server to load it. When the request is complete, the page is unloaded. From one end of the life cycle to the other, the goal is to render appropriate HTML output back to the requesting browser. The life cycle of a page is marked by the following events, each of which you can handle yourself or leave to default handling by the ASP.NET server:

Initialize
> Initialize is the first phase in the life cycle for any page or control. It is here that any settings needed for the duration of the incoming request are initialized.

Load ViewState
> The ViewState property of the control is populated. The ViewState information comes from a hidden variable on the control, used to persist the state across round trips to the server. The input string from this hidden variable is parsed by the page framework, and the ViewState property is set. The ViewState property can be modified via the LoadViewState() method, which allows ASP.NET to manage the state of your control across page loads so that each control is not reset to its default state each time the page is posted.

Process Postback Data
> During this phase, the data sent to the server in the posting is processed. If any of this data results in a requirement to update the ViewState, that update is performed via the LoadPostData() method.

Load
> CreateChildControls() is called, if necessary, to create and initialize server controls in the control tree. State is restored, and the form controls show client-side data. You can modify the load phase by handling the Load event with the OnLoad() method.

Send Postback Change Modifications
> If there are any state changes between the current state and the previous state, change events are raised via the RaisePostDataChangedEvent() method.

Handle Postback Events
> The client-side event that caused the postback is handled.

PreRender
> This is the phase just before the output is rendered to the browser. It is essentially your last chance to modify the output prior to rendering using the OnPreRender() method.

Save State

Near the beginning of the life cycle, the persisted view state was loaded from the hidden variable. Now it is saved back to the hidden variable, persisting as a string object that will complete the round trip to the client. You can override this using the SaveViewState( ) method.

Render

This is where the output to be sent back to the client browser is generated. You can override it using the Render( ) method. CreateChildControls( ) is called, if necessary, to create and initialize server controls in the control tree.

Dispose

This is the last phase of the life cycle. It gives you an opportunity to do any final cleanup and release references to any expensive resources, such as database connections. You can modify it using the Dispose( ) method.

Creating a Web Form

To create the simple Web Form that will be used in Example 15-1, start up Visual Studio .NET and open a New Project named *ProgrammingVBWeb*. In the Project Types window, select the Visual Basic .NET Projects folder (because Visual Basic .NET is your language of choice). In the Templates window, select ASP.NET Web Application, and enter the name of your project (*ProgrammingVBWeb*) in the Name text box. Visual Studio .NET will display *http://localhost/* as the default Location, but you can create a subdirectory if you choose to, as shown in Figure 15-1.

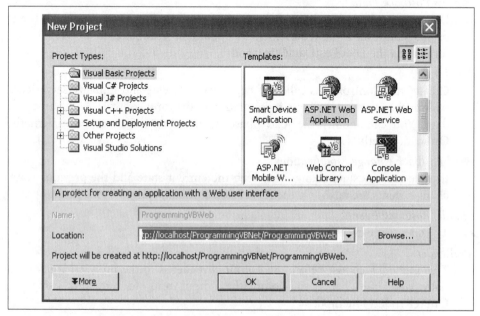

Figure 15-1. Creating a project in the New Project window of Visual Studio .NET

Visual Studio places nearly all the files it creates for the project in a folder within your local machine's default web site; for example, *c:\Inetpub\wwwroot\ProgrammingVBNET\ProgrammingVBWeb*.

> In Visual Studio .NET, a solution is a set of projects; each project will create a dynamic link library (DLL) or an executable (EXE). All projects are created in the context of a solution, and solutions are managed by *.sln* and *.suo* files.

The solution files and other Visual Studio-specific files are stored in *<drive>\Documents and Settings\<username>\My Documents\Visual Studio Projects* (where *<drive>* and *<username>* are specific to your machine).

> You must have IIS and the FrontPage Server extensions installed on your computer to use Web Forms. To configure the FrontPage Server extensions, open the Internet Service Manager and right-click the web site. Select `All Tasks->Configure Server Extensions`. For further information, please check *http://www.microsoft.com*.

When the application is created, Visual Studio places a number of files in your project. The Web Form itself is stored in a file named *WebForm1.aspx*. This file will contain only HTML. A second, equally important file, *WebForm1.aspx.vb*, stores the Visual Basic .NET code associated with your form; this is the code-behind file.

Notice that the code-behind file does *not* appear in the Solution Explorer. To see the code-behind (*.vb*) file, you must place the cursor within Visual Studio .NET, right-click the form, and choose "View Code" in the pop-up menu. You can now tab back and forth between the form itself, *WebForm1.aspx*, and the Visual Basic .NET code-behind file, *WebForm1.aspx.vb*. When viewing the form, *WebForm1.aspx*, you can choose between Design mode and HTML mode by clicking the tabs at the bottom of the Editor window. Design mode lets you drag controls onto your form; HTML mode allows you to view and edit the HTML code directly.

Let's take a closer look at the *.aspx* and code-behind files that Visual Studio creates. Start by renaming *WebForm1.aspx* to *HelloWeb.aspx*. To do this, close *WebForm1. aspx,* and then right-click its name in the Solution Explorer. Choose Rename and enter the name *HelloWeb.aspx*. After you rename it, open *HelloWeb.aspx* and view the code; you will find that the code-behind file has been renamed as well to *HelloWeb.aspx.vb*.

When you create a new Web Form application, Visual Studio .NET will generate a bit of boilerplate code to get you started, as shown in Example 15-1.

Example 15-1. Wizard-generated code for a Web Form

```
<%@ Page Language="vb"
    AutoEventWireup="false"
    Codebehind="HelloWeb.aspx.vb"
```

Example 15-1. Wizard-generated code for a Web Form (continued)

```
    Inherits="ProgrammingVBWeb.WebForm1"%>
<!DOCTYPE HTML PUBLIC "-//W3C//DTD HTML 4.0 Transitional//EN">
<html>
  <head>
    <title>WebForm1</title>
    <meta name="GENERATOR" content="Microsoft Visual Studio.NET 7.0">
    <meta name="CODE_LANGUAGE" content="Visual Basic 7.0">
    <meta name=vs_defaultClientScript content="JavaScript">
    <meta name=vs_targetSchema content="http://schemas.microsoft.com/intellisense/ie5">
  </head>
  <body MS_POSITIONING="GridLayout">

    <form id="Form1" method="post" runat="server">

    </form>

  </body>
</html>
```

What you see is typical boilerplate HTML except for the first line, which contains the following ASP.NET code:

```
<%@ Page Language="vb"
    AutoEventWireup="false"
    Codebehind="HelloWeb.aspx.vb"
    Inherits="ProgrammingVBWeb.WebForm1"%>
```

The Language attribute indicates that the language used on the code-behind page is Visual Basic .NET. The Codebehind attribute designates that the filename of that page is *HelloWeb.aspx.vb*, and the Inherits attribute indicates that this page derives from WebForm1. WebForm1 is a class declared in *HelloWeb.aspx.vb*:

```
Public Class WebForm1
    Inherits System.Web.UI.Page
```

As the Visual Basic .NET code makes clear, WebForm1 inherits from System.Web.UI.Page, which is the class that defines the properties, methods, and events common to all server-side pages.

Returning to the HTML view of *HelloWeb.aspx*, you see that a form has been specified in the body of the page using the standard HTML form tag:

```
<form id="Form1" method="post" runat="server">
```

Web Forms assumes that you need at least one form to manage the user interaction, and creates one when you open a project. The attribute runat="server" is the key to the server-side magic. Any tag that includes this attribute is considered a server-side control to be executed by the ASP.NET framework on the server.

Having created an empty Web Form, the first thing you might want to do is add some text to the page. By switching to HTML view, you can add script and HTML directly to the file just as you could with classic ASP. Adding the following line to the body segment of the HTML page will cause it to display a greeting and the current local time:

```
Hello World! It is now <% = DateTime.Now.ToString( ) %>
```

The <% and %> marks work just as they did in classic ASP, indicating that code (in this case, Visual Basic .NET) falls between them. The equals sign (=) immediately following the opening tag causes ASP.NET to display the value, just like a call to Response. Write( ). You could just as easily write the line as:

```
Hello World! It is now
<% Response.Write(DateTime.Now.ToString( )) %>
```

Run the page by pressing F5 (or save it and navigate to it in your browser). You should see the string printed to the browser, as in Figure 15-2.

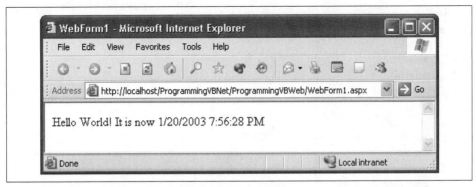

Figure 15-2. Output generated by the HelloWorld.aspx file

Adding Controls

You can add server-side controls to a Web Form in two ways: manually (by writing HTML into the HTML page), or by dragging controls from the toolbox to the Design page. For example, suppose you want to use buttons to let the user choose one of three Shippers provided in the Northwinds database. You could write the following HTML into the <form> element in the HTML window:

```
<asp:RadioButton GroupName="Shipper" id="Airborne"
    text = "Airborne Express" Checked="True" runat="server">
</asp:RadioButton>
<asp:RadioButton GroupName="Shipper" id="UPS"
    text = "United Parcel Service" runat="server">
</asp:RadioButton>
<asp:RadioButton GroupName="Shipper" id="Federal"
    text = "Federal Express" runat="server">
</asp:RadioButton>
```

The asp tags declare server-side ASP.NET controls that are replaced with normal HTML when the server processes the page. When you run the application, the browser displays three radio buttons in a button group; pressing one will deselect the others.

You can create the same effect more easily by dragging three buttons from the Visual Studio toolbox onto the Form, as illustrated in Figure 15-3.

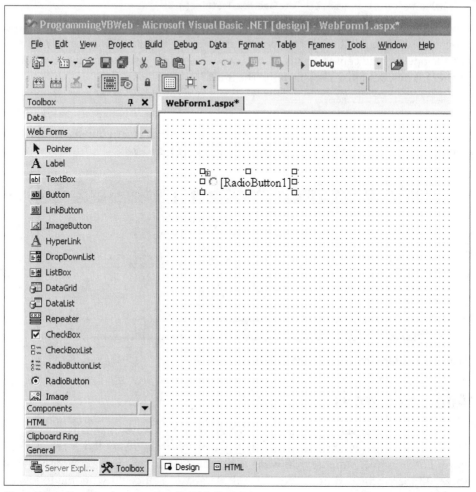

Figure 15-3. Dragging buttons onto the Web Form

You can add controls to a page in one of two modes. The default mode is GridLayout. When you add controls in GridLayout mode, they are arranged in the browser using absolute positioning (x and y coordinates).

The alternative mode is FlowLayout. With FlowLayout, the controls are added to the form from top to bottom, as in a Microsoft Word document. To change from GridLayout to FlowLayout or back, change the pageLayout property of the document in Visual Studio .NET.

Web Forms offers two types of server-side controls. The first is server-side HTML controls, also called Web Controls. These are standard HTML controls that you tag with the attribute runat="server".

The alternative to Web Controls is ASP.NET Server Controls, also called ASP Controls. ASP Controls have been designed to replace the standard HTML controls. ASP Controls provide a more consistent object model and more consistently named attributes. For example, with HTML controls, there are myriad different ways to handle input:

```
<input type="radio">
<input type="checkbox">
<input type="button">
<input type="text">
<textarea>
```

Each of these behaves differently and takes different attributes. The ASP Controls try to normalize the set of controls, using attributes consistently throughout the ASP control object model. The ASP Controls that correspond to the preceding HTML server-side controls are:

```
<asp:RadioButton>
<asp:CheckBox>
<asp:Button>
<asp:TextBox rows="1">
<asp:TextBox rows="5">
```

The remainder of this chapter focuses on ASP Controls.

Data Binding

Various technologies have offered programmers the opportunity to bind controls to data so that as the data is modified, the controls respond automatically. As Rocky used to say to Bullwinkle, "But that trick never works." Bound controls often provided only limited control over their look and feel, and performance was usually pretty terrible. The ASP.NET designers set out to solve these problems and provide a suite of robust data-bound controls, which simplify display and modification of data, sacrificing neither performance nor control over the UI.

In the previous section, you hardcoded radio buttons onto a form, one for each of three Shippers in the Northwinds database. That can't be the best way to do it; if you change the Shippers in the database, you have to go back and rewire the controls. This section shows how you can create these controls dynamically and then bind them to data in the database.

You might want to create the radio buttons based on data in the database because you can't know at design time what text the buttons will have, or even how many buttons you'll need. To accomplish this, use a RadioButtonList. RadioButtonList is a control that allows you to create radio buttons programatically; you provide the name and values for the buttons, and ASP.NET takes care of the plumbing.

Delete the radio buttons already on the form, and drag and drop a RadioButtonList in their place. Once it is there, you can use the Properties window to rename it to rbl1.

Setting Initial Properties

Web Forms programming is event-based; you write your code to respond to various events. Typically, the events you're responding to are user-initiated. For example, when the user clicks a button, a button-click event is generated.

The most important initial event is the Page_Load event, which is fired every time a Web Form is loaded. When the page is loaded, you want to fill the radio buttons with values from the database. For example, if you are creating a purchase form, you might create one radio button for each possible shipping method, such as UPS, FedEx, and so forth. You should therefore put your code into the Page_Load() method to create the buttons.

You only want to load these values into the radio buttons the first time the page is loaded. If the user clicks a button or takes another action that sends the page back to the server, you do not want to retrieve the values again when the page is reloaded.

ASP.NET can differentiate the first time the page is displayed from subsequent displays after a client postback of the page to the server. Every Web Form page has the property IsPostBack, which will be true if the page is being loaded in response to a client postback, and false if it is being loaded for the first time.

You can check the value of IsPostBack. If it is false, you know that this is the first time the page is being displayed, and it's therefore time to get the values out of the database:

```
Private Sub Page_Load( _
    ByVal sender As System.Object, _
    ByVal e As System.EventArgs) _
    Handles MyBase.Load

    If Not IsPostBack Then
        '...
    End If

End Sub
```

The arguments to the Page_Load() method are the normal arguments for events, as discussed in Chapter 12.

Connecting to the Database

The code for making the connection to the database and filling a data set will look very familiar; it is almost identical to what you saw in Chapter 13. There is no difference in creating a data set for Web Forms and creating a data set for Windows Forms.

Start by declaring the member variables you need:

```
Private myConnection As System.Data.SqlClient.SqlConnection
Private myDataSet As System.Data.DataSet
Private myCommand As System.Data.SqlClient.SqlCommand
Private dataAdapter As System.Data.SqlClient.SqlDataAdapter
```

As in Chapter 13, use the Structured Query Language (SQL) versions of SqlConnection and dataAdapter. Create the connectionString for the Northwinds database, and use that to instantiate and open the SQLConnection object:

```
Dim connectionString As String = _
    "server=Mozart; " & _
    "uid=sa; " & _
    "pwd=secret; " & _
    "database=northwind"
myConnection = _
    New System.Data.SqlClient.SqlConnection( _
        connectionString)
myConnection.Open( )
```

Create the data set and set it to handle case-sensitive queries:

```
myDataSet = New System.Data.DataSet( )
myDataSet.CaseSensitive = True
```

Next, create the SqlCommand object and assign it the connection object and the Select statement, which are needed to get the ShipperID and company name identifying each potential shipper. Use the name as the text for the radio button and the ShipperID as the value:

```
myCommand = New System.Data.SqlClient.SqlCommand( )
myCommand.Connection = myConnection
myCommand.CommandText = "Select ShipperID, CompanyName from Shippers"
```

Now create the dataAdapter object, set its SelectCommand property with your command object, and add the Shippers table to its table mappings:

```
dataAdapter = New System.Data.SqlClient.SqlDataAdapter( )
dataAdapter.SelectCommand = myCommand
dataAdapter.TableMappings.Add("Table", "Shippers")
```

Finally, fill the dataAdapter with the results of the query:

```
dataAdapter.Fill(myDataSet)
```

This is all virtually identical to what you saw in Chapter 13. This time, however, you're going to bind this data to the RadioButtonList you created earlier.

The first step is to set the properties on the RadioButtonList object. The first property of interest tells the RadioButtonList how to flow the radio buttons on the page:

```
rbl1.RepeatLayout = _
    System.Web.UI.WebControls.RepeatLayout.Flow
```

Flow is one of the two possible values in the RepeatLayout enumeration. The other is Table, which displays the radio buttons using a tabular layout. Next you must tell the RadioButtonList which values from the dataset are to be used for display (the DataTextField) and which is the value to be returned when selected by the user (the DataValueField):

```
rbl1.DataTextField = "CompanyName"
rbl1.DataValueField = "ShipperID"
```

The final steps are to tell the RadioButtonList which view of the data to use. For this example, use the default view of the Shippers table within the dataset:

```
rbl1.DataSource = myDataSet.Tables("Shippers").DefaultView
```

With that done, you're ready to bind the RadioButtonList to the dataset:

```
rbl1.DataBind( )
```

Finally, you should ensure that one of the radio buttons is selected, so select the first:

```
rbl1.Items(0).Selected = True
```

This statement accesses the Items collection within the RadioButtonList, chooses the first item (the first radio button), and sets its Selected property to true.

When you run the program and navigate to the page in your browser, the buttons will be displayed, as shown in Figure 15-4.

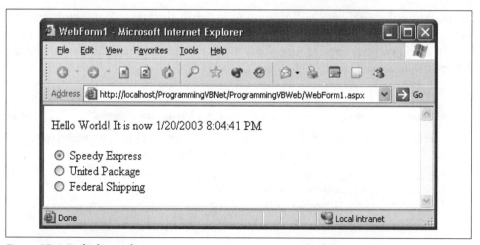

Figure 15-4. Radio button list

If you examine the page source, you will not find a RadioButtonList. Instead, standard HTML radio buttons have been created, and each has been given a shared ID. This allows the browser to treat them as a group. Their labels have been created, and each radio button and its label have been wrapped in a <span> tag:

```
<span id="rbl1" style="...">
<input id="rbl1_0" type="radio" name="rbl1"
        value="1" checked="checked" />
```

```
<label for="rbl1_0">Speedy Express</label>
<br>
<!-- remaining buttons omitted for brevity -->
</span>
```

This HTML is generated by the server by combining the RadioButtonList you added to your HTML with the processing of the code-behind page. When the page is loaded, the Page_Load() method is called and the data adapter is filled. When you assign the rbl1.DataTextField to CompanyName and the rbl1.DataValueField to ShipperID and assign the rbl1.DataSource to the Shipper's table default view, you prepare the radio button list to generate the buttons. When you call DataBind, the radio buttons are created from the data in the data source.

By adding just a few more controls, you can create a complete form with which users can interact. You will do this by adding a more appropriate greeting ("Welcome to NorthWind"), a text box to accept the name of the user, two new buttons (Order and Cancel), and text that provides feedback to the user. Figure 15-5 shows the finished form.

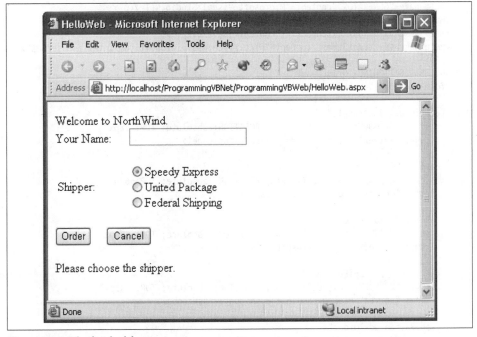

Figure 15-5. The finished form

This form will not win any awards for design, but its use will illustrate a number of key points about Web Forms.

I've never known a developer who didn't think he could design a perfectly fine UI. At the same time, I've never known one who actually could. UI design is one of those skills (such as teaching) that we all think we can do, but only a few very talented folks are good at it. As a developer, I know my limitations; I write the code, someone else lays it out on the page.

Example 15-2 is the complete HTML for the *.aspx* file.

Example 15-2. The .aspx page

```
<%@ Page Language="vb"
    AutoEventWireup="false"
    Codebehind="HelloWeb.aspx.vb"
    Inherits="ProgrammingVBWeb.WebForm1"%>
<!DOCTYPE HTML PUBLIC "-//W3C//DTD HTML 4.0 Transitional//EN">
<HTML>
  <HEAD>
    <title>WebForm1</title>
    <meta name="GENERATOR" content="Microsoft Visual Studio.NET 7.0">
    <meta name="CODE_LANGUAGE" content="Visual Basic 7.0">
    <meta name=vs_defaultClientScript content="JavaScript">
    <meta name=vs_targetSchema content="http://schemas.microsoft.com/intellisense/ie5">
  </HEAD>
  <body MS_POSITIONING="GridLayout">
    <form id="Form1" method="post" runat="server">

      <asp:Label id="Label1"
        style="Z-INDEX: 101; LEFT: 20px; POSITION: absolute; TOP: 28px"
        runat="server">Welcome to NorthWind.</asp:Label>

      <asp:Label id="Label2"
        style="Z-INDEX: 102; LEFT: 20px; POSITION: absolute; TOP: 67px"
        runat="server">Your Name:</asp:Label>

      <asp:Label id="Label3"
        style="Z-INDEX: 103; LEFT: 20px; POSITION: absolute; TOP: 134px"
        runat="server">Shipper:</asp:Label>

      <asp:Label id="lblFeedBack"
        style="Z-INDEX: 104; LEFT: 20px; POSITION: absolute; TOP: 241px"
        runat="server">Please choose the shipper.</asp:Label>

      <asp:Button id="Order"
        style="Z-INDEX: 105; LEFT: 20px; POSITION: absolute; TOP: 197px"
        runat="server" Text="Order"></asp:Button>

      <asp:Button id="Cancel"
        style="Z-INDEX: 106; LEFT: 128px; POSITION: absolute; TOP: 197px"
        runat="server" Text="Cancel"></asp:Button>

      <asp:TextBox id="txtName"
        style="Z-INDEX: 107; LEFT: 128px; POSITION: absolute; TOP: 64px"
```

Example 15-2. The .aspx page (continued)

```
        runat="server"></asp:TextBox>

    <asp:RadioButtonList id="rbl1"
        style="Z-INDEX: 108; LEFT: 112px; POSITION: absolute; TOP: 130px"
        runat="server"></asp:RadioButtonList>

    </form>

  </body>
</HTML>
```

The <asp:Button> controls will be converted into a standard HTML <input> tag. Again, the advantage of using ASP controls is that they provide a more consistent object model for the programmer and yet they generate standard HTML that every browser can display. Because they are marked with the runat="server" attribute as well as given an id attribute, you can access these buttons programmatically in server-side code if you choose to do so. Example 15-3 is the complete code-behind page to support this HTML.

Example 15-3. The code-behind page supporting the HTML

```
Imports System
Imports System.Collections
Imports System.ComponentModel
Imports System.Data
Imports System.Drawing
Imports System.Web
Imports System.Web.SessionState
Imports System.Web.UI
Imports System.Web.UI.WebControls
Imports System.Web.UI.HtmlControls


Public Class WebForm1
    Inherits System.Web.UI.Page

#Region " Web Form Designer Generated Code "
#End Region

    Protected Label1 As System.Web.UI.WebControls.Label
    Protected Label2 As System.Web.UI.WebControls.Label
    Protected Label3 As System.Web.UI.WebControls.Label
    Protected lblFeedBack As System.Web.UI.WebControls.Label
    Protected WithEvents Order As System.Web.UI.WebControls.Button
    Protected Cancel As System.Web.UI.WebControls.Button
    Protected txtName As System.Web.UI.WebControls.TextBox
    Protected rbl1 As System.Web.UI.WebControls.RadioButtonList

    Private myConnection As System.Data.SqlClient.SqlConnection
    Private myDataSet As System.Data.DataSet
    Private myCommand As System.Data.SqlClient.SqlCommand
    Private dataAdapter As System.Data.SqlClient.SqlDataAdapter
```

Example 15-3. The code-behind page supporting the HTML (continued)

```
Private Sub Page_Load( _
    ByVal sender As Object, _
    ByVal e As System.EventArgs) _
    Handles MyBase.Load
    ' the first time we load the page, get the data and
    ' set the radio buttons
    If Not IsPostBack Then
        ' connect to my local server, northwind db
        Dim connectionString As String = _
            "server=Mozart; " + _
            "uid=sa; " + _
            "pwd=secret; " + _
            "database=northwind"
        myConnection = _
          New System.Data.SqlClient.SqlConnection(connectionString)
        myConnection.Open( )

        ' create the data set and set a property
        myDataSet = New System.Data.DataSet( )
        myDataSet.CaseSensitive = True

        ' create the SqlCommand object and assign the
        ' connection and the select statement
        myCommand = New System.Data.SqlClient.SqlCommand( )
        myCommand.Connection = myConnection
        myCommand.CommandText = _
          "Select ShipperID, CompanyName from Shippers"

        ' create the dataAdapter object and pass in the
        ' SqlCommand object and establish the data mappings
        dataAdapter = New System.Data.SqlClient.SqlDataAdapter( )
        dataAdapter.SelectCommand = myCommand
        dataAdapter.TableMappings.Add("Table", "Shippers")

        ' Tell the dataAdapter object to fill the dataSet
        dataAdapter.Fill(myDataSet)

        ' set up the properties for the RadioButtonList
        rbl1.RepeatLayout = System.Web.UI.WebControls.RepeatLayout.Flow
        rbl1.DataTextField = "CompanyName"
        rbl1.DataValueField = "ShipperID"

        ' set the data source and bind to i
        rbl1.DataSource = myDataSet.Tables("Shippers").DefaultView
        rbl1.DataBind( )

        ' select the first button
        rbl1.Items(0).Selected = True
    End If
End Sub 'Page_Load

Private Sub Order_Click( _
```

Example 15-3. The code-behind page supporting the HTML (continued)

```
        ByVal sender As System.Object, _
        ByVal e As System.EventArgs) Handles Order.Click
        Dim msg As String
        msg = "Thank you " + txtName.Text + ". You chose "
        ' iterate over the radio buttons
        Dim i As Integer
        For i = 0 To rbl1.Items.Count - 1
            ' if it is selected, add it to the msg.
            If rbl1.Items(i).Selected Then
                msg = msg + rbl1.Items(i).Text
                lblFeedBack.Text = msg
            End If ' end if selected
        Next i ' end for loop
    End Sub
End Class 'WebForm1 ' end class WebForm1
```

Responding to Postback Events

The <asp:Button> objects automatically postback when clicked. You need not write any code to handle that event unless you want to do something more than postback to the server. If you take no other action, the page will simply be re-sent to the client.

Normally, when a page is redrawn, each control is redrawn from scratch. The Web is stateless, and if you want to manage the state of a control (e.g., redraw the user's text in the text box), you must do so yourself. In classic ASP, the programmer was responsible for managing this state, but ASP.NET provides some assistance. When the page is posted, a hidden element named ViewState is automatically added to the page:

```
<input type="hidden" name="__VIEWSTATE"
value="YTB6LTI5MTE3ODE1N19hMHpfaHo1ejF4X2Ewel9oejV6NXhfYTB6YTB6YTB6aHpSZXBlYXRMYXlvdX
RfU3lzdGVtLldlYi5VSS5XZWJDb25Ocm9scy5SZXBlYXRMYXlvdXR6VGFibGV4X0RhdGFWYWx1ZUZpZWxkX1N
oaXBwZXJJJRF9EYXRhVGVceHRGaWVsZF9Db21wYW55TmFtZXhfX3hfYTB6YTB6YXpTcGVlZHkgRVx4cHJlc3Nf
MV94X2F6VW5pdGVkIFBhY2thZ2VfMl94X2F6RmVkZXJhbCBTaGlwcGluZ18zX3hfeF94X3hfX3h4X3hfX
3hcdDUwX1N5c3RlbS5TdHJpbmc=a15204ed" />
```

This element represents the state of the form (the values already chosen by the user). When the page is redrawn on the client, ASP.NET uses the view state to return the controls to their previous state.

When the user clicks the Order button, the page is posted and the event handler assigned to that button is invoked:

```
Private Sub Order_Click( _
    ByVal sender As System.Object, _
    ByVal e As System.EventArgs) Handles Order.Click
    Dim msg As String
    msg = "Thank you " + txtName.Text + ". You chose "
    ' iterate over the radio buttons
    Dim i As Integer
```

```
    For i = 0 To rbl1.Items.Count - 1
        ' if it is selected, add it to the msg.
        If rbl1.Items(i).Selected Then
            msg = msg + rbl1.Items(i).Text
            lblFeedBack.Text = msg
        End If ' end if selected
    Next i ' end for loop
End Sub
```

 The easiest way to create the event handler is to double-click the Order button in Design mode in Visual Studio .NET. This will cause Visual Studio to add the WithEvents keyword to the declaration of the button:

```
Protected WithEvents Order As _
    System.Web.UI.WebControls.Button
```

It will also create a skeleton Order_Click() event-handler method for you. Alternatively, you can do this all by hand.

The Order_Click() handler creates a message based on the name you enter and the shipper you choose, and puts that message into the Feedback label. When the form first comes up, it looks like Figure 15-5. If I fill in my name, pick United Package, and press Order, the form will be submitted and then redisplayed. The result is shown in Figure 15-6.

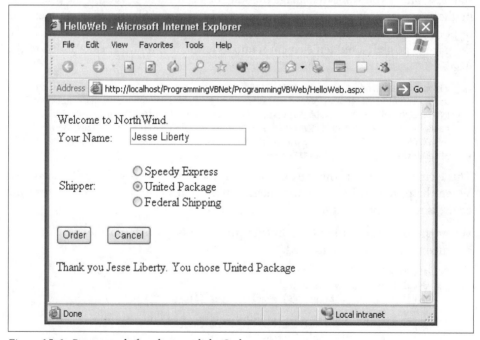

Figure 15-6. Page posted after the user clicks Order

The form automatically remembers the state of the radio button and text controls (this is what the VIEWSTATE field is for) and that the event handler has been called and run on the server; the label is updated accordingly.

 ASP programmers take note: there is no code in the *.aspx* file nor in the *.vb* file to manage the state. Nowhere do you stash away the state of the radio buttons or the text field; all this is managed automatically for you by ASP.NET.

CHAPTER 16

Programming Web Services

.NET Web Services expand on the concept of distributed processing to build components whose methods can be invoked across the Internet. These components can be built in any .NET language, and they communicate using open protocols that are platform-independent.

For example, a stock exchange server might provide a web service method that takes a stock ticker symbol as a parameter and returns a quote. An application might combine that service with another service from a different company that also takes a stock symbol but that returns background data about the company. The application developer can concentrate on adding value to these services, rather than duplicating the same service for his own application.

The list of web services that might be useful to developers and end users seems boundless. A bookstore might provide a web service that takes an ISBN and returns the price and availability of a title. A hotel's web service might take a date range and number of guests and return a reservation. Another web service might take a telephone number and return a name and address. Yet another might provide information about the weather or shuttle launches.

In such a world, a single application might draw on and stitch together the services of hundreds of small web services distributed all over the world. This takes the Web to an entirely new dimension: not only is information retrieved and exchanged, but also methods are invoked and applications are executed.

While .NET Web Services are a complex topic, the fundamentals are straightforward, and will be reviewed in this chapter. (For more complete coverage, see *Programming ASP.NET* by Jesse Liberty and Dan Hurwitz, O'Reilly.)

SOAP, WSDL, and Discovery

What is needed to make web services possible is a simple, universally accepted protocol for exposing, finding, and invoking web service functions. In 1999, Simple

Object Access Protocol (SOAP) was proposed to the World Wide Web Consortium. SOAP has the advantages of being based on XML and of using standard Internet communications protocols. SOAP is a lightweight, message-based protocol built on XML, HTTP, and SMTP.

Two other protocols are desirable, but not required, for a client to use a SOAP-enabled web service: Discovery and Description.

It is through the discovery process that web service clients learn that a service exists, what its capabilities are, and how to properly interact with it. A Discovery (*.disco*) file provides information to help browsers determine the URLs at any web site at which web services are available. When a server receives a request for a *.disco* file, it generates a list of some or all of the URLs at that site that provide web services.

The description of the methods provided by a particular service that can be understood and acted upon by clients is provided in .NET by the Web Service Description Language (WSDL) protocol, jointly developed by Microsoft, IBM, and others. WSDL is an XML schema used to describe the available methods—the interface—of a web service.

Server-Side Support

The plumbing necessary to discover and invoke web services is integrated into the .NET Framework and provided by classes within the System.Web.Services namespace. Creating a web service requires no special programming on your part; you need only write the implementing code, add the [WebMethod] attribute, and let the server do the rest. You can read about attributes in detail in Chapter 18.

Client-Side Support

You make use of a web service by writing client code that acts as though it were communicating directly with a local class. However, in reality, the client interacts with a *proxy*. The job of the proxy is to represent the server on the client machine, to bundle client requests into SOAP messages that are sent on to the server, and to retrieve the responses that contain the result. Proxies and the details of dealing with objects on other machines are covered in detail in Chapter 19.

Building a Web Service

To illustrate the techniques used to implement a web service in Visual Basic .NET using the services classes of the .NET Framework, you will build a simple calculator and then make use of its functions over the Web.

Begin by specifying the web service. To do so, define a class that inherits from System.Web.Services.WebService. The easiest way to create this class is to open Visual

Studio and create a new ASP.NET Web Service project. The default name that Visual Studio provides is WebService1, but you might want to choose something more appropriate.

Visual Studio .NET creates a skeleton web service and even provides a .NET Web Service example method for you to replace with your own code, as shown in Example 16-1.

Example 16-1. Skeleton web class generated by Visual Studio .NET

```
Option Strict On
Imports System

Imports System.Web.Services

<WebService(Namespace := "http://tempuri.org/")> _
Public Class Service1
    Inherits System.Web.Services.WebService

#Region " Web Services Designer Generated Code "

    Public Sub New( )
        MyBase.New( )

        'This call is required by the Web Services Designer.
        InitializeComponent( )

        'Add your own initialization code after the InitializeComponent( ) call

    End Sub

    'Required by the Web Services Designer
    Private components As System.ComponentModel.IContainer

    'NOTE: The following procedure is required by the Web Services Designer
    'It can be modified using the Web Services Designer.
    'Do not modify it using the code editor.
    <System.Diagnostics.DebuggerStepThrough( )> Private Sub InitializeComponent( )
        components = New System.ComponentModel.Container( )
    End Sub

    Protected Overloads Overrides Sub Dispose(ByVal disposing As Boolean)
        'CODEGEN: This procedure is required by the Web Services Designer
        'Do not modify it using the code editor.
        If disposing Then
            If Not (components Is Nothing) Then
                components.Dispose( )
            End If
        End If
        MyBase.Dispose(disposing)
    End Sub

#End Region
```

```
' WEB SERVICE EXAMPLE
' The HelloWorld( ) example service returns the string Hello World.
' To build, uncomment the following lines then save and build the project.
' To test this web service, ensure that the .asmx file is the start page
' and press F5.
'
'<WebMethod( )> Public Function HelloWorld( ) As String
'    HelloWorld = "Hello World"
' End Function
```

```
End Class
```

Create five methods: Add(), Sub(), Mult(), Div(), and Pow(). Each takes two parameters of type Double, performs the requested operation, and then returns a value of the same type. For example, here is the code for raising a number to some specified power:

```
Function Pow(ByVal x As Double, ByVal y As Double) As Double
    Dim retVal As Double = x
    Dim i As Integer
    For i = 0 To (y - 1) - 1
        retVal *= x
    Next i
    Return retVal
End Function 'Pow
```

To expose each method as a web service, you simply add the <WebMethod> attribute before each method declaration (attributes are discussed in Chapter 18). You are not required to expose all the methods of your class as web methods. You can pick and choose, adding the <WebMethod> attribute only to those methods you want to expose.

That's all you need to do; .NET takes care of the rest.

WSDL and Namespaces

Your web service will use a Web Service Description Language (WSDL) XML document to describe the web-callable end points. Within any WSDL document, an XML namespace must be used to ensure that the end points have unique names. The default XML namespace is *http://tempuri.org*, but you will want to modify this before making your web service publicly available.

You can change the XML namespace by using the WebService attribute:

```
<WebService(Namespace := _
    "http://www.LibertyAssociates.com/webServices/")>
```

You can read about attributes in detail in Chapter 18.

Example 16-2 shows the complete source code for the Calculator web service.

Example 16-2. Calculator web service program

```
Option Strict On
Imports System
Imports System.Web.Services

<WebService(Namespace := "http://tempuri.org/")> _
Public Class Service1
    Inherits System.Web.Services.WebService

#Region " Web Services Designer Generated Code "
#End Region
    <WebMethod(Description:="Add two numbers")> Public _
    Function Add(ByVal x As Double, ByVal y As Double) As Double
        Return x + y
    End Function 'Add

    <WebMethod(Description:="Subtract two numbers")> Public _
    Function Subtract(ByVal x As Double, ByVal y As Double) As Double
        Return x - y
    End Function 'Sub

    <WebMethod(Description:="Multiply two numbers")> Public _
    Function Mult(ByVal x As Double, ByVal y As Double) As Double
        Return x * y
    End Function 'Mult

    <WebMethod(Description:="Divide two numbers")> Public _
    Function Div(ByVal x As Double, ByVal y As Double) As Double
        Return x / y
    End Function 'Div

    <WebMethod(Description:="Raise a number to a power")> Public _
        Function Pow(ByVal x As Double, ByVal y As Double) As Double
        Dim retVal As Double = x
        Dim i As Integer
        For i = 0 To (y - 1) - 1
            retVal *= x
        Next i
        Return retVal
    End Function 'Pow

End Class
```

When you build this project with Visual Studio .NET, a DLL is created in the appropriate subdirectory of your Internet server (e.g., *c:\InetPub\wwwroot\ VBWSCals\bin*). A quick check of the base directory reveals that a *.vsdisco* file has also been added.

There is nothing magical about using Visual Studio .NET; you can create your server in Notepad if you like. Visual Studio .NET simply saves you the work of creating the directories, creating the *.vsdisco* file, and so forth. Visual Studio .NET is particularly helpful when creating the client files, as you'll see shortly.

Testing Your Web Service

If you open a browser to your web service's URL (or invoke the browser by running the program in Visual Studio .NET), you get an automatically generated, server-side web page that describes the web service, as shown in Figure 16-1. Test pages such as this offer a good way to test your web service. (The next section illuminates the seeming hocus-pocus that produces these pages.)

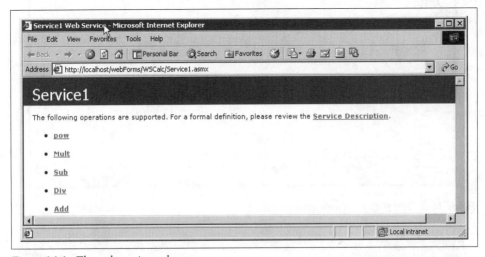

Figure 16-1. The web service web page

Notice that the description that you added to the WebMethod attribute is used here to provide a description of each method. Clicking a method brings you to a page that allows you to invoke it by typing in parameters and pressing the Invoke button. Figure 16-2 illustrates.

If you type 38 into the first value field and 4 into the second field, you will have asked the web service to raise 38 to the power of 4. The result is an XML page describing the output, as shown in Figure 16-3.

Notice that the URL encodes the parameters of 38 and 4, and the output XML shows the result of 2085136 ($38 \times 38 \times 38 \times 38 = 2085136$).

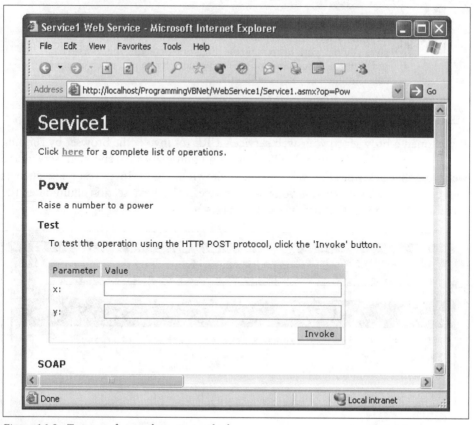

Figure 16-2. Test page for a web service method

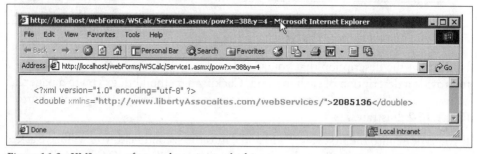

Figure 16-3. XML output for a web service method

Viewing the WSDL Contract

A lot of work is being done for you automatically. HTML pages describing your web service and its methods are generated, and these pages include links to pages in which the methods can be tested. How is this done?

As noted earlier, the web service is described in WSDL. You can see the WSDL document by appending ?wsdl to the web service URL, like this:

```
http://localhost/ProgrammingVBNET/VBWSCalc/Service1.asmx?wsdl
```

The browser displays the WSDL document, as shown in Figure 16-4.

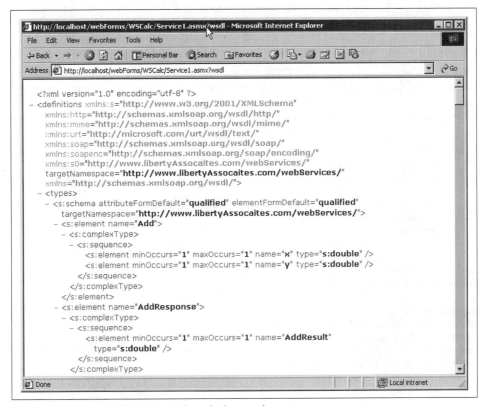

Figure 16-4. Sample WSDL output for calculator web service

The details of the WSDL document are beyond the scope of this book, but you can see that each method is fully described in a structured XML format. This is the information used by SOAP to allow the client browser to invoke your web service methods on the server.

Creating the Proxy

Before you can create a client application to interact with the calculator web service, you must first create a proxy class. Once again, you can do this by hand, but that would be hard work. The folks at Microsoft have provided a tool called *wsdl* that generates the source code for the proxy based on the information in the WSDL file.

To create the proxy, enter *wsdl* at the Visual Studio .NET command-line prompt followed by the path to the WSDL contract and the */l:vb* flag:

```
wsdl <url> /l:vb
```

For example, you might enter:

```
wsdl http://localhost/VBWSCalc/Service1.asmx?wsdl /l:vb
```

The flag */l:vb* tells *wsdl* to produce a Visual Basic .NET file.

The result is the creation of a Visual Basic .NET client file named *Service1.vb,* an excerpt of which appears in Example 16-3. You must add the namespace WSCalc because you'll need it when you build your client (the tool does not insert it for you).

Example 16-3. Sample client code to access the calculator web service

```
'------------------------------------------------------------------------
' <autogenerated>
'     This code was generated by a tool.
'     Runtime Version: 1.0.3705.288
'
'     Changes to this file may cause incorrect behavior and will be lost if
'     the code is regenerated.
' </autogenerated>
'------------------------------------------------------------------------


Option Strict Off
Option Explicit On

Imports System
Imports System.ComponentModel
Imports System.Diagnostics
Imports System.Web.Services
Imports System.Web.Services.Protocols
Imports System.Xml.Serialization

'
'This source code was auto-generated by wsdl, Version=1.0.3705.288.
'

'<remarks/>
Namespace VBWSCalc

    <System.Diagnostics.DebuggerStepThroughAttribute(), _
    System.ComponentModel.DesignerCategoryAttribute("code"), _
    System.Web.Services.WebServiceBindingAttribute(Name:="Service1Soap", [Namespace]:
="http://tempuri.org/")> _
    Public Class Service1
        Inherits System.Web.Services.Protocols.SoapHttpClientProtocol

        '<remarks/>
        Public Sub New( )
            MyBase.New( )
            Me.Url = "http://localhost/ProgrammingVBNET/VBWSCalc/Service1.asmx"
```

Example 16-3. Sample client code to access the calculator web service (continued)

```
        End Sub

        '<remarks/>
        <System.Web.Services.Protocols.SoapDocumentMethodAttribute("http://tempuri.org/
Add", RequestNamespace:="http://tempuri.org/", ResponseNamespace:="http://tempuri.org/",
Use:=System.Web.Services.Description.SoapBindingUse.Literal, ParameterStyle:=System.Web.
Services.Protocols.SoapParameterStyle.Wrapped)> _
        Public Function Add(ByVal x As Double, ByVal y As Double) As Double
            Dim results() As Object = Me.Invoke("Add", New Object() {x, y})
            Return CType(results(0), Double)
        End Function

        '<remarks/>
        Public Function BeginAdd(ByVal x As Double, ByVal y As Double, ByVal callback As
System.AsyncCallback, ByVal asyncState As Object) As System.IAsyncResult
            Return Me.BeginInvoke("Add", New Object() {x, y}, callback, asyncState)
        End Function

        '<remarks/>
        Public Function EndAdd(ByVal asyncResult As System.IAsyncResult) As Double
            Dim results() As Object = Me.EndInvoke(asyncResult)
            Return CType(results(0), Double)
        End Function

        '<remarks/>
        <System.Web.Services.Protocols.SoapDocumentMethodAttribute("http://tempuri.org/
Subtract", RequestNamespace:="http://tempuri.org/", ResponseNamespace:="http://tempuri.
org/", Use:=System.Web.Services.Description.SoapBindingUse.Literal, ParameterStyle:
=System.Web.Services.Protocols.SoapParameterStyle.Wrapped)> _
        Public Function Subtract(ByVal x As Double, ByVal y As Double) As Double
            Dim results() As Object = Me.Invoke("Subtract", New Object() {x, y})
            Return CType(results(0), Double)
        End Function

        '<remarks/>
        Public Function BeginSubtract(ByVal x As Double, ByVal y As Double, ByVal callback
As System.AsyncCallback, ByVal asyncState As Object) As System.IAsyncResult
            Return Me.BeginInvoke("Subtract", New Object() {x, y}, callback, asyncState)
        End Function

        '<remarks/>
        Public Function EndSubtract(ByVal asyncResult As System.IAsyncResult) As Double
            Dim results() As Object = Me.EndInvoke(asyncResult)
            Return CType(results(0), Double)
        End Function

        '<remarks/>
        <System.Web.Services.Protocols.SoapDocumentMethodAttribute("http://tempuri.org/
Mult", RequestNamespace:="http://tempuri.org/", ResponseNamespace:="http://tempuri.org/",
Use:=System.Web.Services.Description.SoapBindingUse.Literal, ParameterStyle:=System.Web.
Services.Protocols.SoapParameterStyle.Wrapped)> _
        Public Function Mult(ByVal x As Double, ByVal y As Double) As Double
```

```
            Dim results() As Object = Me.Invoke("Mult", New Object() {x, y})
            Return CType(results(0), Double)
        End Function


        '<remarks/>
        Public Function BeginMult(ByVal x As Double, ByVal y As Double, ByVal callback As
System.AsyncCallback, ByVal asyncState As Object) As System.IAsyncResult
            Return Me.BeginInvoke("Mult", New Object() {x, y}, callback, asyncState)
        End Function


        '<remarks/>
        Public Function EndMult(ByVal asyncResult As System.IAsyncResult) As Double
            Dim results() As Object = Me.EndInvoke(asyncResult)
            Return CType(results(0), Double)
        End Function


        '<remarks/>
        <System.Web.Services.Protocols.SoapDocumentMethodAttribute("http://tempuri.org/
Div", RequestNamespace:="http://tempuri.org/", ResponseNamespace:="http://tempuri.org/",
Use:=System.Web.Services.Description.SoapBindingUse.Literal, ParameterStyle:=System.Web.
Services.Protocols.SoapParameterStyle.Wrapped)> _
        Public Function Div(ByVal x As Double, ByVal y As Double) As Double
            Dim results() As Object = Me.Invoke("Div", New Object() {x, y})
            Return CType(results(0), Double)
        End Function


        '<remarks/>
        Public Function BeginDiv(ByVal x As Double, ByVal y As Double, ByVal callback As
System.AsyncCallback, ByVal asyncState As Object) As System.IAsyncResult
            Return Me.BeginInvoke("Div", New Object() {x, y}, callback, asyncState)
        End Function


        '<remarks/>
        Public Function EndDiv(ByVal asyncResult As System.IAsyncResult) As Double
            Dim results() As Object = Me.EndInvoke(asyncResult)
            Return CType(results(0), Double)
        End Function


        '<remarks/>
        <System.Web.Services.Protocols.SoapDocumentMethodAttribute("http://tempuri.org/
Pow", RequestNamespace:="http://tempuri.org/", ResponseNamespace:="http://tempuri.org/",
Use:=System.Web.Services.Description.SoapBindingUse.Literal, ParameterStyle:=System.Web.
Services.Protocols.SoapParameterStyle.Wrapped)> _
        Public Function Pow(ByVal x As Double, ByVal y As Double) As Double
            Dim results() As Object = Me.Invoke("Pow", New Object() {x, y})
            Return CType(results(0), Double)
        End Function


        '<remarks/>
        Public Function BeginPow(ByVal x As Double, ByVal y As Double, ByVal callback As
System.AsyncCallback, ByVal asyncState As Object) As System.IAsyncResult
            Return Me.BeginInvoke("Pow", New Object() {x, y}, callback, asyncState)
```

Example 16-3. Sample client code to access the calculator web service (continued)

```
        End Function

        '<remarks/>
        Public Function EndPow(ByVal asyncResult As System.IAsyncResult) As Double
            Dim results() As Object = Me.EndInvoke(asyncResult)
            Return CType(results(0), Double)
        End Function
    End Class
End Namespace
```

This complex code is produced by the *wsdl* tool to build the proxy DLL you will need when you build your client. The file uses attributes extensively (see Chapter 18), but with your working knowledge of Visual Basic .NET you can extrapolate at least how some of it works.

The file starts by declaring the Service1 class that derives from the class SoapHttpClientProtocol, which occurs in the namespace called System.Web.Services.Protocols:

```
    Public Class Service1
        Inherits System.Web.Services.Protocols.SoapHttpClientProtocol
```

The constructor sets the URL property inherited from SoapHttpClientProtocol to the URL of the *.asmx* page you created earlier.

The Add() method is declared with a host of attributes that provide the SOAP plumbing to make the remote invocation work.

The WSDL application has also provided asynchronous support for your methods. For example, for the Add() method, it also created BeginAdd() and EndAdd(). This allows you to interact with a web service without performance penalties.

To build the proxy, place the code generated by WSDL into a Visual Basic .NET Library project in Visual Studio .NET and then build the project to generate a DLL. You may need to add a reference to System.Web.Services. In any case, be sure to write down the location of that DLL, as you will need it when you build the client application.

To test the web service, create a very simple Visual Basic .NET console application. The only trick is that in your client code you need to add a reference to the proxy DLL just created. Once that is done, you can instantiate the web service, just like any locally available object:

```
    Dim theWebSvc As _
        New ClassLibrary1.VBWSCalc.Service1( )
```

You can then invoke the Pow() method as if it were a method on a locally available object:

```
    Dim i As Integer
    Dim j As Integer
    For i = 2 To 10
```

```
        For j = 1 To 10
            Console.WriteLine("{0} to the power of {1} = {2}", _
                i, j, theWebSvc.Pow(i, j))
        Next
    Next
```

This simple loop creates a table of the powers of the numbers 2 through 9, displaying for each the powers 1 through 9. The complete source code and an excerpt of the
output is shown in Example 16-4.

Example 16-4. A client program to test the calculator web service

```
Class Tester
    Public Sub Run( )
        Dim theWebSvc As _
            New ClassLibrary1.VBWSCalc.Service1( )
        Dim i As Integer
        Dim j As Integer
        For i = 2 To 10
            For j = 1 To 10
                Console.WriteLine("{0} to the power of {1} = {2}", _
                    i, j, theWebSvc.Pow(i, j))
            Next
        Next
    End Sub

    Public Shared Sub Main( )
        Dim t As New Tester( )
        t.Run( )
    End Sub

End Class

Output (excerpt):
2 to the power of 1 = 2
2 to the power of 2 = 4
2 to the power of 3 = 8
2 to the power of 4 = 16
2 to the power of 5 = 32
2 to the power of 6 = 64
2 to the power of 7 = 128
2 to the power of 8 = 256
2 to the power of 9 = 512
2 to the power of 10 = 1024
3 to the power of 1 = 3
3 to the power of 2 = 9
3 to the power of 3 = 27
3 to the power of 4 = 81
3 to the power of 5 = 243
3 to the power of 6 = 729
3 to the power of 7 = 2187
3 to the power of 8 = 6561
3 to the power of 9 = 19683
3 to the power of 10 = 59049
```

Your calculator service is now more available than you might have imagined (depending on your security settings) through the web protocols of HTTP-Get, HTTP-Post, or SOAP. Your client uses the SOAP protocol, but you could certainly create a client that would use HTTP-Get:

```
http://localhost/VBWSCalc/Service1.asmx/Add?x=23&y=22
```

In fact, if you put that URL into your browser, the browser will respond with the following answer:

```
<?xml version="1.0" encoding="utf-8"?>
<double xmlns="http://www.libertyAssociates.com/webServices/">45</double>
```

The key advantage SOAP has over HTTP-Get and HTTP-Post is that SOAP can support a rich set of datatypes, including all of the Visual Basic .NET intrinsic types (Integer, Double, etc.), as well as enumerations, classes, structures, and ADO.NET DataSets, and arrays of any of these types.

Also, while HTTP-Get and HTTP-Post protocols are restricted to name/value pairs of primitive types and enums, SOAP's rich XML grammar offers a more robust alternative for data exchange.

PART III

VB.NET and the .NET CLR

CHAPTER 17

Assemblies and Versioning

The basic unit of .NET programming is the *assembly*. An assembly is a collection of files that appears to the user to be a single dynamic link library (DLL) or executable (EXE). DLLs are collections of classes and methods that are linked into your running program only when they are needed.

Assemblies are the .NET unit of reuse, versioning, security, and deployment. This chapter discusses assemblies in detail, including the architecture and contents of assemblies, private assemblies, and shared assemblies.

In addition to the object code for the application, assemblies contain resources such as *gif* files, type definitions for each class you define, as well as metadata about the code and data.

PE Files

On disk, assemblies are Portable Executable (PE) files. PE files are not new. The format of a .NET PE file is exactly the same as a normal Windows PE file. PE files are implemented as DLLs or EXEs. Logically (as opposed to physically), assemblies consist of one or more modules. Note, however, that an assembly must have exactly one entry point—DLLMain, WinMain, or Main DLLMain is the entry point for DLLs, WinMain is the entry point for Windows applications, and Main is the entry point for DOS and Console applications.

Modules are created as DLLs and are the constituent pieces of assemblies. Standing alone, modules cannot be executed; they must be combined into assemblies to be useful.

You deploy and reuse the entire contents of an assembly as a unit. Assemblies are loaded on demand and will not be loaded if not needed.

Metadata

Metadata is information stored in the assembly that describes the types and methods of the assembly and provides other useful information about the assembly. Assemblies are said to be *self-describing* because the metadata fully describes the contents of each module. Metadata is explored in detail in Chapter 18.

Security Boundary

Assemblies form security boundaries as well as type boundaries. That is, an assembly is the scope boundary for the types it contains, and types cannot cross assemblies. You can, of course, refer to types across assembly boundaries by adding a reference to the required assembly, either in the Integrated Development Environment (IDE) or on the command line, at compile time. What you cannot do is have the definition of a type span two assemblies.

Versioning

Each assembly has a version number, and versions cannot transcend the boundary of the assembly. That is, a version can refer only to the contents of a single assembly. All types and resources within the assembly change versions together.

Manifests

As part of its metadata, every assembly has a *manifest*. This describes what is in the assembly, including identification information (name, version, etc.), a list of the types and resources in the assembly, a map to connect public types with the implementing code, and a list of assemblies referenced by this assembly.

Even the simplest program has a manifest. You can examine that manifest using ILDasm, which is provided as part of your development environment. When you open it in ILDasm, the EXE program created by Example 12-3 looks like Figure 17-1.

Notice the manifest (second line from the top). Double-clicking the manifest opens a Manifest window, as shown in Figure 17-2.

This file serves as a map of the contents of the assembly. You can see in the first line the reference to the mscorlib assembly, which is referenced by this and every .NET application. The mscorlib assembly is the core library assembly for .NET and is available on every .NET platform.

The manifest references a number of libraries used in the program such as Microsoft.VisualBasic, System, System.Data, and System.XML. Finally, towards the bottom of the image, you see a a reference to the assembly from Example 12-3. You can also see that this assembly consists of a single module. You can ignore the rest of the metadata for now.

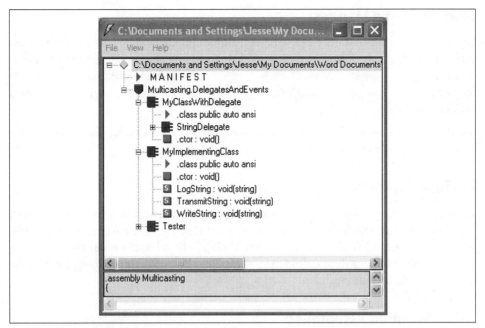

Figure 17-1. ILDasm of Example 12-3

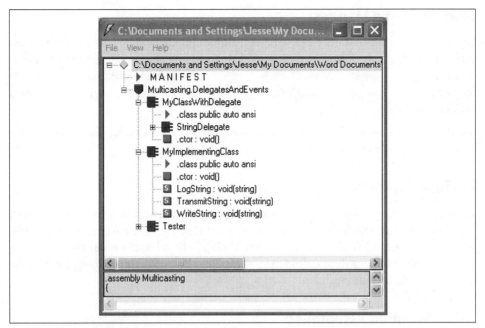

Figure 17-2. The manifest window

Modules in the Manifest

Assemblies can consist of more than one module. In such a case, the manifest includes a hash code identifying each module to ensure that when the program executes, only the proper version of each module is loaded. If you have multiple versions of a given module on your machine, the hash code ensures that your program will load properly.

The hash is a numeric representation of the code for the module, and if the code is changed, the hash will not match.

Module Manifests

Each module has a manifest of its own that is separate from the assembly manifest. The module manifest lists the assemblies referenced by that particular module. In addition, if the module declares any types, these are listed in the manifest along with the code to implement the module. A module can also contain resources, such as the images needed by that module.

Other Required Assemblies

The assembly manifest also contains references to other required assemblies. Each such reference includes the name of the other assembly, the version number and required culture, and, optionally, the other assembly's originator. The originator is a digital signature for the developer or company that provided the other assembly.

 Culture is an object representing the language and national display characteristics for the person using your program. It is culture that determines, for example, whether dates are in month/date/year format or date/month/year format.

Multi-Module Assemblies

A single-module assembly has a single file that can be an EXE or DLL file. This single module contains all the types and implementations for the application. The assembly manifest is embedded within this module.

A multi-module assembly consists of multiple files (zero or one EXE and zero or more DLL files, though you must have at least one EXE or DLL). The assembly manifest in this case can reside in a standalone file, or it can be embedded in one of the modules. When the assembly is referenced, the runtime loads the file containing the manifest and then loads the required modules as needed.

Benefitting from Multi-Module Assemblies

Multi-module assemblies have advantages for real-world programs, especially if they are developed by multiple developers or are very large.

Imagine that 25 developers are working on a single project. If they were to create a single-module assembly to build and test the application, all 25 programmers would have to check in their latest code simultaneously, and the entire mammoth application would be built. That creates a logistical nightmare.

If they each build their own modules, however, the program can be built with the latest available module from each programmer. This relieves the logistics problems; each module can be checked in when it is ready.

Perhaps more importantly, multiple modules make it easier to deploy and to maintain large programs. Imagine that each of the 25 developers builds a separate module, each in its own DLL. The person responsible for building the application would then create a 26th module with the manifest for the entire assembly. These 26 files can be deployed to the end user. The end user then need only load the one module with the manifest, and he can ignore the other 25. The manifest will identify which of the 25 modules has each method, and the appropriate modules will be loaded as methods are invoked. This will be transparent to the user.

As modules are updated, the programmers need only send the updated modules (and a module with an updated manifest). Additional modules can be added and existing modules can be deleted; the end user continues to load only the one module with the manifest.

In addition, it is entirely likely that not all 25 modules will need to be loaded into the program. By breaking the program into 25 modules, the loader can load only those parts of the program that are needed. This makes it easy to shunt aside code that is only rarely needed into its own module, which might not be loaded at all in the normal course of events. Although this was the theory behind DLLs all along, .NET accomplishes this without "DLL Hell," a monumental achievement described later in this chapter.

Building a Multi-Module Assembly

To demonstrate the use of multi-module assemblies, Example 17-1 creates a couple of very simple modules that you can then combine into a single assembly. The first module is a Fraction class. This simple class will allow you to create and manipulate common fractions.

Example 17-1. The Fraction class

```
Option Strict On
Imports System
```

Example 17-1. The Fraction class (continued)

```
Namespace ProgVB

    Public Class Fraction

        Public Sub New(numerator As Integer, denominator As Integer)
            Me.numerator = numerator
            Me.denominator = denominator
        End Sub 'New

        Public Function Add(rhs As Fraction) As Fraction
            If rhs.denominator <> Me.denominator Then
                Throw New ArgumentException("Denominators must match")
            End If

            Return New Fraction(Me.numerator + rhs.numerator, Me.denominator)
        End Function 'Add

        Public Overrides Function ToString() As String
            Return numerator.ToString() + "/" + denominator.ToString()
        End Function 'ToString

        Private numerator As Integer
        Private denominator As Integer
    End Class 'Fraction
End Namespace 'ProgVB
```

Notice that the Fraction class is in the ProgVB namespace. The full name for the class is ProgVB.Fraction.

The Fraction class takes two values in its constructor: a numerator and a denominator. There is also an Add() method, which takes a second Fraction and returns the sum, assuming the two share a common denominator. This class is simplistic, but it will demonstrate the functionality necessary for this example.

The second class is the myCalc class, which stands in for a robust calculator. Example 17-2 illustrates.

Example 17-2. The calculator

```
Option Strict On
Imports System

Namespace ProgVB

    Public Class myCalc

        Public Function Add(val1 As Integer, val2 As Integer) As Integer
            Return val1 + val2
        End Function 'Add

        Public Function Mult(val1 As Integer, val2 As Integer) As Integer
            Return val1 * val2
```

Example 17-2. The calculator (continued)

```
      End Function 'Mult
   End Class 'myCalc
End Namespace 'ProgVB
```

Once again, myCalc is a very stripped-down class to keep things simple. Notice that calc is also in the ProgVB namespace.

This is sufficient to create an assembly. Use an *AssemblyInfo.vb* file to add some metadata to the assembly. The use of metadata is covered in Chapter 18. An example *AssemblyInfo.vb* file is shown in Example 17-3.

Example 17-3. AssemblyInfo.vb

```
Option Strict On
Imports System.Reflection
Imports System.Runtime.InteropServices

<Assembly: AssemblyTitle("")>
<Assembly: AssemblyDescription("")>
<Assembly: AssemblyCompany("")>
<Assembly: AssemblyProduct("")>
<Assembly: AssemblyCopyright("")>
<Assembly: AssemblyTrademark("")>
<Assembly: Guid("401658E1-6FC7-4BB4-AE86-8463FEB1703B")>
<Assembly: AssemblyVersion("1.0.*")>
```

 You can write your own *AssemblyInfo.vb* file, but the simplest approach is to let Visual Studio generate one for you automatically by creating a dummy application and then just borrowing the resulting *AssemblyInfo.vb* file.

Visual Studio creates single-module assemblies by default. You can create a multi-module resource option using the command-line compiler with the */addModules* option. The easiest way to compile and build a multi-module assembly is with a makefile, which you can create with Notepad or any text editor.

 If you are unfamiliar with makefiles, don't worry; this is the only example that needs a makefile, and that is only to get around the current limitation of Visual Studio creating only single-module assemblies. If necessary, you can just use the makefile as offered without fully understanding every line.

Example 17-4 shows the complete makefile (which is explained in detail immediately afterward). To run this example, put the makefile (with the name *makefile*) in a directory together with a copy of *Calc.vb*, *Fraction.vb*, and *AssemblyInfo.vb*. Start up a .NET command window and *cd* to that directory. Invoke *nmake* without any command switches. You will find the *SharedAssembly.dll* in the *bin* subdirectory.

Example 17-4. The makefile

```
ASSEMBLY= MySharedAssembly.dll

BIN=.\bin
SRC=.
DEST=.\bin

VBC=vbc /nologo /debug+ /debug:full

MODULETARGET=/t:module
LIBTARGET=/t:library
EXETARGET=/t:exe

REFERENCES=System.dll

MODULES=$(DEST)\Fraction.dll $(DEST)\Calc.dll
METADATA=$(SRC)\AssemblyInfo.vb

all: $(DEST)\MySharedAssembly.dll

# Assembly metadata placed in same module as manifest
$(DEST)\$(ASSEMBLY): $(METADATA) $(MODULES) $(DEST)
    $(VBC) $(LIBTARGET) /addmodule:$(MODULES: =,) /out:$@ %s

# Add Calc.dll module to this dependency list
$(DEST)\Calc.dll: Calc.vb $(DEST)
    $(VBC) $(MODULETARGET) /r:$(REFERENCES: =;) /out:$@ %s

# Add Fraction
$(DEST)\Fraction.dll: Fraction.vb $(DEST)
    $(VBC) $(MODULETARGET) /r:$(REFERENCES: =;) /out:$@ %s

$(DEST)::
!if !EXISTS($(DEST))
        mkdir $(DEST)
!endif
```

The makefile begins by defining the assembly you want to build:

```
ASSEMBLY= MySharedAssembly.dll
```

It then defines the directories you'll use, putting the output in a *bin* directory beneath the current directory and retrieving the source code from the current directory:

```
BIN=.\bin
SRC=.
DEST=.\bin
```

Build the assembly as follows:

```
$(DEST)\$(ASSEMBLY): $(METADATA) $(MODULES) $(DEST)
    $(VBC) $(LIBTARGET) /addmodule:$(MODULES: =,) /out:$@ %s
```

This places the assembly (*MySharedAssembly.dll*) in the destination directory (*bin*). It tells *nmake* (the program that executes the makefile) that the assembly consists of the metadata and the modules, and it provides the command line required to build the assembly.

The metadata is defined earlier as:

```
METADATA=$(SRC)\AssemblyInfo.vb
```

The modules are defined as the two DLLs:

```
MODULES=$(DEST)\Fraction.dll $(DEST)\Calc.dll
```

The compile line builds the library and adds the modules, putting the output into the assembly file *MySharedAssembly.dll*:

```
$(DEST)\$(ASSEMBLY): $(METADATA) $(MODULES) $(DEST)
    $(VBC) $(LIBTARGET) /addmodule:$(MODULES: =,) /out:$@ %s
```

To accomplish this, *nmake* needs to know how to make the modules. Start by telling *nmake* how to create *calc.dll*. You need the *calc.vb* source file for this; tell *nmake* on the command line to build that DLL:

```
$(DEST)\Calc.dll: Calc.vb $(DEST)
    $(VBC) $(MODULETARGET) /r:$(REFERENCES: =;) /out:$@ %s
```

Then do the same thing for *fraction.dll*:

```
$(DEST)\Fraction.dll: Fraction.vb $(DEST)
    $(VBC) $(MODULETARGET) /r:$(REFERENCES: =;) /out:$@ %s
```

The result of running *nmake* on this makefile is to create three DLLs: *fraction.dll*, *calc.dll*, and *MySharedAssembly.dll*. If you open *MySharedAssembly.dll* with ILDasm, you'll find that it consists of nothing but a manifest, as shown in Figure 17-3.

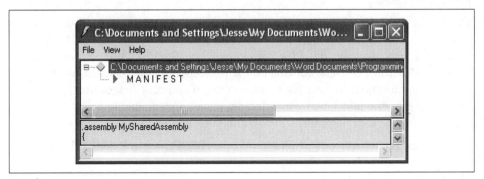

Figure 17-3. MySharedAssembly.dll

If you examine the manifest, you see the metadata for the libraries you created, as shown in Figure 17-4.

You first see an external assembly for the core library (mscorlib), followed by the two modules, ProgVB.Fraction and ProgVB.myCalc.

You now have an assembly that consists of three DLL files: *MySharedAssembly.dll* with the manifest, and *Calc.dll* and *Fraction.dll* with the types and implementation needed.

```
/ MANIFEST                                                              [□][□][X]
.module extern Fraction.dll
.module extern Calc.dll
.assembly extern mscorlib
{
    .publickeytoken = (B7 7A 5C 56 19 34 E0 89 )                // .z\U.4..
    .ver 1:0:3300:0
}
.assembly extern Microsoft.VisualBasic
{
    .publickeytoken = (B0 3F 5F 7F 11 D5 0A 3A )                // .?_....:
    .ver 7:0:3300:0
}
.assembly extern System
{
    .publickeytoken = (B7 7A 5C 56 19 34 E0 89 )                // .z\U.4..
    .ver 1:0:3300:0
}
.assembly MySharedAssembly
{
    // --- The following custom attribute is added automatically, do not uncomment -------
    // .custom instance void [mscorlib]System.Diagnostics.DebuggableAttribute::.ctor(bool,
    //                                                           bool) = ( 01 00 01 01 00 00 )
    .custom instance void [mscorlib]System.Runtime.InteropServices.GuidAttribute::.ctor(string) = ( 01 00 24 34 30 31 36 35 38 45
                                                                           2D 34 42 42 34 2D 41 45 38 36
                                                                           45 42 31 37 30 33 42 00 00 )
    .custom instance void [mscorlib]System.Reflection.AssemblyTrademarkAttribute::.ctor(string) = ( 01 00 00 00 00 00 )
    .custom instance void [mscorlib]System.Reflection.AssemblyCopyrightAttribute::.ctor(string) = ( 01 00 00 00 00 00 )
    .custom instance void [mscorlib]System.Reflection.AssemblyProductAttribute::.ctor(string) = ( 01 00 00 00 00 00 )
    .custom instance void [mscorlib]System.Reflection.AssemblyCompanyAttribute::.ctor(string) = ( 01 00 00 00 00 00 )
    .custom instance void [mscorlib]System.Reflection.AssemblyDescriptionAttribute::.ctor(string) = ( 01 00 00 00 00 00 )
    .custom instance void [mscorlib]System.Reflection.AssemblyTitleAttribute::.ctor(string) = ( 01 00 00 00 00 00 )
    .hash algorithm 0x00008004
    .ver 1:0:997:16287
}
.file Fraction.dll
    .hash = (C2 3E E3 4D B1 5C 34 9E 49 98 A0 4F F0 27 7A C6    // .>.M.\4.I..0.'z.
             7D A4 D0 E4 )                                      // }...
.file Calc.dll
    .hash = (B9 D7 EA 29 16 C3 61 4F E9 A6 52 D2 18 05 F8 C5    // ...)..a0..R.....
             41 AF 98 58 )                                      // A..X
.class extern public ProgVB.Fraction
{
    .file Fraction.dll
    .class 0x02000002
}
.class extern public ProgVB.myCalc
{
```

Figure 17-4. The manifest for MySharedAssembly

Testing the assembly

To use these modules, you need to create a driver program that will load in the modules as needed. Create a new Console application in Visual Studio .NET in the same directory as the *dll* files and name it *TestVB*. Add a reference to MySharedAssembly by right-clicking on the References in the Solution window, and then clicking on the Add References pop-up menu choice. Click on the Projects tab and Browse to the *.dll*. Once you select it, it will appear in the Selected Components window, and clicking OK will add it to your references.

Create a new file called *module1.vb* and add the code shown in Example 17-5.

Example 17-5. TestVB

```
Option Strict On
Imports System

Namespace ProgVB

    Public Class Test

        ' main will not load the shared assembly
        Shared Sub Main( )
```

Example 17-5. TestVB (continued)

```
        Dim t As New Test()
        t.UseCS()
        t.UseFraction()
    End Sub 'Main

    ' calling this loads the myCalc assembly
    ' and the mySharedAssembly assembly as well
    Public Sub UseCS()
        Dim calc As New ProgVB.myCalc()
        Console.WriteLine("3+5 = {0}" + _
            ControlChars.Lf + "3*5 = {1}", _
            calc.Add(3, 5), calc.Mult(3, 5))
    End Sub 'UseCS

    ' calling this adds the Fraction assembly
    Public Sub UseFraction()
        Dim frac1 As New ProgVB.Fraction(3, 5)
        Dim frac2 As New ProgVB.Fraction(1, 5)
        Dim frac3 As ProgVB.Fraction = frac1.Add(frac2)
        Console.WriteLine("{0} + {1} = {2}", frac1, frac2, frac3)
    End Sub 'UseFraction
  End Class 'Test
End Namespace 'ProgrammingVB
```

For the purposes of this demonstration, it is important not to put any code in Main( ) that depends on your modules. You do not want the modules loaded when Main( ) loads, so no Fraction or Calc objects are placed in Main( ). When you call into UseFraction and UseCS, you'll be able to see that the modules are individually loaded.

Loading the assembly

An assembly is loaded into its application by the AssemblyResolver through a process called *probing*. The assembly resolver is called by the .NET Framework automatically; you do not call it explicitly. Its job is to resolve the assembly name to an EXE program and load your program.

With a private assembly, the AssemblyResolver looks only in the application load directory and its subdirectories—that is, the directory in which you invoked your application.

 The three DLLs produced earlier must be in the directory in which Example 17-5 executes or in a subdirectory of that directory.

Put a break point on the second line in Main( ), as shown in Figure 17-5.

Execute to the break point and open the Modules window. Only two modules are loaded, as shown circled in Figure 17-6.

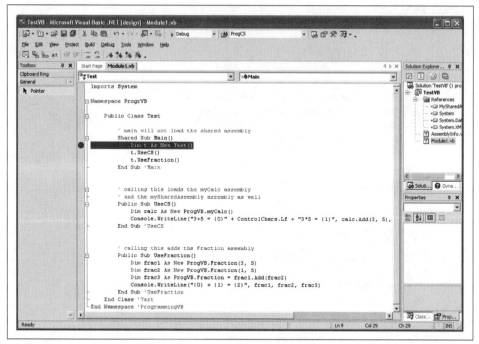

Figure 17-5. Setting the breakpoint

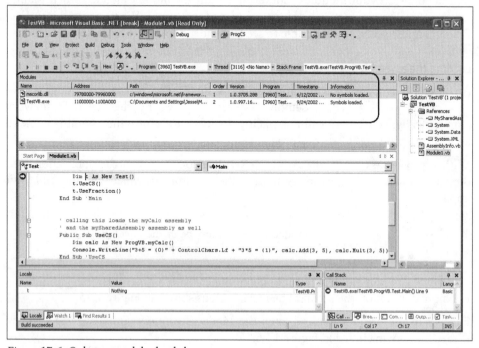

Figure 17-6. Only two modules loaded

Step into the first method call and watch the modules window. As soon as you step into UseCS, the AssemblyLoader recognizes that it needs an assembly from MySharedAssembly.Dll. The DLL is loaded, and from that assembly's manifest the AssemblyLoader finds that it needs Calc.dll, which is loaded as well, as shown in Figure 17-7.

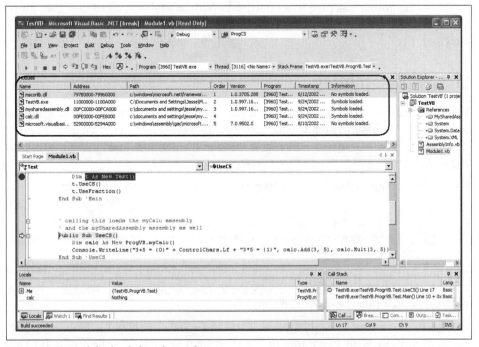

Figure 17-7. Modules loaded on demand

When you step into Fraction, the final DLL is loaded. The advantage of multi-module assemblies is that a module is loaded only when it is needed.

Private Assemblies

Assemblies come in two flavors: *private* and *shared*. Private assemblies are intended to be used by only one application; shared assemblies are intended to be shared among many applications.

All the assemblies you've built so far are private. By default, when you compile a Visual Basic .NET application, a private assembly is created. The files for a private assembly are all kept in the same folder (or in a tree of subfolders). This tree of folders is isolated from the rest of the system, as nothing other than the one application depends on it, and you can redeploy this application to another machine just by copying the folder and its subfolders.

A private assembly can have any name you choose. It does not matter if that name clashes with assemblies in another application; the names are local only to a single application.

In the past, DLLs were installed on a machine and an entry was made in the Windows Registry. It was difficult to avoid corrupting the Registry, and reinstalling the program on another machine was nontrivial. With assemblies, all of that goes away. With private assemblies, installing is as simple as copying the files to the appropriate directory. Period.

Shared Assemblies

You can create assemblies that can be shared by other applications. You might want to do this if you have written a generic control or a class that might be used by other developers. If you want to share your assembly, it must meet certain stringent requirements.

First, your assembly must have a *strong name*. Strong names are globally unique.

 No one else can generate the same strong name as you because an assembly generated with one private key is guaranteed to have a different name than any assembly generated with another private key.

Second, your shared assembly must be protected against newer versions trampling over it, and so it must have version control.

Finally, to share your assembly, place it in the *Global Assembly Cache* (GAC) (pronounced GACK). This is an area of the filesystem set aside by the Common Language Runtime (CLR) to hold shared assemblies.

The End of DLL Hell

Assemblies mark the end of DLL Hell. Remember this scenario: You install Application A on your machine, and it loads a number of DLLs into your Windows directory. It works great for months. You then install Application B on your machine, and suddenly, unexpectedly, Application A breaks. Application B is in no way related to Application A. So what happened? It turns out, you later learn, that Application B replaced a DLL that Application A needed, and suddenly Application A begins to stagger about, blind and senseless.

When DLLs were invented, disk space was at a premium and reusing DLLs seemed like a good idea. The theory was that DLLs would be backward-compatible, so automatically upgrading to the new DLL would be painless and safe. As my old boss Pat Johnson used to say, "In theory, theory and practice are the same. But in practice, they never are."

When the new DLL was added to the computer, the old application, which was happily minding its own business in another corner of your machine, suddenly linked to a DLL that was incompatible with its expectations and hey! Presto! It went into the dance of death. This phenomenon led customers to be justifiably leery of installing new software, or even of upgrading existing programs, and it is one of the reasons Windows machines are perceived to be unstable. With assemblies, this entire nightmare goes away.

Versions

Shared assemblies in .NET are uniquely identified by their names and their versions. The GAC allows for "side-by-side" versions in which an older version of an assembly is available alongside a newer version. This allows particular applications to say "give me the newest" or "give me the latest build of Version 2," or even "give me only the version I was built with."

 Side-by-side versioning applies only to items in the GAC. Private assemblies do not need this feature and do not have it.

A version number for an assembly might look like this: 1:0:2204:21 (four numbers, separated by colons). The first two numbers (1:0) are the major and minor version. The third number (2204) is the build, and the fourth (21) is the revision.

When two assemblies have different major or minor numbers, they are considered to be incompatible. When they have different build numbers, they might or might not be compatible, and when they have different revision numbers, they are considered *definitely* compatible with each other.

Revision numbers are intended for bug fixes. If you fix a bug and are prepared to certify that your DLL is fully backward-compatible with the existing version, you should increment the revision. When an application loads an assembly, it specifies the major and minor version that it wants, and the AssemblyResolver finds the highest build and revision numbers.

Strong Names

In order to use a shared assembly, you must meet three requirements:

- You need to be able to specify the exact assembly you want to load. Therefore, you need a globally unique name for the shared assembly.
- You need to ensure that the assembly has not been tampered with. That is, you need a digital signature for the assembly when it is built.

- You need to ensure that the assembly you are loading is the one authored by the actual creator of the assembly. You therefore need to record the identity of the originator.

All these requirements are met by *strong names*. Strong names are globally unique and use public key encryption to ensure that the assembly hasn't been tampered with and was written by the creator. A strong name is a string of hexadecimal digits and is not meant to be human-readable.

To create a strong name, a public-private key pair is generated for the assembly. A hash is taken of the names and contents of the files in the assembly. The hash is then encrypted with the private key for the assembly and placed in the manifest. This is known as *signing the assembly*. The public key is incorporated into the strong name of the assembly.

Public Key Encryption

Strong names are based on public key encryption technology. The essence of public key encryption is that your data is encoded with a complex mathematical formula that returns two keys. Data encrypted with the first key can only be decrypted with the second. Data encrypted with the second key can only be decrypted with the first.

Distribute your first key as a *public key* that anyone can have. Keep your second key as a *private key* that no one but you can have access to.

The reciprocal relationship between the keys allows anyone to encrypt data with your public key, and then you can decrypt it with your private key. No one else has access to the data once it is encrypted, including the person who encrypted it.

Similarly, you can encrypt data with your private key, and then anyone can decrypt that data with your public key. Although this makes the data freely available, it ensures that only you could have created it. This is called a *digital signature*.

When an application loads the assembly, the CLR uses the public key to decode the hash of the files in the assembly to ensure that they have not been tampered with. This also protects against name clashes.

You can create a strong name with the *sn* utility:

```
sn -k c:\myStrongName.snk
```

The *–k* flag indicates that you want a new key pair written to the specified file. You can call the file anything you like. Remember, a strong name is a string of hexadecimal digits and is not meant to be human-readable.

You can associate this strong name with your assembly by using an attribute:

```
import System.Runtime.CompilerServices;
<assembly: AssemblyKeyFile("c:\myStrongName.key")>
```

Attributes are covered in detail in Chapter 18. For now, you can just put this code at the top of your file to associate the strong name you generated with your assembly.

The Global Assembly Cache

Once you've created your strong name and associated it with your assembly, all that remains is to place the assembly in the GAC, which is a reserved system directory. You can do that with the *gacutil* utility:

```
gacutil /i MySharedAssembly.dll
```

Or you can open your File Explorer and drag your assembly into the GAC. To see the GAC, open the File Explorer and navigate to *%SystemRoot%\assembly*. Navigating to this directory causes Explorer to function as a GAC utility.

Building a Shared Assembly

The best way to understand shared assemblies is to build one. Let's return to the earlier multi-module project (see Examples 17-1 through 17-5) and navigate to the directory that contains the files *calc.vb* and *fraction.vb*.

Try this experiment: Locate the *bin* directory for the driver program and make sure that you do not have a local copy of the MySharedAssembly DLL files.

 The referenced assembly (MySharedAssembly) should have its Copy-Local property set to false.

Run the program. It should fail with an exception saying it cannot load the assembly:

```
Unhandled Exception: System.IO.FileNotFoundException: File or assembly name
MySharedAssembly, or one of its dependencies
, was not found.
File name: "MySharedAssembly"
   at TestVB.ProgrVB.Test.UseCS( )
   at TestVB.ProgrVB.Test.Main( ) in C:\...\Programming VB.NET\source\Assemblies\
TestVB\Module1.vb:line 10

Fusion log follows:
=== Pre-bind state information ===
LOG: DisplayName = MySharedAssembly, Version=1.0.997.16287, Culture=neutral,
PublicKeyToken=null
 (Fully-specified)
LOG: Appbase = C:\...\Programming VB.NET\source\Assemblies\TestVB\bin\
LOG: Initial PrivatePath = NULL
Calling assembly : TestVB, Version=1.0.997.16041, Culture=neutral,
PublicKeyToken=null.
===

LOG: Application configuration file does not exist.
```

```
LOG: Policy not being applied to reference at this time (private, custom, partial, or
location-based assembly bind).
LOG: Post-policy reference: MySharedAssembly, Version=1.0.997.16287, Culture=neutral,
PublicKeyToken=null
LOG: Attempting download of new URL file:///C:.../Programming VB.NET/source/
Assemblies/TestVB/bin/MySharedAssembly.DLL.
LOG: Attempting download of new URL file:///C:.../Programming VB.N
ET/source/Assemblies/TestVB/bin/MySharedAssembly/MySharedAssembly.DLL.
LOG: Attempting download of new URL file:///C:.../Programming VB.N
ET/source/Assemblies/TestVB/bin/MySharedAssembly.EXE.
LOG: Attempting download of new URL file:///C:.../Programming VB.N
ET/source/Assemblies/TestVB/bin/MySharedAssembly/MySharedAssembly.EXE.
```

Now copy the DLLs into the driver program's directory tree, run it again, and this time you should find that it works fine.

Let's make the MySharedAssembly into a shared assembly. This is done in two steps. First, create a strong name for the assembly, and then you put the assembly into the GAC.

Step 1: Create a strong name

Create a key pair by opening a command window and entering:

```
sn -k keyFile.snk
```

Now open the *AssemblyInfo.vb* file in the project for the *MySharedAssembly.dll* and add this line:

```
<Assembly: AssemblyKeyFile(".\\keyFile.snk")>
```

This sets the key file for the assembly. Rebuild with the same makefile as earlier, and then open the resulting DLL in ILDasm and open the manifest. You should see a public key, as shown in Figure 17-8.

By adding the strong name, you have signed this assembly (your exact values will be different). You now need to get the strong name from the DLL. To do this, navigate to the directory with the DLL and enter the following at a command prompt:

```
sn -T MySharedAssembly.dll
```

 Note that *sn* is case-sensitive. Do not write *sn -t*.

The response should be something like this:

```
Public key token is de3bc3f3da9fe75a
```

This value is an abbreviated version of the assembly's public key, called the *public key token*.

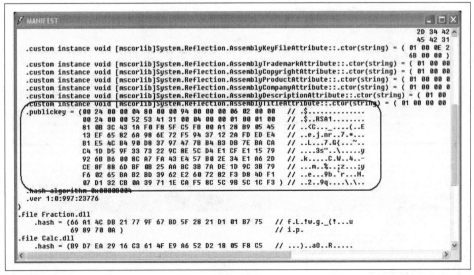

```
2D 34 42
45 42 31
.custom instance void [mscorlib]System.Reflection.AssemblyKeyFileAttribute::.ctor(string) = ( 01 00 0E 2
                                                                                             6B 00 00 )
.custom instance void [mscorlib]System.Reflection.AssemblyTrademarkAttribute::.ctor(string) = ( 01 00 00
.custom instance void [mscorlib]System.Reflection.AssemblyCopyrightAttribute::.ctor(string) = ( 01 00 00
.custom instance void [mscorlib]System.Reflection.AssemblyProductAttribute::.ctor(string) = ( 01 00 00 0
.custom instance void [mscorlib]System.Reflection.AssemblyCompanyAttribute::.ctor(string) = ( 01 00 00 0
.custom instance void [mscorlib]System.Reflection.AssemblyDescriptionAttribute::.ctor(string) = ( 01 00
.custom instance void [mscorlib]System.Reflection.AssemblyTitleAttribute::.ctor(string) = ( 01 00 00 00
.publickey = (00 24 00 00 04 80 00 00 94 00 00 00 06 02 00 00   // .$..............
              00 24 00 00 52 53 41 31 00 04 00 00 01 00 01 00   // .$..RSA1........
              81 0B 3C 43 1A F0 F8 5F C5 FB 00 A1 28 B9 05 45   // ..<C..._....(..E
              13 EF 65 82 6A 98 6E 72 F5 94 37 12 2A FD ED E4   // ..e.j.nr..7.*...
              B1 E5 4C B4 90 D8 37 97 47 7B B4 B3 DB 7E BA CA   // ..L...7.G{...~..
              C4 1D D5 9F 33 73 22 9C 8E 5C D4 E1 CF E1 15 79   // ....3s"..\.....y
              92 6B B6 00 8C A7 FA 43 E4 57 B0 2E 34 E1 A6 2D   // .k.....C.W..4..-
              CE 8F 88 6D BF 0B 25 AA BC 3B 7A DE 1D 9C 3B 79   // ...m..%..;z...;y
              F6 02 65 BA B2 BD 39 62 E2 60 72 82 F3 D8 4D F1   // ..e...9b.`r...M.
              07 D1 32 CB 0A 39 71 1E CA F5 8C 5C 9B 5C 1C F3 ) // ..2..9q....\.\..
.hash algorithm 0x00008004
.ver 1:0:997:23776
}
.file Fraction.dll
  .hash = (66 A1 4C DB 21 77 9F 67 BD 5F 28 21 D1 01 B7 75   // f.L.!w.g._(!...u
           69 89 70 0A )                                      // i.p.
.file Calc.dll
  .hash = (B9 D7 EA 29 16 C3 61 4F E9 A6 52 D2 18 05 F8 C5   // ...)..aO..R.....
```

Figure 17-8. The originator in the manifest of MySharedAssembly.dll

Remove the DLLs from the test program's directory structure and run it again. It should fail again. Although you've given this assembly a strong name, you've not yet registered it in the GAC.

Step 2: Put the shared assembly in the GAC

The next step is to drag the library into the GAC. To do so, open an Explorer window and navigate to the *%SystemRoot%* directory (e.g., on Windows XP, C:\Windows). When you double-click the Assembly subdirectory, Explorer will turn into a GAC viewer.

You can drag and drop into the GAC viewer, or you can invoke this command-line utility:

```
Gacutil /i mySharedAssembly.dll
```

In either case, be sure to check that your assembly was loaded into the GAC, and that the originator value shown in the GAC viewer matches the value you got back from sn:

```
Public key token is de3bc3f3da9fe75a
```

This is illustrated in Figure 17-9.

Once this is done, you have a shared assembly that can be accessed by any client. Refresh the client by building it again and look at its manifest, as shown in Figure 17-10.

There's MySharedAssembly, listed as an external assembly, and the public key now matches the value shown in the GAC. Very nice; time to try it.

assembly
File Edit View Favorites Tools Help
Back Search Folders
Address C:\WINDOWS\assembly
Go
Folders
aim95
AppPatch
assembly
Config
Connection Wizard
Cursors
Debug
Global Assembly Name
Type
Version
Culture
Public Key Token
MSDDSLMP 7.0.3300.0 b03f5f7f11d50a3a
MSDDSP 7.0.3300.0 b03f5f7f11d50a3a
MySharedAssembly 1.0.997.23776 de3bc3f3da9fe75a
Office 7.0.3300.0 b03f5f7f11d50a3a
Regcode 1.0.3300.0 b03f5f7f11d50a3a
SoapSudsCode 1.0.3300.0 b03f5f7f11d50a3a
stdole 7.0.3300.0 b03f5f7f11d50a3a
System Native Images 1.0.3300.0 b77a5c561934e089

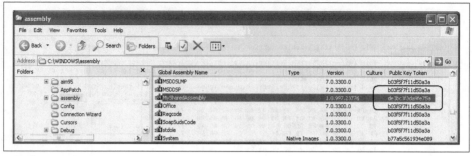

Figure 17-9. The GAC

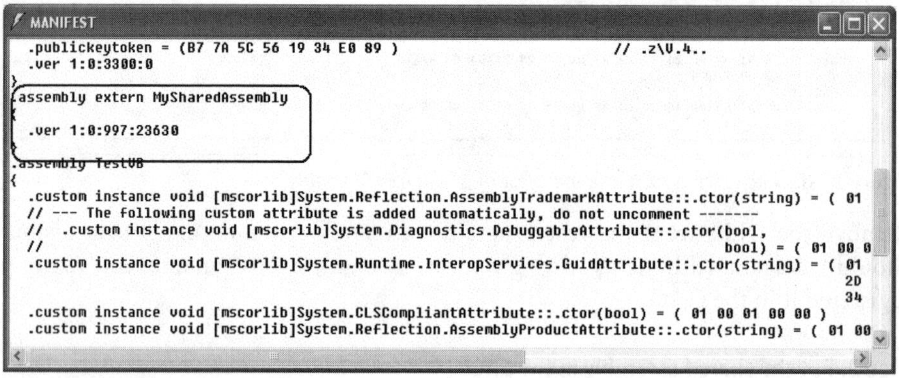

MANIFEST
.publickeytoken = (B7 7A 5C 56 19 34 E0 89) // .z\V.4..
.ver 1:0:3300:0
}
.assembly extern MySharedAssembly
{
.ver 1:0:997:23630
}
.assembly TestVB
{
.custom instance void [mscorlib]System.Reflection.AssemblyTrademarkAttribute::.ctor(string) = (01
// --- The following custom attribute is added automatically, do not uncomment -------
// .custom instance void [mscorlib]System.Diagnostics.DebuggableAttribute::.ctor(bool,
// bool) = (01 00 0
.custom instance void [mscorlib]System.Runtime.InteropServices.GuidAttribute::.ctor(string) = (01
2D
34
.custom instance void [mscorlib]System.CLSCompliantAttribute::.ctor(bool) = (01 00 01 00 00)
.custom instance void [mscorlib]System.Reflection.AssemblyProductAttribute::.ctor(string) = (01 00

Figure 17-10. The manifest

Close ILDasm and compile and run your code. It should work fine, even though there are no DLLs for this library in its immediate path. You have just created and used a shared assembly.

CHAPTER 18

Attributes and Reflection

Throughout this book, I have emphasized that a .NET application contains code, data, and metadata. *Metadata* is information about the data—that is, information about the types, code, assembly, and so forth—stored along with your program. This chapter explores how some of that metadata is created and used.

Attributes are a mechanism for adding metadata, such as compiler instructions and other data about your data, methods, and classes, to the program itself. Attributes are inserted into the metadata and are visible through *ILDasm* and other metadata-reading tools.

Reflection is the process by which a program can read its own metadata. A program is said to reflect on itself, extracting metadata from its assembly and using that metadata either to inform the user or to modify its own behavior.

Attributes

An attribute is an object that represents data you want to associate with an element in your program. The element to which you attach an attribute is referred to as the target of that attribute. For example, the attribute:

```
<NoIDispatch>
```

is associated with a class or an interface to indicate that the target class should derive from IUnknown rather than IDispatch when exporting to COM.

In Chapter 17, you saw this attribute:

```
<assembly: AssemblyKeyFile("c:\myStrongName.key")>
```

This inserts metadata into the assembly to designate the program's StrongName.

Intrinsic Attributes

Attributes come in two flavors: *intrinsic* and *custom*. *Intrinsic* attributes are supplied as part of the Common Language Runtime (CLR), and they are integrated into .NET. *Custom* attributes are attributes you create for your own purposes.

Most programmers will use only intrinsic attributes, though custom attributes can be a powerful tool when combined with reflection, described later in this chapter.

Attribute targets

If you search through the CLR, you'll find a great many attributes. Some attributes are applied to an assembly, others to a class or interface, and some, such as <WebMethod>, are applied to class members. These are called the *attribute targets*. Possible attribute targets are detailed in Table 18-1.

Table 18-1. Possible attribute targets

Member name	Usage
All	Applied to any of the following elements: assembly, class, constructor, delegate, enum, event, field, interface, method, module, parameter, property, return value, or struct
Assembly	Applied to the assembly itself
Class	Applied to instances of the class
Constructor	Applied to a given constructor
Delegate	Applied to the delegated method
Enum	Applied to an enumeration
Event	Applied to an event
Field	Applied to a field
Interface	Applied to an interface
Method	Applied to a method
Module	Applied to a single module
Parameter	Applied to a parameter of a method
Property	Applied to a property (both get and set, if implemented)
ReturnValue	Applied to a return value
Struct	Applied to a struct

Applying attributes

Apply attributes to their targets by placing them in angle brackets immediately before the target item. You can combine attributes by stacking one on top of another:

```
<assembly: AssemblyDelaySign(false)>
<assembly: AssemblyKeyFile(".\keyFile.snk")>
```

This can also be done by separating the attributes with commas:

```
<assembly: AssemblyDelaySign(false),
    assembly: AssemblyKeyFile(".\keyFile.snk")>
```

You must place assembly attributes after all using statements and before any code.

Many intrinsic attributes are used for interoperating with COM. You've already seen use of one attribute (<WebMethod>) in Chapter 16. You'll see other attributes, such as the <Serializable> attribute, used in the discussion of serialization in Chapter 19.

The System.Runtime namespace offers a number of intrinsic attributes, including attributes for assemblies (such as the keyname attribute), for configuration (such as debug to indicate the debug build), and for version attributes.

You can organize the intrinsic attributes by how they are used. The principal intrinsic attributes are those used for COM, those used to modify the Interface Definition Language (IDL) file from within a source-code file, those used by the ATL Server classes, and those used by the Visual Basic .NET compiler.

Perhaps the attribute you are most likely to use in your everyday Visual Basic .NET programming (if you are not interacting with COM) is <Serializable>. As you'll see in Chapter 19, all you need to do to ensure that your class can be serialized to disk or to the Internet is add the <Serializable> attribute to the class:

```
<Serializable> _
Class MySerializableClass
```

The attribute tag is put in angle brackets immediately before its target—in this case, the class declaration.

The key fact about intrinsic attributes is that you know when you need them; the task will dictate their use.

Custom Attributes

You are free to create your own custom attributes and use them at runtime as you see fit. Suppose, for example, that your development organization wants to keep track of bug fixes. You already keep a database of all your bugs, but you'd like to tie your bug reports to specific fixes in the code.

You might add comments to your code along the lines of:

```
// Bug 323 fixed by Jesse Liberty 1/1/2005.
```

This would make it easy to see in your source code, but there is no enforced connection to Bug 323 in the database. A custom attribute might be just what you need. You would replace your comment with something like this:

```
<BugFixAttribute(107, "Jesse Liberty", "01/04/05", _
Comment:="Fixed off by one errors")>
```

You could then write a program to read through the metadata to find these bug-fix notations and update the database. The attribute would serve the purposes of a comment, but would also allow you to retrieve the information programmatically through tools you'd create.

Declaring an attribute

Attributes, like most things in Visual Basic .NET, are embodied in classes. To create a custom attribute, derive your new custom attribute class from System.Attribute:

```
Public Class BugFixAttribute
    Inherits System.Attribute
```

You need to tell the compiler which kinds of elements this attribute can be used with (the attribute target). Specify this with (what else?) an attribute:

```
<AttributeUsage(AttributeTargets.Class Or _
AttributeTargets.Constructor Or _
AttributeTargets.Field Or _
AttributeTargets.Method Or _
AttributeTargets.Property, AllowMultiple:=True)> _
```

Notice the line continuation character at the end of the AttributeUsage attribute. In Visual Basic .NET attributes do not stand alone; they must immediately be followed by their target, in this case the class declaration. Thus, the entire statement is:

```
<AttributeUsage(AttributeTargets.Class Or _
AttributeTargets.Constructor Or _
AttributeTargets.Field Or _
AttributeTargets.Method Or _
AttributeTargets.Property, AllowMultiple:=True)> _
Public Class BugFixAttribute
    Inherits System.Attribute
```

AttributeUsage is an attribute applied to attributes: a meta-attribute. It provides, if you will, meta-metadata—that is, data about the metadata. For the AttributeUsage attribute constructor, you pass two arguments. The first argument is a set of flags that indicate the target—in this case, the class and its constructor, fields, methods, and properties. The second argument is a flag that indicates whether a given element might receive more than one such attribute. In this example, AllowMultiple is set to true, indicating that class members can have more than one BugFixAttribute assigned.

Naming an attribute

The new custom attribute in this example is named BugFixAttribute. The convention is to append the word Attribute to your attribute name. The compiler supports this by allowing you to call the attribute with the shorter version of the name. Thus, you can write:

```
<BugFix(107, "Jesse Liberty", "01/04/05", _
Comment:="Fixed off by one errors")>
```

The compiler will first look for an attribute named BugFix and, if it does not find that, will then look for BugFixAttribute.

Constructing an attribute

Every attribute must have at least one constructor. Attributes take two types of parameters: *positional* and *named.* In the BugFix example, the bug ID, the programmer's name and the date are positional parameters, and comment is a named parameter. Positional parameters are passed in through the constructor and must be passed in the order declared in the constructor:

```
Public Sub New( _
    ByVal bugID As Integer, _
    ByVal programmer As String, _
    ByVal theDate As String)

    mBugID = bugID
    mProgrammer = programmer
    mDate = theDate

End Sub 'New
```

Named parameters are implemented as properties:

```
Public Property Comment( ) As String
    Get
        Return mComment
    End Get
    Set(ByVal Value As String)
        mComment = Value
    End Set
End Property
```

It is common to create read-only properties for the positional parameters:

```
Public ReadOnly Property BugID( ) As Integer
    Get
        Return mBugID
    End Get
End Property
```

Using an attribute

Once you have defined an attribute, you can put it to work by placing it immediately before its target. To test the BugFixAttribute of the preceding example, the following program creates a simple class named MyMath and gives it two functions. Assign BugFixAttributes to the class to record its code-maintenance history:

```
<BugFixAttribute(121, "Jesse Liberty", "01/03/05"), _
 BugFixAttribute(107, "Jesse Liberty", "01/04/05", _
 Comment:="Fixed off by one errors")> _
Public Class MyMath
```

These attributes will be stored with the metadata. Example 18-1 shows the complete program.

Example 18-1. Custom attributes

```
Option Strict On
Imports System
Imports System.Reflection

' create custom attribute to be assigned to class members
<AttributeUsage(AttributeTargets.Class Or _
AttributeTargets.Constructor Or _
AttributeTargets.Field Or _
AttributeTargets.Method Or _
AttributeTargets.Property, AllowMultiple:=True)> _
Public Class BugFixAttribute
    Inherits System.Attribute

    ' private member data
    Private mBugID As Integer
    Private mComment As String
    Private mDate As String
    Private mProgrammer As String

    Public Sub New( _
        ByVal bugID As Integer, _
        ByVal programmer As String, _
        ByVal theDate As String)

        mBugID = bugID
        mProgrammer = programmer
        mDate = theDate

    End Sub 'New

    ' accessor
    Public ReadOnly Property BugID() As Integer
        Get
            Return mBugID
        End Get
    End Property

    ' property for named parameter

    Public Property Comment() As String
        Get
            Return mComment
        End Get
        Set(ByVal Value As String)
            mComment = Value
        End Set
    End Property
```

Example 18-1. Custom attributes (continued)

```
    ' accessor
    Public ReadOnly Property theDate( ) As String
        Get
            Return mDate
        End Get
    End Property

    ' accessor

    Public ReadOnly Property Programmer( ) As String
        Get
            Return mProgrammer
        End Get
    End Property

End Class 'BugFixAttribute

' ********* assign the attributes to the class ********
<BugFixAttribute(121, "Jesse Liberty", "01/03/05"), _
 BugFixAttribute(107, "Jesse Liberty", "01/04/05", _
 Comment:="Fixed off by one errors")> _
Public Class MyMath

    Public Function DoFunc1(ByVal param1 As Double) As Double
        Return param1 + DoFunc2(param1)
    End Function 'DoFunc1

    Public Function DoFunc2(ByVal param1 As Double) As Double
        Return param1 / 3
    End Function 'DoFunc2

End Class 'MyMath

Public Class Tester

    Public Shared Sub Main( )
        Dim mm As New MyMath( )
        Console.WriteLine("Calling DoFunc(7). Result: {0}", mm.DoFunc1(7))
    End Sub 'Main
End Class 'Tester

Output:
Calling DoFunc(7). Result: 9.33333333333333
```

As you can see, the attributes had absolutely no impact on the output. In fact, for the moment, you have only my word that the attributes exist at all. A quick look at the metadata using ILDasm does reveal that the attributes are in place, however, as shown in Figure 18-1. You'll see how to get at this metadata and use it in your program in the next section.

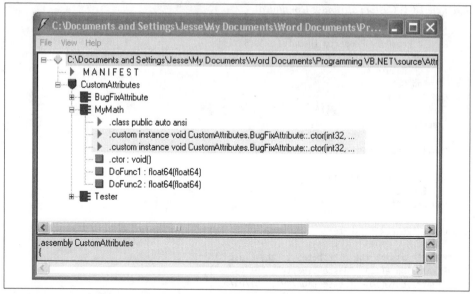

Figure 18-1. *The metadata in the assembly*

Reflection

For the attributes in the metadata to be useful, you need a way to access them, ideally during runtime. The classes in the Reflection namespace, along with the System.Type and System.TypedReference classes, provide support for examining and interacting with the metadata.

Reflection is generally used for any of four tasks:

Viewing metadata
This might be used by tools and utilities that wish to display metadata.

Performing type discovery
This allows you to examine the types in an assembly and interact with or instantiate those types. This can be useful in creating custom scripts. For example, you might want to allow your users to interact with your program using a script language, such as JavaScript, or a scripting language you create yourself.

Late binding to methods and properties
This allows the programmer to invoke properties and methods on objects dynamically instantiated based on type discovery. This is also known as *dynamic invocation*.

Creating types at runtime (reflection emit)
The ultimate use of reflection is to create new types at runtime and then to use those types to perform tasks. You might do this when a custom class, created at runtime, will run significantly faster than more generic code created at compile time. An example is offered later in this chapter.

Viewing MetaData

In this section, you will use the Visual Basic .NET Reflection support to read the metadata in the MyMath class.

Start by initializing an object of the type MemberInfo. This object, in the System. Reflection namespace, is provided to discover the attributes of a member and to provide access to the metadata:

```
Dim inf As System.Reflection.MemberInfo = GetType(MyMath)
```

Call the GetType operator on the MyMath type, which returns an object of type Type, which derives from MemberInfo.

> The Type class is the root of the reflection classes. Type encapsulates a representation of the type of an object. The Type class is the primary way to access metadata. Type derives from MemberInfo and encapsulates information about the members of a class (e.g., methods, properties, fields, events, etc.).

The next step is to call GetCustomAttributes on this MemberInfo object, passing in the type of the attribute you want to find. You get back an array of objects, each of type BugFixAttribute:

```
Dim attributes() As Attribute
attributes = inf.GetCustomAttributes(GetType(BugFixAttribute), False)
```

You can now iterate through this array, printing out the properties of the BugFixAttribute object. Example 18-2 replaces the Tester class from Example 18-1.

Example 18-2. Using reflection

```
Public Class Tester

    Public Shared Sub Main( )
        Dim mm As New MyMath( )
        Console.WriteLine("Calling DoFunc(7). Result: {0}", mm.DoFunc1(7))

        Dim inf As System.Reflection.MemberInfo = GetType(MyMath)

        Dim attributes() As Attribute
        attributes = _
           inf.GetCustomAttributes(GetType(BugFixAttribute), False)

        ' iterate through the attributes, retrieving the
        ' properties
        Dim attribute As [Object]
        For Each attribute In attributes
            Dim bfa As BugFixAttribute = CType(attribute, BugFixAttribute)
            Console.WriteLine(ControlChars.Lf + "BugID: {0}", bfa.BugID)
            Console.WriteLine("Programmer: {0}", bfa.Programmer)
            Console.WriteLine("Date: {0}", bfa.theDate)
```

Example 18-2. Using reflection (continued)

```
            Console.WriteLine("Comment: {0}", bfa.Comment)
        Next attribute
    End Sub 'Main
End Class 'Tester
```

When you put this replacement code into Example 18-1 and run it, you can see the metadata printed as you'd expect:

```
Output:
Calling DoFunc(7). Result: 9.33333333333333

BugID: 107
Programmer: Jesse Liberty
Date: 01/04/05
Comment: Fixed off by one errors

BugID: 121
Programmer: Jesse Liberty
Date: 01/03/05
Comment:
```

Type Discovery

You can use reflection to explore and examine the contents of an assembly. You can find the types associated with a module; the methods, fields, properties, and events associated with a type, as well as the signatures of each of the type's methods; the interfaces supported by the type; and the type's base class.

To start, load an assembly dynamically with the Assembly.Load() static method. The Assembly class encapsulates the actual assembly itself, for purposes of reflection. The signature for the Load() method is:

```
Overloads Public Shared Function Load(AssemblyName) As Assembly
```

For the next example, pass in the Core Library to the Load() method. MsCorLib.dll has the core classes of the .NET Framework. Because Assembly is both a keyword and a class name, you'll need to enclose the class name in square brackets:

```
Dim a As [Assembly] = [Assembly].Load("Mscorlib.dll")
```

Once the assembly is loaded, you can call GetTypes() to return an array of Type objects. The Type object is the heart of reflection. Type represents type declarations (classes, interfaces, arrays, values, and enumerations):

```
Dim theTypes As Type() = a.GetTypes()
```

The assembly returns an array of types that you can display in a For Each loop, as shown in Example 18-3. Because this listing uses the Type class, you will want to add an Imports statement for the System.Reflection namespace.

Example 18-3. Reflecting on an assembly

```
Option Strict On
Imports System
Imports System.Reflection

Public Class Tester

    Public Shared Sub Main( )
        ' what is in the assembly
        Dim a As [Assembly] = [Assembly].Load("Mscorlib.dll")
        Dim theTypes As Type( ) = a.GetTypes( )
        Dim t As Type
        For Each t In theTypes
            Console.WriteLine("Type is {0}", t)
        Next t
        Console.WriteLine("{0} types found", theTypes.Length)
    End Sub 'Main
End Class 'Tester
```

The output from this would fill many pages. Here is a short excerpt:

```
Type is System.TypeCode
Type is System.Security.Util.StringExpressionSet
Type is System.Runtime.InteropServices.COMException
Type is System.Runtime.InteropServices.SEHException
Type is System.Reflection.TargetParameterCountException
Type is System.Text.UTF7Encoding
Type is System.Text.UTF7Encoding+Decoder
Type is System.Text.UTF7Encoding+Encoder
Type is System.ArgIterator
1430 types found
```

This example obtained an array filled with the types from the Core Library and printed them one by one. The array contained 1,430 entries on my machine.

Reflecting on a Type

You can reflect on a single type in the mscorlib assembly as well. To do so, extract a type from the assembly with GetType( ) method, as shown in Example 18-4.

Example 18-4. Reflecting on a type

```
Option Strict On
Imports System
Imports System.Reflection

Public Class Tester
    Public Shared Sub Main( )
        Dim t As Type = Type.GetType("System.Reflection.Assembly")
        Console.WriteLine("Single type is {0}", t)
    End Sub 'Main
End Class 'Tester
```

Finding all type members

You can ask the Assembly type for all its members using the GetMembers() method of the Type class, which lists all the methods, properties, and fields, as shown in Example 18-5.

Example 18-5. Reflecting on the members of a type

```
Option Strict On
Imports System
Imports System.Reflection

Public Class Tester
    Public Shared Sub Main( )
        Dim t As Type = Type.GetType("System.Reflection.Assembly")
        Console.WriteLine("Single type is {0}", t)
        Dim mbrInfoArray As MemberInfo( ) = t.GetMembers( )
        Dim inf As MemberInfo
        For Each inf In mbrInfoArray
            Console.WriteLine("{0} is a {1}", _
                inf, inf.MemberType)
        Next
    End Sub 'Main
End Class 'Tester
```

Once again the output is quite lengthy, but within the output you see fields, methods, constructors, and properties, as shown in this excerpt:

```
Boolean IsDefined(System.Type, Boolean) is a Method
System.Object<> GetCustomAttributes(Boolean) is a Method
System.Object<> GetCustomAttributes(System.Type, Boolean) is a Method
System.Security.Policy.Evidence get_Evidence( ) is a Method
System.String get_Location( ) is a Method
```

Finding type methods

You might want to focus on methods only, excluding the fields, properties, and so forth. To do so, remove the call to GetMembers():

```
Dim mbrInfoArray As MemberInfo( ) = t.GetMembers( )
```

and add a call to GetMethods( ):

```
Dim mbrInfoArray As MemberInfo( ) = t.GetMethods( )
```

The output now is nothing but the methods:

```
Output (excerpt):
Boolean Equals(System.Object) is a Method
System.String ToString( ) is a Method
System.String CreateQualifiedName(
        System.String, System.String) is a Method
Boolean get_GlobalAssemblyCache( ) is a Method
```

Finding particular type members

Finally, to narrow it down even further, you can use the FindMembers method to find particular members of the type. For example, you can narrow your search to methods whose names begin with "Get".

To narrow the search, use the FindMembers method, which takes four parameters: MemberTypes, BindingFlags, MemberFilter, and object.

MemberTypes
> A MemberTypes object that indicates the type of the member to search for. These include All, Constructor, Custom, Event, Field, Method, NestedType, Property, and TypeInfo. You will also use the MemberTypes method to find a method.

BindingFlags
> An enumeration that controls the way searches are conducted by reflection. There are a great many BindingFlag values, including IgnoreCase, Instance, Public, Static, and so forth.

MemberFilter
> A delegate (see Chapter 12) that is used to filter the list of members in the MemberInfo array of objects. The filter you'll use is Type.FilterName, a field of the Type class used for filtering on a name.

Object
> A string value that will be used by the filter. In this case you'll pass in "Get*" to match only those methods that begin with "Get".

The complete listing for filtering on these methods is shown in Example 18-6.

Example 18-6. Finding particular methods

```
Option Strict On
Imports System
Imports System.Reflection

Public Class Tester
    Public Shared Sub Main( )
        Dim t As Type = Type.GetType("System.Reflection.Assembly")

        Dim mbrInfoArray As MemberInfo( ) = t.FindMembers( _
            MemberTypes.Method, _
            BindingFlags.Public Or _
            BindingFlags.Static Or _
            BindingFlags.NonPublic Or _
            BindingFlags.Instance Or _
            BindingFlags.DeclaredOnly, _
            Type.FilterName, "Get*")

        Dim inf As MemberInfo
        For Each inf In mbrInfoArray
```

Example 18-6. Finding particular methods (continued)

```
            Console.WriteLine("{0} is a {1}", _
                inf, inf.MemberType)
        Next
    End Sub 'Main
End Class 'Tester
```

Here is an excerpt of the output:

```
System.Object[] GetCustomAttributes(Boolean) is a Method
System.Object[] GetCustomAttributes(System.Type, Boolean) is a Method
System.IO.Stream GetManifestResourceStream(System.String, System.Threading.
StackCrawlMark ByRef, Boolean) is a Method
GetManifestResourceInfo(System.String) is a Method
System.String[] GetManifestResourceNames() is a Method
System.IO.FileStream[] GetFiles(Boolean) is a Method
System.IO.FileStream[] GetFiles() is a Method
System.IO.FileStream GetFile(System.String) is a Method
System.String GetFullName() is a Method
Byte* GetResource(System.String, UInt64 ByRef, System.Threading.StackCrawlMark ByRef,
Boolean) is a Method
```

Late Binding

Once you have discovered a method, it's possible to invoke it using reflection. For example, you might like to invoke the Cos() method of System.Math, which returns the cosine of an angle.

> You could, of course, call Cos() in the normal course of your code, but reflection allows you to bind to that method at runtime. This is called late-binding and offers the flexibility of choosing at runtime which object you will bind to and invoking it programmatically. This can be useful when creating a custom script to be run by the user or when working with objects that might not be available at compile time. For example, by using late-binding, your program can interact with the spellchecker or other components of a running commercial word processing program such as Microsoft Word.

To invoke Cos(), you will first get the Type information for the System.Math class:

```
Dim theMathType As Type = Type.GetType("System.Math")
```

With that type information, you could dynamically load an instance of a class by using a static method of the Activator class. Since Cos() is static, you don't need to construct an instance of System.Math (and you can't, since System.Math has no public constructor).

The Activator class contains four methods, all static, which you can use to create objects locally or remotely, or to obtain references to existing objects. The four methods are CreateComInstanceFrom, CreateInstanceFrom, GetObject, and CreateInstance:

CreateComInstanceFrom
Used to create instances of COM objects.

CreateInstanceFrom
Used to create a reference to an object from a particular assembly and type name.

GetObject
Used when marshaling objects. Marshaling is discussed in detail in Chapter 19.

CreateInstance
Used to create local or remote instances of an object.

For example:

```
Dim theObj As Object = Activator.CreateInstance(someType)
```

Back to the Cos() example, you now have one object in hand: a Type object named theMathType, which you created by calling GetType.

Before you can invoke a method on the object, you must get the method you need from the Type object, theMathType. To do so, you'll call GetMethod(), and you'll pass in the signature of the Cos method.

The signature, you will remember, is the name of the method (Cos) and its parameter types. In the case of Cos(), there is only one parameter: a double. However, Type.GetMethod takes two parameters. The first represents the name of the method you want, and the second represents the parameters. The name is passed as a string; the parameters are passed as an array of types:

```
Dim ConsineInfo As MethodInfo = _
    theMathType.GetMethod("Cos", paramTypes)
```

Before calling GetMethod, you must prepare the array of types:

```
Dim paramTypes(0) As Type
paramTypes(0) = Type.GetType("System.Double")
```

This code declares the array of Type objects and then fills the first element (paramTypes(0)) with a Type representing a Double. Obtain the type representing a Double by calling the static method Type.GetType(), and passing in the string "System.Double".

You now have an object of type MethodInfo on which you can invoke the method. To do so, you must pass in the object to invoke the method on and the actual value of the parameters, again in an array. Since this is a static method, pass in theMathType. (If Cos() was an instance method, you could use theObj instead of theMathType.)

```
Dim parameters(0) As Object
parameters(0) = 45 * (Math.PI / 180) '45 degrees in radians
Dim returnVal As Object = _
    ConsineInfo.Invoke(theMathType, parameters)
```

Note that you've created two arrays. The first, paramTypes, holds the type of the parameters. The second, parameters, holds the actual value. If the method had taken two arguments, you'd have declared these arrays to hold two values.

Example 18-7 illustrates dynamically calling the Cos() method.

Example 18-7. Dynamically invoking a method

```
Option Strict On
Imports System
Imports System.Reflection

Public Class Tester
    Public Shared Sub Main()

        ' Sine System.Math has no public constructor you can not call
        ' Activator.CreateInstance(theMathType)
        Dim theMathType As Type = Type.GetType("System.Math")

        Dim paramTypes(0) As Type
        paramTypes(0) = Type.GetType("System.Double")

        Dim ConsineInfo As MethodInfo = _
            theMathType.GetMethod("Cos", paramTypes)

        Dim parameters(0) As Object
        parameters(0) = 45 * (Math.PI / 180) '45 degrees in radians
        Dim returnVal As Object

        returnVal = ConsineInfo.Invoke(theMathType, parameters)
        Console.WriteLine("The cosine of a 45 degree angle is {0}", _
            returnVal)

    End Sub 'Main
End Class 'Tester
```

That was a lot of work just to invoke a single method. The power, however, is that you can use reflection to discover an assembly on the user's machine, to query what methods are available, and to invoke one of those members dynamically!

Reflection Emit

So far we've seen reflection used for three purposes: viewing metadata, type discovery, and dynamic invocation. You might use these techniques when building tools (such as a development environment) or when processing scripts. The most powerful use of reflection, however, is with reflection emit.

Reflection emit supports the dynamic creation of new types at runtime. You can define an assembly to run dynamically or to save itself to disk, and you can define modules and new types with methods that you can then invoke.

The use of dynamic invocation and reflection emit should be considered an advanced topic. Most developers will never have need to use reflection emit. This demonstration is based on an example provided at a Microsoft Author's Summit.

To understand the power of reflection emit, you must first consider a slightly more complicated example of dynamic invocation.

Problems can have general solutions that are relatively slow and specific solutions that are fast. To keep things manageably simple, consider a DoSum() method, which provides the sum of a string of integers from 1 to n, where n will be supplied by the user.

Thus, DoSum(3) is equal to 1+2+3, or 6. DoSum(10) is 55. Writing this in Visual Basic .NET is very simple:

```vb
Public Function DoSum1(n As Integer) As Integer
    Dim result As Integer = 0
    Dim i As Integer
    For i = 1 To n
        result += i
    Next i
    Return result
End Function 'DoSum1
```

The method simply loops, adding the requisite number. If you pass in 3, the method adds 1 + 2 + 3 and returns an answer of 6.

With large numbers, and when run many times, this might be a bit slow. Given the value 20, this method would be considerably faster if you removed the loop:

```vb
Public Function DoSum2() As Integer
    Return 1 + 2 + 3 + 4 + 5 + 6 + 7 + 8 + 9 + 10 + 11 + 12 + 13 + 14 + _
    15 + 16 + 17 + 18 + 19 + 20
End Function 'DoSum2
```

DoSum2 runs more quickly than DoSum1 does. How much more quickly? To find out, you'll need to put a timer on both methods. To do so, use a DateTime object to mark the start time and a TimeSpan object to compute the elapsed time.

For this experiment, you need to create two DoSum() methods; the first will use the loop and the second will not. Call each 1,000,000 times. (Computers are very fast, so to see a difference you have to work hard!) Then compare the times. Example 18-8 illustrates the entire test program.

Example 18-8. Comparing loop to brute force

```vb
Option Strict On
Imports System
Imports System.Diagnostics
Imports System.Threading
```

Example 18-8. Comparing loop to brute force (continued)

```vb
Public Class MyMath

    ' sum numbers with a loop
    Public Function DoSum(ByVal n As Integer) As Integer
        Dim result As Integer = 0
        Dim i As Integer
        For i = 1 To n
            result += i
        Next i
        Return result
    End Function 'DoSum

    ' brute force by hand
    Public Function DoSum2() As Integer
        Return 1 + 2 + 3 + 4 + 5 + 6 + 7 + 8 + 9 + 10 _
        + 11 + 12 + 13 + 14 + 15 + 16 + 17 + 18 + 19 + 20
    End Function 'DoSum2
End Class 'MyMath

Public Class TestDriver

    Public Shared Sub Main()

        Const val As Integer = 20 ' val to sum
        ' 1,000,000 iterations
        Const iterations As Integer = 1000000

        ' hold the answer
        Dim result As Integer = 0

        Dim m As New MyMath()

        ' mark the start time
        Dim startTime As DateTime = DateTime.Now

        ' run the experiment
        Dim i As Integer
        For i = 0 To iterations - 1
            result = m.DoSum(val)
        Next i

        ' mark the elapsed time
        Dim elapsed As TimeSpan = DateTime.Now.Subtract(startTime)

        ' display the results
        Console.WriteLine("Loop: Sum of ({0}) = {1}", val, result)
        Console.WriteLine(("The elapsed time in milliseconds is: " _
          & elapsed.TotalMilliseconds.ToString()))

        ' mark a new start time
        startTime = DateTime.Now
```

Example 18-8. Comparing loop to brute force (continued)

```
        ' run the experiment
        Dim j As Integer
        For j = 0 To iterations - 1
            result = m.DoSum2()
        Next j

        ' mark the new elapsed time
        elapsed = DateTime.Now.Subtract(startTime)

        ' display the results
        Console.WriteLine( _
          "Brute Force: Sum of ({0}) = {1}", val, result)
        Console.WriteLine("The elapsed time in milliseconds is: " _
          & elapsed.TotalMilliseconds.ToString())
    End Sub 'Main
End Class 'TestDriver
```

As you can see, both methods returned the same answer (one million times!), but the brute-force method was six times faster.

Is there a way to avoid the loop and still provide a general solution? In traditional programming, the answer would be no, but with reflection you do have one other option. You can, at runtime, take the value the user wants (20, in this case) and write out to disk a class that implements the brute-force solution. You can then use dynamic invocation to invoke that method.

There are at least three ways to achieve this result, each increasingly elegant. The third, reflection emit, is the best, but a close look at two other techniques is instructive. If you are pressed for time, you might wish to jump ahead to the section entitled "Dynamic Invocation with Reflection Emit."

Dynamic invocation with InvokeMember( )

The first approach will be to dynamically create a class named BruteForceSums at runtime. The BruteForceSums class will contain a method, ComputeSum(), that implements the brute-force approach. You'll write that class to disk, compile it, and then use dynamic invocation to invoke its brute-force method by means of the InvokeMember() method of the Type class. The key point is that *BruteForceSums.vb* won't exist until you run the program. You'll create it when you need it and supply its arguments then.

To accomplish this, you'll create a new class named ReflectionTest. The job of the ReflectionTest class is to create the BruteForceSums class, write it to disk, and compile it. ReflectionTest has only two methods: DoSum and GenerateCode.

ReflectionTest.DoSum is a public method that returns the sum, given a value. That is, if you pass in 10, it returns the sum of 1+2+3+4+5+6+7+8+9+10. It does this by creating the BruteForceSums class and delegating the job to its ComputeSum method.

ReflectionTest has two private fields:

```
Private theType As Type = Nothing
Private theClass As Object = Nothing
```

The first is an object of type Type, which you use to load your class from disk; the second is an object of type object, which you use to dynamically invoke the ComputeSums( ) method of the BruteForceSums class you'll create.

The driver program instantiates an instance of ReflectionTest and calls its DoSum method, passing in the value. For this version of the program, the value is increased to 200.

The DoSum method checks whether theType is nothing; if it is, the class has not been created yet. DoSum calls the helper method GenerateCode to generate the code for the BruteForceSums class and the class's ComputeSums method. GenerateCode then writes this newly created code to a *.vb* file on disk and runs the compiler to turn it into an assembly on disk. Once this is completed, DoSum can call the method using reflection.

Once the class and method are created, load the assembly from disk and assign the class type information to theType—DoSum can use that to invoke the method dynamically to get the correct answer.

You begin by creating a constant for the value to which you'll sum:

```
Const val As Integer = 200
```

Each time you compute a sum, it will be the sum of the values 1 to 200.

Before you create the dynamic class, you need to go back and re-create MyMath:

```
Dim m As New MyMath( )
```

Give MyMath a method DoSumLooping, much as you did in the previous example:

```
Public Class MyMath

    ' sum numbers with a loop
    Public Function DoSumLooping(ByVal initialVal As Integer) As Integer
        Dim result As Integer = 0
        Dim i As Integer
        For i = 1 To initialVal
            result += i
        Next i
        Return result
    End Function 'DoSumLooping
End Class 'MyMath
```

This serves as a benchmark against which you can compare the performance of the brute-force method.

Now you're ready to create the dynamic class and compare its performance with the looping version. First, instantiate an object of type ReflectionTest and invoke the DoSum() method on that object:

```
Dim t As New ReflectionTest()
result = t.DoSum(val)
```

ReflectionTest.DoSum checks to see if its Type field, theType, is nothing. If it is, you haven't yet created and compiled the BruteForceSums class and must do so now:

```
If theType Is Nothing Then
    GenerateCode(theValue)
End If
```

The GenerateCode method takes the value (in this case, 200) as a parameter to know how many values to add.

GenerateCode begins by creating a file on disk. For now, I'll walk you through this quickly. First, call the static method File.Open, and pass in the filename and a flag indicating that you want to create the file. File.Open returns a Stream object:

```
Dim fileName As String = "BruteForceSums"
Dim s As Stream = File.Open(fileName & ".vb", FileMode.Create)
```

Once you have the Stream, you can create a StreamWriter so that you can write into that file:

```
Dim wrtr As New StreamWriter(s)
```

You can now use the WriteLine methods of StreamWriter to write lines of text into the file. Begin the new file with a comment:

```
wrtr.WriteLine(" ' Dynamically created BruteForceSums class")
```

This writes the comment:

```
' Dynamically created BruteForceSums class
```

to the file you've just created (*BruteForceSums.vb*). Next, write out the class declaration:

```
Dim className As String = "BruteForceSums"
wrtr.WriteLine("class {0}", className)
```

Within the definition of the class, create the ComputeSum method:

```
wrtr.WriteLine(ControlChars.Tab & _
    "public Function ComputeSum() as Integer")
wrtr.WriteLine(ControlChars.Tab & "' Brute force sum method")
wrtr.WriteLine(ControlChars.Tab & "' For value = {0}", theVal)
```

Now it is time to write out the addition statements. When you are done, you want the file to have this line:

```
return 0+1+2+3+4+5+6+7+8+9...
```

continuing up to value (in this case, 200):

```
wrtr.Write(ControlChars.Tab + "return 0")
Dim i As Integer
```

```
For i = 1 To theVal
    wrtr.Write("+ {0}", i)
Next i
```

Notice how this works. What will be written to the file is:

```
ControlChars.Tab return 0+ 1+ 2+ 3+...
```

The initial ControlChars.Tab causes the code to be indented in the source file.

When the loop completes, end the return statement and end the method and then end the class:

```
wrtr.WriteLine("")
wrtr.WriteLine(ControlChars.Tab & "End Function") ' end method
wrtr.WriteLine("End Class") ' end class
```

Close the streamWriter and the stream, thus closing the file:

```
wrtr.Close( )
s.Close( )
```

When this runs, the *BruteForceSums.vb* file will be written to disk. It will look like this:

```
' Dynamically created BruteForceSums class
class BruteForceSums
    public Function ComputeSum( ) as Integer
    ' Brute force sum method
    ' For value = 200
    return 0+ 1+ 2+ 3+ 4+ 5+ 6+ 7+ 8+ 9+ 10+ 11+ 12+ 13+ 14+ 15+ 16+ 17+ 18+ 19+ 20+
21+ 22+ 23+ 24+ 25+ 26+ 27+ 28+ 29+ 30+ 31+ 32+ 33+ 34+ 35+ 36+ 37+ 38+ 39+ 40+ 41+
42+ 43+ 44+ 45+ 46+ 47+ 48+ 49+ 50+ 51+ 52+ 53+ 54+ 55+ 56+ 57+ 58+ 59+ 60+ 61+ 62+
63+ 64+ 65+ 66+ 67+ 68+ 69+ 70+ 71+ 72+ 73+ 74+ 75+ 76+ 77+ 78+ 79+ 80+ 81+ 82+ 83+
84+ 85+ 86+ 87+ 88+ 89+ 90+ 91+ 92+ 93+ 94+ 95+ 96+ 97+ 98+ 99+ 100+ 101+ 102+ 103+
104+ 105+ 106+ 107+ 108+ 109+ 110+ 111+ 112+ 113+ 114+ 115+ 116+ 117+ 118+ 119+ 120+
121+ 122+ 123+ 124+ 125+ 126+ 127+ 128+ 129+ 130+ 131+ 132+ 133+ 134+ 135+ 136+ 137+
138+ 139+ 140+ 141+ 142+ 143+ 144+ 145+ 146+ 147+ 148+ 149+ 150+ 151+ 152+ 153+ 154+
155+ 156+ 157+ 158+ 159+ 160+ 161+ 162+ 163+ 164+ 165+ 166+ 167+ 168+ 169+ 170+ 171+
172+ 173+ 174+ 175+ 176+ 177+ 178+ 179+ 180+ 181+ 182+ 183+ 184+ 185+ 186+ 187+ 188+
189+ 190+ 191+ 192+ 193+ 194+ 195+ 196+ 197+ 198+ 199+ 200
    End Function
End Class
```

This accomplishes the goal of dynamically creating a class with a method that finds the sum through brute force.

The only remaining task is to build the file and then use the method. To build the file, you must start a new process (processes are explained in some detail in Chapter 20). The best way to launch this process is with a ProcessStartInfo class that will hold the command line. Instantiate a ProcessStartInfo and set its filename to *cmd.exe*:

```
Dim psi As New ProcessStartInfo( )
psi.FileName = "cmd.exe"
```

You need to pass in the string you want to invoke at the command line. The ProcessStartInfo.Arguments property specifies the command-line arguments to use when starting the program. The command-line argument to the *cmd.exe* program will be */c* to tell *cmd.exe* to exit after it executes the command. The command for *cmd.exe* is the command-line compiler:

```
Dim compileString As String = "/c {0}vbc /optimize+ "
compileString += "/target:library "
compileString += "{1}.vb > compile.out"
```

The string compileString will invoke the Visual Basic .NET compiler (*vbc*), telling it to optimize the code (after all, you're doing this to gain performance) and to build a dynamic link library (DLL) file (*/target:library*). Redirect the output of the compile to a file named *compile.out* so that you can examine it if there are errors.

Combine compileString with the filename, using the static method Format of the string class, and assign the combined string to psi.Arguments. The first placeholder, {0}, holds the location of the compiler (*%SystemRoot%\Microsoft.NET\Framework\ <version>*), and the second placeholder, {1}, holds the source code filename:

```
Dim frameworkDir As String = RuntimeEnvironment.GetRuntimeDirectory()
psi.Arguments = String.Format(compileString, frameworkDir, fileName)
```

The effect of all this is to set the Arguments property of the ProcessStartInfo object psi to:

```
/c vbc /optimize+ /target:library
BruteForceSums.vb > compile.out
```

Before invoking *cmd.exe,* set the WindowStyle property of psi to Minimized so that when the command executes, the window does not flicker onto and then off of the user's display:

```
psi.WindowStyle = ProcessWindowStyle.Minimized
```

You are now ready to start the *cmd.exe* process—wait until it finishes before proceeding with the rest of the GenerateCode method:

```
Dim proc As Process = Process.Start(psi)
proc.WaitForExit()
```

Once the process is done, you can get the assembly; from the assembly, you can get the class you've created. Finally, you can ask that class for its type and assign that to your theType member variable:

```
Dim a As [Assembly] = [Assembly].LoadFrom((fileName & ".dll"))
theClass = a.CreateInstance(className)
theType = a.GetType(className)
```

You can now delete the *.vb* file you generated:

```
File.Delete(fileName & ".vb")
```

You've now filled theType, and you're ready to return to DoSum to invoke the ComputeSum method dynamically. The Type object has a method, InvokeMember(), which can be used to invoke a member of the class described by the Type object. The InvokeMember method is overloaded; the version you'll use takes five arguments:

```
Overloads Public Function InvokeMember( _
    ByVal name As String, _
    ByVal invokeAttr As BindingFlags, _
    ByVal binder As Binder, _
    ByVal target As Object, _
    ByVal args() As Object _
) As Object
```

name

The name of the method you wish to invoke.

invokeAttr

A bit mask of BindingFlags that specify how the search of the object is conducted. In this case, you'll use the InvokeMethod flag OR'd with the flag. These are the standard flags for invoking a method dynamically.

binder

Used to assist in type conversions. By passing in nothing, you'll specify that you want the default binder.

target

The object on which you'll invoke the method. In this case, you'll pass in theClass, which is the class you just created from the assembly you just built.

args

An array of arguments to pass to the method you're invoking.

The complete invocation of InvokeMember looks like this:

```
Dim arguments() As Object
Dim retVal As Object = _
  theType.InvokeMember( _
    "ComputeSum", _
    BindingFlags.Default Or BindingFlags.InvokeMethod, _
    Nothing, theClass, arguments)

    Return CDbl(retVal)
```

The result of invoking this method is assigned to the local variable retVal, which is then returned, as a double, to the driver program. The complete listing is shown in Example 18-9.

Example 18-9. Dynamic invocation with Type and InvokeMethod()

```
Option Strict On
Imports System
Imports System.Diagnostics
Imports System.IO
Imports System.Reflection
```

Example 18-9. Dynamic invocation with Type and InvokeMethod() (continued)

```vb
Imports System.Runtime.InteropServices ' provides RuntimeEnvironment

' benchmark the looping approach
Public Class MyMath

    ' sum numbers with a loop
    Public Function DoSumLooping(ByVal initialVal As Integer) As Integer
        Dim result As Integer = 0
        Dim i As Integer
        For i = 1 To initialVal
            result += i
        Next i
        Return result
    End Function 'DoSumLooping
End Class 'MyMath

' responsible for creating the BruteForceSums
' class and compiling it and invoking the
' DoSums method dynamically
Public Class ReflectionTest

    Private theType As Type = Nothing
    Private theClass As Object = Nothing

    ' the public method called by the driver
    Public Function DoSum(ByVal theValue As Integer) As Double
        ' if you don't have a reference
        ' to the dynamically created class
        ' create it
        If theType Is Nothing Then
            GenerateCode(theValue)
        End If

        ' with the reference to the dynamically
        ' created class you can invoke the method
        Dim arguments() As Object
        Dim retVal As Object = _
         theType.InvokeMember( _
            "ComputeSum", _
            BindingFlags.Default Or BindingFlags.InvokeMethod, _
            Nothing, theClass, arguments)
        Return CDbl(retVal)
    End Function 'DoSum


    ' generate the code and compile it
    Private Sub GenerateCode(ByVal theVal As Integer)
        ' open the file for writing
        Dim fileName As String = "BruteForceSums"
        Dim s As Stream = File.Open(fileName & ".vb", FileMode.Create)
        Dim wrtr As New StreamWriter(s)
        wrtr.WriteLine(" ' Dynamically created BruteForceSums class")
```

Example 18-9. Dynamic invocation with Type and InvokeMethod() (continued)

```
        ' create the class
        Dim className As String = "BruteForceSums"
        wrtr.WriteLine("class {0}", className)

        ' create the method
        wrtr.WriteLine(ControlChars.Tab & _
          "public Function ComputeSum( ) as Integer")
        wrtr.WriteLine(ControlChars.Tab & "' Brute force sum method")
        wrtr.WriteLine(ControlChars.Tab & "' For value = {0}", theVal)

        ' write the brute force additions
        wrtr.Write(ControlChars.Tab & "return 0")
        Dim i As Integer
        For i = 1 To theVal
            wrtr.Write("+ {0}", i)
        Next i
        wrtr.WriteLine("")
        wrtr.WriteLine(ControlChars.Tab & "End Function") ' end method
        wrtr.WriteLine("End Class") ' end class
        ' close the writer and the stream
        wrtr.Close( )
        s.Close( )

        ' Build the file
        Dim psi As New ProcessStartInfo( )
        psi.FileName = "cmd.exe"

        Dim compileString As String = "/c {0}vbc /optimize+ "
        compileString += "/target:library "
        compileString += "{1}.vb > compile.out"

        Dim frameworkDir As String = _
        RuntimeEnvironment.GetRuntimeDirectory( )
        psi.Arguments = [String].Format(compileString, _
            frameworkDir, fileName)
        psi.WindowStyle = ProcessWindowStyle.Minimized

        Dim proc As Process = Process.Start(psi)
        proc.WaitForExit( )

        ' Open the file, and get a
        ' pointer to the method info
        Dim a As [Assembly] = [Assembly].LoadFrom((fileName & ".dll"))
        theClass = a.CreateInstance(className)
        theType = a.GetType(className)
        ' File.Delete(fileName + ".vb")
    End Sub 'GenerateCode
End Class 'ReflectionTest

Public Class TestDriver

    Public Shared Sub Main( )
```

Example 18-9. Dynamic invocation with Type and InvokeMethod( ) (continued)

```
            Const val As Integer = 200 ' 1..200
            Const iterations As Integer = 100000
            Dim result As Double = 0

            ' run the benchmark
            Dim m As New MyMath( )
            Dim startTime As DateTime = DateTime.Now
            Dim i As Integer
            For i = 0 To iterations - 1
                result = m.DoSumLooping(val)
            Next i
            Dim elapsed As TimeSpan = DateTime.Now.Subtract(startTime)
            Console.WriteLine("Sum of ({0}) = {1}", val, result)
            Console.WriteLine("Looping. Elapsed milliseconds: " & _
            elapsed.TotalMilliseconds.ToString( ) _
              & " for {0} iterations", iterations)

            ' run our reflection alternative
            Dim t As New ReflectionTest( )

            startTime = DateTime.Now
            For i = 0 To iterations - 1
                result = t.DoSum(val)
            Next i

            elapsed = DateTime.Now.Subtract(startTime)
            Console.WriteLine("Sum of ({0}) = {1}", val, result)
            Console.WriteLine("Brute Force. Elapsed milliseconds: " & _
              elapsed.TotalMilliseconds.ToString( ) & _
            " for {0} iterations", iterations)
    End Sub 'Main
End Class 'TestDriver

Output:
Sum of (200) = 20100
Looping. Elapsed milliseconds: 46.875 for 100000 iterations
Sum of (200) = 20100
Brute Force. Elapsed milliseconds: 1406.25 for 100000 iterations
```

Notice that the dynamically invoked method is *far* slower than the loop. This is not a surprise; writing the file to disk, compiling it, reading it from disk, and invoking the method all bring significant overhead. You accomplished your goal, but it was a pyrrhic victory.

Dynamic invocation with interfaces

It turns out that dynamic invocation is particularly slow. You want to maintain the general approach of writing the class at runtime and compiling it on the fly. But rather than using dynamic invocation, you'd just like to call the method. One way to speed things up is to use an interface to call the ComputeSums( ) method directly.

To accomplish this, you need to change ReflectionTest.DoSum() from:

```
Public Function DoSum(ByVal theValue As Integer) As Double
    ' if you don't have a reference
    ' to the dynamically created class
    ' create it
    If theType Is Nothing Then
        GenerateCode(theValue)
    End If

    ' with the reference to the dynamically
    ' created class you can invoke the method
    Dim arguments() As Object
    Dim retVal As Object = _
     theType.InvokeMember( _
        "ComputeSum", _
        BindingFlags.Default Or BindingFlags.InvokeMethod, _
        Nothing, theClass, arguments)
    Return CDbl(retVal)
End Function 'DoSum
```

to the following:

```
Public Function DoSum(ByVal theValue As Integer) As Double
    If theComputer Is Nothing Then
        GenerateCode(theValue)
    End If

    Return theComputer.ComputeSum()
End Function 'DoSum
```

In this example, theComputer is an interface to an object of type BruteForceSums. It must be an interface and not an object because when you compile this program, the-Computer won't yet exist; you'll create it dynamically.

Remove the declarations for theType and theClass and replace them with:

```
Private theComputer As IComputer = Nothing
```

This declares theComputer to be an IComputer interface. At the top of your program, declare the interface:

```
Public Interface IComputer
    Function ComputeSum() As Integer
End Interface
```

When you create the BruteForceSum class, you must make it implement IComputer:

```
Dim className As String = "BruteForceSums"
wrtr.WriteLine("class {0}", className)
wrtr.WriteLine( _
    "Implements ReflectionEmit2.Programming_VBNET.IComputer")
```

You must also modify the implementation of ComputeSums to indicate that it implements the method from the interface:

```
wrtr.WriteLine( _
  ControlChars.Tab & _
```

```
        "Public Function ComputeSum( ) as Integer _ ")
    wrtr.WriteLine( _
        "Implements ReflectionEmit2.Programming_VBNET.IComputer.ComputeSum ")
```

Save your program in a project file named *ReflectionEmit2*, and modify compileString in GenerateCode as follows:

```
Dim compileString As String = "/c {0}vbc /optimize+ "
compileString += "/r:ReflectionEmit2.exe "
compileString += "/target:library "
compileString += "{1}.vb > compile.out"
```

The compile string will need to reference the *ReflectionEmit2* program itself (*ReflectionEmit2.exe*) so that the dynamically called compiler will know where to find the declaration of IComputer.

After you build the assembly, you will no longer assign the instance to theClass and then get the type for theType, as these variables are gone. Instead, you will assign the instance to the interface IComputer:

```
theComputer = a.CreateInstance(className)
```

Use the interface to invoke the method directly in DoSum:

```
Return theComputer.ComputeSum( )
```

Example 18-10 is the complete source code.

Example 18-10. Dynamic invocation with interfaces

```
Option Strict On
Imports System
Imports System.Diagnostics
Imports System.IO
Imports System.Reflection
Imports System.Runtime.InteropServices ' provides RuntimeEnvironment

Namespace Programming_VBNET

    Public Interface IComputer
        Function ComputeSum( ) As Integer
    End Interface

    ' benchmark the looping approach
    Public Class MyMath

        ' sum numbers with a loop
        Public Function DoSumLooping(ByVal initialVal As Integer) _
            As Integer
            Dim result As Integer = 0
            Dim i As Integer
            For i = 1 To initialVal
                result += i
            Next i
            Return result
        End Function 'DoSumLooping
```

Example 18-10. Dynamic invocation with interfaces (continued)

```
End Class 'MyMath


' responsible for creating the BruteForceSums
' class and compiling it and invoking the
' DoSums method dynamically
Public Class ReflectionTest

    Private theComputer As IComputer = Nothing

    ' the public method called by the driver
    Public Function DoSum(ByVal theValue As Integer) As Double
        If theComputer Is Nothing Then
            GenerateCode(theValue)
        End If

        Return theComputer.ComputeSum( )
    End Function 'DoSum

    ' generate the code and compile it
    Private Sub GenerateCode(ByVal theVal As Integer)
        ' open the file for writing
        Dim fileName As String = "BruteForceSums"
        Dim s As Stream = File.Open(fileName & ".vb", FileMode.Create)
        Dim wrtr As New StreamWriter(s)
        wrtr.WriteLine(" ' Dynamically created BruteForceSums class")

        ' create the class
        Dim className As String = "BruteForceSums"
        wrtr.WriteLine("class {0}", className)
        wrtr.WriteLine( _
            "Implements ReflectionEmit2.Programming_VBNET.IComputer")


        ' create the method
        wrtr.WriteLine( _
            ControlChars.Tab + _
          "Public Function ComputeSum( ) as Integer _ ")
        wrtr.WriteLine( _
  "Implements ReflectionEmit2.Programming_VBNET.IComputer.ComputeSum ")
        wrtr.WriteLine( _
            ControlChars.Tab & "' Brute force sum method")
        wrtr.WriteLine( _
            ControlChars.Tab & "' For value = {0}", theVal)

        ' write the brute force additions
        wrtr.Write(ControlChars.Tab & "return 0")
        Dim i As Integer
        For i = 1 To theVal
            wrtr.Write("+ {0}", i)
        Next i
        wrtr.WriteLine("")
        wrtr.WriteLine(ControlChars.Tab & "End Function") ' end method
```

Example 18-10. Dynamic invocation with interfaces (continued)

```
            wrtr.WriteLine("End Class") ' end class
            ' close the writer and the stream
            wrtr.Close( )
            s.Close( )

            ' Build the file
            Dim psi As New ProcessStartInfo( )
            psi.FileName = "cmd.exe"

            Dim compileString As String = "/c {0}vbc /optimize+ "
            compileString += "/r:ReflectionEmit2.exe "
            compileString += "/target:library "
            compileString += "{1}.vb > compile.out"

            Dim frameworkDir As String = _
            RuntimeEnvironment.GetRuntimeDirectory( )
            Dim args As String = _
            [String].Format(compileString, frameworkDir, fileName)
            psi.Arguments = args
            psi.WindowStyle = ProcessWindowStyle.Minimized

            Dim proc As Process = Process.Start(psi)
            proc.WaitForExit( )

            ' Open the file, and get a
            ' pointer to the method info
            Dim a As [Assembly] = [Assembly].LoadFrom((fileName & ".dll"))
            theComputer = a.CreateInstance(className)
            ' File.Delete(fileName & ".vb")
        End Sub 'GenerateCode
    End Class 'ReflectionTest

Public Class TestDriver

    Public Shared Sub Main( )
        Const val As Integer = 200 ' 1..200
        Const iterations As Integer = 100000
        Dim result As Double = 0

        ' run the benchmark
        Dim m As New MyMath( )
        Dim startTime As DateTime = DateTime.Now
        Dim i As Integer
        For i = 0 To iterations - 1
            result = m.DoSumLooping(val)
        Next i
        Dim elapsed As TimeSpan = DateTime.Now.Subtract(startTime)
        Console.WriteLine("Sum of ({0}) = {1}", val, result)
        Console.WriteLine("Looping. Elapsed milliseconds: " & _
            elapsed.TotalMilliseconds.ToString() _
          & " for {0} iterations", iterations)
```

Example 18-10. Dynamic invocation with interfaces (continued)

```
              ' run our reflection alternative
              Dim t As New ReflectionTest( )

              startTime = DateTime.Now
              For i = 0 To iterations - 1
                  result = t.DoSum(val)
              Next i

              elapsed = DateTime.Now.Subtract(startTime)
              Console.WriteLine("Sum of ({0}) = {1}", val, result)
              Console.WriteLine("Brute Force. Elapsed milliseconds: " & _
                elapsed.TotalMilliseconds.ToString( ) & _
                  " for {0} iterations", iterations)
          End Sub 'Main
      End Class 'TestDriver
End Namespace

Output:
Sum of (200) = 20100
Looping. Elapsed milliseconds: 46.875 for 100000 iterations
Sum of (200) = 20100
Brute Force. Elapsed milliseconds: 375 for 100000 iterations
```

This output is much more satisfying; our dynamically created brute-force method now runs a bit faster, but still not as fast as the loop does. The solution to this is to use reflection emit.

Dynamic invocation with reflection emit

So far you've created an assembly on the fly by writing its source code to disk and then compiling that source code. You then dynamically invoked the method you wanted to use from that assembly, which was compiled on disk. That brings a lot of overhead, and what have you accomplished? When you're done with writing the file to disk, you have source code you can compile; when you're done compiling, you have IL (Intermediate Language) op codes on disk that you can ask the .NET Framework to run.

Reflection emit allows you to skip a few steps and just "emit" the op codes directly. This is writing assembly code directly from your Visual Basic .NET program and then invoking the result. It just doesn't get any cooler than that.

You start much as you did in the previous examples. Create a constant for the number to add to (200) and the number of iterations (1,000,000). You then re-create the myMath class as a benchmark.

Once again you have a ReflectionTest class, and once again you call DoSum, passing in the value:

```
Dim t As New ReflectionTest( )
result = t.DoSum(val)
```

DoSum itself is virtually unchanged:

```
Public Function DoSum(ByVal theValue As Integer) As Double
    If theComputer Is Nothing Then
        GenerateCode(theValue)
    End If

    ' call the method through the interface
    Return theComputer.ComputeSum()
End Function 'DoSum
```

As you can see, you will use an interface again, but this time you are not going to write a file to disk.

GenerateCode is quite different now. You no longer write the file to disk and compile it; instead you call the helper method EmitAssembly and get back an assembly. You then create an instance from that assembly and cast that instance to your interface:

```
Public Sub GenerateCode(ByVal theValue As Integer)
    Dim theAssembly As [Assembly] = EmitAssembly(theValue)
    theComputer = _
        CType(theAssembly.CreateInstance("BruteForceSums"), _
        IComputer)
End Sub 'GenerateCode
```

As you might have guessed, the magic is stashed away in the EmitAssembly method:

```
Private Function EmitAssembly(ByVal theValue As Integer) As [Assembly]
```

The value you pass in is the sum you want to compute. To see the power of reflection emit, you'll increase that value from 200 to 2,000.

The first thing to do in EmitAssembly is to create an object of type AssemblyName and give that AssemblyName object the name "DoSumAssembly":

```
Dim assemblyName As New AssemblyName()
assemblyName.Name = "DoSumAssembly"
```

An AssemblyName is an object that fully describes an assembly's unique identity. As discussed in Chapter 17, an assembly's identity consists of a simple name (DoSumAssembly), a version number, a cryptographic key pair, and a supported culture.

With this object in hand, you can create a new AssemblyBuilder object. To do so, call DefineDynamicAssembly on the current domain, which is done by calling the static GetDomain() method of the Thread object. Domains are discussed in detail in Chapter 19.

The parameters to the GetDomain() method are the AssemblyName object you just created and an AssemblyBuilderAccess enumeration value (one of Run, RunAndSave, or Save). You'll use Run in this case to indicate that the assembly can be run but not saved:

```
Dim newAssembly As AssemblyBuilder = _
    Thread.GetDomain().DefineDynamicAssembly( _
        assemblyName, AssemblyBuilderAccess.Run)
```

With this newly created AssemblyBuilder object, you are ready to create a ModuleBuilder object. The job of the ModuleBuilder, not surprisingly, is to build a module dynamically. Modules are discussed in Chapter 17. Call the DefineDynamicModule method, passing in the name of the method you want to create:

```
Dim newModule As ModuleBuilder = _
    newAssembly.DefineDynamicModule("Sum")
```

Now, given that module, you can define a public class and get back a TypeBuilder object. TypeBuilder is the root class used to control the dynamic creation of classes. With a TypeBuilder object, you can define classes and add methods and fields:

```
Dim myType As TypeBuilder = _
    newModule.DefineType("BruteForceSums", TypeAttributes.Public)
```

You are now ready to mark the new class as implementing the IComputer interface:

```
myType.AddInterfaceImplementation(GetType(IComputer))
```

You're almost ready to create the ComputeSum method, but first you must set up the array of parameters. Because you have no parameters at all, create an array of zero length:

```
Dim paramTypes() As Type
```

Then create a Type object to hold the return type for your method:

```
Dim returnType As Type = GetType(Integer)
```

You're ready to create the method. The DefineMethod() method of TypeBuilder will both create the method and return an object of type MethodBuilder, which you will use to generate the IL code:

```
Dim simpleMethod As MethodBuilder = _
    myType.DefineMethod("ComputeSum", MethodAttributes.Public _
    Or MethodAttributes.Virtual, returnType, paramTypes)
```

Pass in the name of the method, the flags you want (public and virtual), the return type (Integer), and the paramTypes (the zero length array).

Then use the MethodBuilder object you created to get an ILGenerator object:

```
Dim generator As ILGenerator = _
    simpleMethod.GetILGenerator()
```

With your precious ILGenerator object in hand, you are ready to emit the op codes. These are the very op codes that the Visual Basic .NET compiler would have created. (In fact, the best way to get the op codes is to write a small Visual Basic .NET program, compile it, and then examine the op codes in ILDasm!)

First emit the value 0 to the stack. Then loop through the number values you want to add (1 through 200), adding each to the stack in turn, adding the previous sum to the new number, and leaving the result on the stack:

```
generator.Emit(OpCodes.Ldc_I4, 0)
Dim i As Integer
```

```
For i = 1 To theValue
    generator.Emit(OpCodes.Ldc_I4, i)
    generator.Emit(OpCodes.Add)
Next i
```

The value that remains on the stack is the sum you want, so you'll return it:

```
generator.Emit(OpCodes.Ret)
```

You're ready now to create a MethodInfo object that will describe the method:

```
Dim computeSumInfo As MethodInfo = _
    GetType(IComputer).GetMethod("ComputeSum")
```

Now you must specify the implementation that will implement the method. Call DefineMethodOverride on the TypeBuilder object you created earlier, passing in the MethodBuilder you created along with the MethodInfo object you just created:

```
myType.DefineMethodOverride(simpleMethod, computeSumInfo)
```

You're just about done; create the class and return the assembly:

```
myType.CreateType( )
Return newAssembly
```

OK, I didn't say it was easy, but it is really cool, and the resulting code runs very fast. Example 18-11 is the full source code.

Example 18-11. Dynamic invocation with reflection emit

```
Option Strict On
Imports System
Imports System.Diagnostics
Imports System.IO
Imports System.Reflection
Imports System.Reflection.Emit
Imports System.Runtime.InteropServices ' provides RuntimeEnvironment
Imports System.Threading

Namespace Programming_VBNET

    Public Interface IComputer
        Function ComputeSum( ) As Integer
    End Interface

    ' benchmark the looping approach
    Public Class MyMath
        ' sum numbers with a loop
        Public Function DoSumLooping(ByVal initialVal As Integer) _
            As Integer
            Dim result As Integer = 0
            Dim i As Integer
            For i = 1 To initialVal
                result += i
            Next i
            Return result
```

Example 18-11. Dynamic invocation with reflection emit (continued)

```
        End Function 'DoSumLooping
    End Class 'MyMath

    ' responsible for creating the BruteForceSums
    ' class and compiling it and invoking the
    ' DoSums method dynamically
    Public Class ReflectionTest

        Private theComputer As IComputer = Nothing
        ' the private method which emits the assembly
        ' using op codes
        Private Function EmitAssembly( _
        ByVal theValue As Integer) As [Assembly]
            ' Create an assembly name
            Dim assemblyName As New AssemblyName( )
            assemblyName.Name = "DoSumAssembly"

            ' Create a new assembly with one module
            Dim newAssembly As AssemblyBuilder = _
                Thread.GetDomain( ).DefineDynamicAssembly( _
                    assemblyName, AssemblyBuilderAccess.Run)
            Dim newModule As ModuleBuilder = _
                newAssembly.DefineDynamicModule("Sum")

            '  Define a public class named "BruteForceSums "
            '  in the assembly.
            Dim myType As TypeBuilder = _
                newModule.DefineType( _
            "BruteForceSums", TypeAttributes.Public)

            ' Mark the class as implementing IComputer.
            myType.AddInterfaceImplementation(GetType(IComputer))

            ' Define a method on the type to call. Pass an
            ' array that defines the types of the parameters,
            ' the type of the return type, the name of the
            ' method, and the method attributes.
            Dim paramTypes( ) As Type
            Dim returnType As Type = GetType(Integer)
            Dim simpleMethod As MethodBuilder = _
                myType.DefineMethod("ComputeSum", MethodAttributes.Public _
                Or MethodAttributes.Virtual, returnType, paramTypes)

            ' Get an ILGenerator. This is used
            ' to emit the IL that you want.
            Dim generator As ILGenerator = _
                simpleMethod.GetILGenerator( )

            ' Emit the IL that you'd get if you
            ' compiled the code example
            ' and then ran ILDasm on the output.
            ' Push zero onto the stack. For each 'i'
```

Example 18-11. Dynamic invocation with reflection emit (continued)

```
    ' less than 'theValue',
    ' push 'i' onto the stack as a constant
    ' add the two values at the top of the stack.
    ' The sum is left on the stack.
    generator.Emit(OpCodes.Ldc_I4, 0)
    Dim i As Integer
    For i = 1 To theValue
        generator.Emit(OpCodes.Ldc_I4, i)
        generator.Emit(OpCodes.Add)
    Next i

    ' return the value
    generator.Emit(OpCodes.Ret)

    'Encapsulate information about the method and
    'provide access to the method's metadata
    Dim computeSumInfo As MethodInfo = _
        GetType(IComputer).GetMethod("ComputeSum")

    ' specify the method implementation.
    ' Pass in the MethodBuilder that was returned
    ' by calling DefineMethod and the methodInfo
    ' just created
    myType.DefineMethodOverride(simpleMethod, computeSumInfo)

    ' Create the type.
    myType.CreateType( )
    Return newAssembly
End Function 'EmitAssembly

' check if the interface is nothing
' if so, call Setup.
Public Function DoSum(ByVal theValue As Integer) As Double
    If theComputer Is Nothing Then
        GenerateCode(theValue)
    End If

    ' call the method through the interface
    Return theComputer.ComputeSum( )
End Function 'DoSum

' emit the assembly, create an instance
' and get the interface
Public Sub GenerateCode(ByVal theValue As Integer)
    Dim theAssembly As [Assembly] = EmitAssembly(theValue)
    theComputer = _
        CType(theAssembly.CreateInstance("BruteForceSums"), _
        IComputer)
End Sub 'GenerateCode

' private member data
```

Example 18-11. Dynamic invocation with reflection emit (continued)

```
    End Class 'ReflectionTest

    Public Class TestDriver

        Public Shared Sub Main( )
            Const val As Integer = 200 ' 1..200
            Const iterations As Integer = 100000
            Dim result As Double = 0

            ' run the benchmark
            Dim m As New MyMath( )
            Dim startTime As DateTime = DateTime.Now
            Dim i As Integer
            For i = 0 To iterations - 1
                result = m.DoSumLooping(val)
            Next i
            Dim elapsed As TimeSpan = DateTime.Now.Subtract(startTime)
            Console.WriteLine("Sum of ({0}) = {1}", val, result)
            Console.WriteLine("Looping. Elapsed milliseconds: " & _
                elapsed.TotalMilliseconds.ToString( ) & _
                    " for {0} iterations", iterations)

            ' run our reflection alternative
            Dim t As New ReflectionTest( )
            startTime = DateTime.Now
            For i = 0 To iterations - 1
                result = t.DoSum(val)
            Next i
            elapsed = DateTime.Now.Subtract(startTime)
            Console.WriteLine("Sum of ({0}) = {1}", val, result)
            Console.WriteLine("Brute Force. Elapsed milliseconds: " & _
                elapsed.TotalMilliseconds.ToString( ) & _
                    " for {0} iterations", iterations)
        End Sub 'Main
    End Class 'TestDriver
End Namespace
```

```
Output:
Sum of (2000) = 2001000
Looping. Elapsed milliseconds: 11468.75 for 1000000 iterations
Sum of (2000) = 2001000
Brute Force. Elapsed milliseconds: 406.25 for 1000000 iterations
```

Reflection emit is a powerful technique for emitting op codes. Although today's compilers are very fast and today's machines have lots of memory and processing speed, it is comforting to know that when you must, you can get right down to the virtual metal.

CHAPTER 19

Marshaling and Remoting

The days of integrated programs all running in a single process on a single machine are, if not dead, at least seriously wounded. Today's programs consist of complex components running in multiple processes, often across the network. The Web has facilitated distributed applications in a way that was unthinkable even a few years ago, and the trend is toward distribution of responsibility.

A second trend is toward centralizing business logic on large servers. Although these trends appear to be contradictory, in fact they are synergistic: business objects are being centralized while the user interface and even some middleware are being distributed.

The net effect is that objects need to be able to talk with one another at a distance. Objects running on a server handling the web user interface need to be able to interact with business objects living on centralized servers at corporate headquarters.

The process of moving an object across a boundary is called *remoting*. Boundaries exist at various levels of abstraction in your program. The most obvious boundary is between objects running on different machines.

The process of preparing an object to be remoted is called *marshaling*. On a single machine, objects might need to be marshaled across context, app domain, or process boundaries.

A *process* is essentially a running application. If an object in your word processor wants to interact with an object in your spreadsheet, they must communicate across process boundaries.

Processes are divided into *application domains* (often called "app domains"); these in turn are divided into various *contexts*. App domains act like lightweight processes, and contexts create boundaries that objects with similar rules can be contained within. At times, objects will be marshaled across both context and app domain boundaries, as well as across process and machine boundaries. (Processes, app domains, and contexts are all explained in greater detail later in this chapter.)

When an object is remoted, it appears to be sent through the wire from one computer to another, much like Captain Kirk being teleported down to the surface of a planet some miles below the orbiting USS Enterprise.

In Star Trek, Kirk was actually sent to the planet, but in the .NET edition it is all an illusion. If you are standing on the surface of the planet, you might think you are seeing and talking with the real Kirk, but you are not talking to Kirk at all; you are talking to a proxy, or a simulation whose job is to take your message and beam it up to the Enterprise where it is relayed to the real Kirk. Between you and Kirk there are also a number of "sinks."

A *sink* is an object whose job is to enforce policy. For example, if Kirk tries to tell you something that might influence the development of your civilization, the prime-directive sink might disallow the transmission.

When the real Kirk responds, he passes his response through various sinks until it gets to the proxy and the proxy tells you. It seems to you as though Kirk is really there, but he's actually sitting on the bridge, yelling at Scotty that he needs more power.

The actual transmission of your message is done by a *channel*. The channel's job is to know how to move the message from the Enterprise to the planet. The channel works with a *formatter*, which makes sure the message is in the right format. Perhaps you speak only Vulcan, and the poor Captain does not. The formatter can translate your message into Federation Standard, and translate Kirk's response from Federation Standard back to Vulcan. You appear to be talking with one another, but the formatter is silently facilitating the communication.

This chapter demonstrates how your objects can be marshaled across various boundaries, and how proxies and stubs can create the illusion that your object has been squeezed through the network cable to a machine across the office or around the world. In addition, this chapter explains the role of formatters, channels, and sinks, and how to apply these concepts to your programming.

Application Domains

A *process* is, essentially, a running application. Each .NET application runs in its own process. If you have Word, Excel, and Visual Studio open, you have three processes running. If you open another copy of Word, another process starts up. Each process is subdivided into one or more *application domains* (or *app domains*). An app domain acts like a process but uses fewer resources.

App domains can be independently started and halted; they are secure, lightweight, and versatile. An app domain can provide fault tolerance; if you start an object in a second app domain and it crashes, it will bring down the app domain but not your entire program. You can imagine that web servers might use app domains for running users' code; if the code has a problem, the web server can maintain operations.

An app domain is encapsulated by an instance of the AppDomain class, which offers a number of methods and properties. A few of the most important are listed in Table 19-1.

Table 19-1. Methods and properties of the AppDomain class

Method or property	Details
CurrentDomain	Public static property that returns the current application domain for the current thread
CreateDomain( )	Overloaded public static method that creates a new application domain
GetCurrentThreadID( )	Public static method that returns the current thread identifier
Unload( )	Public static method that removes the specified app domain
FriendlyName	Public property that returns the friendly name for this app domain
DefineDynamicAssembly( )	Overloaded public method that defines a dynamic assembly in the current app domain
ExecuteAssembly( )	Public method that executes the designated assembly
GetData( )	Public method that gets the value stored in the current application domain given a key
Load( )	Public method that loads an assembly into the current app domain
SetAppDomainPolicy( )	Public method that sets the security policy for the current app domain
SetData( )	Public method that puts data into the specified app domain property

App domains also support a variety of events—including AssemblyLoad, AssemblyResolve, ProcessExit, and ResourceResolve—that are fired as assemblies are found, loaded, run, and unloaded.

Every process has an initial app domain, and can have additional app domains as you create them. Each app domain exists in exactly one process. Until now, all the programs in this book have been in a single app domain: the default app domain. Each process has its own default app domain. In many, perhaps in most of the programs you write, the default app domain will be all that you'll need.

However, there are times when a single domain is insufficient. You might create a second app domain if you need to run a library written by another programmer. Perhaps you don't trust the library, and want to isolate it in its own domain so that if a method in the library crashes the program, only the isolated domain will be affected. If you were the author of Internet Information Server (IIS, Microsoft's web hosting software), you might spin up a new app domain for each plug-in application or each virtual directory you host. This would provide fault tolerance, so that if one web application crashed, it would not bring down the web server.

It is also possible that the other library might require a different security environment; creating a second app domain allows the two security environments to co-exist. Each app domain has its own security, and the app domain serves as a security boundary.

App domains are not threads and should be distinguished from threads. A thread exists in one app domain at a time, and a thread can access (and report) which app domain it is executing in. App domains are used to isolate applications; within an app domain there might be multiple threads operating at any given moment (see Chapter 20).

To see how app domains work, let's set up an example. Suppose you wish your program to instantiate a Shape class, but in a second app domain.

 There is no good reason for this Shape class to be put in a second app domain, except to illustrate how these techniques work. It is possible, however, that more complex objects might need a second app domain to provide a different security environment. Further, if you are creating classes that might engage in risky behavior, you might like the protection of starting them in a second app domain.

Normally, you'd load the Shape class from a separate assembly, but to keep this example simple, you'll just put the definition of the Shape class into the same source file as all the other code in this example (see Chapter 17). Further, in a production environment, you might run the Shape class methods in a separate thread, but for simplicity, you'll ignore threading for now. (Threading is covered in detail in Chapter 20.) By sidestepping these ancillary issues, you can keep the example straightforward and focus on the details of creating and using application domains and marshaling objects across app domain boundaries.

Creating and Using App Domains

Create a new app domain by calling the static method CreateDomain() on the App-Domain class:

```
Dim ad2 As AppDomain = AppDomain.CreateDomain("Shape Domain")
```

This creates a new app domain with the *friendly name* Shape Domain. The friendly name is a convenience to the programmer; it is a way to interact with the domain programmatically without knowing the internal representation of the domain. You can check the friendly name of the domain you're working in with the property System.AppDomain.CurrentDomain.FriendlyName.

Once you have instantiated an AppDomain object, you can create instances of classes, interfaces, and so forth using its CreateInstance() method. Here's the signature:

```
<ClassInterface(ClassInterfaceType.None)>
NotOverridable Overloads Public Function CreateInstance( _
    ByVal assemblyName As String, _
    ByVal typeName As String, _
    ByVal ignoreCase As Boolean, _
    ByVal bindingAttr As BindingFlags, _
```

```
        ByVal binder As Binder, _
        ByVal args() As Object, _
        ByVal culture As CultureInfo, _
        ByVal activationAttributes() As Object, _
        ByVal securityAttributes As Evidence _
    ) As ObjectHandle Implements _AppDomain.CreateInstance
```

And here's how to use it:

```
Dim oh As ObjectHandle = _
    ad2.CreateInstance( _
        "Marshaling", _
        "Marshaling.NSMarshaling.Shape", _
        False, _
        System.Reflection.BindingFlags.CreateInstance, _
        Nothing, _
        New Object() {3, 5}, _
        Nothing, Nothing, Nothing)
```

The first parameter (Marshaling) is the name of the assembly, and the second (Marshaling.Shape) is the name of the class. The class name must be fully qualified. In this case, Marshaling is the name of the assembly, NSMarshaling is the name of the name space, and Shape is the name of the class.

A *binder* is an object that enables dynamic binding of an assembly at runtime. Its job is to allow you to pass in information about the object you want to create, to create that object for you, and to bind your reference to that object. In the vast majority of cases, including this example, you'll use the default binder, which is accomplished by passing in Nothing.

It is possible, of course, to write your own binder, which might, for example, check your ID against special permissions in a database and reroute the binding to a different object, based on your identity or your privileges.

> *Binding* typically refers to attaching an object name to an object. *Dynamic binding* refers to the ability to make that attachment when the program is running, as opposed to when it is compiled. In this example, the Shape object is bound to the instance variable at runtime, through the app domain's CreateInstance() method.

Binding flags help the binder fine-tune its behavior at binding time. In this example, use the BindingFlags enumeration value CreateInstance. The default binder normally only looks at public classes for binding, but you can add flags to have it look at private classes if you have the right permissions.

When you bind an assembly at runtime, do not specify the assembly to load at compile time; rather, determine which assembly you want programmatically, and bind your variable to that assembly when the program is running.

The constructor you're calling takes two integers, which must be put into an object array (New Object() {3, 5}). You can send Nothing for the culture because you'll use the default (en) culture and won't specify activation attributes or security attributes.

You get back an *object handle*, which is a type that is used to pass an object (in a wrapped state) between multiple app domains without loading the metadata for the wrapped object in each object through which the ObjectHandle travels. You can get the actual object itself by calling Unwrap() on the object handle, and casting the resulting object to the actual type—in this case, Shape.

The CreateInstance() method provides an opportunity to create the object in a new app domain. If you were to create the object with New, it would be created in the current app domain.

Marshaling Across App Domain Boundaries

You've created a Shape object in the Shape domain, but you're accessing it through a Shape object in the original domain. To access the shape object in another domain, you must marshal the object across the domain boundary.

Marshaling is the process of preparing an object to move across a boundary, once again like Captain Kirk teleporting to the planet's surface. Marshaling is accomplished in two ways: *by value* or *by reference*. When an object is marshaled by value, a copy is made. It is as if I called you on the phone and asked you to send me your calculator, and you called up the hardware store and had them send me one that is identical to yours. I can use the copy just as I would the original, but entering numbers on my copy has no effect on your original.

Marshaling by reference is almost like sending me your own calculator. Here's how it works. You do not actually give me the original, but instead keep it in your house and send me a proxy. The proxy is very smart: when I press a button on my proxy calculator, it sends a signal to your original calculator, and the number appears over there. Pressing buttons on the proxy looks and feels to me just like I reached through the telephone wire between us and touched your original calculator.

Understanding marshaling with proxies

The Captain Kirk and hardware analogies are fine as far as analogies go, but what actually happens when you marshal by reference? The Common Language Runtime (CLR) provides your calling object with a *transparent proxy* (TP).

The job of the TP is to take everything known about your method call (the return value, the parameters, etc.) off of the stack and stuff it into an object that implements the IMessage interface. That IMessage is passed to a RealProxy object.

RealProxy is an abstract base class from which all proxies derive. You can implement your own real proxy or any of the other objects in this process except for the transparent proxy. The default real proxy will hand the IMessage to a series of *sink* objects.

Any number of sinks can be used, depending on the number of policies you wish to enforce, but the last sink in a chain will put the IMessage into a Channel. Channels are split into client-side and server-side channels, and their job is to move the message across the boundary. Channels are responsible for understanding the transport protocol. The actual format of a message as it moves across the boundary is managed by a *formatter*. The .NET Framework provides two formatters: a Simple Object Access Protocol (SOAP) formatter, which is the default for HTTP channels, and a Binary formatter, which is the default for TCP/IP channels. You are free to create your own formatters and, if you are truly a glutton for punishment, your own channels.

Once a message is passed across a boundary, it is received by the server-side channel and formatter, which reconstitute the IMessage and pass it to one or more sinks on the server side. The final sink in a sink chain is the StackBuilder, whose job is to take the IMessage and turn it back into a stack frame so that it appears to be a function call to the server.

Specifying the marshaling method

To illustrate the distinction between marshaling by value and marshaling by reference, in the next example you'll tell the Shape object to marshal by reference but give it a member variable of type Point, which you'll specify as marshal by value.

Note that each time you create an object that might be used across a boundary, you must choose how it will be marshaled. Normally, objects cannot be marshaled at all; you must take action to indicate that an object can be marshaled, either by value or by reference.

The easiest way to make an object marshal by value is to mark it with the Serializable attribute:

```
<Serializable()> _
Public Class Point
```

When an object is serialized, its internal state is written out to a stream, either for marshaling or for storage. The details of serialization are covered in Chapter 20.

The easiest way to make an object marshal by reference is to derive its class from:

```
Public Class Shape
    Inherits MarshalByRefObject
```

The Shape class will have just one member variable, upperLeft. This variable will be a Point object, which will hold the coordinates of the upper-left corner of the shape.

The constructor for Shape will initialize its Point member:

```
Public Sub New(ByVal upperLeftX As Integer, ByVal upperLeftY As Integer)
    Console.WriteLine("[{0}] {1}", _
```

```
        System.AppDomain.CurrentDomain.FriendlyName, _
        "Shape constructor")
    upperLeft = New Point(upperLeftX, upperLeftY)
End Sub 'New
```

Provide Shape with a method for displaying its position:

```
Public Sub ShowUpperLeft()
    Console.WriteLine("[{0}] Upper left: {1},{2}", _
        System.AppDomain.CurrentDomain.FriendlyName, _
        upperLeft.X, upperLeft.Y)
End Sub 'ShowUpperLeft
```

Also provide a second method for returning its upperLeft member variable:

```
Public Function GetUpperLeft() As Point
    Return upperLeft
End Function 'GetUpperLeft
```

The Point class is very simple as well. It has a constructor that initializes its two member variables and accessors to get their value.

Once you create the Shape, ask it for its coordinates:

```
s1.ShowUpperLeft()      ' ask the object to display
```

Then ask it to return its upperLeft coordinate as a Point object that you'll change:

```
Dim localPoint As Point = s1.GetUpperLeft()

localPoint.X = 500
localPoint.Y = 600
```

Ask that Point to print its coordinates, and then ask the Shape to print *its* coordinates. So, will the change to the local Point object be reflected in the Shape? That will depend on how the Point object is marshaled. If it is marshaled by value, the localPoint object will be a copy, and the Shape object will be unaffected by changing the localPoint variables' values. If, on the other hand, you change the Point object to marshal by reference, you'll have a proxy to the actual upperLeft variable, and changing that will change the Shape. Example 19-1 illustrates. Make sure you build Example 19-1 in a project named Marshaling. When Main() instantiates the Shape object, the method is looking for *Marshaling.exe*.

Example 19-1. Marshaling across app domain boundaries

```
Option Strict On
Imports System
Imports System.Runtime.Remoting

Imports System.Reflection

Namespace NSMarshaling

    ' for marshal by reference, comment out
    ' the attribute, and uncomment the base class
```

Example 19-1. Marshaling across app domain boundaries (continued)

```
<Serializable( )> _
Public Class Point
    ' Inherits MarshalByRefObject

    Private mX As Integer
    Private mY As Integer

    Public Sub New(ByVal x As Integer, ByVal y As Integer)
        Console.WriteLine("[{0}] {1}", _
            System.AppDomain.CurrentDomain.FriendlyName, _
            "Point constructor")
        Me.mX = x
        Me.mY = y
    End Sub 'New


    Public Property X( ) As Integer
        Get
            Console.WriteLine("[{0}] {1}", _
                System.AppDomain.CurrentDomain.FriendlyName, _
                "Point x.get")
            Return Me.mX
        End Get

        Set(ByVal Value As Integer)
            Console.WriteLine("[{0}] {1}", _
                System.AppDomain.CurrentDomain.FriendlyName, _
                "Point x.set")
            Me.mX = Value
        End Set
    End Property


    Public Property Y( ) As Integer
        Get
            Console.WriteLine("[{0}] {1}", _
                System.AppDomain.CurrentDomain.FriendlyName, _
                "Point y.get")
            Return Me.mY
        End Get

        Set(ByVal Value As Integer)
            Console.WriteLine("[{0}] {1}", _
                System.AppDomain.CurrentDomain.FriendlyName, _
                "Point y.set")
            Me.mY = Value
        End Set
    End Property

End Class 'Point

' the shape class marshals by reference
```

Example 19-1. Marshaling across app domain boundaries (continued)

```
Public Class Shape
    Inherits MarshalByRefObject

    Public Sub New( _
        ByVal upperLeftX As Integer, ByVal upperLeftY As Integer)
        Console.WriteLine("[{0}] {1}", _
            System.AppDomain.CurrentDomain.FriendlyName, _
            "Shape constructor")
        upperLeft = New Point(upperLeftX, upperLeftY)
    End Sub 'New

    Public Function GetUpperLeft( ) As Point
        Return upperLeft
    End Function 'GetUpperLeft

    Public Sub ShowUpperLeft( )
        Console.WriteLine("[{0}] Upper left: {1},{2}", _
            System.AppDomain.CurrentDomain.FriendlyName, _
            upperLeft.X, upperLeft.Y)
    End Sub 'ShowUpperLeft

    Private upperLeft As Point
End Class 'Shape

Public Class Tester

    Public Shared Sub Main( )

        Console.WriteLine("[{0}] {1}", _
            System.AppDomain.CurrentDomain.FriendlyName, _
        "Entered Main")

        ' create the new app domain
        Dim ad2 As AppDomain = AppDomain.CreateDomain("Shape Domain")

        ' Dim a As Assembly = Assembly.LoadFrom("Marshaling.exe")
        ' Dim theShape As Object = a.CreateInstance("Shape")
        ' instantiate a Shape object
        Dim oh As ObjectHandle = _
            ad2.CreateInstance( _
                "Marshaling", _
                "Marshaling.NSMarshaling.Shape", _
                False, _
                System.Reflection.BindingFlags.CreateInstance, _
                Nothing, _
                New Object( ) {3, 5}, _
                Nothing, Nothing, Nothing)

        Dim s1 As Shape = CType(oh.Unwrap( ), Shape)

        s1.ShowUpperLeft( ) ' ask the object to display
```

Example 19-1. Marshaling across app domain boundaries (continued)

```
                ' get a local copy? proxy?
                Dim localPoint As Point = s1.GetUpperLeft( )

                ' assign new values
                localPoint.X = 500
                localPoint.Y = 600

                ' display the value of the local Point object
                Console.WriteLine("[{0}] localPoint: {1}, {2}", _
                    System.AppDomain.CurrentDomain.FriendlyName, _
                    localPoint.X, localPoint.Y)

                s1.ShowUpperLeft( ) ' show the value once more
            End Sub 'Main
        End Class 'Tester
End Namespace
```

```
Output:
[Marshaling.exe] Entered Main
[Shape Domain] Shape constructor
[Shape Domain] Point constructor
[Shape Domain] Point x.get
[Shape Domain] Point y.get
[Shape Domain] Upper left: 3,5
[Marshaling.exe] Point x.set
[Marshaling.exe] Point y.set
[Marshaling.exe] Point x.get
[Marshaling.exe] Point y.get
[Marshaling.exe] localPoint: 500, 600
[Shape Domain] Point x.get
[Shape Domain] Point y.get
[Shape Domain] Upper left: 3,5
```

Read through the code, or better yet, put it in your debugger and step through it. The output reveals that the Shape and Point constructors run in the Shape domain, as does the access of the values of the Point object in the Shape.

The property is set in the original app domain, setting the local copy of the Point object to 500 and 600. Because Point is marshaled by value, however, you are setting a copy of the Point object. When you ask the Shape to display its upperLeft member variable, it is unchanged.

To complete the experiment, comment out the attribute at the top of the Point declaration and uncomment the base class:

```
    '<Serializable( )> _
    Public Class Point
        Inherits MarshalByRefObject
```

Now run the program again. The output is quite different:

```
    [Marshaling.exe] Entered Main
    [Shape Domain] Shape constructor
```

```
[Shape Domain] Point constructor
[Shape Domain] Point x.get
[Shape Domain] Point y.get
[Shape Domain] Upper left: 3,5
[Shape Domain] Point x.set
[Shape Domain] Point y.set
[Shape Domain] Point x.get
[Shape Domain] Point y.get
[Marshaling.exe] localPoint: 500, 600
[Shape Domain] Point x.get
[Shape Domain] Point y.get
[Shape Domain] Upper left: 500,600
```

This time you get a proxy for the Point object and the properties are set through the proxy on the original Point member variable. Thus, the changes are reflected within the Shape itself.

Context

App domains themselves are subdivided into *contexts*. Contexts can be thought of as boundaries within which objects share usage rules. These usage rules include synchronization transactions, and so forth.

Context-Bound and Context-Agile Objects

Objects are either *context-bound* or they are *context-agile*. If they are context-bound, they exist in a context, and to interact with them the message must be marshaled. If they are context-agile, they act within the context of the calling object; that is, their methods execute in the context of the object that invokes the method and so marshaling is not required.

Suppose you have an object A that interacts with the database and so is marked to support transactions. This creates a context. All method calls on A occur within the context of the protection afforded by the transaction. Object A can decide to roll back the transaction, and all actions taken since the last commit are undone.

Suppose that you have another object, B, which is context-agile. Now suppose that object A passes a database reference to object B and then calls methods on B. Perhaps A and B are in a call-back relationship, in which B will do some work and then call A back with the results. Because B is context-agile, B's method operates in the context of the calling object; thus it will be afforded the transaction protection of object A. The changes B makes to the database will be undone if A rolls back the transaction, because B's methods execute within the context of the caller. So far, so good.

Should B be context-agile or context-bound? In the case examined so far, B worked fine being agile. Suppose one more class exists: C. C does not have transactions, and it calls a method on B that changes the database. Now A tries to roll back, but unfortunately, the work B did for C was in C's context and thus was not afforded the support of transactions. Uh-oh: that work can't be undone.

If B was marked context-bound when A created it, B would have inherited A's context. In that case, when C invoked a method on B it would have to be marshaled across the context boundary, but then when B executed the method it would have been in the context of A's transaction. Much better.

This would work if B were context-bound but without attributes. B of course could have its own context attributes, and these might force B to be in a different context from A. For example, B might have a transaction attribute marked RequiresNew. In this case, when B is created it gets a new context, and thus cannot be in A's context. Thus, when A rolled back, B's work could not be undone. You might mark B with the RequiresNew enumeration value because B is an audit function. When A takes an action on the database it informs B, which updates an audit trail. You do not want B's work undone when A undoes its transaction. You want B to be in its own transaction context, rolling back only its own mistakes, not A's.

An object thus has three choices. The first option is to be context-agile. A context-agile object operates in the context of its caller. Option two is to be context-bound (accomplished by deriving from ContextBoundObject) but have no attributes, and thus operate in the context of the creator. Option three is to be context-bound with context attributes, and thus operate only in the context that matches the attributes.

Which you decide upon depends on how your object will be used. If your object is a simple calculator that cannot possibly need synchronization or transactions or any context support, it is more efficient to be context-agile. If your object should use the context of the object that creates it, you should make that object context-bound with no attributes. Finally, if your object has its own context requirements, you should give it the appropriate attributes.

Marshaling Across Context Boundaries

No proxy is needed when accessing context-agile objects within a single app domain. When an object in one context accesses a context-bound object in a second context, it does so through a proxy, and at that time the two context policies are enforced. It is in this sense that a context creates a boundary; the policy is enforced at the boundary between contexts.

For example, when you mark a context-bound object with the System.Enterprise-Services.Synchronization attribute, you indicate that you want the system to manage synchronization for that object. All objects outside that context must pass through the context boundary to touch one of the objects, and at that time the policy of synchronization will be applied.

Strictly speaking, marking two classes with the Synchronization attribute does not guarantee that they will end up in the same context. Each attribute gets to vote on whether it is happy with the current context at activation. If two objects are marked for synchronization but one is pooled, they will be forced into different contexts.

Objects are marshaled differently across context boundaries, depending on how they are created:

- Typical objects are not marshaled at all; within app domains they are context-agile.

- Objects marked with the Serializable attribute are marshaled by value across app domains and are context-agile.

- Objects that derive from MarshalByRefObject are marshaled by reference across app domains and are context-agile.

- Objects derived from ContextBoundObject are marshaled by reference across app domains as well as by reference across context boundaries.

Remoting

In addition to being marshaled across context and app domain boundaries, objects can be marshaled across process boundaries, and even across machine boundaries. When an object is marshaled, either by value or by proxy, across a process or machine boundary, it is said to be *remoted*.

Understanding Server Object Types

There are two types of server objects supported for remoting in .NET: *well-known* and *client-activated*. The communication with well-known objects is established each time a message is sent by the client. There is no permanent connection with a well-known object, as there is with client-activated objects.

Well-known objects come in two varieties: *singleton* and *single-call*. With a well-known singleton object, all messages for the object, from all clients, are dispatched to a single object running on the server. The object is created when the server is started and is there to provide service to any client that can reach it. Well-known objects must have a default (parameterless) constructor.

With a well-known single-call object, each new message from a client is handled by a new object. This is highly advantageous on server farms, where a series of messages from a given client might be handled in turn by different machines depending on load balancing.

Client-activated objects are typically used by programmers who are creating dedicated servers, which provide services to a client they are also writing. In this scenario, the client and the server create a connection, and they maintain that connection until the needs of the client are fulfilled.

Specifying a Server with an Interface

The best way to understand remoting is to walk through an example. We will build a simple four-function calculator class, like the one used in an earlier discussion on web services (see Chapter 16), that implements the interface shown in Example 19-2.

Example 19-2. The Calculator interface

```
Option Strict On
Imports System

Namespace Programming_VBNET
    Public Interface ICalc
        Function Add(x As Double, y As Double) As Double
        Function Subtract (x As Double, y As Double) As Double
        Function Mult(x As Double, y As Double) As Double
        Function Div(x As Double, y As Double) As Double
    End Interface 'ICalc
End Namespace 'Programming_VBNET
```

Save this in a file named *ICalculator.vb* and compile it into a file named *ICalculatorDLL.dll*. To create and compile the source file in Visual Studio, create a new project of type Visual Basic .NET Class Library, enter the interface definition in the Edit window, and then select Build->Build Solution on the Visual Studio menubar. Alternatively, if you have entered the source code using Notepad, you can compile the file at the command line by entering:

```
vbc /t:library ICalculatorDLL.vb
```

There are tremendous advantages to implementing a server through an interface. If you implement the calculator as a class, the client must link to that class in order to declare instances on the client. This greatly diminishes the advantages of remoting because changes to the server require the class definition to be updated on the client. In other words, the client and server would be tightly coupled. Interfaces help decouple the two objects; in fact, you can later update that implementation on the server, and as long as the server still fulfills the contract implied by the interface, the client need not change at all.

Building a Server

To build the server used in this example, create *CalcServer.vb* in a new project of type Visual Basic .NET Console Application (be sure to include a reference to *ICalc.dll*) and then compile it by selecting Build->Build on the Visual Studio menu bar. Or, you can enter the code in Notepad, save it to a file named *CalcServer.vb*, and enter the following at the command-line prompt:

```
vbc /t:exe /r:ICalculatorDLL.dll CalcServer.vb
```

The Calculator class implements ICalc. It derives from MarshalByRefObject so that it will deliver a proxy of the calculator to the client application:

```
Public Class Calculator
    Inherits MarshalByRefObject
    Implements ICalculatorDLL.Programming_VBNET.ICalc
```

The implementation consists of little more than a constructor and simple methods to implement the four functions.

In this example, you'll put the logic for the server into the Main() method of *CalcServer.vb*.

Your first task is to create a channel. Use HTTP as the transport because it is simple and you don't need a sustained TCP/IP connection. You can use the HTTPChannel type provided by .NET:

```
Dim chan As New HttpChannel(65100)
```

 You'll need to include a reference to System.Runtime.Remoting in your project.

Notice that you register the channel on TCP/IP port 65100 (see the discussion of port numbers in Chapter 20).

Next, register the channel with the CLR ChannelServices using the static method RegisterChannel:

```
ChannelServices.RegisterChannel(chan)
```

This step informs .NET that you will be providing HTTP services on port 65100, much as IIS does on port 80. Because you've registered an HTTP channel and not provided your own formatter, your method calls will use the SOAP formatter by default.

Now you are ready to ask the RemotingConfiguration class to register your well-known object. You must pass in the type of the object you want to register, along with an *endpoint*. An *endpoint* is a name that RemotingConfiguration will associate with your type. It completes the address. If the IP address identifies the machine and the port identifies the channel, the endpoint identifies the actual application that will be providing the service. To get the type of the object, you can call the static method GetType() of the Type class, which returns a Type object. Pass in the full name of the object whose type you want:

```
Dim calcType As Type = _
    Type.GetType("CalcServer.Programming_VBNET.Calculator")
```

Also pass in the enumerated type that indicates whether you are registering a Single-Call or Singleton:

```
RemotingConfiguration.RegisterWellKnownServiceType( _
    calcType, "theEndPoint", WellKnownObjectMode.Singleton)
```

The call to RegisterWellKnownServiceType does not put one byte on the wire. It simply uses reflection to build a proxy for your object.

Now you're ready to rock and roll. Example 19-3 provides the entire source code for the server.

Example 19-3. The Calculator server

```
Option Strict On
Imports System
Imports System.Runtime.Remoting
Imports System.Runtime.Remoting.Channels
Imports System.Runtime.Remoting.Channels.Http

Namespace Programming_VBNET
    ' implement the calculator class
    Public Class Calculator
        Inherits MarshalByRefObject
        Implements ICalculatorDLL.Programming_VBNET.ICalc

        Public Sub New( )
            Console.WriteLine("Calculator constructor")
        End Sub 'New

        ' implement the four functions
        Public Function Add( _
            ByVal x As Double, ByVal y As Double) As Double _
            Implements ICalculatorDLL.Programming_VBNET.ICalc.Add
            Console.WriteLine("Add {0} + {1}", x, y)
            Return x + y
        End Function 'Add

        Public Function Subtract( _
            ByVal x As Double, ByVal y As Double) As Double _
            Implements ICalculatorDLL.Programming_VBNET.ICalc.Subtract
            Console.WriteLine("Sub {0} - {1}", x, y)
            Return x - y
        End Function 'Sub

        Public Function Mult( _
            ByVal x As Double, ByVal y As Double) As Double _
            Implements ICalculatorDLL.Programming_VBNET.ICalc.Mult
            Console.WriteLine("Mult {0} * {1}", x, y)
            Return x * y
        End Function 'Mult

        Public Function Div( _
            ByVal x As Double, ByVal y As Double) As Double _
```

Example 19-3. The Calculator server (continued)

```
            Implements ICalculatorDLL.Programming_VBNET.ICalc.Div
            Console.WriteLine("Div {0} / {1}", x, y)
            Return x / y
        End Function 'Div
    End Class 'Calculator

    Public Class ServerTest

        Public Shared Sub Main( )
            ' create a channel and register it
            Dim chan As New HttpChannel(65100)
            ChannelServices.RegisterChannel(chan)

            Dim calcType As Type = _
                Type.GetType("CalcServer.Programming_VBNET.Calculator")

            ' register our well-known type and tell the server
            ' to connect the type to the endpoint "theEndPoint"
            RemotingConfiguration.RegisterWellKnownServiceType( _
                calcType, "theEndPoint", WellKnownObjectMode.Singleton)

            ' "They also serve who only stand and wait." (Milton)
            Console.WriteLine("Press [enter] to exit...")
            Console.ReadLine( )
        End Sub 'Main
    End Class 'ServerTest
End Namespace 'Programming_VBNET
```

When you run this program, it prints its self-deprecating message:

```
    Press [enter] to exit...
```

and then waits for a client to ask for service.

Building the Client

The client must also register a channel, but because you are not listening on that channel, you can use channel 0:

```
Dim chan As New HttpChannel(0)
ChannelServices.RegisterChannel(chan)
```

The client now need only connect through the remoting services, passing a Type object representing the type of the object it needs (in our case, the ICalc interface) and the URI (Uniform Resource Identifier) of the implementing class:

```
Dim obj As MarshalByRefObject = _
    CType(RemotingServices.Connect( _
        GetType(ICalculatorDLL.Programming_VBNET.ICalc), _
        "http://localhost:65100/theEndPoint"), _
        MarshalByRefObject)
```

In this case the server is assumed to be running on your local machine, so the URI is *http://localhost*, followed by the port for the server (65100), followed in turn by the endpoint you declared in the server (theEndPoint).

The remoting service should return an object representing the interface you've requested. You can then cast that object to the interface and begin using it. Because remoting cannot be guaranteed (the network might be down, the host machine may not be available, and so forth), you should wrap the usage in a try block:

```
Try
    Dim calc As ICalculatorDLL.Programming_VBNET.ICalc = obj

    Dim sum As Double = calc.Add(3.0, 4.0)
    Dim difference As Double = calc.Subtract(3, 4)
    Dim product As Double = calc.Mult(3, 4)
    Dim quotient As Double = calc.Div(3, 4)

    Console.WriteLine("3+4 = {0}", sum)
    Console.WriteLine("3-4 = {0}", difference)
    Console.WriteLine("3*4 = {0}", product)
    Console.WriteLine("3/4 = {0}", quotient)
Catch ex As System.Exception
    Console.WriteLine("Exception caught: ")
    Console.WriteLine(ex.Message)
End Try
```

You now have a proxy of the Calculator operating on the server, but usable on the client, across the process boundary and, if you like, across the machine boundary. Example 19-4 shows the entire client (to compile it, you must include a reference to *ICalc.dll* as you did with *CalcServer.vb*).

Example 19-4. The remoting Calculator client

```
Option Strict On
Imports System
Imports System.Runtime.Remoting
Imports System.Runtime.Remoting.Channels
Imports System.Runtime.Remoting.Channels.Http

Namespace Programming_VBNET

    Public Class CalcClient

        Public Shared Sub Main()

            Dim myIntArray(3) As Integer

            Console.WriteLine("Watson, come here I need you...")

            ' create an Http channel and register it
            ' uses port 0 to indicate won't be listening
            Dim chan As New HttpChannel(0)
            ChannelServices.RegisterChannel(chan)
```

Example 19-4. The remoting Calculator client (continued)

```
                    ' get my object from across the http channel
                    ' uses GetType operator
                    Dim obj As MarshalByRefObject = _
                        CType(RemotingServices.Connect( _
                            GetType(ICalculatorDLL.Programming_VBNET.ICalc), _
                            "http://localhost:65100/theEndPoint"), _
                            MarshalByRefObject)

                Try
                        ' cast the object to our interface
                        Dim calc As ICalc.Programming_VBNET.ICalc = obj

                        ' use the interface to call methods
                        Dim sum As Double = calc.Add(3.0, 4.0)
                        Dim difference As Double = calc.Subtract(3, 4)
                        Dim product As Double = calc.Mult(3, 4)
                        Dim quotient As Double = calc.Div(3, 4)

                        ' print the results
                        Console.WriteLine("3+4 = {0}", sum)
                        Console.WriteLine("3-4 = {0}", difference)
                        Console.WriteLine("3*4 = {0}", product)
                        Console.WriteLine("3/4 = {0}", quotient)
                Catch ex As System.Exception
                        Console.WriteLine("Exception caught: ")
                        Console.WriteLine(ex.Message)
                End Try
            End Sub 'Main
        End Class 'CalcClient
End Namespace 'Programming_VBNET
```

The server starts up and waits for the user to press Enter to signal that it can shut down. The client starts and displays a message to the console. The client then calls each of the four operations. You see the server printing its message as each method is called, and then the results are printed on the client.

It is as simple as that; you now have code running on the server and providing services to your client.

Using SingleCall

To see the difference that SingleCall makes versus Singleton, change one line in the server's Main() method. Here's the existing code:

```
RemotingConfiguration.RegisterWellKnownServiceType( _
    calcType, "theEndPoint", WellKnownObjectMode.Singleton)
```

Change the object to SingleCall:

```
RemotingConfiguration.RegisterWellKnownServiceType( _
    calcType, "theEndPoint", WellKnownObjectMode.SingleCall)
```

Using Fully Qualified Names

Note that in Example 19-4 we use the GetType operator. You can also call the GetType( ) method on the TypeClass, but you must pass in a fully qualified name. The correct syntax for a fully qualified type name is:

```
TopNamespace.SubNamespace.ContainingClass+NestedClass, AssemblyName
```

The fully qualified name for the Calc type would therefore be:

```
"ICalculatorDLL.Programming_VBNET.ICalc, ICalc"
```

You could therefore write:

```
Dim calcType As Type = _
    Type.GetType( _
        "ICalculatorDLL.Programming_VBNET.ICalc, ICalculatorDLL")

Dim obj As MarshalByRefObject = _
    CType(RemotingServices.Connect( _
        calcType, "http://localhost:65100/theEndPoint"), _
        MarshalByRefObject)
```

Either approach will work; the latter approach allows you to examine the Type object you get back from the Assembly.

The output reflects that a new object is created to handle each request:

```
Press [enter] to exit..
Calculator constructor
Calculator constructor
Add 3 + 4
Calculator constructor
Sub 3 - 4
Calculator constructor
Mult 3 * 4
Calculator constructor
Div 3 / 4
```

Understanding RegisterWellKnownServiceType

When you called the RegisterWellKnownServiceType( ) method on the server, what actually happened? Remember that you created a Type object for the Calculator class:

```
Dim calcType As Type = _
    Type.GetType("CalcServer.Programming_VBNET.Calculator")
```

You then called RegisterWellKnownServiceType( ), passing in that Type object along with the endpoint and the Singleton enumeration. This signals the CLR to instantiate your Calculator and then to associate it with an endpoint.

To do that work yourself, you would need to modify Example 19-3, changing Main() to instantiate a Calculator and then passing that Calculator to the Marshal() method of RemotingServices with the endpoint to which you want to associate that instance of Calculator. The modified Main() is shown in Example 19-5 and, as you can see, its output is identical to that of Example 19-3.

Example 19-5. Manually instantiating and associating Calculator with an endpoint

```
Public Shared Sub Main( )
    Dim chan As New HttpChannel(65100)
    ChannelServices.RegisterChannel(chan)

    Dim calc As Calculator = New Calculator( )
    RemotingServices.Marshal(calc, "theEndPoint")

    ' "They also serve who only stand and wait." (Milton)
    Console.WriteLine("Press [enter] to exit...")
    Console.ReadLine( )
End Sub 'Main
```

The net effect is that you have instantiated a calculator object, and associated a proxy for remoting with the endpoint you've specified.

Understanding Endpoints

What is going on when you register this endpoint? Clearly, the server is associating that endpoint with the object you've created. When the client connects, that endpoint is used as an index into a table so that the server can provide a proxy to the correct object (in this case, the Calculator).

If you don't provide an endpoint for the client to talk to, you can instead write all the information about your calculator object to a file and physically give that file to your client. For example, you could send it to your buddy by email, and he could load it on his local computer.

The client can deserialize the object and reconstitute a proxy, which it can then use to access the calculator on your server! (The following example was suggested to me by Mike Woodring of DevelopMentor, who uses a similar example to drive home the idea that the endpoint is simply a convenience for accessing a marshaled object remotely.)

To see how you can invoke an object without a known endpoint, modify the Main() method of Example 19-3 once again. This time, rather than calling Marshal() with an endpoint, just pass in the object:

```
Dim myObjRef As ObjRef = RemotingServices.Marshal(calculator)
```

Marshal() returns an ObjRef object. An ObjRef object stores all the information required to activate and communicate with a remote object. When you do supply an endpoint, the server creates a table that associates the endpoint with an ObjRef so that the server can create the proxy when a client asks for it. ObjRef contains all the information needed by the client to build a proxy, and objRef itself is serializable.

Open a file stream for writing to a new file and create a new SOAP formatter. You can serialize your ObjRef to that file by invoking the Serialize() method on the formatter, passing in the file stream and the ObjRef you got back from Marshal. Presto! You have all the information you need to create a proxy to your object written out to a disk file. The complete replacement for Main() is shown in Example 19-6. You will also need to add two using statements to *CalcServer.vb*:

```
Imports System.IO
Imports System.Runtime.Serialization.Formatters.Soap
```

Make sure you add references in your Server project to System.Runtime.Remoting and System.Runtime.Serializaiton.Formatters.Soap.

Example 19-6. Marshaling an object without a well-known endpoint

```
Public Shared Sub Main( )
    ' create a channel and register it
    Dim chan As New HttpChannel(65100)
    ChannelServices.RegisterChannel(chan)
    ' make your own instance and call Marshal directly
    Dim calculator As New Calculator( )

    Dim myObjRef As ObjRef = RemotingServices.Marshal(calculator)

    Dim fileStream As New FileStream( _
        "calculatorSoap.txt", FileMode.Create)

    Dim soapFormatter As New SoapFormatter( )

    soapFormatter.Serialize(fileStream, myObjRef)
    fileStream.Close( )

    '   "They also serve who only stand and wait." (Milton)
    Console.WriteLine( _
        "Exported to CalculatorSoap.txt. Press ENTER to exit...")
    Console.ReadLine( )
End Sub 'Main
```

When you run the server, it writes the file *calculatorSoap.txt* to the disk. The server then waits for the client to connect. It might have a long wait.

You can take that file to your client and reconstitute it on the client machine. To do so, copy the file into the *bin* directory of your client. Again create a channel and register it. This time, however, open a fileStream on the file you just copied from the server:

```
Dim fileStream As New FileStream( _
    "calculatorSoap.txt", FileMode.Open)
```

Then instantiate a SoapFormatter and call Deserialize() on the formatter, passing in the filename and getting back an ICalc:

```
Dim soapFormatter As New SoapFormatter( )

Try
    Dim calc As ICalculatorDLL.Programming_VBNET.ICalc = _
        CType( _
            soapFormatter.Deserialize(fileStream), _
            ICalculatorDLL.Programming_VBNET.ICalc)
```

You are now free to invoke methods on the server through that ICalc, which acts as a proxy to the calculator object running on the server that you described in the *calculatorSoap.txt* file. The complete replacement for the client is shown in Example 19-7. You will also need to add two using statements to *CalcClient.vb*:

```
Imports System.IO
Imports System.Runtime.Serialization.Formatters.Soap
```

Make sure you add references in your Client project to System.Runtime.Remoting and System.Runtime.Serializaiton.Formatters.Soap.

Example 19-7. Replacement client

```
Option Strict On
Imports System
Imports System.IO
Imports System.Runtime.Serialization.Formatters.Soap
Imports System.Runtime.Remoting
Imports System.Runtime.Remoting.Channels
Imports System.Runtime.Remoting.Channels.Http


Namespace Programming_VBNET

    Public Class CalcClient

        Public Shared Sub Main( )

            Dim myIntArray(3) As Integer

            Console.WriteLine("Watson, come here I need you...")

            ' create an Http channel and register it
            ' uses port 0 to indicate you won't be listening
            Dim chan As New HttpChannel(0)
            ChannelServices.RegisterChannel(chan)

            Dim fileStream As New FileStream( _
                "calculatorSoap.txt", FileMode.Open)
            Dim soapFormatter As New SoapFormatter( )

            Try
                Dim calc As ICalculatorDLL.Programming_VBNET.ICalc = _
```

Example 19-7. Replacement client (continued)

```
                CType( _
                    soapFormatter.Deserialize(fileStream), _
                    ICalculatorDLL.Programming_VBNET.ICalc)

            ' use the interface to call methods
            Dim sum As Double = calc.Add(3.0, 4.0)
            Dim difference As Double = calc.Subtract(3, 4)
            Dim product As Double = calc.Mult(3, 4)
            Dim quotient As Double = calc.Div(3, 4)

            ' print the results
            Console.WriteLine("3+4 = {0}", sum)
            Console.WriteLine("3-4 = {0}", difference)
            Console.WriteLine("3*4 = {0}", product)
            Console.WriteLine("3/4 = {0}", quotient)
        Catch ex As System.Exception
            Console.WriteLine("Exception caught: ")
            Console.WriteLine(ex.Message)
        End Try
    End Sub 'Main

  End Class 'CalcClient
End Namespace 'Programming_VBNET
```

When the client starts up, the file is read from the disk and the proxy is unmarshaled. This is the mirror operation to marshaling and serializing the object on the server. Once you have unmarshalled the proxy, you are able to invoke the methods on the calculator object running on the server.

CHAPTER 20
Threads and Synchronization

Threads are relatively lightweight processes responsible for multitasking within a single application. The System.Threading namespace provides a wealth of classes and interfaces to manage multithreaded programming. The majority of programmers might never need to manage threads explicitly, however, because the Common Language Runtime (CLR) abstracts much of the threading support into classes that greatly simplify most threading tasks.

The first part of this chapter shows you how to create, manage, and kill threads. Even if you don't create your own threads explicitly, you'll want to ensure that your code can handle multiple threads if it's run in a multithreading environment. This concern is especially important if you are creating components that might be used by other programmers in a program that supports multithreading. It is particularly significant to web services developers. Although web services (covered in Chapter 16) have many attributes of desktop applications, they are run on the server, generally lack a user interface, and force the developer to think about server-side issues such as efficiency and multithreading.

The second part of this chapter focuses on synchronization. When you have a limited resource, you may need to restrict access to that resource to one thread at a time. A classic analogy is to a restroom on an airplane. You want to allow access to the restroom for only one person at a time. This is done by putting a lock on the door. When passengers want to use the restroom, they try the door handle; if it is locked, they either go away and do something else, or they wait patiently in line with others who want access to the resource. When the resource becomes free, one person is taken off the line and given the resource, which is then locked again.

At times, various threads might want to access a resource in your program, such as a file. It might be important to ensure that only one thread has access to your resource at a time, and so you will lock the resource, allow a thread access, and then unlock the resource. Programming locks can be fairly sophisticated, ensuring a fair distribution of resources.

Threads

Threads are typically created when you want a program to do two things at once. For example, assume you are calculating *pi* (3.141592653589...) to the 10 billionth place. The processor will happily begin computing this, but nothing will write to the user interface while it is working. Because computing *pi* to the 10 billionth place will take a few million years, you might like the processor to provide an update as it goes. In addition, you might want to provide a Stop button so that the user can cancel the operation at any time. To allow the program to handle the click on the Stop button, you will need a second thread of execution.

 An apartment is a logical container within a process, and is used for objects that share the same thread-access requirements. Objects in an apartment can all receive method calls from any object in any thread in the apartment. The .NET Framework does not use apartments, and managed objects (objects created within the CLR) are responsible for thread safety. The only exception to this is when managed code talks to COM.

Another common place to use threading is when you must wait for an event, such as user input, a read from a file, or receipt of data over the network. Freeing the processor to turn its attention to another task while you wait (such as computing another 10,000 values of *pi*) is a good idea, and it makes your program appear to run more quickly.

On the flip side, note that in some circumstances, threading can actually slow you down. Assume that in addition to calculating *pi*, you also want to calculate the Fibonacci series (1,1,2,3,5,8,13,21...). If you have a multiprocessor machine, this will run faster if each computation is in its own thread. If you have a single-processor machine (as most users do), computing these values in multiple threads will certainly run *slower* than computing one and then the other in a single thread, because the processor must switch back and forth between the two threads. This thread switching incurs some overhead.

Starting Threads

The simplest way to create a thread is to create a new instance of the Thread class. The Thread constructor takes a single argument: a delegate type. The CLR provides the ThreadStart delegate class specifically for this purpose, which points to a method you designate. This allows you to construct a thread and to say to it, "When you start, run this method." The ThreadStart delegate declaration is:

```
Public Delegate Sub ThreadStart( )
```

As you can see, the sub you attach to this delegate must take no parameters. Thus, you might create a new thread like this:

```
Dim t1 As Thread = _
    New Thread(New ThreadStart(AddressOf Incrementer))
```

Incrementer must be a sub that takes no parameters and returns Nothing.

For example, you might create two worker threads, one that counts up from zero:

```
' demo function, counts up to 1K
Public Sub Incrementer()

    Dim i As Integer
    For i = 0 To 1000
        Console.WriteLine("Incrementer: {0}", i)
    Next
End Sub
```

and one that counts down from 10:

```
' demo function, counts down from 1k
Public Sub Decrementer()
    Dim i As Integer
    For i = 1000 To 0 Step -1
        Console.WriteLine("Decrementer: {0}", i)
    Next
End Sub
```

To run these in threads, create two new threads, each initialized with a ThreadStart delegate. These in turn would be initialized to the respective member functions:

```
Dim t1 As Thread = _
    New Thread(New ThreadStart(AddressOf Incrementer))

Dim t2 As Thread = _
    New Thread(New ThreadStart(AddressOf Decrementer))
```

Instantiating these threads does not start them running. To do so you must call the Start method on the Thread object itself:

```
t1.Start()
t2.Start()
```

 If you don't take further action, the thread will stop when the method returns. You'll see how to stop a thread before the method ends later in this chapter.

Example 20-1 is the full program and its output. You will need to add an Imports statement for System.Threading to make the compiler aware of the Thread class. Notice the output, where you can see the processor switching from t1 to t2.

Example 20-1. Using threads

```
Option Strict On
Imports System
Imports System.Threading

Namespace Programming_VBNET

    Public Class Tester

        Shared Sub Main( )
            ' make an instance of this class
            Dim t As Tester = New Tester( )

            ' run outside static Main
            t.DoTest( )
        End Sub

        Public Sub DoTest( )

            ' create a thread for the Incrementer
            ' pass in a ThreadStart delegate
            ' with the address of Incrementer
            Dim t1 As Thread = _
              New Thread(New ThreadStart(AddressOf Incrementer))

            ' create a thread for the Decrementer
            ' pass in a ThreadStart delegate
            ' with the address of Decrementer
            Dim t2 As Thread = _
                New Thread(New ThreadStart(AddressOf Decrementer))

            ' start the threads
            t1.Start( )
            t2.Start( )

        End Sub

        ' demo function, counts up to 1K
        Public Sub Incrementer( )

            Dim i As Integer
            For i = 0 To 1000
                Console.WriteLine("Incrementer: {0}", i)
            Next
        End Sub

        ' demo function, counts down from 1k
        Public Sub Decrementer( )
            Dim i As Integer
            For i = 1000 To 0 Step -1
                Console.WriteLine("Decrementer: {0}", i)
            Next
        End Sub
```

Example 20-1. Using threads (continued)

```
    End Class
End Namespace

Output (excerpt):
Incrementer: 595
Incrementer: 596
Incrementer: 597
Incrementer: 598
Incrementer: 599
Incrementer: 600
Incrementer: 601
Incrementer: 602
Incrementer: 603
Decrementer: 585
Decrementer: 584
Decrementer: 583
Decrementer: 582
Decrementer: 581
```

The processor allows the first thread to run long enough to count up to 106. Then, the second thread kicks in, counting down from 1,000 for a while. Then the first thread is allowed to run. When I run this with larger numbers, I notice that each thread is allowed to run for about 100 numbers before switching. The actual amount of time devoted to any given thread is handled by the thread scheduler and will depend on many factors, such as the processor speed, demands on the processor from other programs, and so forth.

Joining Threads

When you tell a thread to stop processing and wait until a second thread completes its work, you are said to be joining the first thread to the second. It is as if you tied the tip of the first thread on to the tail of the second—hence "joining" them.

To join thread 1 (t1) onto thread 2 (t2), write:

```
t2.Join( )
```

If this statement is executed in a method in thread t1, t1 will halt and wait until t2 completes and exits. For example, we might ask the thread in which Main() executes to wait for all our other threads to end before it writes its concluding message. In this next code snippet, assume you've created a collection of threads named myThreads. Iterate over the collection, joining the current thread to each thread in the collection in turn:

```
Dim t As Thread
For Each t In myThreads
    t.Join( )
Next t

Console.WriteLine("All my threads are done.")
```

The final message ("All my threads are done") will not be printed until all the threads have ended. In a production environment, you might start up a series of threads to accomplish some task (e.g., printing, updating the display, etc.) and not want to continue the main thread of execution until the worker threads are completed.

Suspending Threads

At times, you want to suspend your thread for a short while. You might, for example, like your clock thread to suspend for about a second in between testing the system time. This lets you display the new time about once a second without devoting hundreds of millions of machine cycles to the effort.

The Thread class offers a public static method, Sleep, for just this purpose. The method is overloaded; one version takes an Integer, the other a timeSpan object. Each represents the number of milliseconds you want the thread suspended for, expressed either as an Integer representing milliseconds (e.g., 2,000 milliseconds equals 2 seconds) or as a timeSpan.

Although timeSpan objects can measure *ticks* (100 nanoseconds), the Sleep() method's granularity is in milliseconds (1,000,000 nanoseconds).

To cause your thread to sleep for one second, you can invoke the static method of Thread, Sleep, which suspends the thread in which it is invoked:

```
Thread.Sleep(1000)
```

At times, you'll tell your thread to sleep for zero milliseconds. You would do this to signal to the thread scheduler that you'd like your thread to yield to another thread, even if the thread scheduler might otherwise give your thread a bit more time.

If you modify Example 20-1 to add a Thread.Sleep(0) statement after each WriteLine(), the output changes significantly:

```
Dim i As Integer
For i = 0 To 1000
    Console.WriteLine("Incrementer: {0}", i)
    Thread.Sleep(0)
Next
```

This small change is sufficient to give each thread an opportunity to run. The output reflects this change:

```
Incrementer: 0
Incrementer: 1
Decrementer: 1000
Incrementer: 2
Decrementer: 999
Incrementer: 3
Decrementer: 998
Incrementer: 4
Decrementer: 997
Incrementer: 5
```

```
Decrementer: 996
Incrementer: 6
Decrementer: 995
```

Killing Threads

Typically, threads die after running their course. You can, however, ask a thread to kill itself by calling its Abort() method. This causes a ThreadAbortException exception to be thrown, which the thread can catch, and thus provides the thread with an opportunity to clean up any resources it might have allocated:

```
Catch e As ThreadAbortException
    Console.WriteLine("***Thread {0} aborted! Cleaning up...", _
        Thread.CurrentThread.Name)
```

The thread ought to treat the ThreadAbortException exception as a signal that it is time to exit, and as quickly as possible. You don't so much kill a thread as politely request that it commit suicide.

You might wish to kill a thread in reaction to an event, such as the user pressing the Cancel button. The event handler for the Cancel button might be in thread T0. In your event handler, you can call Abort on T0:

```
T0.Abort()
```

An exception will be raised in T0's currently running method that T0 can catch. This gives T0 the opportunity to free its resources and then exit gracefully.

In Example 20-2, three threads are created and stored in an array of Thread objects. Before the Threads are started, the IsBackground property is set to true. Each thread is then started and named (e.g., Thread0, Thread1, etc.). A message is displayed indicating that the thread is started, and then the main thread sleeps for 50 milliseconds before starting up the next thread.

After all three threads are started and another 50 milliseconds have passed, the first thread is aborted by calling Abort(). The main thread then joins all three of the running threads. The effect of this is that the main thread will not resume until all the other threads have completed. When they do complete, the main thread prints a message: All my threads are done. The complete source is displayed in Example 20-2.

Example 20-2. Interrupting a thread

```
Option Strict On
Imports System
Imports System.Threading

Class Tester

    Shared Sub Main()
        ' make an instance of this class
```

Example 20-2. Interrupting a thread (continued)

```
    Dim t As New Tester( )

    ' run outside static Main
    t.DoTest( )
End Sub 'Main

Public Sub DoTest( )
    ' create an array of unnamed threads
    Dim myThreads As Thread( ) = _
        {New Thread(New ThreadStart(AddressOf Decrementer)), _
         New Thread(New ThreadStart(AddressOf Incrementer)), _
         New Thread(New ThreadStart(AddressOf Incrementer))}

    ' start each thread
    Dim ctr As Integer = 0
    Dim myThread As Thread
    For Each myThread In myThreads
        myThread.IsBackground = True
        myThread.Start( )
        myThread.Name = "Thread" + ctr.ToString( )
        ctr += 1
        Console.WriteLine("Started thread {0}", myThread.Name)
        Thread.Sleep(50)
    Next myThread

    ' having started the threads
    ' tell thread 1 to abort
    myThreads(0).Abort( )

    ' wait for all threads to end before continuing
    Dim t As Thread
    For Each t In myThreads
        t.Join( )
    Next t

    ' after all threads end, print a message
    Console.WriteLine("All my threads are done.")
End Sub 'DoTest


' demo function, counts down from 1k
Public Sub Decrementer( )
    Try
        Dim i As Integer
        For i = 1000 To 0 Step -1
            Console.WriteLine("Thread {0}. Decrementer: {1}", _
                Thread.CurrentThread.Name, i)
            Thread.Sleep(0)
        Next i
    Catch e As ThreadAbortException
        Console.WriteLine("***Thread {0} aborted! Cleaning up...", _
            Thread.CurrentThread.Name)
```

Example 20-2. Interrupting a thread (continued)

```
        Finally
            Console.WriteLine("Thread {0} Exiting. ", _
                Thread.CurrentThread.Name)
        End Try
    End Sub 'Decrementer


    ' demo function, counts up to 1K
    Public Sub Incrementer()
        Try
            Dim i As Integer
            For i = 0 To 9999
                Console.WriteLine("Thread {0}. Incrementer: {1}", _
                    Thread.CurrentThread.Name, i)
                Thread.Sleep(0)
            Next i
        Catch
        Finally
            Console.WriteLine("Thread {0} Exiting. ", _
                Thread.CurrentThread.Name)
        End Try
    End Sub 'Incrementer
End Class 'Tester
```

```
Output (excerpts):
Started thread Thread0
Thread Thread0. Decrementer: 1000
Thread Thread0. Decrementer: 999
Thread Thread0. Decrementer: 998
Thread Thread0. Decrementer: 997
Thread Thread0. Decrementer: 982
Thread Thread0. Decrementer: 981
Started thread Thread1
Thread Thread1. Incrementer: 0
Thread Thread0. Decrementer: 980
Thread Thread1. Incrementer: 1
Thread Thread0. Decrementer: 979
Thread Thread0. Decrementer: 957
Thread Thread0. Decrementer: 955
Started thread Thread2
Thread Thread1. Incrementer: 26
Thread Thread2. Incrementer: 0
Thread Thread0. Decrementer: 954
Thread Thread1. Incrementer: 27
Thread Thread2. Incrementer: 1
Thread Thread2. Incrementer: 25
Thread Thread1. Incrementer: 49
***Thread Thread0 aborted! Cleaning up...
Thread Thread0 Exiting.
Thread Thread1. Incrementer: 50
Thread Thread2. Incrementer: 26
Thread Thread1. Incrementer: 9999
Thread Thread2. Incrementer: 9975
```

Example 20-2. Interrupting a thread (continued)

```
Thread Thread1 Exiting.
Thread Thread2. Incrementer: 9998
Thread Thread2. Incrementer: 9999
Thread Thread2 Exiting.
All my threads are done.
Press any key to continue
```

You see the first thread start and decrement from 1,000 to 998. The second thread starts, and the two threads are interleaved for a while until the third thread starts. After a short while, however, Thread0 reports that it has been aborted, and then it reports that it is exiting. The two remaining threads continue until they are done. They then exit naturally, and the main thread, which was joined on all three, resumes to print its exit message.

Synchronization

At times, you might want to control access to a resource, such as an object's properties or methods, so that only one thread at a time can modify or use that resource. Your object is similar to the airplane restroom discussed earlier, and the various threads are like the people waiting in line. Synchronization is provided by a lock on the object, which prevents a second thread from barging in on your object until the first thread is finished with it.

In this section you examine three synchronization mechanisms provided by the CLR: the Interlock class, the Visual Basic .NET Lock statement, and the Monitor class. But first, you need to simulate a shared resource, such as a file or printer, with a simple integer variable: counter. Rather than opening the file or accessing the printer, you'll increment counter from each of two threads.

To start, declare the member variable and initialize it to 0:

```
Private counter As Integer = 0
```

Modify the Incrementer method to increment the counter member variable:

```
Public Sub Incrementer( )
    Try
        While counter < 1000
            Dim temp As Integer = counter
            temp += 1 ' increment

            Thread.Sleep(0)

            counter = temp
            Console.WriteLine("Thread {0}. Incrementer: {1}", _
                Thread.CurrentThread.Name, counter)
        End While
```

The idea here is to simulate the work that might be done with a controlled resource. Just as we might open a file, manipulate its contents, and then close it, here we read the value of counter into a temporary variable, increment the temporary variable, suspend the thread to simulate work (Thread.Sleep(0)), and then assign the incremented value back to counter.

The problem is that your first thread will read the value of counter (0) and assign that to a temporary variable. It will then increment the temporary variable. While it is doing its work, the second thread will read the value of counter (still 0) and assign that value to a temporary variable. The first thread finishes its work, then assigns the temporary value (1) back to counter and displays it. The second thread does the same. What is printed is 1,1. In the next go around, the same thing happens. Rather than having the two threads count 1,2,3,4, we see 1,1,2,2,3,3. Example 20-3 shows the complete source code and output for this example.

Example 20-3. Simulating a shared resource

```
Option Strict On
Imports System
Imports System.Threading

Class Tester
    Private counter As Integer = 0

    Shared Sub Main( )
        ' make an instance of this class
        Dim t As New Tester( )

        ' run outside static Main
        t.DoTest( )
    End Sub 'Main

    Public Sub DoTest( )
        Dim t1 As New Thread(New ThreadStart(AddressOf Incrementer))
        t1.IsBackground = True
        t1.Name = "ThreadOne"
        t1.Start( )
        Console.WriteLine("Started thread {0}", t1.Name)

        Dim t2 As New Thread(New ThreadStart(AddressOf Incrementer))
        t2.IsBackground = True
        t2.Name = "ThreadTwo"
        t2.Start( )
        Console.WriteLine("Started thread {0}", t2.Name)
        t1.Join( )
        t2.Join( )

        ' after all threads end, print a message
        Console.WriteLine("All my threads are done.")
    End Sub 'DoTest
```

Example 20-3. Simulating a shared resource (continued)

```
    ' demo function, counts up to 1K
    Public Sub Incrementer()
        Try
            While counter < 1000
                Dim temp As Integer = counter
                temp += 1 ' increment
                ' simulate some work in this method
                Thread.Sleep(0)

                ' assign the decremented value
                ' and display the results
                counter = temp
                Console.WriteLine("Thread {0}. Incrementer: {1}", _
                    Thread.CurrentThread.Name, counter)
            End While
        Catch e As ThreadInterruptedException
            Console.WriteLine("Thread {0} interrupted! Cleaning up...", _
                Thread.CurrentThread.Name)

        Finally
            Console.WriteLine("Thread {0} Exiting. ", _
                Thread.CurrentThread.Name)
        End Try
    End Sub 'Incrementer
End Class 'Tester

Output (excerpt) :
Started thread ThreadOne
Started thread ThreadTwo
Thread ThreadTwo. Incrementer: 1
Thread ThreadOne. Incrementer: 1
Thread ThreadTwo. Incrementer: 2
Thread ThreadOne. Incrementer: 2
Thread ThreadTwo. Incrementer: 3
Thread ThreadOne. Incrementer: 3
Thread ThreadTwo. Incrementer: 4
Thread ThreadOne. Incrementer: 4
Thread ThreadTwo. Incrementer: 5
Thread ThreadOne. Incrementer: 5
Thread ThreadTwo. Incrementer: 6
Thread ThreadOne. Incrementer: 6
Thread ThreadTwo. Incrementer: 7
Thread ThreadOne. Incrementer: 7
Thread ThreadTwo. Incrementer: 8
Thread ThreadOne. Incrementer: 8
Thread ThreadTwo. Incrementer: 9
Thread ThreadOne. Incrementer: 9
```

Assume your two threads are accessing a database record rather than reading a member variable. For example, your code might be part of an inventory system for a book retailer. A customer asks if *Programming Visual Basic .NET* is available. The first thread reads the value and finds that there is one book on hand. The customer wants to buy the book, so the thread proceeds to gather credit card information and validate the customer's address.

While this is happening, a second thread asks if this wonderful book is still available. The first thread has not yet updated the record, so one book still shows as available. The second thread begins the purchase process. Meanwhile, the first thread finishes and decrements the counter to zero. The second thread, blissfully unaware of the activity of the first, also sets the value back to zero. Unfortunately, you have now sold the same copy of the book twice.

As noted earlier, you need to synchronize access to the counter object (or to the database record, file, printer, etc.).

Using Interlocked

The CLR provides a number of synchronization mechanisms. These include the common synchronization tools such as critical sections (called *Locks* in .NET), as well as more sophisticated tools such as a Monitor class. Each is discussed later in this chapter.

Incrementing and decrementing a value is such a common programming pattern, and one which so often needs synchronization protection, that Visual Basic .NET offers a special class, Interlocked, just for this purpose. Interlocked has two methods, Increment and Decrement, which not only increment or decrement a value, but also do so under synchronization control.

Modify the Incrementer method from Example 20-3 as follows:

```
Public Sub Incrementer( )
    Try
        While counter < 1000
            Interlocked.Increment(counter)
            Console.WriteLine("Thread {0}. Incrementer: {1}", _
                Thread.CurrentThread.Name, counter)
            Thread.Sleep(0)
        End While
```

The catch and finally blocks and the remainder of the program are unchanged from the previous example.

Interlocked.Increment( ) expects a single parameter: a reference to an Integer. The Increment( ) method is overloaded and can take a reference to a long, rather than to an Integer, if that is more convenient.

Once this change is made, access to the counter member is synchronized, and the output is what we'd expect.

```
Output (excerpts):
Started thread ThreadOne
Started thread ThreadTwo
```

```
Thread ThreadOne. Incrementer: 1
Thread ThreadTwo. Incrementer: 2
Thread ThreadOne. Incrementer: 3
Thread ThreadTwo. Incrementer: 4
Thread ThreadTwo. Incrementer: 5
Thread ThreadOne. Incrementer: 6
Thread ThreadTwo. Incrementer: 7
Thread ThreadOne. Incrementer: 8
Thread ThreadTwo. Incrementer: 9
Thread ThreadOne. Incrementer: 10
```

Using the SyncLock Statement

Although the Interlocked object is fine if you want to increment or decrement a value, there will be times when you want to control access to other objects as well. What is needed is a more general synchronization mechanism. This is provided by the .NET SyncLock object.

A SyncLock marks a critical section of your code, providing synchronization to an object you designate while the lock is in effect. The syntax of using a SyncLock statement is to request a SyncLock on an object and then to execute a statement or block of statements. The SyncLock is removed at the end of the statement block.

Visual Basic .NET provides direct support for locks through the SyncLock keyword. For example, you can modify Incrementer once again to use a lock statement, as follows:

```
Public Sub Incrementer()
    Try
        While counter < 1000
            SyncLock Me
                Dim temp As Integer = counter
                temp += 1
                Thread.Sleep(0)
                counter = temp
                Console.WriteLine("Thread {0}. Incrementer: {1}", _
                    Thread.CurrentThread.Name, counter)
            End SyncLock
        End While
```

The catch and finally blocks and the remainder of the program are unchanged from the previous example.

The output from this code is identical to that produced using Interlocked.

Using Monitors

The objects used so far will be sufficient for most needs. For the most sophisticated control over resources, you might want to use a *monitor*. A monitor lets you decide when to enter and exit the synchronization, and it lets you wait for another area of your code to become free.

A monitor acts as a smart lock on a resource. When you want to begin synchronization, call the Enter() method of the monitor, passing in the object you want to lock:

```
Monitor.Enter(Me)
```

If the monitor is unavailable, the object protected by the monitor is in use. You can do other work while you wait for the monitor to become available and then try again. You can also explicitly choose to Wait(), suspending your thread until the moment the monitor is free. Wait() helps you control thread ordering.

For example, suppose you are downloading and printing an article from the Web. For efficiency, you'd like to print in a background thread, but you want to ensure that at least 10 pages have downloaded before you begin.

Your printing thread will wait until the get-file thread signals that enough of the file has been read. You don't want to Join the get-file thread because the file might be hundreds of pages. You don't want to wait until it has completely finished downloading, but you do want to ensure that at least 10 pages have been read before your print thread begins. The Wait() method is just the ticket.

To simulate this, rewrite Tester and add back the decrementer method. Your incrementer will count up to 10. The decrementer method will count down to zero. It turns out you don't want to start decrementing unless the value of counter is at least 5.

In Decrementer, call Enter on the monitor. Then check the value of counter, and if it is less than 5, call Wait on the monitor:

```
If counter < 5 Then
    Console.WriteLine( _
        "[{0}] In Decrementer. Counter: {1}. Gotta Wait!", _
        Thread.CurrentThread.Name, counter)
    Monitor.Wait(Me)
End If
```

This call to Wait() frees the monitor, but signals to the CLR that you want the monitor back the next time it is free. Waiting threads will be notified of a chance to run again if the active thread calls Pulse():

```
Monitor.Pulse(Me)
```

Pulse() signals to the CLR that there has been a change in state that might free a thread that is waiting. The CLR will keep track of the fact that the earlier thread asked to wait, and threads will be guaranteed access in the order in which the waits were requested. ("Your wait is important to us and will be handled in the order received.")

When a thread is finished with the monitor, it can mark the end of its controlled area of code with a call to Exit():

```
Monitor.Exit(Me)
```

Example 20-4 continues the simulation, providing synchronized access to a counter variable using a Monitor.

Example 20-4. Using a Monitor object

```
Option Strict On
Imports System
Imports System.Threading

Class Tester

    Shared Sub Main( )
        ' make an instance of this class
        Dim t As New Tester( )

        ' run outside static Main
        t.DoTest( )
    End Sub 'Main

    Public Sub DoTest( )
        ' create an array of unnamed threads
        Dim myThreads As Thread( ) = _
        {New Thread(New ThreadStart(AddressOf Decrementer)), _
        New Thread(New ThreadStart(AddressOf Incrementer))}

        ' start each thread
        Dim ctr As Integer = 1
        Dim myThread As Thread
        For Each myThread In myThreads
            myThread.IsBackground = True
            myThread.Start( )
            myThread.Name = "Thread" & ctr.ToString( )
            ctr += 1
            Console.WriteLine("Started thread {0}", myThread.Name)
            Thread.Sleep(50)
        Next myThread

        ' wait for all threads to end before continuing
        Dim t As Thread
        For Each t In myThreads
            t.Join( )
        Next t

        ' after all threads end, print a message
        Console.WriteLine("All my threads are done.")
    End Sub 'DoTest

    Sub Decrementer( )
        Try
            ' synchronize this area of code
            Monitor.Enter(Me)

            ' if counter is not yet 5
```

Example 20-4. Using a Monitor object (continued)

```
            ' then free the monitor to other waiting
            ' threads, but wait in line for your turn
            If counter < 5 Then
                Console.WriteLine( _
                    "[{0}] In Decrementer. Counter: {1}. Gotta Wait!", _
                    Thread.CurrentThread.Name, counter)
                Monitor.Wait(Me)
            End If

            While counter > 0
                Dim temp As Long = counter
                temp -= 1
                Thread.Sleep(0)
                counter = temp
                Console.WriteLine("[{0}] In Decrementer. Counter: {1}. ", _
                Thread.CurrentThread.Name, counter)
            End While

        Finally
            Monitor.Exit(Me)
        End Try
    End Sub 'Decrementer

    Sub Incrementer( )
        Try
            Monitor.Enter(Me)
            While counter < 10
                Dim temp As Long = counter
                temp += 1
                Thread.Sleep(0)
                counter = temp
                Console.WriteLine("[{0}] In Incrementer. Counter: {1}", _
                Thread.CurrentThread.Name, counter)
            End While

            ' I'm done incrementing for now, let another
            ' thread have the Monitor
            Monitor.Pulse(Me)
        Finally
            Console.WriteLine("[{0}] Exiting...", _
            Thread.CurrentThread.Name)
            Monitor.Exit(Me)
        End Try
    End Sub 'Incrementer
    Private counter As Long = 0
End Class 'Tester
```

In this example, Decrementer is started first. In the output you see Thread1 (the decrementer) start up and then realize that it has to wait. You then see Thread2 start up. Only when Thread2 pulses does Thread1 begin its work.

Try some experiments with this code. First, comment out the call to Pulse(). You'll find that Thread1 never resumes. Without Pulse() there is no signal to the waiting threads.

As a second experiment, rewrite Incrementer to pulse and exit the monitor after each increment:

```
Sub Incrementer()
    Try
        While counter < 10
            Monitor.Enter(Me)
            Dim temp As Long = counter
            temp += 1
            Thread.Sleep(0)
            counter = temp
            Console.WriteLine("[{0}] In Incrementer. Counter: {1}", _
            Thread.CurrentThread.Name, counter)

            Monitor.Pulse(Me)
            Monitor.Exit(Me)
        End While
```

Rewrite Decrementer as well, changing the If statement to a While statement and knocking down the value from 10 to 5:

```
While counter < 5
    Console.WriteLine( _
        "[{0}] In Decrementer. Counter: {1}. Gotta Wait!", _
        Thread.CurrentThread.Name, counter)
    Monitor.Wait(Me)
End While
```

The net effect of these two changes is to cause Thread2, the Incrementer, to pulse the Decrementer after each increment. While the value is smaller than five, the Decrementer must continue to wait; once the value goes over five, the Decrementer runs to completion. When it is done, the Incrementer thread can run again. The output is shown here:

```
Started thread Thread1
[Thread1] In Decrementer. Counter: 0. Gotta Wait!
Started thread Thread2
[Thread2] In Incrementer. Counter: 1
[Thread1] In Decrementer. Counter: 1. Gotta Wait!
[Thread2] In Incrementer. Counter: 2
[Thread1] In Decrementer. Counter: 2. Gotta Wait!
[Thread2] In Incrementer. Counter: 3
[Thread1] In Decrementer. Counter: 3. Gotta Wait!
[Thread2] In Incrementer. Counter: 4
[Thread1] In Decrementer. Counter: 4. Gotta Wait!
[Thread2] In Incrementer. Counter: 5
[Thread1] In Decrementer. Counter: 4.
[Thread1] In Decrementer. Counter: 3.
[Thread1] In Decrementer. Counter: 2.
[Thread1] In Decrementer. Counter: 1.
```

```
[Thread1] In Decrementer. Counter: 0.
[Thread2] In Incrementer. Counter: 1
[Thread2] In Incrementer. Counter: 2
[Thread2] In Incrementer. Counter: 3
[Thread2] In Incrementer. Counter: 4
[Thread2] In Incrementer. Counter: 5
[Thread2] In Incrementer. Counter: 6
[Thread2] In Incrementer. Counter: 7
[Thread2] In Incrementer. Counter: 8
[Thread2] In Incrementer. Counter: 9
[Thread2] In Incrementer. Counter: 10
[Thread2] Exiting...
All my threads are done.
```

Race Conditions and Deadlocks

The .NET library provides sufficient thread support that you will rarely find yourself creating your own threads and managing synchronization manually.

Thread synchronization can be tricky, especially in complex programs. If you do decide to create your own threads, you must confront and solve all the traditional problems of thread synchronization, such as race conditions and deadlock.

Race Conditions

A *race condition* exists when the success of your program depends on the uncontrolled order of completion of two independent threads.

Suppose, for example, that you have two threads—one is responsible for opening a file and the other is responsible for writing to the file. It is important that you control the second thread so that it's assured that the first thread has opened the file. If not, under some conditions the first thread will open the file, and the second thread will work fine; under other unpredictable conditions, the first thread won't finish opening the file before the second thread tries to write to it, and you'll throw an exception (or worse, your program will simply seize up and die). This is a race condition, and race conditions can be very difficult to debug.

You cannot leave these two threads to operate independently; you must ensure that Thread1 will have completed before Thread2 begins. To accomplish this, you might Join() Thread2 on Thread1. As an alternative, you can use a Monitor and Wait() for the appropriate conditions before resuming Thread2.

Deadlock

When you wait for a resource to become free, you are at risk of *deadlock*, also called a *deadly embrace*. In a deadlock, two or more threads are waiting for each other, and neither can become free.

Suppose you have two threads, ThreadA and ThreadB. ThreadA locks down an Employee object and then tries to get a lock on a row in the database. It turns out that ThreadB already has that row locked, so ThreadA waits.

Unfortunately, ThreadB can't update the row until it locks down the Employee object, which is already locked down by ThreadA. Neither thread can proceed, and neither thread will unlock its own resource. They are waiting for each other in a deadly embrace.

As described, the deadlock is fairly easy to spot and to correct. In a program running many threads, deadlock can be very difficult to diagnose, let alone solve. One guideline is to get all the locks you need or to release all the locks you have. That is, as soon as ThreadA realizes that it can't lock the Row, it should release its lock on the Employee object. Similarly, when ThreadB can't lock the Employee, it should release the Row. A second important guideline is to lock as small a section of code as possible and to hold the lock as briefly as possible.

Index

Symbols

+ addition operator, 55, 60
= assignment operator, 55, 61
\ backslash (left-facing) division
    operator, 55–57
^ caret, 243
: colon, 243
> comparison operator, 55
& concatenation operator, 60, 230
+ concatenation operator, 231
. dot operator, 12
= equality operator, 61
= equals sign, 61, 395
^ exponentiation operator, 59
/ forward slash (right-facing) division
    operator, 55–57
> greater-than operator, 60
>= or => greater-than or equal to
    operator, 61
< less-than operator, 61
<= or =< less-than or equal to operator, 61
<% %> marks, 395
+ multiplication operator, 55
<> not equal operator, 61
( ) parentheses (see parentheses)
' single quote, 13
- subtraction operator, 55
_ underscore, 26
| vertical bar, 243

A

Abort( ) method, 514
abstract classes, 127–130
    designating as, 128
    vs. interfaces, 148
abstract methods, 127–130
AcceptChanges( ) method, 379
Access (Microsoft), 353
access modifiers, 78, 87, 121
accessor-body, 106
Activator class, 458
Add( ) method
    ArrayLists class, 211
    Collection class, 213
addition operator (+), 55
    for string concatenation, 60
ADO.NET, 353–386
    object model for, 357
    working with, 358–362
    XML and, 386
aggregation of classes, 71
And operator, 62
AppDomain class, 485
Append( ) method, 241
AppendFormat( ) method, 241, 242
application domain boundaries, marshaling
    across, 488–494
application domains (app domains), 483,
    484–494
    creating/using, 486–488
Application Folder, 348
applications
    building/writing, 13–20
    client-server (two-tier), 307

multi-module assemblies, 428–437
    testing, 434
multicasting, 290–294
multidimensional arrays, 170, 182–190
multiple inheritance, not supported in
    VB.NET, 153
multiplication operator (*), 55
MustInherit keyword, 128, 130
MustOverride keyword, 127
My Documents folder, 349

N

named parameters, 449
names
    for application domains, 486
    fully qualified, 503
    of interfaces, I prefixing, 147
    method, ( ) in, 10
    strong, 439–441
        creating, 442
namespaces, 11
    XML, 411
    (see also entries at System...)
narrowing casts, 25
nested classes, 135
nested If statements, 38
.NET Framework, 5–7
.NET platform, 3, 4
.NET Web Services (see web services)
New keyword, 78
New Project window (Visual Studio .NET
    IDE), 312
Next statement, in For loops, 53
non-postback events, 390
normalization, 354
Northwind sample database, 353
not equal operator (<>), 61
Not operator, 62
notation systems
    Camel, 26
    Hungarian, 22
    Pascal, 26
Notepad, 13
    Web Forms, creating with, 389
    Windows applications, creating
        with, 308–312
NotInheritable keyword, 130, 227
n-tier applications, 307
Numeric types, default value for, 28

O

Object class, 131–133
object handles, 488
object-oriented programming, 68–75
    three pillars of, 71–74
objects, 10, 70, 76–114
    capabilities of, 69
    context-agile/context-bound, 494
    garbage collection for, 99
    instantiating, 78–80
    interface implementation testing
        and, 156–160
offsets, 175
OLE DB Managed Provider, 362
On Error statement, 255
one-dimensional arrays, 170
OnPreRender( ) method, 391
OOP (see object-oriented programming)
operators, 54–67
    logical, 61
    mathematical, 55–61
    order of precedence for, 65–67
    self-assignment, 57
Option Strict On, 22
Or operator, 62
order of precedence for operators, 65–67
OrElse keyword, 63
outer classes, 135
outer joins, 356
overloading methods/constructors, 100–102

P

PadLeft( ) method, 228
PadRight( ) method, 228
Page_Load( ) method, 398
Page_Load events, 398
ParamArray keyword, 180–182
parameters
    passing
        by reference, 89, 110
        by value, 89, 108–110
        variable number of, 180–182
    positional/named, 449
parentheses ( )
    accessing arrays and, 175
    in method names, 10
    nesting, 66
    in regular expressions, 243
Pascal notation, 26
pattern matching, 242
PE files, 425

Peek( ) method
    Queue class, 217
    Stack class, 220
performance, multi-module assemblies
        and, 429
polymorphism (OOP), 71–73, 121–127
Pop( ) method, 220
populating arrays, 173
Portable Executable (PE) files, 425
positional parameters, 449
postback events, 390, 391, 405–407
primary keys, 354, 369
primitive types, 22, 23–26
    default values for, 90
Private access modifier, 87, 121
private assemblies, 437–438
private keys, 440
private member variables, 103
probing, 435
problem domain, 68
procedural programming languages, 355
processes, 483, 484
programming
    component-oriented, 8
    event-driven, 274, 299
    eXtreme, 74
    OOP, 68–75
programming languages, 3
    declarative vs. procedural, 355
    SQL, 355–357
    strongly typed, 22
    (see also ADO.NET)
programs (see applications)
properties, 103
    dynamic invocation for, 458–460
    encapsulating with, 103–108
Properties window (Visual Studio .NET
        IDE), 313
    application opening dialog box and, 352
Protected access modifier, 88, 121
Protected Friend access modifier, 88
protocols for web services, 408
proxies, 409
    creating, 415–421
    for marshaling, 488
Public access modifier, 87, 121
public classes, 121
public key encryption, 440
public key tokens, 442
public keys, 440
publishing events, 299–302
Pulse( ) method, 522, 525
Push( ) method, 220

Q

queries, 355
Queue class, 217
queues, 216–220
    elements of, copying to arrays, 223–225

R

race conditions, 526
RAD (Rapid Application Development), 308,
        388
RaisePostDataChangedEvent( ) method, 391
raising events, 299, 390
Rank property, 190
Rapid Application Development (RAD), 308,
        388
ReadOnly property, 107
RealProxy class, 488
records, 372–387
    creating, 380–387
    deleting, 379
    exception handling for, 378
    updating, 377–379
rectangular arrays, 183–186
ReDim keyword, 172
redimensioning arrays, 172
reference types, 23, 81, 108
    boxing/unboxing value types
        and, 133–135
    default values and, 173–174
    passing by value, 111–114
ReferenceEquals( ) method, 131
reflection, 445
    tasks performed by (list), 452
reflection emit, 460–482
    using for dynamic invocation, 476–482
Reflection namespace, 452
Regex class, 243–253
RegisterWellKnownServiceType( )
        method, 503
Registry, caution with, 350
regular expressions, 226, 242–253
relational databases, 353–357
relational operators, 60
    order of precedence for, 65
remoting, 483, 496–507
Remove( ) method
    Collection class, 213
    String class, 228
    StringBuilder class, 241
RemoveAt( ) method, 211
Render( ) method, 392

System.Object root class, 5
System.Text.RegularExpressions
    namespace, 243
System.Threading namespace, 508
System.Web.Services namespace, 409
System.Web.Services.WebService
    namespace, 409

T

tables, 353–357
    combining, 369–373
text editors, 14
Thread class, 509
ThreadAbortException exception, 514
threads, 508–527
    interrupting, 514–517
three-tier applications, 307
Throw keyword, 256
throwing exceptions, 254
time
    class for, 86
    culture objects and, 428
ToArray( ) method
    ArrayLists class, 211
    Queue class, 217
    Stack class, 220
ToCharArray( ) method, 228
ToLower( ) method, 228
Toolbox window (Visual Studio .NET
    IDE), 312
tools (see utilities)
ToString( ) method, 227
    Object class, 131–133
ToUpper( ) method, 228
TP (transparent proxies), 488
TreeNode objects, 323
TreeView controls, populating, 323–326
TreeView events (FileCopier
    utility), 326–329
Trim( ) method, 228
TrimEnd( ) method, 228
TrimStart( ) method, 228
troubleshooting thread synchronization, 526
try/catch blocks, 254, 257–259
    dedicated catch blocks and, 261–263
    finally blocks and, 263
    rethrowing exceptions and, 270–273
    stacks and, 259–261
two-dimensional arrays, 171, 182
two-tier applications, 307
type boundaries, 426
Type class, 453

type discovery, 454
TypeOf( ) function, 135
TypeOf…Is expression, 157–160
types, 22–26
    creating at runtime, 460–482
    mapping to underlying types, 23
    polymorphism support for, 121
    reflection and, 454–458

U

UI forms, creating, 321
UML (Unified Modeling Language), 116
unboxing value types, 133–135
unconditional branching, 33
underscore (_), leading identifiers, 26
Unified Modeling Language (UML), 116
Unload( ) method, 485
Update( ) method, 379
user-defined types, 22
user interface forms (UI forms), creating, 321
user interface, managing during application
    setup, 351
user interface (UI), Web Forms and, 389
utilities
    gacutil, 441
    ILDasm, 426, 445
    wsdl, 415–419

V

value types, 23, 81, 108
    boxing/unboxing, 133–135
    default values for, 173–174
values
    comparing, relational operators for, 60
    default, 28
variables, 27
    interim, 66
Variant type (VB6), not available in
    VB.NET, 21
.vb files, 393
VB.NET (see Visual Basic .NET)
versions/versioning, 126, 425–444
    shared assemblies and, 439
vertical bar (|), in regular expressions, 243
ViewState element, 405
ViewState property, 391
virtual methods, 122–126
Visual Basic .NET (VB.NET)
    vs. C#, 4
    language fundamentals of, 21–67
    vs. VB6, 21

About the Author

Jesse Liberty is the author of a dozen books, including the best-selling *Programming C#* and *Programming ASP.NET*, both from O'Reilly. Jesse is the president of Liberty Associates, Inc. (*http://www.LibertyAssociates.com*), where he provides .NET training, contract programming, and consulting services. He is a former vice president of electronic delivery for Citibank and a former Distinguished Software Engineer and architect for AT&T, Ziff Davis, Xerox, and PBS.

Colophon

Our look is the result of reader comments, our own experimentation, and feedback from distribution channels. Distinctive covers complement our distinctive approach to technical topics, breathing personality and life into potentially dry subjects.

The animal on the cover of *Programming Visual Basic .NET*, Second Edition, is a catfish. Catfish can be found all over the world, most often in freshwater environments. Catfish are identified by their whiskers, called "barbels," as well by as their scaleless skin; fleshy, rayless posterior fins; and sharp, defensive spines in the dorsal and shoulder fins. Catfish have complex bones and sensitive hearing. They are omnivorous feeders and skilled scavengers. A marine catfish can taste with any part of its body.

Though most madtom species of catfish are no more than 5 inches in length, some Danube catfish (called wels or sheatfish) reach lengths of up to 13 feet and weigh as much as 400 pounds. Wels catfish (found mostly in the United Kingdom) are dark, flat, and black in color, with white bellies. They breed in the springtime in shallow areas near rivers and lakes. The females leave their eggs on plants for the males to guard. Two to three weeks later, the eggs hatch into tadpole-like fish, which grow quickly in size. The largest recorded wels catfish was 16 feet long and weighed 675 pounds.

Jane Ellin was the production editor and proofreader for *Programming Visual Basic .NET*, Second Edition. Rachel Wheeler and Emily Quill provided quality control. Sue Willing provided production support. Brenda Miller wrote the index.

Pam Spremulli designed the cover of this book, based on a series design by Edie Freedman. The cover image is a 19th-century engraving from the Dover Pictorial Archive. Emma Colby produced the cover layout with QuarkXPress 4.1 using Adobe's ITC Garamond font.

Bret Kerr designed the interior layout, based on a series design by David Futato. Joe Wizda converted the files from Microsoft Word to FrameMaker 5.5.6, using tools created by Mike Sierra. The text font is Linotype Birka; the heading font is Adobe Myriad Condensed; and the code font is LucasFont's TheSans Mono Condensed. The illustrations that appear in the book were produced by Robert Romano and Jessamyn Read using Macromedia FreeHand 9 and Adobe Photoshop 6. The tip and warning icons were drawn by Christopher Bing.

Other Titles Available from O'Reilly

Microsoft .NET Programming

Mastering Visual Studio .NET

*By Ian Griffiths, Jon Flanders
& Chris Sells
1st Edition March 2003 (est.)
352 pages (est.), ISBN 0-596-00360-9*

Mastering Visual Studio .NET provides you, as an experienced programmer, with all the information needed to get the most out of the latest and greatest development tool from Microsoft. Written by experienced developers and trainers John Flanders, Ian Griffiths, and Chris Sells, this book not only covers the fundamentals, but also shows how to customize and extend the toolkit to your specific needs.

Programming C#, 2nd Edition

*By Jesse Liberty
2nd Edition February 2002
650 pages, ISBN 0-596-00309-9*

The first part of *Programming C#*, 2nd Edition introduces C# fundamentals, then goes on to explain the development of desktop and Internet applications, including Windows Forms, ADO.NET, ASP.NET (including Web Forms), and Web Services. Next, this book gets to the heart of the .NET Framework, focusing on attributes and reflection, remoting, threads and synchronization, streams, and finally, it illustrates how to interoperate with COM objects.

Learning Visual Basic .NET

*By Jesse Liberty
1st edition October 2002
320 pages, ISBN 0-596-00386-2*

Learning Visual Basic .NET is a complete introduction to VB.NET and object-oriented programming. By using hundreds of examples, this book demonstrates how to develop various kinds of applications—including those that work with databases—and web services. *Learning Visual Basic .NET* will help you build a solid foundation in .NET.

Programming ASP.NET

*By Jesse Liberty & Dan Hurwitz
1st Edition February 2002
960 pages, ISBN 0-596-00171-1*

The ASP.NET technologies are so complete and flexible; your main difficulty may lie simply in weaving the pieces together for maximum efficiency. *Programming ASP.NET* shows you how to do just that. Jesse Liberty and Dan Hurwitz teach everything you need to know to write web applications and web services using both C# and Visual Basic .NET.

C# in a Nutshell

*By Peter Drayton & Ben Albarhari
1st Edition March 2002
856 pages, ISBN 0-596-00181-9*

C# is likely to become one of the most widely used languages for building .NET applications. *C# in a Nutshell* contains a concise introduction to the language and its syntax, plus brief tutorials used to accomplish common programming tasks. It also includes O'Reilly's classic-style, quick-reference material for all the types and members in core .NET namespaces, including System, System.Text, System.IO, and System.Collections.

ASP.NET in a Nutshell

*By G. Andrew Duthie &
Matthew MacDonald
1st Edition June 2002
816 pages, ISBN 0-596-00116-9*

As a quick reference and tutorial in one, *ASP.NET in a Nutshell* goes beyond the published documentation to highlight little-known details, stress practical uses for particular features, and provide real-world examples that show how features can be used in a working application. This book covers application and web service development, custom controls, data access, security, deployment, and error handling. There is also an overview of web-related class libraries.

O'REILLY®

To order: *800-998-9938* • *order@oreilly.com* • *www.oreilly.com*
Online editions of most O'Reilly titles are available by subscription at *safari.oreilly.com*
Also available at most retail and online bookstores.

How to stay in touch with O'Reilly

1. Visit our award-winning web site

http://www.oreilly.com/

★ "Top 100 Sites on the Web"—PC Magazine
★ CIO Magazine's Web Business 50 Awards

Our web site contains a library of comprehensive product information (including book excerpts and tables of contents), downloadable software, background articles, interviews with technology leaders, links to relevant sites, book cover art, and more. File us in your bookmarks or favorites!

2. Join our email mailing lists

Sign up to get email announcements of new books and conferences, special offers, and O'Reilly Network technology newsletters at:

http://elists.oreilly.com

It's easy to customize your free elists subscription so you'll get exactly the O'Reilly news you want.

3. Get examples from our books

To find example files for a book, go to:

http://www.oreilly.com/catalog

select the book, and follow the "Examples" link.

4. Work with us

Check out our web site for current employment opportunities:

http://jobs.oreilly.com/

5. Register your book

Register your book at:

http://register.oreilly.com

6. Contact us

O'Reilly & Associates, Inc.
1005 Gravenstein Hwy North
Sebastopol, CA 95472 USA
TEL: 707-827-7000 or 800-998-9938
        (6am to 5pm PST)
FAX: 707-829-0104

order@oreilly.com
For answers to problems regarding your order or our products. To place a book order online visit:

http://www.oreilly.com/order_new/

catalog@oreilly.com
To request a copy of our latest catalog.

booktech@oreilly.com
For book content technical questions or corrections.

corporate@oreilly.com
For educational, library, government, and corporate sales.

proposals@oreilly.com
To submit new book proposals to our editors and product managers.

international@oreilly.com
For information about our international distributors or translation queries. For a list of our distributors outside of North America check out:

http://international.oreilly.com/distributors.html

adoption@oreilly.com
For information about academic use of O'Reilly books, visit:

http://academic.oreilly.com

Learning Resources
Centre

O'REILLY®